VOID

Library of
Davidson College

Partners in
East-West
Economic Relations

Pergamon Policy Studies on the Soviet Union and Eastern Europe

Abouchar *Economic Evaluation of Soviet Socialism*
Allworth *Ethnic Russia in the USSR*
Blazynski *Flashpoint Poland*
Dismukes & McConnell *Soviet Naval Diplomacy*
Douglass *Soviet Military Strategy in Europe*
Duncan *Soviet Policy in the Third World*
Francisco, Laird & Laird *The Political Economy of Collectivized Agriculture*
Kahan & Ruble *Industrial Labor in the USSR*
Katsenelinboigen *Soviet Economic Thought and Political Power in the USSR*
Koropeckyj & Schroeder *Economics of Soviet Regions*
McCagg & Silver *Soviet Asian Ethnic Frontiers*
Neuberger & Tyson *The Impact of International Economic Disturbances on the Soviet Union and Eastern Europe*
Schulz & Adams *Political Participation in Communist Systems*

Related Titles

Brezhnev *L.I. Brezhnev — Selected Speeches and Writings on Foreign Affairs*
Close *Europe Without Defense?*
Gorshkov *Sea Power of the State*
Laszlo & Kurtzman *Eastern Europe and the New International Economic Order*
Strickland *Soviet and Western Perspectives in Social Psychology*

 ON THE SOVIET UNION AND EASTERN EUROPE

Partners in East-West Economic Relations
The Determinants of Choice

Edited by
Zbigniew M. Fallenbuchl
Carl H. McMillan

Pergamon Press
NEW YORK • OXFORD • TORONTO • SYDNEY • FRANKFURT • PARIS

Pergamon Press Offices:

U.S.A. Pergamon Press Inc., Maxwell House, Fairview Park, Elmsford, New York 10523, U.S.A.

U.K. Pergamon Press Ltd., Headington Hill Hall, Oxford OX3 0BW, England

CANADA Pergamon of Canada, Ltd., 150 Consumers Road, Willowdale, Ontario M2J, 1P9, Canada

AUSTRALIA Pergamon Press (Aust) Pty. Ltd., P O Box 544, Potts Point, NSW 2011, Australia

FRANCE Pergamon Press SARL, 24 rue des Ecoles, 75240 Paris, Cedex 05, France

FEDERAL REPUBLIC OF GERMANY Pergamon Press GmbH, 6242 Kronberg/Taunus, Pferdstrasse 1, Federal Republic of Germany

Copyright © 1980 Pergamon Press Inc.

Library of Congress Cataloging in Publication Data

Main entry under title:

Partners in East-West economic relations.

  (Pergamon policy studies)
  Bibliography: p.
  Includes indexes.
  1. East-West trade (1945-   )—Addresses, essays, lectures. 2. International economic relations—Addresses, essays, lectures. I. Fallenbuchl, Zbigniew M. II. McMillan, Carl H.
HF1411.P313 1979   382'.09171'301717   79-13150
ISBN 0-08-022497-0

All Rights reserved. No part of this publication may be reproduced, stored in a retrieval system or transmitted in any form or by any means: electronic, electrostatic, magnetic tape, mechanical, photocopying, recording or otherwise, without permission in writing from the publishers.

Printed in the United States of America

Contents

Introduction		ix
Part I:	The Changing International Environment and East-West Economic Relations	
Chapter		
1	The CMEA Countries in the Changing International Economic Climate Oleg T. Bogomolov	5
2	Commentary on Professor Bogomolov's Position John P. Hardt	18
3	From the Present Crisis Towards the Establishment of a New International Economic Order: Theses for Discussion Costin Murgescu	28
4	East-West Economic Relations and the International Division of Labor Hugo K. Radice	34
5	The Significance of Economic Interdependence Arising from East-West Relations Peter Knirsch	51
6	Comments Jeanne Kirk Laux and Alan A. Abouchar	76

CONTENTS

Part II:	Changing Actors and Roles in a New International Division of Labor	
7	Changing Roles of International Institutional Actors in East-West and North-South Relations Max Baumer and Hanns-Dieter Jacobsen	91
8	Legal and Organizational Factors in the Participation of Western Multinationals in East-West Trade and Industrial Cooperation David Winter	111
9	Organizational Problems of Multinational Corporations in East-West Trade G. Peter Lauter	131
10	Western Multinational Corporations in Eastern Europe and CMEA Integration Paul Marer	144
11	Comments Egon Neuberger, Sylvain P. Wickham, and Angela M. Conning	170
Part III:	The Choice of Partners: The Experiences of Some Selected Countries	
12	The Trade-Partner Composition of Soviet Trade with the West Philip Hanson	185
13	Choice of Partners in International Economic Relations: The Hungarian Experience Mihaly Simai	219
14	Traditional and Nontraditional Trade: The Case of Czechoslovakia Jaroslav Nykryn	236
15	Factors Influencing Trade with the West: Albania, Mongolia, North Korea, and Vietnam Adi Schnytzer	253

CONTENTS

16	Comments Thomas A. Wolf, Agota Gueullette, and Friedrich Levcik	278
Part IV:	Factors Affecting the Choice of Partners	
17	The Importance of Country Size: A Question But Not a Subject Peter J. D. Wiles	297
18	Balance of Payments Constraints on Socialist Countries: Their Impact on the Choice of Trade Partners Zbigniew Kamecki	317
19	Advanced Technology and the Choice of Trade Partners: The Soviet Policy Eugene Zaleski	343
20	In Search of a Criterion for the Coalition in International Trade Henri Dunajewski and Christian Arnal	370
21	Parallels Between Different Systems in International Economic Relations Detlef Lorenz	393
22	The Influence of the Socioeconomic System on East-West Economic Relations: Poland Jan Mujzel	415
23	Comments Richard Portes, Allen J. Lenz, Antonio Guccione, Alan A. Brown, and Morris Bornstein	427
Name Index		443
Subject Index		447
About the Contributors		457

Introduction

This volume consists of the papers and proceedings of an international conference which took place at Montebello, Quebec over a three-day period, April 26-29, 1978. The conference, entitled "The Choice of Partners in East-West Economic Relations," was jointly organized by the Institute of Soviet and East European Studies, Carleton University in Ottawa, and the Department of Economics at the University of Windsor, Ontario.

The Montebello Conference brought together a group of leading international experts to address three interrelated sets of issues in contemporary international economic relations. In all three areas, the conference was designed to break new ground. It sought to place East-West relations in a broader context, with special reference to an emerging new international economic order, and within that framework to analyze the principal geographic, economic, and political determinants of the choice of partners. At the same time, it was designed to examine common areas in the experience of countries in the East and South, with particular regard to the internationalization of production through the medium of large Western multinational companies.

The three interrelated sets of issues were:

1. <u>The reintegration of the economics of the Soviet Union and Eastern Europe into the international division of labor.</u> The rapid evolution of East-West relations has taken place in an international setting which is in flux. East-West relations have both affected and been affected by the emergence of a new institutional framework for world trade and investment. The papers and discussion at the conference were intended to examine areas of interaction between East-West relations and the emerging new international economic order, and thus to interrelate issues in East-West and North-South relations.

2. <u>The determinants of the choice of partners in East-West relations at the national and subnational levels</u>. The conference explored the principal determinants of the choice of partners in contemporary relations between systematically divergent economics. It sought to examine how comparative costs are affected by differences in size, levels of development, and the economic system. Some contributors approached these questions as case studies on the basis of the experience of individual countries. Others analyzed the roles of functional factors, such as technology, financing, and even bilateral political relations.

3. <u>The similarities and differences between partnerships in the East-West and North-South contexts</u>. Rather than limit itself to stressing the uniqueness of East-West relations in terms of the linkage which they establish among different economic and social systems, the conference was planned so as to differentiate between factors connected with the size of partners and their production structures and those of a primarily systemic nature. The perspective of many Eastern European countries on commercial, financial, and technological relationships with large Western companies is often quite similar to the perspective of Third World countries. Foremost among the common problem is the relationship between smaller, more open economies and the large multinational corporations which control much of the technology, credits, and markets in the West.

To address these questions, the conference organizers sought to bring together specialists actively engaged as practitioners in business, government, and international organizations, as well as scholars. Efforts were made to obtain the participation of experts from a number of Eastern and Western countries, selected so that an essential range of national perspectives and experience could be reflected in the discussions. Academic specialists on the international political economy of the Third World countries were invited to serve as discussants on many of the panels and to draw parallels with their own research findings and experience. Participants included scholars and other experts from the following countries: Austria, Australia, Canada, Czechoslovakia, France, the Federal Republic of Germany, Hungary, Poland, Romania, the Soviet Union, the United Kingdom, and the United States. On this basis, a crossfertilization of information and ideas between East European and Western economists and also between researchers concerned with North-South and East-West economic relations was attained.

When it came time to publish the proceedings of the conference, the editors decided that it would be possible to include almost all of the papers presented. The conference program was conceived to ensure a logical construction for the book, and participants had been

INTRODUCTION

asked to prepare contributions with the proposed publication in mind. As a result, most papers were of a caliber suitable for publication after relatively minor revision. The decision was also taken to include commentaries by assigned discussants, where they drew attention to controversial methodological points or the tentative nature of conclusions; when they contributed special insights drawn, e.g., from practical, personal experience in East-West commerce; or where they treated subject matter not covered elsewhere in the volume.

This volume of papers from Montebello is organized into four parts. The first part includes papers and commentaries discussing East-West economic relations against the background of the current, unstable international economic climate. The analyses of the underlying factors and trends often reflect the political and ideological commitments of the authors, and interesting differences in perspective emerge. There seems to be a consensus, however, that East-West and North-South relations have been similarly affected by developments in the world economy and, in turn, have contributed both to the solution of some problems and the creation of others for any new international economic order.

Part Two examines multinational institutions as actors in this changing international setting. The topics here include the changing role of the Council for Mutual Economic Assistance (CMEA) countries in multilateral organizations, the participation of multinational corporations in East-West relations, and the influence of regional economic groupings.

The experience of selected countries in the choice of economic partners is examined in Part Three. The case studies focus on the Soviet Union, Hungary, and Czechoslovakia, as well as on several smaller, centrally planned economies which are often neglected in Western analysis: Albania, Mongolia, North Korea, and Vietnam.

In Part Four, several functional factors which affect the choice of partners have been selected for more detailed analysis. These include country size, balance of payments constraints, availability of advanced technology, complementarities, and systemic factors. Many of the conclusions remain tentative, and the studies clearly show the great need for further research in this area.

As indicated earlier, an important secondary objective of the conference was to undertake a comparative analysis of the central themes as they apply in North-South and East-West relations. These comparisons were drawn largely in the conference discussions and, therefore, are not fully reflected in the formal contributions published here. Participants specializing in the political economy of the developing countries and drawing on their Third World experience argued that in the long run, the development of the Eastern economies could be adversely affected by close links with Western multinationals. The technologies so acquired might be inappropriate to the production and distributional structures and requirements of the Eastern countries. Such links could also restrain the development of independent R&D capabilities which might develop more rapidly if economic relations with the West remained more traditional, i.e., of an "arms-length" nature. In reply, other participants argued that such reasoning tended to ignore the Eastern defense mechanisms of more extensive R&D facilities, central controls over domestic and foreign investment, and state trading mechanisms which enhance bargaining power <u>vis-a-vis</u> the multinationals in contrast to the developing countries' mechanisms. They conceded, however, that important differences in this regard exist among Eastern countries and that little evidence is available on the nature of the impact of technology transferred via multinationals on the level and development of technology in the Eastern countries.

The Montebello Conference was intended to shed new light on these complex issues, and the editors hope that the publication of the proceedings will not only be of value to the international community at large, but also will serve to stimulate broader interest in these issues. Not all relevant topics have been covered in this book. Some important aspects could not be discussed at sufficient length or depth. Many methodological points could not be followed up, and conclusions drawn were far from satisfactory in some cases. It is hoped, however, that despite such limitations, the publication of these papers will prove useful and will induce further research and discussion of these important subjects.

This book would not have been possible without the assistance of a number of organizations and individuals. The Montebello Conference was made possible by the generous financial support of Electrovert Ltd., of Montreal, the American Council of Learned Societies, the International Exchanges and Research Board (IREX), the Canada Council, the German Marshall Fund of the United States, and the Department of External Affairs of Canada. Carleton University bore many of the administrative costs of the conference organization.

The conference was designed to follow up some of the issues raised at an international conference held in October 1976, at Indiana University on "CMEA Integration and East-West Trade." The organizers of that conference, and in particular Paul Marer, gave valuable encouragement and advice. Philip Hanson provided an excellent written summary of his impressions of the conference, which were very helpful to the organizers who could not be present throughout all the sessions. John Hannigan and Bruce Morgan of the Institute of Soviet and East European Studies at Carleton gave invaluable assistance in

INTRODUCTION xiii

the organization of the conference and were ably joined during the conference by David Dunn and David Stinson.

The editors wish to acknowledge with thanks the excellent cooperation of the authors, who met close deadlines and thereby contributed decisively to timely publication of the book. Professor Sinclair Robinson of the Department of French at Carleton University translated the contributions of Eugene Zaleski, Henri Dunajewski, and Sylvain Wickham into English. Special thanks are due to Mrs. Marilyn Stewart, who with two other secretaries in the Department of Economics at the University of Windsor, Mrs. Maureen Marchini and Miss Susan Capela, retyped most of the papers, handled correspondence, and participated in many editorial decisions. Without their help, and the cooperation of the University and the Department, which assumed the financial cost of editorial and secretarial work, the editing of this book would have been impossible.

I

The Changing International Environment and East-West Economic Relations

Introduction

This part describes broad trends in the international environment under which East-West relations are developing and defines the issues they pose from various national and individual perspectives. It includes contributions from the Soviet Union, the United States, Romania, the United Kingdom, the German Federal Republic, and Canada.

In the first chapter Professor Bogomolov describes -- on the basis of official statistics constructed according to Marxist definitions of national income, industrial production, and so on -- economic progress in the countries belonging to the Council for Mutual Economic Assistance (CMEA), the role of foreign trade in their development, trends in their economic integration, and their involvement in East-West trade. He also gives a clear, concise presentation of the position of the CMEA countries on the present world economic crisis, a new economic order, and cooperation with the Third World.

Instead of limiting himself to simply discussing the paper presented in Chapter 1, in the next chapter Dr. Hardt has provided a commentary on various writings of Professor Bogomolov and has presented his own analysis of developments within CMEA and in East-West economic relations, including an interesting agenda of issues. This is, in effect, an original and valuable contribution which certainly deserves a separate chapter.

Chapter 3 presents another contribution from the CMEA countries, written by a distinguished Romanian economist, Costin Murgescu, who analyzes the nature and roots of the present global crisis, suggests some possible remedies such as strengthening the role of the United Nations, and outlines the Romanian positions on the issue of a new economic order.

Chapter 4 provides a provocative discussion of East-West economic relations against the background of recent and probable future changes in the world economy. Approaching the subject from a very broad point of view of ideology, economics, and international relations, Hugo Radice analyzes the roots of some fundamental maladjustments in the international economic system and points out that the present state of the world economy is by itself a serious obstacle for the development of East-West economic relations.

In Chapter 5, Professor Knirsch discusses the important problem of economic interdependence resulting from East-West economic relations, on the basis of a detailed analysis of the relative strengths and weaknesses of each side.

Finally, Professor Laux provides interesting comments on certain issues raised by Professor Murgescu, and Professor Abouchar addresses himself to the difficult task of measuring economic dependence and interdependence in connection with Professor Knirsch's contribution.

1 The CMEA Countries in the Changing International Economic Climate
Oleg T. Bogomolov

The functioning of the world economy is a source of rising apprehension. Although the exchange of goods and technology among countries has been growing together with the international flow of capital and internationalization of industrial activity, the symptoms of the malaise which has been eating away at the mechanism of the world economy are ever more pronounced. This mechanism is failing to cope with problems such as bridging the widening gap between the industrialized and the developing countries; nonequivalent international exchange; the continued inflation and depreciation of the currencies; provision of scarce raw materials, energy resources, and food; and equal access for all countries to the latest scientific and technical achievements. The blame for this falls on the irresponsible and egoistic behavior of some participants who dominate the world economic relations.

The participation of the CMEA (Council for Mutual Economic Assistance) countries in the world economy has been steadily growing, but one must take into account their relatively still small share in world commercial exchange, something like 10%. Nevertheless, the CMEA countries have been substantially helping to improve the international economic climate, with the activity of the CMEA making a definite contribution to this effort. On the one hand, this collective organization of the socialist countries has promoted, within the framework of its region, the balanced regulation of international economic processes, paving the way for new solutions to a number of global problems. On the other, its international role and experience cannot be ignored in the efforts of all the countries of the world to cope with the scientific, technical, and economic problems facing humanity on the basis of democratic and fair principles.

ECONOMIC GROWTH

During the 1970s, the CMEA countries' economic development has gone forward at a high and stable rate. This has led to a change in the correlation of forces in the world economy. Thus, from 1961 to 1976, the CMEA countries' annual average industrial growth was nearly double that of the developed European Economic Community (EEC) countries, and from 1971 to 1976, it was 3.6 times higher. From 1971 to 1976, the CMEA countries' share of the world output of steel went up from 26 to 30%, electric power generation from 20 to 22%, and manufacture of mineral fertilizers from 29 to 34%.

From 1971 to 1977, the annual average increment of the national income in the CMEA countries as a whole (5.9%) and their industrial growth (7.3%) was sufficiently dynamic. The highest annual average national income growth was in Romania (11.3% in 1971-75 and 9.5% in 1976-77), Poland (9.8% and 6.3%, respectively), Bulgaria 7.8% and 6.4%) and Hungary (6.3% and 5.2 to 5.5%).

AGRICULTURAL GROWTH

The agricultural growth was less stable and was marked by greater discrepancies in the results achieved in the various countries. For the whole group of the CMEA countries in the 1971-77 period, the annual average agricultural-output growth came to 2.0-2.1%. In that period, there was a marked growth of the annual average output of agricultural produce as compared with the 1960s. There have been considerable investments in agriculture and a marked growth of its technical equipment. Due to the faster growth of labor productivity in agriculture, as compared with industry, there has been a substantial reduction in all the countries' share of those employed in this branch of social production. This has made it possible to slow down the shortage of manpower resources, which is evident in virtually all the CMEA countries.

A number of countries have high qualitative indicators in the development of key branches of agriculture. Thus, the annual average wheat yield in Bulgaria, Hungary, the German Democratic Republic (GDR), and Czechoslovakia is already close to 40 centners per hectare. However, with the rapid growth of the populations' incomes and the improving structure of nutrition, the consumption of food in the CMEA countries has been growing much faster than their output. As a result, in the past two five-year periods, the annual average positive balance in the CMEA countries' trade with the capitalist countries in food and food raw materials has gone into the red.

INCREASED STANDARD OF LIVING

The large-scale social programs adopted in some CMEA countries over the past several years have led to an accelerated growth in consumption. The sharp increase in the scale of housing construction has to be noted especially. Considerable qualitative advances have been secured in raising living standards. In a number of European CMEA countries the level of consumption has moved markedly closer to the average level of the capitalist countries of Western Europe. Socialist countries are well to the fore in the world in the number of flats being built per 10,000 population. In assessing the achievements in raising living standards, one should also bear in mind that most socialist countries were able to put sizeable resources into this area only in the past 10-20 years. Before that they were forced to emphasize building up a powerful production, scientific, and technical potential.

ECONOMIC RESULTS

It is the use of this potential in the changed conditions that has produced new problems in the development of the CMEA countries' economy as well as the principal possibilities for solving them. The policy of balanced acceleration in the development of heavy industry, which was pursued for a long period, helped to shape a progressive structure of the production apparatus in these countries. Thus, the share of engineering and the chemical industry went up in Bulgaria from 16.1% in 1960 to 32.4% in 1976, in Hungary from 33.8% (in 1965) to 41.7%, in the German Democratic Republic (GDR), from 38.3% to 47.0%, in Poland from 20.5% to 42.1%, in Romania from 30.1% to 45.0%, in the Soviet Union from 20.5% to 31.9%, and in Czechoslovakia from 35.6% to 41.4% of the volume of industrial output. This structure of industry has caused, in particular, the output of engineering to become the most important commodity group in the CMEA countries' trade with each other, while the engineering complex has become the pivot of their economic cooperation and is bound to become even more important in the future.

The high degree to which the CMEA countries are self-sufficient in fuel, energy, and raw material resources is a major achievement of the socialist economy and this will continue to be true in the current five-year period as well. Thus, at present, the CMEA countries cover 99% of their import requirements in hard coal, 77% in oil and oil products, 77% in iron ore, and 81% in saw-timber through trade with each other.

In the basic characteristics, the scientific and technical potential built up in the CMEA countries is no worse, and for some indicators is better, than the scientific and technical potential of the United States. In 1975, the number of those employed in science and scientific services was about 4.9 million persons, and the number of those working in science was about 1.4 million persons. Every year, there are more than 60,000 inventions in the European CMEA countries, which is roughly 20% of the world's total.

The main task of the present stage in the CMEA countries' development is not so much to accelerate the quantitative growth of the production apparatus and the scientific and technical potential as to improve their qualitative characteristics, the balance in their development, and their much more efficient use.

External economic ties have an ever growing role to play in the CMEA countries' economic development. From 1971 to 1977, the total of their foreign trade in current prices went up nearly 2.5-fold. The increase in the quantum of their trade in 1970 prices went up from 8.2% in 1966-70 to 9.4% in 1971-75. The quantum of foreign trade has been growing especially fast in the past six years in Poland, Romania and the Soviet Union.

EXTERNAL ECONOMIC TIES

The CMEA countries are variously involved in the international division of labor (see Table 1.1). External economic ties have the most important role to play in the economic development of Hungary and Bulgaria. To produce a comparable national income unit, Bulgaria has to sell and buy on external markets more than four times more goods than, say, the Soviet Union. In 1976, Hungary traded manufactured goods with other countries worth almost three times as much as the figure for Romania in order to produce a comparable volume of national income.

However, in the 1970s, the role of external economic ties has also grown markedly for the other CMEA countries. Mutual economic ties are the chief priority for the whole of the external economic activity of most CMEA countries. These ties take shape on a stable planned basis and provide a reliable channel for obtaining vital raw

Table 1.1. Ratio of Exports to National Income

	Bulgaria	Hungary	German Democratic Republic	Poland	Romania	Soviet Union	Czechoslovakia
1970	24	29	20	16	18	7	18
1976	34	52	28	25	23	8	26

SOURCE: Estimates of the Institute of Economics of the World Socialist System, USSR Academy of Science, Moscow.

materials, fuels, and equipment, and for marketing export goods, including those which are hard to sell on Western markets because of discriminatory barriers.

The long-term approach and stability are elements characteristic of the CMEA countries' mutual trade as a whole. A growing share of this trade is based on treaties on specialization and cooperation of production, joint construction projects, and scientific and technical cooperation. The development of specialization and cooperation of production have largely promoted the more active use of the advantages of the international division of labor by the CMEA countries' industry.

REDUCTION OF DIFFERENCES IN THE LEVEL OF DEVELOPMENT

Since its establishment, the CMEA has consistently pursued a policy of creating conditions for cooperation to ensure an evening out of the economic-development levels of its members. The effort to overcome the differences in economic-development levels meets both the interests of the less developed countries and those at a higher level of economic development. The latter countries take an interest in this effort not only for moral considerations of equality, but also for purely economic motives. The point is that any great gap tends to reduce the possibilities for using the advantages of the international division of labor with the more developed countries and, in particular, hampers the deepening of international specialization and cooperation of production.

One will appreciate that the evening out of levels can be achieved only with much faster economic growth rates in the less developed countries. The CMEA countries regard the task of bringing the development levels closer together as a common international task, and they also believe that its successful fulfillment depends primarily on the utmost mustering of internal economic-growth reserves in the less developed countries. International assistance and favorable conditions for the international division of labor can materially help to raise the efficiency of internal efforts, but cannot substitute for it.

The CMEA countries' experience shows the share of accumulations in the national incomes of the countries that had inherited a backward economy from the past was, as a rule, higher than that of the others. However, the higher level of accumulations in Bulgaria, Romania, Poland, and Mongolia is not in itself a guarantee of especially high rates of economic growth. Much depended on their use of the accumulations and the economic efficiency of investment. The above-mentioned countries succeeded in accelerating their growth due to the concentration of capital investments in the building of modern branches of industrial production. Industrialization, and stepped-up industrialization in some countries, enabled the CMEA countries which had lagged in their past development to raise the productivity of social labor and improve the sectoral structure of the national economy in a short historical period.

INDUSTRIALIZATION OF LESS DEVELOPED CMEA COUNTRIES

The transfer of technical documentation, modern equipment samples, licenses, and design and development projects free of charge or on easy terms is of tremendous importance for the industrialization of the less developed CMEA countries. According to available estimates, the Soviet Union has transferred free of charge scientific and technical documentation to other Socialist countries with a total value of 9-12.5 billion rubles (at world capitalist market prices). Together with their mutual exchanges of licenses and technical documentation, the CMEA countries have also pooled their scientific and technical potentials for joint fulfillment of various tasks. An important factor favoring the expansion of accumulations in the less developed countries is the CMEA countries' cooperation in the credit sphere. They have made available credits to each other on especially easy terms.

The CMEA countries' purposeful policy has helped them to do much for the practical solution of problems by evening out the levels of their economic growth. I have tried to illustrate the evening-out process with the help of variation coefficients calculated as the ratio of the average quadratic deviation of extreme values to the average value of the given indicator (see Table 1.2). These data show the steady evening out of economic development levels of the European CMEA countries.

Economic Integration

The CMEA countries' strategy is predicated on the assumption that the further deepening of the socialist economic integration is a most important means for solving their key national economic problems in the short and longer term. This implies, above all, an effort to back up their economic growth with fuel, raw material, and energy resources;

Table 1.2. Variation Coefficient Dynamics of Some Economic Development Indicators in the European CMEA Countries

	1950	1955	1960	1965	1970	1974
1. Variation coefficient of share in production of national income:						
a. industry	0.25	0.23	0.19	0.16	0.13	0.11
b. agriculture and forestry	0.36	0.27	0.29	0.31	0.26	0.24
2. Variation coefficient of assets per worker	0.57	0.52	0.48	0.44	0.36	0.31
3. Variation coefficient of social labor productivity	0.34	0.29	0.28	0.25	0.24	0.21
4. Variation coefficient of per head national income	0.34	0.33	0.32	0.23	0.20	0.16

SOURCE: Estimates of the Institute of Economics of the World Socialist System, USSR Academy of Science, Moscow.

an effort to overcome technical lags in the key sectors; an increase in the manufacture of modern machinery and equipment; a solution to the food supply problem; and improvement of supplies of high quality consumer goods for the population. This also implies an effort to consolidate their economic positions, through integration, in their business cooperation with the West and to expand mutually advantageous relations with the developing countries.

International Economic Climate

The CMEA countries, while elaborating ways of further improving their mutually advantageous cooperation, also want to see a steady improvement in the international economic climate. In the past several years, the CMEA countries have increased their share in world trade. Thus, the share of the Western industrialized countries in the CMEA countries' foreign trade went up from 24% in 1970 to 31% in 1976.

The change in the political climate in the world because of international detente has had a definite role to play in this development, and this has made it possible to bring out untapped reserves of business cooperation among countries with opposite social systems. Another important factor is the CMEA countries' urge to markedly use their ties with the developed capitalist countries to raise the technical level of their production. This explains the development of the license trade with their Western partners, the cooperation in production, the supplies of modern complete equipment, and the creation of conditions for direct investment by foreign capital in the national economy of several CMEA countries. In addition, some CMEA countries have vigorously developed their imports of consumer goods and foods from the Western markets for the most efficient fulfillment of their social programs.

It goes without saying that the extension of imports of modern technology from the Western countries cannot be an alternative for the CMEA countries' scientific and technical progress and can merely supplement it. In 1977, the growth in the share of trade with developed capitalist countries stopped, but it is still hard to judge about its development over a long term. Much will depend on the shaping of the international economic climate.

THE WORLD ECONOMIC SYSTEM

The Socialist countries have no stake in world economic chaos. A world economic system based on the principles of equality, justice, nondiscrimination, and mutual advantage fully meets their collective and national state interests. Any restructuring of the world economy cannot be confined to the relations between the industrialized capitalist countries and the Third World. The democratization of the world economic system also requires complete normalization of East-West relations and elimination of factors like artificial restrictions on economic ties among states with different social systems, discrimination in trade for political and ideological motives, and distortion of the international division of labor under the impact of the policies pursued by the Western powers or their economic groupings. Those are the requirements the CMEA countries seek to add to the conceptions of a new international economic order.

Effects on Socialist Countries

The unfair international economic order does much to harm the Socialist countries, which lose tens and even hundreds of millions of dollars in their relations with the non-Socialist world because of the unfavorable export-import prices ratio, the depreciation of capitalist currencies, the discriminatory commercial and credit policies, the bankruptcies and insolvency of capitalist partners, and restrictions on the purchase of new hardware and technology. According to a Club of Rome report, the various types of discriminatory practices in world economic ties have inflicted annual losses of $50-100 billion on the developing countries.

The artificially depressed prices for fuel and raw materials over a period of decades were a highly essential factor in maintaining the high growth rates in the Western countries, modernizing their fuel and raw materials sectors, and reducing costs in their overall reproduction process. It has been estimated that at the beginning of this decade consumers in the industrialized countries annually paid $200 billion for fuel and raw materials imports, while their producers and exporters--the developing countries--received only $30 billion. (1)

Penetration by foreign capital into the developing countries' economy has become a key instrument of their exploitation; Western direct investments in the Third World alone come to $75 billion. Roughly 40% of the developing countries' industrial production and 50% of their exports are controlled by foreign capital, with the transnationals, above all the United States transnationals, having the strongest positions in this area. (2) The scale of their activity is such that they are capable of exerting a tremendous influence not only on the developing countries' economy, but also on their internal political life and foreign policy orientation.

ECONOMIC PROPOSALS

The 1973-74 energy crisis has shown that the existing international system of energy and raw materials supply is extremely vulnerable. The industrialized Western countries consume 20 times more natural resources per head than the developing countries, but according to estimates by Western specialists, have only 30% of the world's oil reserves and roughly 37% of its reserves of 18 key minerals, including iron, nonferrous metals, and phosphorites. Their long-term economic growth is inconceivable without the influx of the lacking resources from outside. However, with the Third World countries' growing economic lag, this cannot be continued on the old economic terms.

The basic content of the programs for a new world economic order put forward by the developing countries consists of two demands: (1) sovereignty over their own natural resources and their use to overcome their backwardness, and (2) creation of an international mechanism for redistributing the earnings from the world economic exchange in favor of the economically lagging countries.

The CMEA countries support the developing countries on the new world economic order, but emphasize the need for progressive social transformations and the mustering of internal potential for economic growth as the chief means for changing their economic condition. The Soviet Union and many other Socialist countries resolutely oppose the diverse utopian projects for a world-wide redistribution of wealth which tend to distract the Third World peoples from the vital tasks of struggling for their national liberation and social emancipation and for the utmost use on that basis of their internal potential for socio-economic progress.

Many of the propositions written into the developing countries' programs for a new international economic order fully or partially meet the interests of the Socialist countries. This relates to points like the unrestricted right to dispose of their national resources, including the nationalization of foreign property; the fixing of stable prices for the developing countries' export products (raw materials and fuels), including the principle of price indexing (an automatic increase in prices for raw materials and fuels proportional to the growth of prices for manufactured goods); the creation of buffer commodity stocks to compensate for the fluctuations in supply and demand, and other measures to stabilize the developing countries' export earnings; greater access for their traditional and new exports to the developed countries' markets; the creation of new channels for the transfer of technology and regulation of the activity of the transnationals; a reform of international trade and the monetary and financial system; and so on.

Socialist Countries and the Third World

However, on the strength of the idea of a universal solidarity, the Socialist countries cannot accept similar claims on all the industrialized countries, regardless of their social system, and the demand that the Socialist countries should accord to the Third World countries' unilateral advantages on the nonreciprocity principle. This kind of approach tends to obscure the fundamental distinction between the Socialist and the capitalist countries, releasing the latter from their responsibility for the colonial past and the present condition of the developing countries. This applies, in particular, to the demand for an elimination of the developing countries' debts and the provision to them of 1% of the industrialized countries' GNP in the form of aid.

Just now the West is siphoning off from the developing countries much more than it is giving them in aid for defense and development purposes. Aid from the West, which does not fully accept the 1%-of-the-GNP demand, can and must be increased in view of its historical responsibility and the scale of its current exploitation of Third World's resources. The Socialist countries have never plundered the developing countries and do not today derive any unilateral advantages from their relations with them. That is why, while urging utmost assistance to Third World countries, we do not and cannot regard the allocation of 1% of our GNP in aid as a "moral duty."

Nor can one ignore the fact that the deepening differentiation among the developing countries tends to increase an element of pragmatism in the policies of some of them, a tendency to conciliation with the leading Western powers, and attempts to put pressure on the Socialist countries, above all on the amount of aid.

The CMEA countries could evidently increase their contributions for development purposes, if progress is achieved in disarmament, and reach agreement to increase the volume of aid, particularly on the deduction of a fixed share of the resources which are now released through the reduction of military budgets. Their interests would be promoted by an increase in credits and technical assistance to the developing countries that would result in a rational division of labor with them and secure new sources of stable imports of raw materials, fuel, and some goods by the CMEA countries, while simultaneously creating a stable prospect for exports to the developing countries of the goods they need.

The economic cooperation between the Socialist countries and the Third World could probably be made more efficient if the assistance is extended not only, or not so much, in building up individual industrial, transport, and other facilities, but in developing intersectoral, territorial, industrial, and agroindustrial complexes and exerting a substantial influence in changing the socioeconomic face of the countries concerned and the structure of their cooperation with the CMEA countries. There are opportunities for new forms of cooperation between Socialist and developing countries, including various forms of mixed and joint enterprises.

Over the next ten or fifteen years, the struggle for a new world economic order will evidently be one of the main lines of international politics. The CMEA countries can make a constructive contribution to the solution of the problems which arise in this connection.

NOTES

1. J. Tinbergen and A. J. Dolman, eds., Reshaping the International Order: A Report to the Club of Rome (New York: Dutton, 1976), p. 34.

2. Ibid., p. 39.

2 Commentary on Professor Bogomolov's Position
John P. Hardt

INTRODUCTION

Professor Bogomolov concludes in Chapter 1, as well as in his previous writings that in effect certain common bases and objectives have developed in the commercial policies of East and West:

1. The emphasis on national economic objectives has shifted from quantitative growth, which characterized the economic strategies of the past, to growth with efficiency. The Stalinist policy of extensive growth has given way to the qualitative, intensive growth strategy in Eastern centrally planned economies. The Western economies are, likewise, increasingly concerned with the changing quality of economic performance and less preoccupied with quantitative growth rates.

2. Global interdependence in economic development has been adopted in lieu of the concept of independence or two markets, which characterized the policies of the past in both East and West. Eastern economic isolation and self-sufficiency have ceased being ends in themselves. Western industrial economies, especially since the oil price rise, have become increasingly aware of the interrelations in the global economy and the trend toward economic interdependence in the world.

3. Global interdependence has been buttressed by a sense of shared East-West responsibility for price stability and economic growth in the international market, in lieu of the

general focus on the national and domestic concerns of the past. Eastern and Western economies have been responsive to the need to follow policies conducive to international and interregional price stability and economic growth in the world economies. Conversely the negative impacts of inflation and recession have been recognized as common problems in both East and West.

4. Attention in the East and West has been focused on the economically developing world and the task of establishing joint responsibility for a New International Economic Order (NIEO). This new perception contrasts with past policies emphasizing national economic independence. While this emphasis on the Third and Fourth World economic problems extends to the oceans as well as land, the development of policies for utilization of fish, mineral, and energy resources of the sea have provided opportunities as well as problems in East-West economic policy.

To be sure each of the shared bases of mutual East-West interest and common objectives contain issues in sharp dispute. However, there is now, more than in the past, a common framework for East-West policy, decisions, negotiations, and adjudication of issues outstanding. The commentary that follows draws from themes in the writings of Professor Bogomolov in this volume and elsewhere and takes his positive view of the mutual benefit of developing East-West commercial relations as a given variable.

CHANGING GENERAL EAST-WEST ENVIRONMENT

Although they are moving toward a common sense of interdependence and mutual obligations, the East and West have certain conflicting trends in their general environment or policy frame of reference.

Improved CMEA commercial and industrial cooperation and financial relations have developed with the West. On the one hand, this new East-West commercial compatibility has provided for advantages of technological, managerial, and financial flows which have enhanced CMEA growth and efficiency. On the other hand, there has been an increased share of hard or convertible goods required to finance the trade turnover. These two developments in part complement each other, but likewise provide some competition with each other in the current environment, especially in view of persistent Eastern deficits and need for hard currency.

The burden of uncertainty in foreign economic relations increased with the expansion of East-West economic relations and increasing ties with the world market in the early 70s. The Eastern traders were affected by the adverse impact of Western recession and inflation. Indeed, "stagflation" took a relatively greater toll in the East than it did in some of the more advanced countries of the West. Likewise, as the commercial prospects have increased for Eastern exporters in the Western market, problems of trade restrictions have become increasingly onerous. Large, successful export programs from the Eastern economies often resulted in Western quotas, increased tariffs, cases of market disruption and dumping, and other trade restrictions instead of stable expanding markets.

On the other hand, the uncertainty and unpredictability of Eastern purchases and sales in the Western markets have often had disruptive effects on price stability and production planning in the West. Most noteworthy in this regard has been the unpredictability of intervention by Soviet grain purchasers in the world market over the last decade. Substantial increases in world grain prices and inability to plan crop plantings in Western grain exporting countries in line with anticipated demand and price changes have been the result. This unpredictable variance in Eastern grain demand has fueled either domestic inflation or agriculture recession in countries such as the United States and Canada.

CHANGING GENERAL INTRA-CMEA ENVIRONMENT

In the post-1973 period of oil price increases, the policies and practices of integration within the Eastern economic alliance (CMEA) have changed terms of alliance in both centrifugal and centripetal ways. The more integrative aspects tying the CMEA together have been the joint projects within the CMEA Comprehensive Program, illustrated by the Orenburg natural gas pipeline project. These joint projects and the mutual interest generated by the CMEA energy and materials programs have tended to tie the East European countries closer to the Soviet economy within CMEA.

Increased requirements for hard goods and modernization within CMEA have led to greater pressures to divert those Eastern goods that could compete in the world market to Western trade and away from intra-CMEA economic relations. In this sense there has been a short run competition within CMEA countries between intra-CMEA

COMMENTARY ON PROF. BOGOMOLOV'S POSITION

needs and requirements for exports to the West. In the longer run, it may be that intra-CMEA activities will increasingly provide for improved joint absorption of advanced Western technology and the increased sale and supply of hard goods with CMEA. Some of the advanced countries in certain sectors may become the preferred entry points for Western technology and appropriate transfer points for Western technology to other members within CMEA under advantageous financial and economic conditions. Thus, in the longer term centripetal and centrifugal forces may offset each other.

Likewise, although current integration appears to be stimulated by the pressures of Soviet energy pricing, intra-CMEA integration involving the smaller Eastern and Western European economies without Soviet influences may come from recent Western relations throughout CMEA. In the automobile industry, for example, FIAT, Citroen, and other Western automotive companies may have provided the common framework for CMEA automotive integration.

COMPARATIVE ADVANTAGES OF THE INTERNATIONAL DIVISION OF LABOR

Relative price and cost have become influential in production and foreign trade decisions in the East as well as the West. Under the concept of international division of labor in the East, as with comparative cost in the West, production and export decisions are based on relative price and cost estimates rather than planning judgments often reflecting noneconomic factors. On the one hand, world market pricing in East-West trade has become advantageous as a measure of efficiency in Eastern European economies. This application of the international division of labor now goes beyond energy to Eastern industrial goods pricing. Moreover, if products can be produced to meet world market standards with available resources, then these goods may be considered preferred in Eastern economic plans and generate financing within the domestic plan as they could provide valuable sources of hard currency earnings. However, when these measures of hard currency trade preferences go beyond comparative advantage or the international division of labor, they tend to distort the structure of Eastern economies since scarcity pricing in Western economies can hardly be an accurate reflection of scarcity or opportunity costs within Eastern economies. Moreover, preferences for foreign hard currency over domestic soft currency markets tend to discriminate against domestic CMEA demands.

In the wake of the world price rise in energy costs, a number of areas of past Eastern discrimination and preference in pricing, as between Western and CMEA sales, became highlighted. The sale of Soviet energy for constant prices, which were lower than the world market prices, in return for soft goods imports suggested a substantial preference or discrimination for Eastern countries within CMEA in energy pricing. This trade preference within CMEA for Eastern suppliers has been historically observable. This preference for soft goods from various CMEA countries within Eastern Europe, that would not be marketable elsewhere without at least substantial prices reductions outside CMEA, has been a form of past discrimination. Each of these areas of preference and discrimination have been narrowed in recent years as intra-CMEA pricing has begun moving toward world market price levels and hard goods have become more important in intra-CMEA trade. No longer can Eastern producers assume CMEA is a captive or exclusive market. Increasingly, competition from outside CMEA is becoming a factor in intra-CMEA trade; thus, discrimination against Western imports has been reduced.

As Eastern economies move toward the efficiency concepts of free trade, many Western economies tend to move toward protectionism. With recession and a reduction of national or individual sector competitiveness, the response is often to restrict or bar entry to cheaper and better foreign products rather than to adopt domestic policies to improve competitiveness. Western restrictions take many forms in tariffs, quantitative restrictions, licensing, and legal actions.

MODERATION OF EAST-WEST SYSTEMIC AND INSTITUTIONAL BARRIERS

Bridging the different economic systems of East and West have been commercial relations and institutional links at a variety of levels. Formal governmental agreements, multilateral and bilateral, have provided a policy umbrella for a variety of East-West agreements at commercial, financial, industrial, and regional levels. These institutional arrangements provide a framework for transmitting information and conducting negotiations which give a stability to the developing East-West commercial relationships. It may seem more important to the Eastern countries to have formal, long-term, governmental agreements with levels of trade and types of transfers spelled out for longer term plan development. However, it is equally important for Western corporate planning to have such relations institutionalized, in the sense that they may be the basis for reducing uncertainty in the financing and trading patterns. International agreements, such as the Helsinki Final Act, and international institutions, such as the Economic Commission for Europe (ECE) and United Nations channels, have likewise assisted this process of the orderly expansion of commercial relations.

From this development of institutional bridges, systemic differences among the Eastern trading monopolies and a characteristically fragmented Western market system have been moderated. In the Eastern economies greater access to end users and suppliers have been provided, as well as more information on current and likely future import needs. At the same time, there are still considerable uncertainties through the control of Eastern plans which may shut off hard currency supplies to an importer, drastically revise Eastern plans for import, and thereby impact negatively on Western export plans.

Western market fragmentation has partly been ameliorated by the development of multinational corporations (MNC) in Western countries. In Western Europe and North Asia close governmental and private economic relations reinforce the more coordinated MNC-dominated pattern of trading from Western economies. By contrast, in North America negative public concerns about government intervention and foreign trade monopolies have tended to reduce this coordination and sharpen differences with Eastern foreign trade monopolies. Still, on balance, Western government/private economic cooperation and the increasing role of multinational corporations have had the effect of drawing the institutional arrangements of the West closer to those of Eastern trading partners. Likewise, the trends toward greater end user access and increased industrial cooperation have reduced the cohesion, discipline, or prohibitively unitary organization of the Eastern market from the standpoint of Western trading companies.

COMMERCIAL, PRODUCTION, AND FINANCIAL COOPERATION

Efficiency, effectiveness of technological transfer, and credit worthiness have all been issues effectively addressed in developing East-West commercial relations. Industrial cooperation providing for quality controls, managerial transfer, and continuous commitment of Western suppliers for the effective absorption and utilization of Western technology have helped improve the effectiveness of technological transfer and its translation into higher quality output in the Eastern economies. Compensation agreements have been developed to deal with the difficult problems of hard currency financing of imports to the East.

On the other hand, compensation agreements have had all of the disadvantages of trade bilateralism in that they distort the production process to meet the needs of financing imports. The lack of flexibility provided to the Eastern suppliers and restrictive production requirements set to meet Western commitments are reinforced by the problems of marketing goods supplied primarily to Western companies to meet commitments in financing exports. The distortions from export for repayment, rather than to satisfy felt domestic needs within the Western market, may be accompanied by undue strains artificially placed on Eastern producers. These export priority pressures may be matched by drains, perceived as critical, on the scarce hard currency supply on the exporters' part and excess stocks generated above the needs of the Western importers in order to repay Western companies under terms of compensation agreements.

Additional sources of benefit, both in terms of financing and technology transfer, may lie in the development and promise of third country cooperation within various areas as diverse in nature as the Arab Oil Producing Export Countries (AOPEC), the developing countries of the Third World, intra-CMEA trade, and intra-Western commercial relations with the oil rich countries. Western technology and Eastern resources and marketing may provide useful mechanisms for earning hard currency for both countries in these cooperative ventures. Developing world trade may likewise provide a mechanism for further development of Eastern economies using Western technology, if financing arrangements can be used to facilitate such arrangements and output in hard goods, such as resources and materials, are forthcoming from the developing world. Intra-CMEA trade may generate returns if the superior ability of Eastern countries to transfer Western technology and to market products within CMEA may be translated into mutually beneficial development. Finally, intra-Western relations may be a part of a process of Eastern countries' enterprises joining the global supply system of large multinational companies of the West.

Issues of economic cooperation join and divide the Eastern and Western economies. On the one hand, in principle the Eastern economies prefer egalitarianism and preferential treatment of the developing countries in the new international economic order. The notion of common heritage and equal sharing of the wealth beneath the seas is an example. The application of the principle, "return according to contributions," in terms of investment and technology would provide more for the Western enterprises' investment as they are able to develop and provide economic returns from these maritime treasures in the short run. This approach involving the principle, "to each according to his contribution," is akin to adoption of the Marxian concept of the "bourgeois right." The common acceptance of a return for contribution approach would facilitate cooperation of East and West in the NIEO. An insistence of the East on an egalitarian approach ("to each according to need") would not facilitate a common East-West policy. The related policy concepts of many of the developing countries, who insist on their presumed rights to nationalize foreign enterprises, to reschedule or renounce payment of debts, and to receive foreign aid "without strings," are likewise issues for which a common policy may develop. However, at present Eastern and Western policies seem to be largely divisive.

COMMERCIAL ORIENTATION OF TRADE AND NON TRADE ACTIVITIES RELATED TO EAST-WEST COMMERCE

The balance of payments and balance of payments deficit have always been factors influencing economic and foreign policies of Western countries, and now in the current era of interdependence they have become factors in the East. Export industries, nontrade sources of income including tourism, merchant marine activities, and sales of scarce metals such as gold, have all become factors in current East-West trade policy. Uneven development of Eastern imports and exports tends to create a degree of instability in Western markets, in part paradoxically related to the success of increased sales of Eastern products and services. Success in expanding Eastern exports to the West can and often does lead to restrictive responses on the part of the West. Quotas for products, such as agriculture goods entering the Common Market, concerns with dumping, legal restrictions, etc., all tend to counter apparent success in increasing commercial relationships.

These commercial restrictions are reinforced by the residual Western political antagonisms toward Eastern trade. In the United States this phenomenon has been referred to as the "Battle Act Drag," or the continuation of the notion that all East-West relations are zero sum games. The increasing acceptance that trade is a positive sum game and that this concept applies especially to East-West commercial relations would tend to counter this traditional psychological climate. Likewise, there is a residual Eastern reluctance to become "economic hostages" of Western suppliers who may use commercial leverage for political purposes.

AGENDA OF ISSUES

A number of issues on the agenda of governments and economic leaders in Western and Eastern economies, such as large scale projects, cooperative mechanisms for technology transfer trade receptivity, credit management, and mutual acceptance of positive sum games, may materially influence the pace and volume of East-West commercial relations.

Large Scale Projects

Large scale long-term CMEA projects, especially in the Soviet Union, as an umbrella for the development of increased trade turnover between CMEA countries and Western economies are significant. Were large scale projects in the Soviet Union, such as energy or metals development in Siberia, to become much more integrated with Western economies, this fact alone would have a significant effect on overall East-West commercial relations.

Cooperative Mechanisms for Technology Transfer

The lack of development of effective stable mechanisms for transfer of Western technology, its absorption, assimilation, and utilization in Eastern economies provides critical constraints on commercial expansion. The kind of flow of technology from advanced to less advanced sectors within the Western economies in the post-World War II period might be emulated in the future technological flow from West to East. However, considerable improvement in the mechanisms, such as industrial cooperation, are necessary to approach this intra-Western level of effectiveness in technology transfer. Significant political and institutional changes are presumably required in both East and West if such flow is desired and is to be attained.

Trade Receptivity

Export generation and import absorption of products from Eastern economies to the West is essential for stimulating and financing increased trade turnover. Improved market management to facilitate substantially improved receptivity and avoid significant restrictions is a critical East-West policy problem.

East-West Credit Management

East-West credit management must be planned, normal, and predictable to satisfy Western bankers and Eastern planners. The financing of commercial relations and the flow of capital from one economy to another according to comparative advantage are normal patterns among Western economies. Due to the probably unresolvable continued systemic differences, greater uncertainties and risks are attached to both Western and Eastern markets than are acceptable for either side under normal conditions. Therefore, government credits and guarantees take on an increasing role of importance. This is especially true in those cases where the development projects are especially large and long-term in character, enhancing the problems of Western market and Eastern plan uncertainty and risk.

Mutual Acceptance of Positive Sum Games

Substantial movement would be required to establish a mutual acceptance of the efficacy of normalization of East-West commercial relations. A requirement exists for an empirical demonstration if there is to be conceptual acceptance that each participant benefits more than the cost in economic as well as other terms.

Once there was a general political acceptance of the desirability of East-West economic interdependence so that a degree of commercial predictability and credit certainty would result. This broadly based mutual benefit in East-West commercial relations might then be expected to provide a stimulus toward a movement to a higher threshold of development and trade turnover. If that were to occur, then interdependence of a world market that would reach from the Atlantic to the Pacific in the Northern Hemisphere might become a reality.

3 From the Present Crisis Towards the Establishment of a New International Economic Order: Theses for Discussion
Costin Murgescu

THREE THESES

The first half of this decade has been dominated by a multitude of serious problems in the world economy: the energy and raw materials crisis, a food crisis in the underdeveloped world, obstacles preventing most of the developing countries to attain their objectives, difficulties of the developed capitalist countries to relaunch their growth after the crisis of 1974-75, a recrudescence of protectionist tendencies in international trade, chronic deficits in trade and current account balances, inflationary pressures that cannot be stopped in a great number of countries, erratic fluctuations of currency exchange rates, and so on. The analysis of these problems is based on three fundamental theses.

Thesis One

The first thesis is that all these phenomena represent a deep, manysided, and overall crisis into which the entire present systen of economic relations has entered. In view of the global character of this crisis and the universal interdependencies among nations, its effects are to be felt under different intensities and forms by all the countries of the world.

One conclusion from this thesis is that the problems that are on the agenda of the present world economy cannot be solved independently. Sectional solutions cannot have but short-term and partial effects, and in the long run they prove to be illusory.

Thesis Two

The real causes of such a global crisis cannot be found in developments that are only its side effects, as was the rapid escalation of the international oil prices in the first half of this decade. It is necessary to examine the historical significance of the fundamental changes that occurred on the world political map after the war, first of all, the development of world forces of Socialism and the collapse of the colonial system of imperialism. Essentially, these transformations express the will of the peoples to decide by themselves their own destinies, to speed up all socioeconomic development, to turn to account the creative national capacity, and to participate alongside with all the other peoples on an equal rights basis in the achievements of contemporary civilization and in all aspects of international life.

This legitimate tendency carries along with it permanent changes in the international balance of forces. It contradicts the interests of those countries that were favored by the old international division of labor, which are now trying to safeguard their privileges in the world market, to resort to neocolonialist practices by attempts to perpetuate in the world the relations for the domination of the weaker or less developed by the more powerful or the more developed ones.

The widening of gaps between advanced and less developed countries is the main factor today that hinders the socioeconomic progress of the entire world, narrows the possibilities of international trade and cooperation, feeds a state of chronic instability in the entire world economy, and induces attempts to create new world spheres of influences between different states of groups of states. The resulting emergence of the world's conflicting spheres will hinder the way to international detente. It will contribute to the acceleration of the arms race and the creation of new hotbeds of tension, thus opening up possibilities of danger for peace and security.

The Romanian concept of a new economic and political international order is based on the analysis of these problems. It places at its core the imperatives of the eradication of underdevelopment and promotion of cooperation among all states, on the basis of strictly observing the principles of independence and national sovereignity, equality in rights, noninterference in internal affairs, and nonrecourse to force and the threat of its use.

In the Romanian conception, the establishment of a new economic order is not a pure desideratum of a certain number of countries in disadvantageous positions as a result of the present international division of labor but is the only realistic way to long-term solutions for the big problems the world is being confronted with today. It is, in fact, a solution objectively imposed by all contemporary historical development and by the requirements to build up a more just and better world for all the peoples for the benefit of social progress in every nation.

Thesis Three

The attainment of the previously mentioned objectives and the improvement of all the mechanisms of international cooperation in keeping with the realities of the world we live in require a global vision and call for solutions to be reached with the participation of all states and their consensus. For this reason it is necessary to democratize and strengthen the role played by the United Nations, which provides the most suitable organizational framework for coping with the problems the world is being faced with today.

TOWARD A NEW INTERNATIONAL ORDER

To place the problems of the eradication of underdevelopment at the top of present day world economic problems means ipso facto to underline the responsibility that the developing countries should take upon themselves. The establishment of a new international economic order is conditioned, to a great extent, by the way in which these countries: (1) effect necessary social changes, (2) formulate and implement an effective internal economic development policy, and (3) are pursuing a policy of international economic cooperation in accordance with their own national interests.

The eradication of underdevelopment requires that each country should elaborate a corresponding system of priorities in employing its own national resources. It should mobilize all its human and material resources in order to set up a modern and harmoniously developed economy according to its particular conditions, and it should allocate for this purpose an important share of its national income for a longer period of time. The Romanian experience is relevant here. In recent five-year plans the country allocated for the accumulation fund approximately 30-34% of its national income. Giving priority to internal factors, President Nicolae Ceausescu has always insisted that the liquidation of gaps implies the maximum mobilization of the country's own means and resources, i.e., joining the efforts, the energy, and the creative capacity of the people to develop the country's production forces with a view to setting up a modern industry and a highly productive agriculture.

At the same time, however, it is important to strengthen the solidarity and cooperation among all developing countries, so that in this way they can increase their growth potential which is often limited by narrow internal markets. An ever increasing role can be played by the agreements for subregional economic collaboration and by the consolidation of subregional economic bodies in Africa, Latin America, and Asia.

The economic international cooperation in the development of less developed countries implies both the promotion of some forms of equitable economic links among all nations and also a real increase in the economic, financial, and technical-scientific aid the advanced industrial countries are granting to developing countries. This aid is imposed by the contemporary universal interdependence, by the fact that the economic-social progress has become as indivisible as world peace is. In this connection it is important to mention the proposal to set up a Development Fund under the United Nations, which was to be primarily channeled to countries with a per capita national income of less than $200. In Romania's view such a fund would be made up of contributions from all states, first of all by the developed ones. One of the additional feeding sources of such a fund could be the unconditioned transfer of one half from sums saved up by cutting down military budgets.

International financial assistance should be used to induce the national efforts of the developing countries. It is, therefore, advisable that the funds should be channeled to those countries which allocate for development a higher share of their national income within their programs covering periods of 10-15 years. Of course, the concrete way in which the funds could be spent by the recipient developing countries should be chosen by the countries themselves in keeping with their priorities established on the basis of the attributes of national sovereignity. The only restriction should be that such funds must be used for development purposes only.

THE ROMANIAN POSITION

Alongside the proposals jointly adopted by the "Group of 77" and other proposals put forward by different individual states, Romania has stated her considerations in the document entitled "Romania's Stand on the Establishment of a New International Economic Order," which was officially released at the Seventh Extraordinary U.N. General Assembly. The common denominator of all Romanian proposals comes from the reason for principles that have been previously formulated: blending of each country's own efforts with wide and equitable economic international cooperation.

Since it is impossible to present here the proposed solutions for all major problems, the spirit of the Romanian position is illustrated in the example of its approach to the solution of the energy and raw materials crisis, which is a problem of vital importance for all countries.

Romania has attempted to solve the energy and raw materials crisis in the field of internal economic policy through the following measures.

1. Romania has been making a huge investment effort for over two decades to increase her own base of raw materials, including exploitation of poor or deep deposits. During the last two five-year plans the total volume of investment in the national economy increased by more than three times and a share of about 3.5% of these investments was allocated to geological explorations within the country.

2. An absolute priority was given to coal in the structure of the thermoelectrical energy utilization. Between 1960 and 1970 Romania's supply of total thermo-electrical energy increased seven times. During the same period, within the structure of fuels, the share of coal increased from 22.4 to 30.5%, while the share of oil decreased from 13.1 to 5%.

3. Strict rules were introduced in all industrial branches in order to reduce material intensity of production processes.

Parallel with the thorough efforts that are being made within the national economy, cooperation with other countries has been advanced: the joint construction with Yugoslavia and Bulgaria of big hydropower stations on the river Danube; the participation in big investment projects in the Soviet Union for the widening of production of some raw materials; and a number of agreements on cooperation in production with developing countries in Africa, Asia, and Latin America.

However, the problem of raw materials is a world problem, and for this reason the third of Romania's action guidelines is the participation in the process of searching for universal solutions with all interested states. These solutions must be based on the observance of national sovereignity and the exercise of national control over natural resources. They should include: the increase of world raw materials and energy reserves by the introduction of modern technical solutions for geological explorations, extraction, and processing; efforts by all states to eliminate fuel and raw materials waste; wide international cooperation in the utilization of deposits lying at the bottom of seas and oceans; and the discovery and use of new energy resources.

It is also necessary to regulate international trade in these products and to eliminate excessively wide fluctuations in prices in the international markets by introducing certain principles and concrete measures to prevent short-run fluctuations and ensure long-term price stability. The problem of raw materials is too important for contemporary economic growth to be left to the anarchic play of the market. The role of long-term international agreements, which would be concluded by the interested states, should be strengthened.

In accordance with such requirements, Romania and the other developing countries have subscribed to "The Integrated Program of Commodities" presented at the Fourth United Nations Conference on Trade and Development (UNICTAD) session at Nairobi in 1976. The objectives of this program could be attained only if all its component elements were carried out, including the setting up of a common fund to finance the buffer stocks. At the same time, a front ranking place should be given to measures meant to establish a correct relation between the prices of raw materials and those of industrial products. Romania is in favor of establishing prices for all the products on the basis of international agreements.

The world we are living in has not only an extremely varied social-political structure, potential, and level of development, but it is also a world that the present technical-scientific revolution turns into an even smaller place. Why shouldn't we conclude and acknowledge the fact that we are living in a world in which the fate of each one is increasingly dependent on that of all the others? In such a world one cannot speak about overcoming the present deadlock -- to say nothing of strengthening of democracy, peace, and international security -- without acknowledging the equal rights of all the nations to progress.

That is the meaning of the movement for the establishment of a new international order and of the appeal launched by President Nicolae Ceausecu. It is this appeal that provides an important concluding thought:

> In this tremendous fight, the progressive forces, all those wishing to set up new relations based on equality and collaboration among peoples and states, irrespective of thier political and philosophical conceptions, religious beliefs, must join their efforts so as to ensure a democratic, progressive development of the human society.

Only in this way shall we be able to overcome the crisis we are faced with at present and bring our contribution to the establishment of a better world.

4
East-West Economic Relations and the International Division of Labor
Hugo K. Radice

INTRODUCTION

If we look at trade flows in the world economy among three groups of countries -- the advanced capitalist countries, the Socialist countries, and the less developed countries -- a simple pattern emerges. If we refer to these three groups for the sake of convenience as the West, the East, and the South, then the pattern of trade between West and South (exchange of manufactured goods, especially producer goods, for primary products and some light manufacture) is essentially similar to the trade between West and East and East and South. A. G. Frank is one recent author who has drawn attention to this pattern, concluding that the "socialist countries occupy an intermediate position in the international division of labour, in this regard not unlike the most developed 'subimperialist' underdeveloped countries like Brazil." (1)

If this is a sufficient preliminary characterization of the structure of East-West-South trade, what are the likely developmental trends in this structure in the coming years? One possible and appealing approach to this vast question involves viewing East-West-South economic relations essentially as but one set of components in a capitalist world economy. In other words, if the East's foreign economic relations place it in an intermediate position in the international division of labor, then the development of the former can in essence be derived from trends in the latter, which in turn is molded by the development of the capitalist system on a world scale.

Objections may be raised that no one would so dismissively accord a purely passive role to the Socialist countries in the world economy, any more than they would on questions of relations of political power, diplomacy, or nuclear strategy. Nevertheless, persuasive arguments can and have been made for viewing economic relations both between West and East and between East and South through one or the other conceptual framework derived from the study of relations between West and South. In the following section, I want to look not so much at the arguments themselves, as at the reasons why they are so persuasive. Following this methodological and ideological inquiry, the remaining part of the paper looks at the substantive issue of trends in the capitalist world economy, the international division of labor, and how the Eastern countries fit into these trends.

THE MARKET-ECONOMY BIAS OF ECONOMICS

My first argument concerns the way in which economists approach the analysis of economic systems and their efficiency or rationality and how this approach colors their appraisal of the Socialist economic system and its relations with the capitalist world economy.

There has been a long and persistent debate about the rationality of the market economy versus the rationality of a planned economy, but at the theoretical level, it is not possible to regard either system as inherently superior to the other. (2) Nevertheless, if we consider how economists in the West have viewed the economic systems of the actually existing Socialist countries, the yardstick by which they assess them has usually been that of the ideal market economy. Nowhere is this more clear than in the debates over the economic reform movement in Eastern Europe. In ideal-type form, the analysis can be summarized as follows. (3) Central planning in a command-economy framework generates inherent contradictions centered on the efficiency criteria which motivate and reward economic actors, particularly with regard to management decisions on the choice of products and techniques of production. This leads to inefficiencies in the allocation of factors of production, sluggish innovation and productivity growth, and a debilitating structural conflict between planners and enterprises. The economic reforms aim to resolve these difficulties by at least a partial return to the rationality of the market. In the ideal "market socialist" model, the scope of administrative central planning is greatly reduced and concentrates on setting desired levels of macroeconomic and sectoral aggregates. Intermediate and enterprise level management is free to make decisions on the basis of market, i.e., profit and criteria with the market conditions molded and constrained by nonselective policy instruments manipulated by the central authorities. Making reference to the supposed shift from extensive to intensive growth in recent years in the Socialist countries, economists for the most part regard the economic reform model as an objective necessary for sustaining the momentum of economic development. It would be fair to say that the approach just outlined is shared by pro-reform economists in the Socialist countries also.

There is at least a strong presumption, therefore, that the socialist economic systems must eventually adopt some form and degree of market rationality. The implications of this for East-West economic relations are particularly clear-cut: A rational market price system extending to foreign trade and the de facto convertibility of currencies would form the optimal, if not necessary, basis for an increasing integration into the capitalist world economy. In line with orthodox international trade theory, this would lead to significant welfare gains through the operation of the law of comparative advantage.

Given this dominant framework of analysis, it is easy to see that economists in general tend to view East-West economic relations as a variant of international capitalist economic relations, hence the optimism of the mid and late sixties and the pessimism of the seventies when it appeared that the economic reform movement had suffered a definitive check, even in Hungary where it had been most, or rather uniquely, comprehensive. It is true that some writers have contended that East-West trade and cooperation may be viewed by Socialist leaders as an alternative to domestic economic reforms, but many would argue that this is a vain hope, because only in the context of the latter can capital goods and technology acquired through the former be effectively utilized. (4) It is true, also, that in sharp contrast to the prevailing orthodoxy, Marxist critics in the West, (5) as well as so-called conservatives in the Socialist countries, have argued that the economic reforms represent a giant step back towards capitalism and that involvement with the capitalist world economy means growing dependence on the West. However, this view constitutes, for the most part, simply a mirror-image of the orthodoxy.

But does this economic approach really give us an adequate understanding of why the reform movement developed and why it was checked? It seems self-evident that social and political factors have to be taken into account to a far greater extent than is usually the case. (6) This is not just a matter of identifying these factors as essentially external constraints imposed by the political leaderships in the Socialist countries, but rather one of analyzing the social and political dimensions internal to the traditional economic system. Putting it very briefly, consideration should be given to whose interests were in fact served by the reform movements and why such narrow limits were in fact placed upon the actual reform achievements. In particular, it seems evident that the hierarchical structure linking enterprise management with local Party and trade union bodies to the central authorities was too important a cornerstone of the social and political structure and it could not be allowed to be weakened by a full-blooded introduction of horizontal economic relations through the market. As a consequence, the achievements of the reform movement have been limited, if we accept their original aim of introducing market relationality into the economic system.

However, again because economics is not everything, this does not mean that the quasi-reformed economic system is not different from the traditional system and capable of ensuring a satisfactory rate of economic growth and development. This does not mean that it is the best possible system from any point of view, but in view of the confusion and disarray of the Western economic system in the past decade, it ill behooves Western economists to demand or expect an optimal system to be adopted in Socialist countries.

Above all, it is rather ridiculous to urge Socialist countries to make significant moves towards convertibility of currencies and free trade under the prevailing circumstances of the capitalist world economy, i.e., the development of piecemeal protectionism, the political brinkmanship over moves to fight the world recession and stabilize international currency markets, and the apparent refusal of the developed capitalist countries to countenance joint control of raw materials markets with the underdeveloped producer countries. If, as international trade theory would have it, a country should act as a rational economic person, then surely at present the Socialist countries are quite right to minimize their structural integration into the capitalist world economy, a conclusion which in no way implies that they should minimize their economic exchanges with the West.

CONVERGENCE

The tendency towards viewing East-West economic relations in terms of mechanisms of the capitalist world economy is also supported in a more general way by the complex of Western social science theory developed around such concepts as Rostow's stages of growth, Kerr's industrialism and postindustrial society, and Bell's end of ideology. (7) The elaboration of such concepts in relation to comparative studies of the Soviet Union and the United States in particular led to a body of literature which can be given the summary title of convergence theory, although this includes some very diverse contributions, depending, of course, precisely upon what two systems are converging according to the author's belief.

By and large, the more simplistic versions of the convergence theory have few adherents today in the social sciences in Western countries since some of their elements are too readily identifiable with an apparently outdated liberal ideology suited to the Cold War period and events in both France and Czechoslovakia in 1968, echoed elsewhere, belied the much celebrated "end of ideology," while at a more theoretical level the functionalism which lay behind much of the convergence theory became unfashionable, especially in radicalized sociology. It, nevertheless, would be fair to say that the plainly observable facts of convergence, for example in economic structure, lifestyles, or environmental problems, provide of themselves persuasive evidence for not going to the other extreme and insisting on the distinguishing features of the two systems.

To elaborate on this a little with regard to the economic systems, the linked theses of development, industrialism, and postindustrialism seemed to founder in the 1970s on the facts of persistent underdevelopment in the Third World and the renewed sharpness with which identifiable capitalist dynamics began to operate in advanced Western economies. The failures of the Keynesian tradition to deal with economic problems, both nationally and internationally, are recorded in increasing unemployment, accelerating inflation, and so on. The emergence of these phenomena, regardless of attempts to control them, were paralleled at the ideological level by the rise of monetarism in Western economic thought, i.e., a return to pre-Keynesian economics. At the same time, structuralist and dependency theories of underdevelopment gained ground with regard to the analysis of less developed economies.

Important trends which formed a part of convergence theories have not, in fact, been dramatically altered. The ideological elements can be removed and still leave a set of observed trends which are not simply to be treated as individual empirical trends, but can be regarded as forming a coherent whole. Thus, the ever expanding role of the state in capitalist economic systems, if it is no longer theorized as post-capitalist, can still be seen as systemic, rather than as an ad hoc response to economic crisis. (8) Paradoxically, in the social sciences it may be the quasi-convergence theorists of the Socialist countries who can best provide this systemic analysis around such concepts as the scientific-technological revolution and extensive-intensive growth. (9)

A good example of "empirical convergence," where the problem can be treated as part of distinct systemic trends in East and West, concerns the role of the state in regulating the transformation of industrial structure in response to shifts in demand, i.e., particularly the problem of dealing with declining industrial sectors. In the West, the baseline for this problem is the judgment of the market in the form of a sectoral crisis of profitability and growth, leading in the absence of state intervention to bankruptcies and closures. In the East, the baseline, at least in the traditional economic system, is in the judgment of central planners, leading to a reallocation of resources away from the declining sector, again perhaps with closures of plants. But in both systems, we find that increasingly the central authorities are faced with a politicization of this seemingly economic problem: resistance to closures and run-downs takes the form of lobbying through the political system, and governments are forced to take steps to mitigate the impact on local communities and other interests. To use the colorful phrase of a British Conservative minister of industry, we all have our lame ducks, and in both East and West there is an increasing tendency to take them under the wing of the state through subsidies and de facto tariff protection, etc. rather than annihilate them. A similar argument also can be applied to the actual foreign trade policy of both systems.

THE INTERNATIONAL RELATIONS APPROACH

The starting point of this approach is the assumption that the key to understanding present world history is in the political interaction of nation-states, particularly great powers. (10) The simple fact that recognized rules and procedures for such interaction exist promotes a strong bias in favor of seeing all parties to this interaction as being part of the same system and subject to the same laws of motion. At the center of the stage is the foreign policy of the different actors (states), obviously to be decomposed into a complex of economic, political, military-strategic, ideological, and other goals. Behind the foreign policy of each actor lies a process of foreign policy making, involving competing formulations and assessments of the national interest with regard to one or more of these goals. It is only behind this still more complex process that we come to the economic, social, and political system of the society in question, and the developmental trends or laws of motion of that system.

This seems to be a topsy-turvey way of looking at the world. It promotes to a high degree an ad hoc procedure of drawing on particular elements of the underlying economic, social, and political forces at work. It harbors a strong and surely unwarranted assumption that these forces can inevitably produce a coherent national interest (note

that the international relations approach is in close harmony with
traditional international trade theory in economics). And it leaves
in the structure of the knowledge which it produces a yawning gap between its abstract theoretical models and its concrete policy oriented
applications to contemporary events. (11) No attempt is made here to
challenge the legitimacy of academics seeking to promote and further
particular national interests or any other interests as they conceive
them. On the contrary, the international relations literature in its
concrete analysis is refreshingly frank in this respect compared to
the economists' tedious and absurd claims to objectivity and a "positive rather than normative" approach. It can, however, be suggested
that we should start from the economic, social, and political forces,
which produce and structure not only the foreign policy agenda but
also the way in which it is pursued. To take an extreme position, the
foreign policy agenda of a dependent state in the Third World today
cannot be regarded as the foreign policy of that state. In short, a
political economic approach to international relations is advocated, in
contrast to a diplomatic approach.

In the case of East-West economic relations, it would not be unfair to say that the Western international relations literature has paid
inadequate attention to the complex of forces governing economic
trends in East and West, particularly the latter. One can still find
in this literature a degree of blind "triumphalism" and ethnocentrism
about the Western economic system which is no less inimical to scientific analysis than the parallel phenomenon in the Eastern literature.
The academic author of the following 1975 quotation can remain anonymous:

> The genuine strength, the self-reliant dynamic vigor of
> Western philosophy as the basis for social democracy, for
> establishing individual freedom, and for safeguarding human rights, imparts an unbounded vitality to the regulative
> principles underlying an individualistic free market economy.

But on a more mundane level, it seems that the East-West relations
literature often seems unable to place the phenomena which it studies
in a proper perspective. Surely the extraordinary optimism in the
United States in the early seventies about the prospects for East-West
trade should have taken more account of the minute significance of
this trade in comparison with American economic activity as a whole.

At a more general level, international relations writers have had
perforce to draw on the work of social scientists whose own analyses
are molded by the influences discussed under the preceding headings,
and their own methodology serves to reinforce these influences.

CONCLUSIONS ON THE CONCEPTUAL FRAMEWORK

There are powerful reasons why Western social scientists should tend to view East-West economic relations in the same terms as they apply to international economic relations in the capitalist world economy. Implicit in these arguments is the view that such a built-in assumption should be avoided. Although no attempt has been made to argue that East-West economic relations should be viewed in an entirely distinct way, it would be much better to start from the initial hypothesis that the dynamics of economic, social, and political development in the Socialist countries are systematically different and that these differences must influence the development of East-West economic relations.

Indeed, in a sense with regard to East-West economic relations, a scientific comparison of the economic systems of East and West can best be made, since it is in the world economy that the two systems actually have to face common conditions. The fact that these common conditions are those of a capitalist world economy thus provides the material basis for the conceptual frameworks discussed previously.

THE CAPITALIST WORLD ECONOMY IN THE 1970s

In retrospect, as far as the West is concerned the period from 1945 to 1970 looks like a capitalist golden age. An unprecedented and almost uninterrupted quarter century of rapid economic growth was accompanied by still more dynamic international trade, encouraged by the postwar liberalization of trade and currency movements and underpinned by the gold dollar standard and the Bretton Woods International Monetary System.

Yet from the mid-1960s instabilities began to develop in the system, which ten years later led to the most serious worldwide recession since the 1930s. Nearly all the industrialized countries experienced rising inflation and slowing growth rates, eventually described as "stagflation." A growing chronic United States deficit, together with persistent structural disequilibriums of foreign trade between other surplus and deficit countries, increasingly undermined the international monetary system and threatened the maintenance of a liberal international trade regime. As a result of increased interdependence through trade and financial flows, sources of instability within different countries increasingly had worldwide effects and the growing simultaneity of economic fluctuations helped to weaken the effectiveness of Keynesian policies in achieving national economic objectives.

In relations between West and South during the same period, there was growing awareness that despite high rates of economic growth, development as defined by Western social scientists was not an automatic consequence of the prevailing international economic system. Most underdeveloped countries of the South continued to rely on export earnings concentrated in one or a few primary products. Industrialization, with rare exceptions, was narrowly based and incoherent. The aid plan was far from achieving its stated objectives. Ironically, however, it was one element of this West-South relation -- the trade in primary products -- which, in the view of some economists, finally triggered the present persistent world recession. The sharp simultaneous boom of 1972-73 in the industrialized countries, running up against inelastic supplies of raw materials, in turn partly the result of worsening terms of trade, created the necessary conditions for the OPEC oil price increases, as well as the sharpest price increases in commodities in general since the Korean War. (12)

Despite many predictions, there is as yet no sign of a full, general recovery in the world economy. There is evidence that in the industrialized West unemployment has to a significant extent replaced inflation as the major problem, although every proposal for expansionary measures brings dire warnings of renewed inflation. There is no sign of a really concerted approach among the Western powers, although the chronic imbalances in trade, especially of manufactured goods, and currency instabilities are clearly common problems. Free-market prescriptions, e.g., "clean" floating of currencies, appear unacceptable, because no one can be certain that domestic economies will adjust towards their presumed equilibrium. Instead, we see a game of bluff and counter bluff, or threat and counter threat, between the United States, Japan, and the EEC when the members of the latter can agree among themselves for long enough.

Relations between West and South are strained in more complicated ways. The prices of some primary products, especially metals, have fallen dramatically, a process in some cases linked to failures to emulate OPEC. The debt burden of the non-OPEC South has escalated alarmingly, particularly with regard to commercial (nongovernmental/intergovernmental) debt, while surplus OPEC revenues have largely gone to shore up Western economies. There seems to be no realistic prospect for the regulation of primary product markets through joint producer-consumer action, e.g., international buffer stock systems. The rhetoric about the New International Economic Order, the North-South dialogue, and so on remains merely rhetoric.

The above summary is not intended to support a prediction of the imminent demise of capitalism. On the contrary, such a demise could only be the result of a social and political upheaval, which is not at present in evidence in the West. It indicates only that if we look at the world economy in terms of the economic conditions, interests, and government policies of its various countries, the present period is one of a crisis in the economic system established in and by the postwar boom. At the level of policy choices, we can all construct alternative scenarios in attempting to predict future developments. (13) It seems more fruitful, however, to examine some underlying economic trends which may be obscured if we focus exclusively on policy alternatives.

A NEW INTERNATIONAL DIVISION OF LABOR

In the context of the sort of analysis given previously, the international division of labor is essentially a given, which is reproduced through international exchange. It implicitly provided us with the basis for outlining the interests expressed in national economic policy positions, but this division of labor, just like that within a national economy, is produced and transformed by the historically specific dynamics of a particular period. Thus, the basic feature of the traditional international division of labor (IDL) between industrial and agrarian/raw material economies was the consequence of the historical development of capitalism in particular areas of the world, which led to the dominance of those areas in the production of manufactured goods, exchanged for primary products and foodstuffs from the remainder of the world economy. The search for raw materials and the need to secure sources of them led to the specific characteristics of the capitalist transformation of the South, classically in the form of export enclaves under colonial political control. This transformation in turn created the conditions for import-substituting industrialization, which turned out to form only a secondary element of the IDL because of the disarticulated and limited nature of economic growth in the primary producing economies. (14)

A growing body of literature argues that the really significant change in the present period is not that there are dislocations and adjustments underway within this traditional IDL, but that it is being transformed into a new IDL. (15) The evidence for this is growing industrialization in the South, particularly export oriented industrialization. (16) The chief institutional feature of this trend is that it is organized and controlled largely by multinational corporations (MNCs), so that it is both created by and integrated into the process of capital accumulation and growth in the West. Export oriented manufacturing in the South is not characterized by a confinement to consumer goods industries, as in the case of import-substituting industrialization; rather, it is based on the relocation of any production process or element thereof which is justified by consideration of costs. Formal ownership of the manufacturing plant is intrinsically less important than its real integration into a process of production, broadly conceived, which is centered elsewhere. The international trade flows generated by such developments will be de facto internal to particular MNCs, and they will be highly dependent on the latter in respect of technology, management, and marketing. (17)

While much has been made in some quarters of the potential of export oriented manufacturing in the South, others argue that although it may expand output, employment, and exports, it does not involve an internally integrated and coherent process of capitalist development, although it may assist such a process where it is already underway, e.g., Brazil. For many mutually reinforcing reasons, it is elsewhere a new form of enclave economy.

This trend towards the relocation of parts of industry to the South can only be promoted by the slowdown of economic growth, the pressures of rising wages, and the vast investment requirements of the new technologies within the advanced economies of the West. Other things being equal, the logic of global rationalization might lead to the relocation of much of the now superseded growth industries, such as iron, steel, and vehicle assembly, as well as more obvious candidates, such as textiles, footwear, and the exotic runaways in electronics. This relocation would especially take advantage of much lower wages, stable labor conditions (e.g., through political repression), and absence of pollution controls, etc., and it would have the effect in the West of releasing capital and labor for accumulation redirected towards the modern growth industries, including the software industries. (18)

The new IDL is clearly not with us yet; there are very many reasons why its advance cannot be smooth and unimpeded. Against lower labor costs, etc. in the South, must be set the costs imposed by lack of infrastructure (or more generally, agglomeration effects), (19) political risks, communications problems, etc.; the acquiescence of labor movements in the West is likewise not guaranteed. At the same time, the old IDL has acquired a new lease on life with the advent of the new Malthusian raw material and energy shortages. However, the manner in which the capitalist world's economy functions under the new IDL involves important discontinuities with the old, particularly in the nature of integration between national economies,

INTERNATIONAL DIVISION OF LABOR   45

i.e., an increasing proportion of trade flows internalized within MNCs; the emergence of technology, or more generally, knowledge as the key component of dependence and interdependence; and the growing irrelevance of the economists' traditional theoretical break between the national economy and the world economy. (20)

SOME IMPLICATIONS FOR EAST-WEST ECONOMIC RELATIONS

In the context of the traditional IDL, the evolving patterns of Eastern trade with the capitalist world economy can be seen in terms of attempts to transform its trade structure through altering its comparative advantages. Discussions along these lines have concerned the static and dynamic gains from trade through increased specialization and the relations between industrial growth, transformation, and specialization with export competitiveness. (21) The standard conclusion is that the main goal is to achieve an export structure comparable to that of advanced Western countries, dominated by exports of manufactured goods, especially machinery, while making due allowance for advantages in primary product exports arising from natural resource endowments.

Given the emphasis on trade flows, this approach implies that the development of the international division of labor and the transformation of the internal industrial structure, while clearly closely articulated, are nonetheless distinct processes and that policies can be constructed that are aimed at an internal transformation, which will in turn alter a country's position in the international division of labor, given, of course, complementary efforts to remove political and institutional barriers to the achievement of this latter.

The model of the new IDL, however, has very different implications. In particular, the patterns of trade and institutional structures created and promoted by MNCs, rooted in firm-specific economic and technological advantages, create much more imposing barriers to any attempt to "climb up the ladder" of the IDL. The parallel to the development of MNCs in East-West economic relations is, of course, the development of East-West industrial cooperation (EWIC) agreements. Although not all Western partners to such agreements are MNCs in the accepted sense of the word, their motivations are those characteristic of MNCs expanding their overseas operations within the capitalist world economy, i.e., a search for markets for goods and technology, and/or lower costs of production. (22)

It is generally agreed that the most significant features of EWIC, from the Eastern point of view, are precisely the advantages which these forms of relation give to the transfer of technology and to the development of exports to the West, although at the same time on both counts, there arises the danger of increased dependence on the West. In the short term, and especially the present period, the problem of the volume of exports is more salient, expressed in the continuing growth of Eastern hard currency indebtedness, but in the longer term, it is surely the question of technology transfer which is more significant.

From the expanding literature on technology transfer between developed and less developed capitalist countries, there emerge the following basic points. (23) First and foremost, technology differs from produced commodities in that the informational requirements of a commodity market are intrinsically unattainable; hence its price can only be a matter of bargaining between buyer and seller. Secondly, the application of technology generally involves a package of hardware and software, and decomposed elements of this package can only be transferred separately if the recipient has the capacity to repackage the elements. Thirdly, while a recipient country must develop its technological capabilities if it is to avoid persistent dependence on imported technology, it will not be able to do so if it has to rely on packaged transfers, especially from MNCs. Fourthly, these technological capabilities are themselves an intrinsic part of the entire process of economic development, involving the educational level and skill structure of the whole work force, and the existence of an internal dynamic of technological progress. Finally, from the point of view of those who offer technology of MNCs, formal ownership of a recipient enterprise is not a necessity if the latter remains dependent on the MNCs' inputs and/or output purchases.

That the Socialist countries are technologically dependent in the sense that they choose to participate in international specialization and exchange of technology is indisputable, but whether they are or might become technologically dependent in terms of the arguments just summarized is a very different matter. Eastern bargaining power vis-a-vis MNCs is undoubtedly qualitatively greater than that of the typical Southern technology recipient in terms of market possibilities, technology assessment capabilities, and the institutional concentration of bargaining resources. Since the general level of economic development is closer to that of the West, it is also much easier for Eastern recipients to purchase "unpackaged" technology and to operate and reproduce specific technologies. What is more at issue is whether the technology transferred can be assimilated fully, which involves both its successful articulation into related industrial branches and its further development and transformation in directions suited to the requirements of the domestic economy.

The ongoing debates over the comparative technological level of industry in the East and the economic and institutional aspects of the innovation process are clearly relevant here. (24) Hanson has suggested two alternative hypotheses concerning Soviet technology imports: one is "that the Soviet leaders have come to perceive Soviet economic progress as critically dependent on the import of advanced Western machinery and know-how"; the other is "that the current emphasis on buying Western technology is no more than a medium-term tactical expedient that will prove as reversible as the Concessions policy of the 1920s." (25) Regardless of the actual policy motives and aims, whether the second approach turns out to have been practical must depend on the existence of an internal dynamic of technological progress.

Two points can be made concerning the comparative technological levels. First, technology cannot be isolated from the social relations of production; it does not in the last analysis determine those relations except at a very abstract level, and at the same time it is not something external to economic processes which can be chosen "off the shelf" as production-function theory suggests. Thus, the technology aspect of the economies of East and West and of East-West economic relations can only be part of a systemic analysis. Secondly, it follows that these caveats are very relevant here; no assumption can be made about the universal applicability of any given innovation system, such as that characteristic of market economies. Perhaps, as Richta argues, only an innovation system qualitatively different from those now in evidence is really adequate for the future. (26)

Whatever the policy constraints which may affect them, the leadership of the Socialist countries have an immeasurably greater capacity to choose whether or not to become part of a new IDL than does any country of the South, because of the internal coherence of their socioeconomic systems and industrial structures, i.e., the fact that these have not developed according to patterns of integration imposed by the capitalist world economy. This constitutes an irreducible system difference.

NOTES

1. A. G. Frank, "Long Live Transideological Enterprise! The Socialist Economies in the Capitalist Division of Labor," Review, 1 (1977): 101.

2. For example, O. Lange and F. Taylor, On the Economic Theory of Socialism (Minneapolis: University of Minnesota Press, 1938).

3. For a summary survey, see K. C. Thalheim, "Balance Sheet," in The New Economic Systems of Eastern Europe, ed. H. H. Hohmann, M. C. Kaser, and K. C. Thalheim (London: C. Hurst & Co., 1975), chapter 17.

4. See P. Hanson, "The East European Interest in Industrial Cooperation" (Paper delivered at a conference on the EEC and Eastern Europe, University of Reading, December 1975), esp. pp. 17 and 24; and the discussion in C. Friesen, The Political Economy of East-West Trade (New York: Praeger, 1976), chapters 2 and 3 and references therein.

5. For example, see C. Bettelheim, "Theoretical Comments" in Unequal Exchange, ed. Arghiri Emmanual (New York: Monthly Review Press, 1972).

6. Some more systematic remarks on such factors are made by J. G. Zielinski, "On System Remodelling in Poland: A Pragmatic Approach," Soviet Studies 30 (1978), sections IV. 3,4; see also M. Rakowski, "Marxism and Soviet Societies," Capital and Class 1 (1977).

7. W. W. Rostow, The Stages of Economic Growth (Cambridge, England: Cambridge University Press, 1965); C. Kerr et al., Industrialism and Industrial Man (Cambridge, Mass: Harvard University Press, 1960); and D. Bell, The End of Ideology (Glencoe: Free Press, 1962).

8. For example, see J. Holloway and S. Picciotto, "Capital, Crisis and the State," Capital and Class 2 (1977).

9. See F. Janossy, The End of the Economic Miracle (White Plains, N. Y.: International Arts and Sciences Press, 1971); and R. Richta et al., Civilization at the Crossroads (White Plains, N. Y.: International Arts and Sciences Press, 1968).

10. A useful recent example is C. Friesen, The Political Economy of East-West Trade (New York: Praeger, 1976).

11. Some closely related points are made by A. Abonyi and I. J. Sylvain, "International Integration Theories and the CMEA: A

Comment from the Political Economy Perspective," in Integration in Eastern Europe and East-West Trade, ed. J.M. Montias and P. Marer (forthcoming).

12. See N. Kaldor, "Inflation and Recession in the World Economy," Economic Journal, 86, no. 4 (1976).

13. See, e.g., J.N. Bhagwati, ed., Economics and World Order: From the 1970's to the 1990's (New York: Macmillan, 1972).

14. See e.g., O. Sunkel, "Underdevelopment in Latin America: Toward the Year 2000," in ibid.

15. J. Annerstedt and R. Gustavsson, Towards a New International Division of Labour? (Roskilde, Denmark: RUC Forlag, 1975); F. Frobel et al., "The Tendency Towards a New International Division of Labor," Review 1, no. 1, (1977); and C. Palloix, Proces de production et crise de capitalisme (Paris: Maspero, 1977), chapter 5.

16. A pioneering study of this process is G. Adam, "Multinational Corporations and Worldwide Sourcing." In International Firms and Modern Imperialism, H. Radice, ed. (London: Penguin, 1975).

17. See Annerstedt and Gustavsson, Towards a New International Division.

18. See C. Palloix, L'internationalisation du capital (Paris: Maspero, 1975), which offers an analysis of this structural shift; see also references in footnote 15 above.

19. See R. Murray, "Underdevelopment, International Firms and the International Division of Labor," Society for International Development, in Towards a New World Economy (Rotterdam: Rotterdam University Press, 1972), esp. Section II.

20. C. Michalet, Le capitalisme mondiale (Paris, 1977) gives an interesting general theoretical framework for analyzing these tendencies.

21. See, e.g., I. Vajda and M. Simai, eds., Foreign Trade in a Planned Economy (Cambridge, England: Cambridge University Press, 1971).

22. A recent contribution aimed specifically at exploring the motivations and experiences of United States' MNCs is E.W. Hayden, Technology Transfer to East Europe: U.S. Corporate Experience (New York: Praeger, 1976).

23. For a summary and detailed references, see Annerstedt and Gustavsson, Towards a New International Division.

24. See e.g., R. Amann et al., eds., The Technological Level of Soviet Industry (New Haven: Yale University Press, 1977); and J. Berliner, The Innovation Decision in Soviet Industry (Cambridge, Mass: M.I.T. Press, 1976).

25. P. Hanson, External Influences on the Soviet Economy Since the Mid-1950's: The Import of Western Technology (Birmingham: Centre for Russian and East European Studies, Discussion Paper No. 7, 1974), p. 1.

26. Richta, Civilization at the Crossroads.

5 The Significance of Economic Interdependence Arising from East-West Relations*
Peter Knirsch

CONCEPT AND FORMS OF INTERDEPENDENCE

Interdependence represents a mutual dependence. (1) For our purposes, therefore, the issue is to clarify how the West is economically dependent on the East and vice versa. The West will include the developed industrial nations of the non-Communist world who are members of the OECD. In the center of this discussion, corresponding to their significance for economic relations with East Europe, will be the countries that comprise the European Economic Community (EEC), plus the United States, Canada, and Japan. The Eastern countries include the Socialist nations of East Europe that are members of CMEA: the Soviet Union, Poland, the German Democratic Republic, Czechoslovakia, Hungary, Romania, and Bulgaria.

Consideration will be given to international dependence between individual countries or groups of states in which 1) economic developments on one side exercise an influence on economic developments on the other side (general economic dependence (2) or 2) one side can influence the economic situation on the other side by means of economic policy measures (politico-economic dependence). (3)

This emphasis on politico-economic dependence arises from the special nature of East-West economic relations: in the East all foreign trade and also domestic economic reactions to foreign trade developments, because of the Soviet-type economic system, are subject

---

* I wish to thank Mary Hess of the Osteuropa-Institut, Freie Universitat Berlin, for her competent translation of this work.

to the control of economic policy, and also in the West foreign trade relations are in general very strongly influenced by government measures, especially in regard to relations with Eastern European states. Hindrance of trade is seen most clearly in embargo regulations or in the maintenance of quantitative restrictions (quotas), while encouragement of trade is observed by how governments exert influence on credit terms for CMEA nations.

Although emphasis will be placed on instances of economic interdependence, the significance of this interdependence does not reside merely in economic advantages or disadvantages or in opportunities to exert economic influence. The great amount of attention which is usually paid to East-West economic relations is due to the consequences these might hold for the political relationship between East and West. In this context it would be possible to speak of "political interdependence" arising from economic interdependence.

Above and beyond this political aspect, the economic relations between East and West also influence technical developments; in this case the concept of "technical interdependence" might be useful. Furthermore, international economic relations can lead to structural changes in the culture and civilization of the respective regions, which in the long run can contribute to an altered social consciousness and changes in the existing structure of the system. In other words, economic interdependence can bring about cultural and technological interdependence between nations.

In addition to the various sociocultural effects which can be associated with economic interdependence, it is possible to set up different kinds of classification criteria for economic interdependence. The most significant of these for our area of concern is the question of how balanced is the interdependence. If the mutual dependence is almost equally important to both regions, then we will speak of balanced or symmetric interdependence. If the interdependence between the two regions is less important to one region than to the other, then we will speak of an unbalanced or asymmetric interdependence. (4) It is evident that this distinction is very important, especially when we consider the political significance of economic interdependence between East and West.

Another distinction which could be important for our deliberations concerns how quickly the respective economies are affected by economic dependence. In many instances, changes in foreign trade relations can affect the economy of the partner nation very rapidly (short-term dependence). In other cases, the effects of the changes are only felt over the long run (long-term dependence). (5)

As a final criterion we can differentiate international economic dependence according to forms of economic relations; we can distinguish between dependence on imports or exports versus financial dependence.

Thus, the following types of dependence play a role in connection with economic interdependence between East and West:

1. Areas of Dependence
    a. Economic dependence
    b. Technical dependence
    c. Political dependence
    d. Cultural-civilizable dependence

2. Forms of Economic Relations
    a. Dependence on imports
    b. Dependence on exports
    c. Financial dependence

3. Balance of Power
    a. Balanced (symmetrical) interdependence
    b. Unbalanced (asymmetrical) interdependence

4. Time Relationship
    a. Short-term dependence
    b. Long-term dependence

This summary includes some important criteria for our study of East-West Economic Relations, although it is possible to conceive of other criteria, such as how natural resources available in a certain economic area affect the ability to be self-sufficient and the dependence of a national economy upon economic trends in other countries. Even though I have taken the special conditions of East-West economic relations into consideration when choosing these criteria, it should be noted that they are also applicable to other cases of international economic interdependence.

THE QUESTION OF MEASURING ECONOMIC INTERDEPENDENCE

The structural criteria outlined above, which could be pertinent to the economic interdependence between East and West, are a necessary prerequisite for even beginning to evaluate such interdependence.

However, whenever the question about the significance of this interdependence is to be answered, and this answer must include not only the economic but also the political significance of interdependence, then politicians and also most economists who have not done much work on this problem almost always expect an exact quantitative answer. Just as when it is assumed that comparing the military potential of East and West, in a manner which may also be very problematic, will provide a measurement of the equilibrium between the two blocs of nations or reveal the superiority of one side, thus the question is also posed in which areas of East-West economic relations one side is dependent on the other and how strong this dependency is. It is no secret that policy makers are very interested in this question to the extent that an answer to it could provide the basis for developing strategies which might weaken the other side or strengthen their own position by intentionally influencing the forms of dependence thus identified.

In this case, as in so many, economic science disappoints policy makers in East and West because at best, exact statements about economic interdependence are only possible in very limited special cases. Since there are incalculable interrelations with countless economic processes, including numerous possibilities for substitutions and side effects, even these attempts are probably a dubious undertaking for the most part; the "exact calculation" of economic dependence as an overall phenomenon is certainly an illusion. Jacobsen and Muller attempt to make the interdependence which results from East-West economic relations quantitatively ascertainable by means of numerous formulas. (6) Their reflections have analytical value insofar as they provide relatively detailed, although not necessarily new, information about which functional relations could be of importance for East-West interdependence. At the end of their deliberations, however, both authors come to the conclusion that too many qualitative factors -- to be perhaps more precise, factors which we have found no way to express in terms of quantities, at least up to this point -- influence this interdependence and that calculations can only provide answers to very limited inquiries. (7)

THE PRESENT STATE OF ECONOMIC INTERDEPENDENCE BETWEEN EAST AND WEST: OVERALL INTERDEPENDENCE

Even though it is not possible to compute "overall interdependence" as resulting from East-West economic relations, some general statements can be made about it. The most general information about this subject is the respective ratio of foreign trade between two regions to their total foreign trade, or more meaningfully to their respective national products. The relative shares of foreign trade in East-West economic relations have been calculated in many different ways. Regardless of how exact the figures obtained may be or how they might fluctuate over a period of time, the following overall picture emerges: East-West trade represents only a small share of world trade. In 1976 it accounted for a mere 4.9% of all world exports. However, it must be taken into consideration that in 1970 its share of world exports was only 3.4%. Eastern Europe's integration into the world economic system is still quite minimal, but nevertheless it did increase significantly during the first half of the seventies. (8)

The ratio of East-West trade to total foreign trade is quite different in East and West. This ratio is considerably higher for the CMEA countries than for the Western industrial nations. In 1976, 34.7% (1970: 26.0%) of CMEA imports came from the West, and 28.2% (1970: 23.8%) of CMEA exports went to Western industrial nations, while only 3.7% (1970: 3.3%) of total Western imports came from the CMEA nations, and only 4.9% (1970: 3.4%) of total Western exports went to CMEA countries. (9) For our purposes the differences in the foreign trade dependence of individual CMEA nations are significant. Measured by total turnover, in 1975 Poland with 41.3% (31.5% of exports and 49.3% of imports) had the largest share of foreign trade with the West, followed by Romania with 36.7% (31.5% of exports, 41.9% of imports). The Soviet Union is above average (30%) with a share of 31.3%, while the German Democratic Republic with 25.9%, Hungary with 24.4%, and Czechoslovakia with 22.4% were below average, and Bulgaria with 17.0% (9.3% of exports, 23.6% of imports) is the CMEA nation with the smallest share of foreign trade turnover with the West. (10) On the part of the West, in 1976 Finland (24%) and Austria (15%) had the largest proportion of exports to East Europe. The Federal Republic of Germany, with 9% of its total exports going to East Europe, is well above average, while the United States with only 2.9% of its exports going to East Europe in 1975 is well below average.

Since the intensity of foreign trade (the share of foreign trade in the gross national product) in the nations concerned differs so much, the ratio of East-West trade to total foreign trade varies greatly in its significance for each of the national economies. Thus, it would be more informative to look at the ratio of East-West trade to GNP in each country. However, as is commonly realized, a meaningful comparison of national incomes is fraught with many problems and such statistics are only accurate enough to give us a general idea of the dimensions involved. According to an estimate for 1973, in Eastern Europe the share of imports from the West in the GNP fluctuates between 0.7% for the Soviet Union and 4.7% for Hungary. (11) Other estimates for the same year arrive at higher values: 1.5% of the Soviet GNP, and in the smaller CMEA countries 5% to 10% of their respective GNPs. (12) In Western nations that trade more extensively with the East, exports to Eastern Europe account for approximately 1% to 1.5% of their GNPs. For our purposes it is sufficient to note that the share of East-West trade in the Soviet Union's national product is very low (only about 1%), while this share is greater in the smaller CMEA countries.

In addition to the foreign trade relations which have been outlined here, other forms of economic relations should also be examined, such as simple compensation transactions, long-term compensation projects, and industrial cooperation, which play a relatively important role. On the whole, all these forms are reflected in foreign trade transactions; in the case of the last two forms, however, effects on foreign trade are delayed for several years. For the sake of our study of interdependence, it will be necessary to take into consideration at a later point how these forms of economic relations influence interdependence. However, in this paper we will not attempt to estimate their quantitative significance, (13) because this involves many problems.

PARTIAL DEPENDENCE IN EAST-WEST ECONOMIC RELATIONS

In addition to the overall share of foreign trade that East-West trade represents, the structure of commodity flows and the balance of payments situation, the latter of which is closely associated with this, are of obvious importance for our study of economic dependence. For our purposes, it will again be sufficient to give a brief summary of the overall dimensions involved. (14) A pronounced complementary character is typical of East-West trade. Roughly speaking, the West supplies primary industrial products and finished goods (SITC 5-8), above all machinery (SITC 7), to the CMEA nations and imports raw materials, fuel, and agricultural products (SITC 0-4). Certain exceptions to this basic structure could be of significance for East-West interdependence. In the case of Soviet imports from the West the structural fluctuations are great, since Soviet agricultural imports are contingent on crop failure. In other words, the share represented by SITC 0 is higher in certain years, primarily at the expense of SITC 5, 6, and 8. As far as the export of the smaller CMEA countries to the West is concerned, over the course of time and probably due for the most part to the EEC's agricultural market policies,

the proportion of agricultural products has dropped sharply, while
the proportion of finished industrial goods exported rose from 15%
in 1961 to 28% in 1975, whereby it should be noted that a shift from
capital goods (SITC 7) to consumer goods (SITC 8) took place. Despite these changes, the complementary imbalance of East-West trade
has continued to be a typical structural feature.

In recent years East-West trade expanded rapidly, but this growth
was to a large extent coupled with high deficits in the trade balances
of the CMEA nations, which in turn were financed by a corresponding
indebtedness to the West. (15) For the purpose of our study, the
exact amount of indebtedness is not of great significance. What does
matter is how this indebtedness might influence the future foreign
trade opportunities of the Eastern European nations. Of special concern is the future burden which debt service will impose on their
balance of payments.

ASSESSING THE SIGNIFICANCE OF THE INTERDEPENDENCE WHICH ARISES FROM EAST-WEST ECONOMIC RELATIONS

Cooper's statement, "It is now commonplace to say that the world is
becoming much more interdependent," (16) is also generally true of
East-West economic relations. Compared with the meager trade flows
between East and West in the fifties, East-West economic relations
intensified considerably after 1965, especially during the first half of
the seventies. Despite this and judging by all that we know, it is very
clear that this interdependence is only partial. Observing the volume
of trade flows, as well as the goods which comprise them, leads to
the conclusion that even a complete and abrupt discontinuance of East-
West economic relations would not lead to the economic collapse of
one of the countries or blocs of nations involved, for national economies are astonishingly resistant entities, as has been proven in times
of war.

It is probably still of some value to exclude these extreme possibilities, for the view that economic sanctions could be employed to
achieve far-reaching political abjectives in the area of East-West
relations has still not been completely eradicated from the minds of
policy makers and the general public, despite the obviously limited
results attained by the embargo policy in the fifties and the present
policy of detente. Therefore, it should first be noted that the interdependence which arises from East-West economic relations does not
make it possible for one side to exert massive political pressure on
the other side. This observation, incidentally, has a very positive

side to it, because this also means East-West economic relations are not important enough to either side to represent a very dangerous potential for conflict.

By eliminating the possibility of total interdependence, we only exclude grossly false interpretations, which fortunately have become rather rare. The state of East-West economic relations outlined previously makes it clear that the structurally unbalanced trade relations between East and West lead to dependence on both sides. The limited share of intersystemic economic relations represented by this volume of trade indicates that the mutual dependence is also of limited significance, that only a partial interdependence exists.

Symmetric interdependence would mean that the dependence involved is of equal significance to both sides. In East-West trade there are clear indications that interdependent relations are not symmetric. Thus, in the CMEA nations, with the exception of the Soviet Union, the ratios of trade with the West to total foreign trade and to the national product are much higher than are the corresponding ratios for Western industrial nations. At least as an initial rough approximation, it can be assumed that East-West interdependence is more important for the CMEA nations than for the OECD nations. The current foreign trade balance deficits and the resulting indebtedness of Eastern Europe also point to a clear asymmetry in East-West economic relations in favor of the West.

An examination also will be made of the special circumstances of East-West relations which counteract this basic asymmetry and might tend to reduce it. Nevertheless, the insight that East-West economic relations are basically unbalanced is very important for this theme. It would certainly be a mistake to infer that this asymmetry arises solely from differences in wealth and development and then to infer that a clear-cut political dependence must exist, as the "Dependencia Theory" postulates for the relationship of the industrial nations (metropolises) to the developing countries (periphery). (17) Despite this, differences in the level of economic development are certainly an important cause of the recognizable asymmetries. Taken as a whole, the Western industrial nations with their higher productivity based on modern technology represent a considerably greater economic potential. Even taking into account the many differences existing among the nations we have listed here as belonging to the West or the East, the West as a whole has reached a higher state of industrial development and is richer than the East; the thought suggests itself that this could lead to the one-sided interdependence structure described previously.

WESTERN DEPENDENCE ON IMPORTS FROM THE EAST

Trade relations are by far the most important form of East-West economic relations. (18) When we examine trade relations more closely to see if they have led to some type of dependence, it seems useful to differentiate between import dependence and export dependence.

If we examine the structure and amounts of Western imports from East Europe more closely, it appears most likely that there might be dependence on imports of raw materials and energy. The main supplier in these areas is the Soviet Union, and oil and gas are clearly the dominant imports. (19) These deliveries have increased greatly over the past few years; in 1976 Soviet oil exports to OECD countries accounted for somewhat more than 50% of total Soviet exports in this area. However, Soviet oil deliveries still accounted for only about 5% of total Western oil imports. In the case of Soviet natural gas deliveries, which, for example, are important for supplying the Federal Republic of Germany because of long-term compensation transactions (pipes for natural gas), the situation is similar; in 1975 Soviet deliveries accounted for less than 10% of the Federal Republic of Germany's total natural gas imports. Other raw materials which the West imports from East Europe are bituminous coal from the Soviet Union and Poland, as well as nonferrous metals, particularly copper. (20)

The raw materials referred to, especially oil, account for a large share of Western imports from East Europe. We can expect that as far as natural gas and gasification of bituminous coal are concerned, deliveries to the countries of West Europe and Japan will continue to increase over the next few years as a result of long-term compensation transactions which have already been concluded. There is no doubt that these imports of raw materials are important to the Western countries; nevertheless, deliveries from East Europe currently, and in the foreseeable future, account and will account for such a small share of total Western imports that no severe economic problems would arise if these deliveries were to cease. It appears possible to substitute other sources for the Eastern Europe supplies, since these products can be obtained elsewhere on the world market and it is very unlikely that the Soviet Union or Poland could exert any real pressure on the West by concluding cartel agreements with the many other suppliers of these products. Therefore, at the most any Western dependence on East European imports would last for only a short time until the necessary conversion to other supplies was made. The West is probably also somewhat dependent on East European imports in terms of cost sensitivity, because the raw material supplied by the Soviet Union may be cheaper in the short run than substitute purchases on the world market. (21)

In the case of all the other products which the West imports from East Europe, primarily consumer-type finished goods and in decreasing amounts foodstuffs from the smaller CMEA countries, any economic sensitivity is very slight. All these goods can be procured domestically or on the world market without any great transitional difficulties, and even price sensitivity should not be significant in the case of important products (clothing, textiles, shoes, furniture), since it should be possible to arrange for substitute deliveries from less developed OECD countries or from developing countries.

Thus, taken as a whole Western dependence on imports from Eastern Europe must be considered very slight. The only, but rather unlikely, way in which the existing interdependence might be exploited for political purposes would be during a transitional period while substitutes for Soviet deliveries of raw materials were being sought.

EASTERN DEPENDENCE ON IMPORTS FROM THE WEST

An examination of the import structure of the CMEA countries suggests that their possible dependence on Western imports might lie in two areas. In the Soviet Union during recent years, imports of foodstuffs, primarily of grain, have made it possible to compensate for crop fluctuations, and Poland and Czechoslovakia also had to import foodstuffs from the West on occasion. In addition, imports of finished industrial products, especially of machinery, were of great significance for the CMEA nations.

We should not underestimate the overall significance of food imports. It is clear that these imports relieve short-term supply problems, and consumer demands have an important influence on the decision to make these imports. Clearly, neither the Soviet Union nor Poland -- when we consider what happened there in the summer of 1976 -- finds it politically feasible to expect its population to put up with a greatly diminished food supply which fluctuates more than the normal food supply, i.e., until the next and possibly better harvest. If this assumption is correct, and the massive use of convertible currency for food imports during recent years seems to bear it out, then the dependence of the Soviet Union and some of the smaller CMEA countries on Western supplies is relatively important. By its very nature, this dependence is a short-term one. However, when we think of the problems the Soviet Union has had up to now in stabilizing its agricultural yields despite genuine efforts to improve the situation, this particular form of dependence could certainly continue to play an important role in the structure of East-West interdependence for some time to come. (22)

In contrast to this, imports of industrial products, mainly investment goods, are of a different nature, and it is quite understandable that they have been considered of decisive importance for East-West relations during recent years. (23) The states of Eastern Europe, probably primarily because of their economic system, have encountered great difficulties in devising technical innovations and applying them efficiently. Importing Western capital goods constitutes a transfer of modern technology as an attempt to compensate for Eastern Europe's own technological inadequacies. (24) Promoting technical progress in Eastern Europe by importing capital goods or buying licenses in the West is so important economically because overall economic growth in East Europe is decisively dependent on the realization of technical progress. This state of affairs is of political significance because the governments of the CMEA nations have assigned very high priority to rapid economic growth in their ranking of economic policy goals. Now that a higher state of economic development has been attained and the growth rate in most of the CMEA nations, especially in the Soviet Union, has slowed, the significance of an adequate economic growth rate has become increasingly greater. In addition to securing external political power on the basis of a sufficiently large economic and military potential, it has become necessary to maintain and improve the standard of living for the general population. In the course of the sixties it apparently became clear in East Europe that domestic resources were not going to be sufficient to guarantee rapid economic growth and, therefore, the nations of East Europe turned to the world market.

The prospects that the CMEA nations will be able to solve these problems by changing their systems partially or by increasing their input in research and development seem to be less than favorable, judged by the experience of the past several decades. In this respect, it appears that the situation in the smaller CMEA nations, including those with a high level of industrial development such as Czechoslovakia and the GDR, is by no means more favorable than in the Soviet Union itself. Only over a longer period of time can imports of technology from the West lead to positive results. In other words, a corresponding dependence on imports will tend to continue for a long time to come.

If the assumptions just made are realistic, imports of Western technology thus represent an exceptionally important political component of interdependence in East-West economic relations. If we consider dependence on imports as an isolated phenomenon, the economic dependence of the West appears to be very slight, while that of the East seems to be quite significant.

WESTERN DEPENDENCE ON EXPORTS TO THE EAST

Since the early sixties the export of Western goods to Eastern Europe has expanded very rapidly. Judged by the total volume of exports of the Western industrial nations, exports to the East still account for a relatively small share, but it is no longer negligible. This is certainly true of at least some Western nations, above all of the Federal Republic of Germany as the largest exporter to Eastern Europe, and it is even truer of certain branches of industry. Thus, in the Federal Republic of Germany exports to Eastern Europe accounted for 8.4% of the total turnover in its iron and steel industry and 5.9% of the total turnover in its engineering industry in 1975, and a total of 333,000 jobs (equivalent to only 1.2% of all employed, but to 30% of the unemployed) is said to depend on exports to East Europe. (25)

Thus, taken as a whole Western exports to Eastern Europe have reached a certain level of economic significance. This significance is influenced by the economic situation in the West. In times of economic prosperity when there is full utilization of capacity, doing without exports to Eastern Europe would be fairly easy in view of the volume involved. On the other hand, when there is a recession, exports to the East can provide essential support in maintaining an acceptable employment rate, at least in certain Western countries. Since Western governments currently assign a high degree of politicoeconomic priority to maintaining employment, this form of dependence on exports definitely could be of political significance. On the whole, the economies of those Western industrial nations which do a significant amount of trade with the East are to a certain extent dependent on Eastern European demand, especially when their domestic economic situation is unfavorable, and the political actions of the Western nations could be influenced by this dependence on exports.

EASTERN DEPENDENCE ON EXPORTS TO THE WEST

If the economies of East Europe should turn out to be in some way dependent on exports to the West, then this dependence would have to be of an entirely different nature than Western dependence on exports.

SIGNIFICANCE OF ECONOMIC INTERDEPENDENCE 63

In all the CMEA nations, there are as a rule no unutilized capacities seeking export opportunities, but on the contrary domestic production usually is not sufficient to meet demand. Thus, in contrast to the West, there is no internal pressure to export. Rather, it can be assumed that the economies of the Eastern European nations would experience an improvement in the strained supply situation if they were not obliged to export.

In this situation the CMEA countries are only dependent on exports because it is necessary to earn foreign currency in order to pay for imports. Because of their negative balance of payments, their dependence on imports from the West makes it necessary to maintain and even increase the level of their exports to nations which pay in hard currency. Here one could speak of indirect dependence. Their definite need to import makes the CMEA nations not only directly sensitive to anything that interferes with their imports, but also indirectly sensitive to anything that interferes with their opportunities to export to the West. This sensitivity could be observed clearly during recent years. The inflationary trend in prices on the world market resulted in an improvement in the terms of trade for the Soviet Union and Poland and a worsening of the terms of trade for the remaining CMEA nations, which varies according to the foreign trade structure of each nation. Of greater significance for the export opportunities of the CMEA nations have been the worsened marketing conditions since 1974 because of the recession in the Western industrial nations. This situation has necessitated even greater efforts to export.

This pressure to export has also caused the CMEA nations to take direct political action. Their efforts to overcome Western obstacles to imports, whether they be customs barriers or quantitative restrictions on imports, can be attributed to this. Because of their specific commodity structures, the dependence of the smaller CMEA nations on exports is especially significant. The originally large share of foodstuffs in their exports was greatly restricted by the EEC's agricultural marketing regulations, and all in all this dependence is probably the main reason that Poland, Romania, and Hungary joined General Agreement on Tariffs and Trade (GATT) between 1967 and 1973 and why in Eastern Europe overall interest in a complete reform of the world economic order has grown during the past few years. (26) The efforts of the nations of East Europe to achieve most-favored-nation status in their trade with the West can also be explained by this dependence on exports.

FINANCIAL DEPENDENCE IN EAST-WEST ECONOMIC RELATIONS

Monetary dependence between East and West can be dealt with quite briefly, not because it is unimportant, but rather because this subject has already been discussed in great detail in the Western literature. (27) The situation is fairly clear. The rapid expansion of East-West trade which occurred after 1970 was possible mainly because credits were granted by the West (at first these were granted by suppliers; later bank loans and money borrowed on Western capital markets became more common), since CMEA exports to the West could not by any means be increased rapidly enough to pay for the increased imports from the West. East European indebtedness to the West had reached a total of about 45-48 billion American dollars by the end of 1977. Naturally this development is merely the financial reflection of the Eastern European import dependence which made it willing to incur debt, as described previously. However, we also see here how much the West depends on exports, so much so that it was willing to grant such credits.

Even though the indebtedness which East Europe has incurred is closely associated with the state of East-West trade relations, it is also important to the economic interdependence between East and West for quite a different reason, namely the potential short-term dependence of the West. The East could interrupt its payment of debts or interest payments, which could create considerable difficulties for the Western lenders, despite the government loan guarantee they hold, and such a move would also exert an unfavorable influence on the already ailing international monetary system and on the general state of the world economy.

A great deal can be said for the assumption that both sides are interested in avoiding any such development. The main reason for this is that the interdependence of economic relations between East and West has grown so much. The East will do everything in its power to avoid any such bankruptcy, because it needs more imports from the West for its own economic growth and, therefore, must maintain its credit standing with the West. On the other hand, Western exporters will strive to prevent any scarcity of convertible currency in East Europe from causing the collapse or even a sharp curtailment of East-West trade. Furthermore, due to the investment problems they are experiencing in the West, Western bankers may well feel that granting still more credit to East Europe is not only the lesser of two evils, but possibly is even a good solution to their problems.

Due to the interdependence which has arisen, the possibility that East Europe might refuse to pay its debts is thus ruled out by most of those concerned. It should also be noted that it is assumed the Soviet Union will stand behind those countries which must pay large shares of their current revenues in convertible currency for debt service. The best-known example is Poland. Obviously the CMEA countries themselves consider their indebtedness to the West a burden and have drawn certain conclusions from this as concerns their economic relations with the West. In 1976-77 they made clear efforts to reduce their trade balance deficit with the West by trying both to prevent further growth in their imports from the West and to increase their exports to the West.

When we consider the forms of dependence described previously, the reduction of imports or at least their stabilization at the current level certainly did not represent an easy decision for the CMEA nations. However, for the purpose of assessing dependence relations this example shows that dependence has its limits, also in sensitive areas, and that the socialist nations are ready, at least temporarily, to reduce those forms of dependence on the West which seem threatening to them even if this requires unpleasant measures. The level at which exports from the West were kept during 1976-77 was certainly not a low one in comparison with previous years. Thus, the measures taken to curb imports were, therefore, probably not too drastic, although it is also possible that people had already gotten accustomed to the continued rapid increase in imports from the West. However, what is noteworthy about this development is that it was not pressure from the West that led to these measures. On the whole, Western willingness to grant credit was unchanged, and due to the unfavorable economic situation, Western businessmen were not especially happy to see either a reduction in their opportunities to export to the East or increased imports from there. To a certain extent, this experience with financial dependence reveals the limits of economic interdependence between East and West.

EAST-WEST INTERDEPENDENCE AND SPECIAL FORMS OF EAST-WEST ECONOMIC RELATIONS

Up to this point we have examined only those forms of dependence which result from East-West trade and credit relations. In addition to these, during the past few years some new forms of East-West economic relations have come into being, and to some extent these have received serious consideration. If we disregard the primitive forms of barter trade (28) which still can be encountered in East-West trade, then above all industrial cooperation, long-term compensation, and mutual capital investments should be mentioned here. Joint ventures, such as Western participation in enterprises in CMEA countries, have been of only marginal significance up to this point. (29) In view of the differences in East-West economic systems, there are no recognizable signs that this form of integration can gain in importance. (30)

Similar difficulties have not arisen in regard to industrial cooperation. Despite this, up to now industrial cooperation has gained ground in only a few of the smaller CMEA countries, particularly Hungary, Poland, and Romania, and even here it represents only a very modest, and in recent years stagnating, share of East-West economic relations. Long-term compensation, in which Western firms deliver complete plants and payment is later made in the form of goods produced by these production facilities, has gained in importance in recent years, especially with regard to the Soviet Union. Both of these forms of interdependence have a similar effect on economic dependence. In contrast to simple foreign trade transactions, they result in greater and longer-term dependence for both sides and thus intensify interdependence. First of all, they represent long-term forms of cooperation, and they should make it possible for the East to adopt modern technology more efficiently. Any breakdown in these forms of interdependence impairs planned economic growth in the respective areas of the economy more strongly than does the nondelivery of imports. The success of the venture for the Western partner depends on carrying out the project exactly as planned. Here also the cooperation partner is hurt more by any breakdown that occurs than is the case with simple trade transactions.

Different phenomena are the direct investments made by Eastern Europe in Western countries. Usually this involves holding an interest in banks or trading companies. At the end of 1977 it was reported that in addition to banks, the capital invested by Eastern Europe in 312 firms totaled about 600 million American dollars. (31) In these cases it can be assumed that the East European investor wishes to preserve his capital investment. Such capital participation by the East tends to intensify East-West interdependence, even though the actual amounts involved are very modest.

ECONOMIC INTERDEPENDENCE AND ITS EFFECT ON TECHNOLOGICAL AND SOCIOCULTURAL DEVELOPMENT

The effects which increased economic interdependence between East and West has on technological development are fairly clear in this context. Up to now this influence has been mostly one-sided, since technology transfer proceeds primarily from West to East. Even if the total volume of technology transfer has been limited, we must nevertheless reckon with far-reaching consequences and with generally strong, long-term influence of Western technology on all the Socialist nations. Two effects appear to be especially important. First, this transfer of technology produces a considerable degree of technological dependence, which in turn results in longer-term economic dependence. Their imports of Western machinery and plants have made it necessary for Eastern Europe to adapt its own technological development to Western norms and procedures, at least to a certain extent. These imports also have a specific effect on technical knowledge in the Socialist countries and necessitate Western deliveries of spare parts or of newly developed supplementary technology.

The second possible effect may well be of primary interest to philosophers or sociologists, but in the long run it can gain greatly in general significance. The technology imported from the West was developed under the efficiency criteria of the capitalist system. It is not known if there is a "capitalist" or a "Socialist" technology, but there is no doubt that there may be interaction between the application of certain technologies and social consciousness. In the case of East-West economic relations one has the feeling that the technology transfer associated with them has so far occurred without any consideration being given in Eastern Europe to the social, and to some extent also the economic, effects it may have, and that this involves unforeseeable consequences for the future development of the Socialist nations.

This problem opens up the entire question of how economic interdependence affects sociocultural development, a question yet to be answered by research. All sorts of speculations are possible in this area. It seems to be a safe assumption that economic relations between countries or regions do exercise an influence on sociocultural development on both sides and that this is at least one effect of increasing East-West interdependence. If appearances are not deceiving, this influence seems to be exerted mainly by the West on the East. The reason for this could be that the West has reached a higher level of economic and technological development. Obviously, importing sophisticated machinery has a more stimulating effect than importing oil. Increased imports from the West have led to the general conclusion in all the CMEA nations that Western goods, especially consumer goods, are of high quality, and it is not uncommon for not only this quality but also Western fashion and forms of consumption (and also foolishness) to be greatly overvalued, uncritically admired, and taken as a model.

A prediction about where these developments will lead -- whether, as some believe, a rapprochement of the systems will be brought about in this manner, whether the leadership of the Communist nations will be able to guide these developments, whether these developments are associated in any significant way with economic interdependence, or whether they are not rather attributable to worldwide industrial-economic developments -- lies beyond this paper.

THE POLITICAL SIGNIFICANCE OF ECONOMIC INTERDEPENDENCE

Studies of economic interdependence always have political implications. When one considers how complex both political and economic East-West relations are, the impression is gained that frequently many people see a much too direct correlation between economics and politics. Nevertheless, it is necessary for the economist to devote attention to this idea, especially since a relationship as important as the one between East and West is concerned.

In order to avoid repeating what has been said about this subject, some propositions are submitted for consideration:

1. The rapid development of East-West economic relations during the past decade was based on the political detente which took place during the same period. The present state of knowledge does not make it possible to decide if this mutual willingness to seek detente was partially or perhaps even primarily motivated by economic concerns.

2. The resulting economic interdependence has certainly not done away with or even tempered ideologically based antagonism between the two blocs of nations. However, it has raised the threshold for hostilities. Economic relations have become important enough to both sides that they cannot be risked thoughtlessly. It does seem likely that economic interdependence can prevent smaller conflicts from arising in East-West relations or at least reduce the effects of these conflicts.

3. However, the decisive factor is that the interdependence which results from East-West economic relations is limited for both sides. As has been said, it is sufficient to (possibly) prevent smaller conflicts from arising, but at least in the short run it does not influence the principles upon which political attitudes in East and West are based.

On balance, the West predominates in economic relations with the East. The East can attempt to at least partly counterbalance this economic dominance by making use of special features in its economic system, such as its monopoly on foreign trade. However, when it needs grain or Western technology, its efforts can meet with only partial success. Nevertheless, the decisive point is that in a concrete situation the East can make use of its absolute political control to force its population to make sacrifices or accept a slowdown in economic growth; i.e. the East is not so economically dependent on the West that it can be manipulated politically when important issues are at stake. Due to the altered social situation in the Socialist nations, it would certainly not be as easy for the East to do without the advantages of trade with the West as it was 20 years ago, but this would still be possible should serious political issues be involved. The experience of the Federal Republic of Germany seems to indicate that it is simpler to win political concessions from Eastern trading partners by making economic concessions than by applying economic sanctions -- a correlation which could well be an interesting subject for political scientists to investigate. (32)

Thus, the political antagonism between East and West will certainly not be eliminated by increasing economic interdependence, but these economic developments have reduced the potential for conflict, which is certainly an important development in world politics.

NOTES

1. For information about literature concerning this subject, I am indebted to a not yet completed working paper by Hanns-Dieter Jacobsen, "Abhangigkeiten in den atlantischen Beziehungen" (Dependence in Atlantic Relations). I also owe various ideas about interdependence to my participation in an advisory capacity in two research projects which analyze concrete aspects of East-West interdependence. These projects are: Jiri Slama, "Perspektiven der regionalen Wirtschafts-integration im RGW im Hinblick auf ihre Bedeutung fur friedlichen Wandel in Osteuropa"

(Prospects for Regional Economic Integration in the CMEA in Regard to their Significance for Peaceful Change in East Europe) (Munich: Osteuropa-Institut); and Klaus Bolz, "Die Bedeutung der wirtschaftlichen Westbeziehungen eines sozialistischen Staates fur dessen wirtschaftliche Entwicklung sowie die Entwicklung seines Wirtschafts- und Gesellschaftssystems - analysiert am Beispiel Ungarn" (The Significance of Economic Relations with the West for a Socialist State in view of its Economic Development as well as the Development of its Economic and Social System - the Case of Hungary) (Hamburg: HWWA-Institut fur Wirtschaftsforschung). See also Connie M. Friesen, The Political Economy of East-West Trade (New York: Praeger, 1976), pp. 4-7.

2. This formulation corresponds to Cooper's definition of interdependence as the "sensitivity of economic events in one country to what is happening in its trading partners...." R.N. Cooper, The Economics of Interdependence: Economic Policy in the Atlantic Community (New York: McGraw-Hill, 1968), p. 10.

3. Friedemann Muller, in Zur Frage der Abhangigkeit in den wirtschaftlichen Ost-West Boziehungen (Concerning Dependence in East-West Economic Relations), SWP-AP 2106 (Ebenhausen: Stiftung Wissenschaft und Politik, 1976), p. 18, reduces dependence to this meaning alone. By his definition, a state of dependence exists when it is possible for the economic partner to intentionally disrupt the internal economic processes of another country, in which connection he considers the individual nations as the "partners" in East-West economic relations (p. 21). Such a limited concept of dependence does not seem practicable to me, since it does not include, for example, the influence which Western economic trends or currency developments can have on East European national economies.

4. See also Peter Knirsch, "Interdependence in East-West Economic Relations," From Marshall Plan to Global Interdependence: New Challenges for the Industrialized Nations (Paris: Organization for Economic Co-operation and Development, 1978), pp. 135-67.

5. Friedemann Muller, in Zur Frage der Abhangigkeit, p. 39, deals with this aspect, although he considers it as part of the issue of policy instrumentation, and he also considers this aspect in "Sicherheitspolitische Aspekte der Ost-West-Wirtschaftsbeziehungen" (Security and Policy Aspects of East-West Economic

Relations), <u>Grunbuch zu den Folgewirkungen der KSZE,</u> Jost Delbruck, Norbert Ropers, Gerd Zellentin, DGFK-Veroffentlichungen, vol. 3 (Cologne: Verlag Wissenschaft und Politik, 1977), pp. 278, 280.

6. See notes 2 and 3.

7. Some examples of parameters which Muller considers "almost impossible" to quantify are the "responsiveness of economic systems" and the "adaptability of the economic structure" (Muller, <u>Zur Frage der Abhangigkeit,</u> p. 34). Jacobsen's factor "political stability" could probably also be included here (p. 55).

8. Compare "Ost-West Handel: Defizitabbau hemmt Expansion" (East-West Trade: Deficit Reduction Slows Expansion), <u>Wochenbericht</u> (Weekly Report), Deutsches Institut fur Wirtschaftsforschung, no. 46 (Berlin (West), 1977), pp. 396-98.

9. Ibid., p. 396.

10. Figures according to Sovet Ekonomiceskoj Vzaimopomosci, ed., <u>Statisticeskij ezegodnik stran-clenov</u> SEV 1976 (Moskva: Izdatel'stvo "Statistika," 1976), p. 341

11. Muller, <u>Zur Frage der Abhangigkeit,</u> p. 11.

12. These are my own calculations, based on Benedikt Askanas, Halina Askanas, and Friedrich Levcik, "Der Aussenhandel der RGW-Lander 1960-1974" (The Foreign Trade of the CMEA Nations: 1960-1974), <u>Monatsberichte</u> (Monthly Report) the Osterreichisches Institut fur Wirtschaftsforschung no. 11 (Wien, 1974), Table 1. Here, differently from the estimate mentioned earlier, the ratio of half the foreign trade turnover to GNP is calculated in terms of domestic and foreign prices. See also Table 17.1 in Peter Wiles' contribution to this Volume, in which total exports (not only West-East trade, as is the case here) are seen as a fraction of GNP.

13. Industrial cooperation has received a great deal of attention in recent years. However, it is of interest because it is a special form of economic relations and not because of its quantitative significance. For more details, see Peter Knirsch, "Vom Ost-West-Handel zur Wirtschaftskooperation?" (From East-West

Trade to Economic Cooperation?), Europa-Archiv 28 Jg., no. 2 (Bonn: 1973): 61-69; Friedrich Levcik and Jan Stankovsky, Industrielle Kooperation zwischen Ost und West (Industrial Cooperation between East and West), Studien über Wirtschafts- und Systemvergleiche, vol. 8, (Wien, New York: Springer Verlag, 1977); and Carl H. McMillan, "East-West Industrial Cooperation," in East European Economies Post-Helsinki, ed. Hardt (Washington, D.C.: Joint Economic Committee, Congress of the United States, 1977), pp. 1175-1224.

14. This subject is treated in greater detail in Jack Brougher, "U.S.S.R. Foreign Trade: A Greater Role for Trade with the West," Soviet Economy in a New Perspective (Washington, D.C.: Joint Economic Committee, Congress of the United States, 1976), pp. 677-94; Thomas A. Wolf, "East-West Economic Relations," East European Economies Post-Helsinki, pp. 1042-54; and DIW Wochenbericht, no. 46 (1977), pp. 397-99.

15. A great deal has been written about East European indebtedness during the past few years. The following publications could be of value in relation to this study: Richard Portes, "East Europe's Debt to the West: Interdependence is a Two-Way Street," Foreign Affairs, July 1977, pp. 751-82; Lawrence J. Brainard, "Eastern Europe's Indebtedness: Policy Choices for East and West" (Paper delivered at the international workshop, "Monetary and Financial Problems in East and West," Budapest, October 16-20, 1977); Joan Parpart Zoeter, "Eastern Europe: The Growing Hard Currency Debt"; and Kathrin Melson and Edwin M. Snell, "Estimating East European Indebtedness to the West," East European Economies Post-Helsinki, pp. 1350-68 and pp. 1369-95, respectively.

16. Richard N. Cooper, "Introduction," in A Reordered World - Emerging International Economic Problems, ed. Richard N. Cooper (Washington, D.C.: Potomac Associates, 1973).

17. The Dependencia Theory, which was primarily influenced by Latin American scholars, has gained a great deal of importance in reference to relations between industrial and developing nations. For a general account, see Roy Preiswerk, "Zum Bruch mit herkommlichen Entwicklungsmodellen" (Breaking away from Conventional Development Models), in Strategien gegen Unterentwicklung zwischen Weltmarkt und Eigenstandigkeit, ed. Alfred Schmidt (Frankfurt; New York: Campus Verlag, 1976), pp. 22-42.

18. The following unpublished essay provided me with some valuable ideas for this section of the paper: Philip Hanson, "East-West Trade and Economic Systems" (Paper delivered at the Round Table Conference of the International Economic Association, "Economic Relations between East and West," Dresden, June 29-July 3, 1976).

19. Concerning the following statistics, Compare Economic Bulletin for Europe 29, no. 1 (Geneva: Economic Commission for Europe - ECE, (1977): 70-90 (quoted according to the prepublication text of November 15, 1977). Concerning oil exports, see "UdSSR vor Erdoldefizit?" (Does the U.S.S.R. Face an Oil Deficit?), DIW Wochenbericht no. 50 (1977).

20. Marshall I. Goldman provides a more differentiated and very informative description in "Autarchy or Integration -- The U.S.S.R. and the World Economy," Soviet Economy in a New Perspective (Washington, D.C.: Joint Economic Committee, Congress of the United States, 1976), pp. 90-93.

21. In 1976 petroleum from the Soviet Union was 8% and natural gas was 20% below the average import price in the Federal Republic of Germany, "RGW-Lander vermindern Handelsbilanzungleichgewicht" (CMEA Nations Reduce Disequilibrium in Balance of Trade), DIW Wochenbericht no. 12 (1977), p. 102. The underlying reasons for these cost factors in international trade dependence are discussed in Albert O. Hirschman, National Power and the Structure of Foreign Trade (Berkeley, Los Angeles: University of California Press, 1945), pp. 17-26. A more recent discussion can be found in Joseph S. Nye, Jr., "Independence and Interdependence," Foreign Policy, Spring 1976, p. 149.

22. See also Goldman's argumentation in "Autarchy or Integration," p. 89 f.

23. For more details, including bibliographical references, see Knirsch, "Interdependence in East-West Economic Relations," especially p. 9 and p. 17 f.

24. The amount of literature about the significance of the East-West technology transfer for the Socialist nations has increased rapidly. For an overview, see East-West Technological Co-operation (Brussels: NATO Directorate of Economic Affairs, 1976).

25. DIW Wochenbericht, no. 12 (1977), p. 105 f. Since the secondary effects cannot be fully ascertained and since the positive effects which a possible simultaneous interruption of imports from Eastern Europe might have on employment are not taken into consideration, these computations are of limited value. At the present time a study is being prepared about how internal German trade affects employment, which concludes that discontinuing this portion of East-West economic relations would have a neutral effect on employment in the Federal Republic of Germany.

26. For more details see Max Baumer and Hanns-Dieter Jacobsen, "CMEA and the World Economy: Institutional Concepts," East European Economies Post-Helsinki, pp. 999-1018, especially pp. 1010-12.

27. R. Portes, "East Europe's Debt to the West" Foreign Affairs 55, no. 4 (1977): 751-82, gives a competent survey of this subject, also in reference to the interdependence problem. Compare also the other sources cited in footnote 18.

28. According to ECE, Economic Bulletin for Europe 29, no. 1: 76, barter trade accounts for about 25 to 30% of the value when there are larger exports to East Europe. Compare in detail Jan Stankovsky, "Die Kompensationen im Ost-West Handel" (Compensation in East-West Trade), Wirtschaftsberichte 12, Jg., no. 6 (Wien: Creditanstalt-Bankverein, 1977): 7-16.

29. McMillan, "East-West Industrial Cooperation," p. 1192. For the current situation see ECE, Economic Bulletin for Europe 29, no. 1 (1977): 75.

30. This is also the general attitude in Hungary, Romania, and Poland where Western capital investments are technically possible. It could be a coincidence that there have been more positive comments by the Hungarian side during the past few months, as for example those by Martos to the Berlin Industrie- und Handelskammer on January 17, 1978 and the comments in "Gemischte Unternehmen in Ungarn - neue Bedingungen fur auslandische Kapitalanlagen" [Mixed Enterprises in Hungary - New Conditions for Foreign Capital Investments], Ungarischer Pressedienst Wien 22, Jg., no. 7 (January 11, 1978).

31. For basic information see Carl H. McMillan, "Direct Soviet and East European Investment in the Industrialized Western Economies,"

Working Paper No. 7 (Ottawa: Carleton University, 1977). See also "Zunehmende COMECON-Direktinvestitionen im Westen" (Increasing Direct Investments by COMECON in the West), Neue Zurcher Zeitung (Zurich, January 27, 1978).

32. The economic accommodations made by the West in the Federal Republic-German Democratic Republic relationship, from paying transit fees to "ransoming" prisoners (and there are many ways of looking at the moral aspects involved in this), have been politically effective, while the restrictive attitude assumed by the West during the fifties brought no political successes. The political failure represented by the cancellation of the interzonal trade agreement in September 1960 was an especially clear illustration of this. Of course, these experiences of the Germans cannot simply be applied to the entire East-West relationship. Concerning these experiences, compare Siegfried Kupper, "Politische Aspekte des innerdeutschen Handels" (Political Aspects of Internal German Trade), in C.-D. Ehlermann, S. Kupper, H. Lambrecht, and G. Illig, Handelspartner DDR - Innerdeutsche Wirtschaftsbeziehungen (The German Democratic Republic as a Trading Partner: Intra-German Economic Relations) (Schriftenreihe Europaische Wirtschaft, Bd. 76, Baden-Baden: Nomos Verlagsgesellschaft, 1975), pp. 11-76.

6 Comments
Jeanne Kirk Laux
and Alan A. Abouchar

My principal thesis emerges directly out of Murgescu's observations on the changing international environment. The world economy, argues Murgescu, is in crisis: an "overall crisis," a crisis of "global character," one of "universal interdependencies." Perhaps these are platitudes, but they have profound implications for the role of the Socialist states. If the world economic crisis is not strictly a crisis of capitalism, then it must be presumed that the Socialist states are implicated and that they are affected, albeit in different forms and to different degrees. Murgescu's characterization of the changing international environment reflects a new premise underlying economic policy making in Eastern Europe.

EASTERN REINTEGRATION INTO THE WORLD CAPITALIST ECONOMY

This leads to the principal thesis: that the political leadership in Eastern Europe (most obviously in Romania, Poland, and Hungary) has already adopted a development strategy which assumes a reintegration into the world capitalist economy. They are now engaged in restructuring industrial production in order to secure an acceptable role in the new international division of labor.

Romanian sources, for example, are highly explicit in espousing this thesis. Romanian News and Notes asserted that "Romania firmly rejects the idea of autarky ... the active participation in the international division of labour being an inseparable facet of ... development of every nation. Proving this fact is the very evolution of foreign trade whose volume grew some 22 times over 1950-1976." (1) What is the objective? All small Socialist states, including Romania, seek to change their comparative advantage, especially vis-a-vis the advanced capitalist economies, altering their trade composition in order to increase the share of manufactured goods, a task which also requires changes in domestic investment patterns in order to modernize process and production technology so as to create goods able to meet the exigencies of Western markets.

When we look at the means selected to reach this objective, we must add a corollary to our principal thesis. The Romanian Communist Party specified three means at its Eleventh Congress in 1974: (a) acquisition of advanced technology, principally imported from the West; (b) increased "export competitiveness"; and (c) industrial cooperation. (2) By 1977 the Romanian Government claimed that its cooperation agreements with western firms accounted for 25% of total exports. Using these means, Romania looks typical rather than unique when compared to the other Socialist states. This choice suggests the following corollary: that Eastern European economic planners have quite consciously recognized the fact that they must fit into an already emergent international division of labor shaped by the global operations of the large corporations in the advanced capitalist countries.

By choosing to emphasize industrial cooperation from licensing to subcontracting to joint equity ventures the Eastern European planners have selected as a key partner the multinational corporation and the large state enterprise in the West. By focusing on export competitiveness to meet their objective of trade restructuring and a more intense participation in the world economy, planners must meet production and marketing standards predefined in the West. Each Socialist economy thus must fit into a niche already chiseled out by the leading Western firms, a requirement reinforced by the criteria for creditworthiness determined by the leading Western lenders. Thus far I see little evidence to prove that imported Western technology is intended for assimilation and eventual technological self-reliance in the new knowledge based industries. I see more evidence to support the interpretation that Western technology is principally intended to allow Eastern European economies to find their place in an international division of labor shaped by others. Hungarian planners, for example, self-consciously chose to streamline industrial production after the oil crisis and opted for a new priority--export oriented development. They looked at the list of 45 products, which had a worldwide volume of sales twice that of the growth rate of world trade, and selected those 16 which Hungary already produced. Now

Hungary will seek to penetrate Western markets, relying heavily on licensing and coproduction ventures with Western firms.

Caveats

Here two caveats must be introduced before any melodramatic conclusions are drawn from the previous assertions. First, reintegration in the world's capitalist economy need not be seen as incompatible with more intense trade and cooperation within the Comecon. Indeed, often the large Western firm will not sell a license to the small Socialist state unless that state already has assured itself a monopoly in the region through Comecon specialization agreements. To use John Hardt's felicitous phrase, we are witnessing Comecon "integration by FIAT."

Secondly, reintegration into the world's capitalist economy does not imply technological sellout. The Socialist economies in question have already developed diversified industrial structures; they already sell technology in the West, from Hungarian pharmaceuticals to Bulgarian fork lifts. Looking at their use of imported Western technology, capital goods and the know-how used to raise the technological level of products intended to make East Europe "export competitive" must be distinguished from those capital goods intended for import substitution, especially turnkey plants or licenses for components to produce consumer goods. For the latter, there is no reason based on the short experience at hand to exclude product modification or even assimilation by the highly competent Eastern European engineering establishment. In the former case, however, despite the fact that export oriented industry usually has linkages to national industry and science -- thus differentiating Eastern Europe from much of the Third World -- it is argued that the new Eastern Europe development strategy involves a basic acceptance of the technological standards and marketing strategies of Western corporations, an acceptance, therefore, of the need to fit into an international division of labor already shaped by others. The stage has already been set; the national role remains only to be interpreted.

If the Eastern European states indeed seek to redefine their role in the international division of labor by changing product lines to promote exports to the advanced capitalist economies, what are the implications for North-South relations? At the same time, after all, Third World states seek to adjust trade and investment patterns to improve their position in the new economic order. Are Eastern and Southern development strategies essentially compatible, as Professor Murgescu implies in his paper, or might they be competitive? Five hypotheses are submitted, no one of which is entirely convincing, yet each of which is plausible, to suggest possible tendencies in North (East)-South relations.

HYPOTHESIS ONE

The first hypothesis postulates that the East and South are engaged in a traditional division of labor in which there is an "unequal" exchange (in the Prebisch sense) between Eastern manufactured goods and Southern raw materials. UNCTAD first signalled a shift in Eastern European development assistance away from promoting projects aimed at import substitution and toward export oriented enterprises, particularly those involved in natural resource development with exports going back to the Comecon countries. More recently, the United Nations report on the Second Development Decade surveyed some 400 industrial cooperation accords between the East and South to conclude that typically the Eastern partner provided engineering skills, machinery, and equipment in exchange for payment in raw materials or semiprocessed goods. (3) Depletion of Eastern European energy sources and the scarcity of hard currency appeared to motivate these East-South ventures.

HYPOTHESIS TWO

The second hypothesis sees compatibility of Eastern and Southern industrial strategies as the East restructures domestic production to specialize in research-intensive manufactures competitive in Western markets, thus opening its domestic markets to Third World manufacturers. Hungary, for example, has chosen to manufacture only specialty clothing items and to import textiles from the Third World. (4) United Nations' trade statistics show that to the extent that primary products have declined slightly in the 1970s as a share of Eastern imports from the Third World, they have declined in favor of textile yarn, fabrics, and clothing. (5)

HYPOTHESIS THREE

The third hypothesis postulated the emergence of a more advanced division of labor, based on specialization within industrial branches, between the East and some of the more industrialized Third World economies. Czechoslovakia, for example, has subcontracted with India for the supply of railroad equipment. (6) Secular trade trends, in fact, show a slight decline in the proportion of SITC categories 1-4 in Comecon country imports from the developing nations. (7). Here the East-South relationship looks highly complementary, rather than one which relegates the South to producer of low technology goods.

HYPOTHESIS FOUR

In direct contradiction with the above evidence, the fourth hypothesis sees some Socialist countries in competition with Third World countries for access to the markets of the advanced capitalist countries. It assumed that Eastern Europe must continue to export processed foods, raw materials (e.g. Polish copper), or textiles (e.g. Romanian synthetic fibers produced under United States license) to cover hard currency trade deficits. In so doing Socialist states compete with the same manufactures from the less developed nations.

HYPOTHESIS FIVE

The fifth, and perhaps the most radical, hypothesis sees Eastern European states playing the role of junior partners to Western corporations, furthering their internationalization of production in the Third World by participating in "tripartite" industrial cooperation arrangements, sometimes called Third Market cooperation. Information on the small number of tripartite arrangements is scarce, but Arkwright and Gutman have interviewed executive officers in forty French firms involved in tripartite deals in 1974. According to their findings, the principal motives for a western firm's combining with a Socialist partner are to win the bid for the contract by lowering the estimate due to cheaper costs in the Socialist states and to benefit from good political relations between Socialist states and the Third World host government. (8) Various benefits accrue to the Socialist partner: managers and engineers involved can familiarize themselves with Western technology and enhance their know-how, and Eastern enterprises can export machinery and equipment embodying low or stable technology as part of the complex package. Third World countries, however, had no direct participation in 75% of the cases surveyed. Where they were involved, their contribution was limited to labor intensive activities, e. g. plant construction. All the while benefiting from their participation, the Socialist countries thus appear to facilitate market penetration by Western multinationals and to sanctify the peripheral role of Third World countries in the global economy.

Clearly the self-conscious effort by Eastern European countries to restructure production and improve their role in the international division of labor has major implications for North-South relations. The fragmentary nature of studies of East-South relations does not permit any unqualified conclusions, but rather raises intriguing questions for the discussion about the likely compatibility or conflict between East and South in the new international economic order.

Jeanne Kirk Laux

Any attempt to quantify as important a concept as interdependence must certainly appeal to the interests of a wide range of economists. Even if a writer concentrates his attention on one aspect of interdependence (economic interdependence) and further reorients the emphasis to economic dependence (the primary concern of Dr. Knirsch) rather than interdependence, he continues to merit the interest and attention of serious scholars. I believe, however, that Dr. Knirsch's paper does not succeed entirely in achieving its appointed goal, partly because of the diversity of interpretations or meanings that can be assigned to the abstract concept of economic dependence. An alternative approach would be to recognize this diversity and attempt to derive a measure for the different types of economic dependence that we might define.

ECONOMIC DEPENDENCE

Thus, we would start by trying to construct an operational definition of economic dependence, which I would propose that we define in terms of the different types of results that we might be interested in studying, i.e., the different relationships in which nations may become involved. Perhaps the three most important questions that might be asked in relation to the three major manifestations of economic dependence are the following:

1. In whose camp would a given third nation find itself in the event of war between two nations or large regional groupings?

2. What is the outlook for expanded trade between two nations?

3. Is there a potential advantage to a particular firm in one nation arising from the economic relationship between two nations?

Clearly, the expression "economic dependence" may arise within the context of any one of these questions. Until it is agreed in any particular situation what is the source of the interest in economic dependence, it really cannot be decided how precisely to go about measuring it empirically. That the measure employed by Dr. Knirsch is not entirely satisfactory, however, can be concluded from the following considerations.

In the discussion to follow, the following terminology is adopted:

X_A, M_A, T_A = Total exports, total imports, and total trade turnover of country A;

$$T_A = X_A + M_A$$

X_{AB}, M_{AB}, T_{AB} = Exports of country A to country B, imports from B to A, and trade turnover between A and B;

$$T_{AB} = X_{AB} + M_{AB}$$

Y_A = GNP of country A

Dr. Knirsch proposes as the basic measure of economic dependence the bilateral turnover/total turnover ratio, i.e., T_{AB}/T_A. As Dr. Knirsch himself recognizes, however, a more meaningful measure of dependence would be the bilateral trade/GNP ratio, T_{AB}/Y_A,

COMMENTS

and his despair of its use is conditioned by the manifest difficulty of trying to standardize GNP measures among countries, especially countries as diverse as those in the First, Second, and Third World camps. Thus, recourse to the bilateral/total ratio is an attempt to make do with the possible. However, as Dr. Knirsch recognizes, very misleading results can be obtained this way since it is possible for a country to have a very high bilateral/total ratio even while total trade is very small in the country's total economic picture. A country may simply be fairly autarkic, engaging in very little trade turnover at all, in which case it is not very meaningful to suggest that the country is dependent upon countries with which it maintains a bilateral trade that is high in relation to its very low total trade turnover.

It remains to ask, however, whether even if GNP could be a standardized measurement and bilateral turnover/GNP ratios could be calculated in a consistent way, if there would be an adequate measure of economic dependence. Accordingly, let us suppose that the problem of GNP standardization does not exist and the bilateral/total turnover ratio moves in perfect agreement with the bilateral trade/GNP ratio, with GNP calculated on the basis of the same concepts and procedures for all countries. In general we would assume that the following relationship holds:

$$\frac{T_{ij}}{T_i} = \alpha(\frac{T_{ij}}{Y_i})$$

That is to say, the bilateral/total trade ratio <u>is</u> a perfect proxy for the bilateral trade/GNP ratio. If a country has a relatively low value of the former, its value of the latter in relation to other countries is also low. It is asked whether even in this situation the measure proposed by Dr. Knirsch is an adequate measure of economic dependence of country A on country B.

A general answer to the last question cannot be given. In this short note an exhaustive analysis of the various possibilities cannot be given in relation to the types of economic dependence that have been posed at the outset as possibly being of concern to the analyst. Moreover, even from any single point of view, the measure of dependence unfortunately must be more microscopic and take into account the composition of the turnover.

POSSIBLE PROBLEMS

A few of the possible problems that arise in the interpretation of the measure for a given pair of countries follow.

Consider the situation in which $\dfrac{T_{AB}}{T_A} > \dfrac{T_{BA}}{T_B}$.

It would concluded that the dependence of A on B was greater than the reverse dependence. Suppose, in the absence of bilaterally balanced trade, the high value of T_{AB}/T_A was caused by a high volume of imports from B to A. To make an inference about dependence requires knowledge of more than that ratio tells about the type of goods being imported. Without meaning to suggest that the following is an exhaustive set of possibilities, assume that the imports are heavily weighted or dominated by one of the four following types of imports: imports of manufactures for the industrial sector, consumption imports for the enclave sector, raw materials, or food imports for national consumption.

High imports of manufactured goods for industry <u>may</u> imply some sort of dependence, given the dependencies of language and customs that the use of B's processes in A implies. This type of trade could not be easily diverted in the short term. High consumption by an enclave sector may also suggest a dependence, since given the preference that the persons belonging to the enclave for imports from B and given the secure position of the enclave, it would probably be correct to assume that one of the definitions of economic dependence, and probably also political dependence, would be implied by the high ratio, since again a serious change would not be expected in the short term. The supply of raw materials, on the other hand, is more easily transferred even in the short term, so that a high import of raw materials is a less valid indicator of economic dependence. Finally, high food imports for the general economy (grain, rice, beans) can readily be transferred, unless possibly reinforced by a strongly entrenched enclave or technological assistance group, which may be the case in developing economies, but which is less likely to be the case in advanced economies, as both the United States and Canada have learned in various experiences over the past five years.

Now consider a relatively high bilateral/total trade ratio caused by high exports. Again, the direction of dependence, or even the applicability of the term dependence at all, cannot be said to be unambiguous. Consider Saudi Arabia and the United States. In the ratio T_{SA-US}/T_{SA}, X_{SA-US} outweighs the imports from the United

States and in any event, is certainly very high. Given the present Saudi Arabian inability to assimilate all its export earnings and given its quite reasonable and repeatedly expressed desire to stretch out the life of its resources - recognizing that even if the rest of the world, and indeed Saudi Arabia itself, is successful in converting to nonfossil forms of energy, there will continue to be a strong demand for the oil reserves as raw industrial inputs - Saudi Arabia can hardly be said to be dependent upon the United States because of its high exports to the United States either in the long term or even in the short. Similarly, the large volume of Saudi Arabian imports now coming from the United States could easily be reoriented and brought from Western Europe. Far from being economically dependent upon the United States, it might argue that the dependency relationship is ideological dependence, which to be sure over the long haul is conditioned by the economic interests of many of the economically important groups within the country and conditions its preference for dealing with the United States as against the Communist world. This preference, however, could also be realized through increased dealings with Western Europe.

It is hoped that the foregoing remarks do not appear overly critical, because as noted at the outset it is desirable to try to say something about economic dependence, which can scarcely be done without some notion of its magnitude in various situations and without some attempt to measure it. It is believed, however, that the measure can be improved upon by considering further the makeup of the basic ratios, and it is urged that further work be done along these lines.

Alan Abouchar

NOTES

1. Romanian News and Notes, August 1977, p. 4.

2. Romanian Communist Party, "Directives of the XI Congress of the Romanian Communist Party concerning the 1976-1980 Five-Year Plan and the Guidelines for the Economic and Social Development of Romania in the 1981-1990 Period" (Bucharest: 1974).

3. United Nations, "Implementation of the International Development Strategy in the Centrally Planned Economies," <u>World Economic Survey (1974)</u>, pp. 168-70.

4. Ibid., p. 176.

5. Ibid., p. 165.

6. Ibid., p. 171.

7. Ibid., p. 162.

8. Patrick Gutman and Francis Arkwright, "La cooperation industrielle tripartite entre pays a systemes economiques et sociaux differentes de l'Ouest, de l'Est et du Sud," <u>Politique estrangere</u>, no. 6 (1975), pp. 621-56.

II

Changing Actors and Roles in a New International Division of Labor

Introduction

This part explores the changing roles of multinational and transnational actors, with contributions from the German Federal Republic, the United Kingdom, the United States, and France.

The first chapter examines the experience of two groups of countries, the less developed countries and the state-trading countries in the world economy; discusses some central issues in East-West economic relations; and describes relations between blocs or groups of countries, with a special stress on relations between CMEA and the European Economic Community. The subsequent three chapters discuss the special role of the multinational corporations in East-West economic relations from the legal, business organization, and economic points of view, respectively.

The last chapter combines comments on the papers dealing with the multinational corporations from the perspective of comparative systems analysis with observations on the nature of East-West economic relations and certain aspects of actual technique by two economists thoroughly familiar with the practical aspects of these relations.

7 Changing Roles of International Institutional Actors in East-West and North-South Relations

Max Baumer and
Hanns-Dieter Jacobsen

INTRODUCTION

When one looks at present political-economic discussions dealing with the creation of a "New International Economic Order," it becomes apparent that these discussions are concentrated around the relationship between less developed and industrialized countries. Although their global economic relevance in relation to world production and world trade has been continually increasing, the state trading countries are far from active participation. The obvious passivity of the Soviet Union and other CMEA members is all the more surprising because there have been phases in the last 35 years in which the Soviet Union showed interest in shaping the world economy and its institutions. Thus, the Soviet Union cooperated in the creation of international economic organizations in the immediate postwar era and took initiatives at the first United Nations Conference on Trade and Development (UNCTAD) in 1964.

In this paper, the causes of the contradictions between the increasing relations of the CMEA state trading countries with the world economy and the unpronounced role of the CMEA countries within international economic organizations will be examined; consequences and possible solutions will then be discussed. (1)

INTERNATIONAL ORGANIZATIONS AND THE WORLD ECONOMY: CHANGING ACTORS AND NEW PROBLEMS

In the postwar period, it was mainly the "General Agreement on Tariffs and Trade" (GATT) and the "International Monetary Fund" (IMF) that, through the codification of international rules, improved the relationship among the trading countries and contributed to the expansion and functioning of world trade.

However, in recent years, the relative significance of global economic institutions has changed, both because new actors appeared, such as the less developed countries (LDCs) and among them the Organization of Petroleum Exporting Countries (OPEC), regional integration systems like the European Economic Community (EEC), and multinational corporations, and because the economic influence of traditional actors either diminished (e.g., the United States) or increased (e.g., the Western European countries and the Council for Mutual Economic Assistance (CMEA) countries). Also, structural changes caused new problems, such as the trend toward mercantile behavior and protectionism, the heavy foreign indebtedness of a number of countries, and the securing and financing of adequate raw material and fuel supplies, etc. Thus, most countries became more dependent on external economic developments, and international economic inter-dependencies have grown. It has become more and more evident that the traditional economic organizations were incapable of coping adequately with these changing conditions or with the national goals and interests of the member countries.

It is not surprising that, consequently, new trends have developed which are not based on the strengthening or altering of existing organizations. Rather, they aim to form factions consisting of countries which share the same interests within those institutions or to form new groups of countries, or reactivate old ones, which have at their disposal a comparable political basis and pursue similar interests. Additionally, apart from the existing organizations, these trends build on informal contacts such as economic summit conferences, etc. As far as international economic organizations are concerned, a polarization process is presently taking place. The global integration phase which characterized the 1960s seems to have ended for the time being. Therefore, the existing institutionalized structure of the world economy can briefly be described as a mixture of global institutions, such as GATT and IMF, which have changed functions or have lost in significance; of increasingly relevant regional or issue referring institutions, such as EEC, OPEC, and OECD; and of bilateral or regional negotiations and agreements. This institutional shifting of weights thus occurred between rising world trade, increased capital flows, and generally increasing international interdependence on the one hand, and growing protectionism which is manifested through national action and counteraction for the protection of the domestic economy on the other hand. The new situation increases the pressure on the participants to find acceptable solutions and avoid threatening conflicts and economic disadvantages for all.

However, the arising problems and the possible solutions for the East-West relations are of a different nature than those for North-South relations.

THE LESS DEVELOPED COUNTRIES

The less developed countries tried to win integration into the worldwide economic system of the industrialized world, and within the framework of developing economic relations, strove not only for nondiscrimination, but beyond this, endeavored to gain preferential treatment. This is illustrated by the following developments: the decades of development of the United Nations, the formation of UNCTAD, the amendments of the statutes of the GATT in favor of the less developed countries (the addition of the chapter, "Trade and Development"), the increase of the "Group of Ten" in the IMF to a "Group of Twenty" in order to better incorporate LDCs' voices in the discussions of institutional reform, and the Lome agreement between the EEC and the ACP countries, etc.

In discussing strategies of doing away with underdevelopment, the concept of "self-reliance" or "endogenous development" plays an increasingly important role. Its fundamental idea is to better mobilize a country's own strength and simultaneously reduce dependency on other countries. Undoubtedly, this will have an effect on the external behavior of countries of the Third World. The concept of "self-reliance" has been used by the LDCs at international conferences, e.g., the "Conference on International Economic Cooperation" (CIEC) which took place in Paris from December, 1975 to June, 1977. During the CIEC, 19 less developed countries, representing the "Group of 77," negotiated with 16 OECD countries (the 9 European Community members appeared as a unit, and the participating industrial countries were spoken of as "Group of 8"). The CMEA members did not participate in that North-South dialogue.

The central means for the realization of the less developed countries' demands for a "New International Economic Order" is expected to be a coherent system of raw material trading agreements, because the developing countries regard their raw materials as an ideal instrument to overcome economic backwardness. In accordance with this "integrated raw material program," ten important raw materials were not to be sold at fluctuating market prices, but rather at regulated prices kept fairly stable through the creation of buffer stocks, thereby stabilizing export earnings for the less developed countries. All ten raw material agreements were to be united within a common fund for the financing of raw material stocks. No solution to this problem was found at the CIEC; the final decision was that the negotiations should be continued at UNCTAD meetings. Concrete solutions have not been found since and are hardly to be expected in the near future because on top of North-South differences of opinion, divergent interests have developed even among Third World exporters of raw materials.

These developmental tendencies are typical of the present day trend. There are various positions of interest, not only with regard to the erosion of the former united world economy, but also within the different blocs, and they include other issues such as debts, energy supply, and transfer of technology, etc. The possibility of finding far-reaching and binding solutions which exceed general codes of conduct seems to be rather limited.

THE STATE TRADING COUNTRIES

The relations of the Soviet Union and the Eastern European countries vis-a-vis the international economic organizations have developed quite differently.

Initially, some of these countries participated in the reorganization of the world economy after World War II (preparation of the Bretton Woods agreement, International Trade Organization, and GATT, etc.). However, the increasing tensions between East and West and the Cold War caused their withdrawal. Only in the late sixties, when detente began to take on shape and the economic relations between East and West increased substantially, were there indications that CMEA countries were reconsidering an integration into global economic organizations (e.g. GATT, IMF) and that they were going to try to improve and to formalize their economic relations with Western countries and institutions. The CMEA took steps by proposing negotiations at the bilateral (e.g., cooperation agreements, joint commissions), as well as the regional (e.g., Romania-EEC, CMEA-EEC), level. (2) The CMEA's leading power, the Soviet Union, acted rather reservedly at the global level, e.g., the Soviet Union never applied for

GATT membership. The underlying rationale seems to be that Soviet policy makers believe that, on the one hand, benefits to be derived from membership in international organizations (e.g., "most-favored-nation" treatment) can be gained in bilateral negotiations as well, whereas on the other hand, membership might restrict their political and economic freedom of action. In this context, it is noteworthy that the Soviet Union still has not explicitly given up Lenin's and Stalin's concept of a second, Socialist world market.

Compared with this, the smaller Eastern European countries are heavily dependent on foreign trade, due to small domestic markets and a lack of natural resources. Therefore, in order to sustain economic growth, it is much more important for these countries to obtain the offered benefits and preferences. Moreover, in joining international economic organizations, these countries may have been hoping to increase their national sovereignty and their margin for economic actions within the Soviet bloc. Even though the experience of the unsuccessful trade negotiations between the Soviet Union and the United States (withdrawal of the United States-Soviet Union trade agreement of 1972 by the Soviet government early in 1975) might suggest that bilateral bargaining does not protect the Soviet Union from attack on matters such as human rights, which have nothing to do with the management of external economic relations, there are no indications of a change in the Soviet policy in this respect. Indeed, as the meager result of the Belgrade meeting of the CSCE demonstrates, the amount of pressure which can be successfully put upon the Soviet Union is rather limited.

In their economic relations with the West, the CMEA countries basically face similar problems and have similar economic objectives as the LDCs: 1) improvement of the export structure - the share of food stuffs, raw materials, and fuel in total exports (SITC 0 - 4) is still higher (except in the cases of the CSSR and the GDR) than the share of industrial products (SITC 5 - 8); 2) long-term stabilization of trade and earnings from trade in order to improve the basis for economic planning; 3) expansion of trade with the advanced countries in the West and removal of barriers to trade established by the Western countries; 4) financing of import surpluses and prevention of possible overindebtedness - in general, a solution to their balance of payments and currency problems; 5) achievement of a smooth and continual transfer of technology from the advanced countries in the West into their countries; and 6) securing and financing adequate raw material and fuel supplies for their national economies. The retrenchment of these problems requires management of additional problems in the case of the state trading countries. Differences not only in the levels of development have to be taken into account, but the differences in the social and economic systems as well. Since most international economic organizations were founded by market type economies and were designed to regulate economic relations among them, these problems are of a principal nature. The functional mechanisms of the international economic organizations were far from being readily adjustable to the central planning of national economies, foreign trade monopolies, nonexistence of tariffs, strictly regulated and inconvertible currencies, prohibition of direct investment and capital transfer, and bilateral balancing of foreign trade, etc.

However, the world economic situation has changed. On the one hand, although low productivity of labor and capital caused the economic reforms in the 1960s, the decision to increase trade and financial relations with the West led to certain changes in industrial organization and in the foreign trade system on the Eastern European side, e.g., better information on economic data, more direct firm-to-firm relations, decentralization of business decision making, wider use of Western currencies, and even possibilities for joint ventures.

On the other hand, the making of economic policy has become more centralized in the Western industrial countries, not only in the sphere of East-West trade. Even in economic relations among OECD countries, the increased use of nontariff barriers to trade and "voluntary" export restrictions have led to a strengthening of the bilateral element and thus, to a gradual renunciation of the concept of free trade. These protectionist measures in the sphere of trade are complemented in the monetary field through restrictions in capital transfer and holdings of foreign currencies, differences in opinion about the proper management of flexible exchange rates, and the future role of Special Drawing Rights (SDRs).

In this respect, apart from political and ideological aspects, the differences between the functioning of the economic systems in the West and in the East have dimished to a certain extent. Complementary to these developments, which could facilitate an institutional integration of the Eastern European countries and the Soviet Union into the world economy, the creation of new instruments at the bilateral (e.g., joint commissions) and the regional (e.g., EEC's responsibility for trade agreements with the state trading countries) level and nongovernmental arrangements (firms, banks, chambers of commerce) should help to promote and regulate the economic relations between the two ideologically opposed camps.

CENTRAL ISSUES OF INTERNATIONAL ECONOMIC RELATIONS: MOST-FAVORED-NATION TREATMENT

Systemic differences, however, between the market economies in the West and the state trading countries in the East are still troubling the institutional structure of the world economy. This will be discussed with regard to two main issues in international trade and international monetary relations.

The characteristic difference between less developed and state trading countries becomes clear when regarding the "most-favored-nation" (MFN) principle, one of the main pillars of world trade and of GATT. The granting of MFN treatment implies that "any advantage, favour, privilege or immunity granted by any contracting party to any product originating in or destined for any other country shall be accorded immediately and unconditionally to the like product originating in or destined for the territories of all other contracting parties." Utilizing this basic principle, GATT emerges as an organization that works toward improvement of the competition between the contracting parties and diminishing the effectiveness of such instruments of economic policy as tariffs, quotas, etc. since the usage of such instruments leads to an impairment of worldwide free trade. The worldwide trade negotiations, which by now have taken place seven times -- the most recent one, the "Tokyo-Round," started in 1973 and seems to be at the final stage -- operate on the "do ut des" principle. The privilege given to a country is returned with reciprocal privileges from the other countries. For the benefit of the less developed countries, the GATT allows an exception to this basic rule (adoption to the GATT statutes of part IV, "Trade and Development," in June 1966) (3) in order to contribute to the development of these countries through preferential treatment of their foreign trade. However, LDCs argue preferential treatment is rhetoric, because following the settlement of the "Kennedy Round" in 1967, they were not able to claim the benefits that industrial nations guaranteed each other. There was no reason to make similar concessions to the Eastern European countries because of their comparatively high level of development. Consequently, securing "effective reciprocity" became the main problem when the state trading countries applied for membership. In state trading countries, tariffs are irrelevant, although Hungary is an exception, because foreign trade which functions through the import plan is directly related to national economic planning in size, structure, and goals and is settled through the foreign trade monopoly. Hence, the basis for a comparison of mutual concessions is missing.

State trading countries behave in a protectionistic manner insofar as they can freely choose either to consider or ignore foreign offers; i.e., the situation is the same as in the case of barriers to trade. Beyond this, Western exporters have greater difficulties obtaining access to the markets of the CMEA countries than the CMEA countries' export organizations in most Western countries. Accordingly, the joining modalities of Poland (1967), Romania (1971), and Hungary (1974) were pragmatically agreed upon, and they are different from one another in their concrete settlements. (4)

The Eastern European countries profit from their membership in GATT in that the effect of increasing protectionism in the world economy is being mitigated. Presently, in the framework of the GATT's "Tokyo Round," control, regulation, and removal of quantitative restrictions are being attempted, and these actions have affected approximately 3 and 5% of world trade. (5) The elimination of these restrictions proves to be much more difficult than the elimination of tariffs. Indeed, the GATT secretariat identified 844 nontariff obstacles, the most frequently noted of which were consulate formalities; industry, health, security, and other norms; quantitative restrictions and import licenses; embargo and other restrictions; harbor and statistical fees; and equalizing assessment of border taxes. (6) The methods used at tariff negotiations (granting bi- or multilateral concessions to all other contracting parties qua MFN treatment) cannot be applied to nontariff trade obstacles. Furthermore, there are considerable limitations to the removal of the nontariff trade obstacles in the deficient legal and organizational provisions of GATT. (7)

Obviously, the state trading countries are now better able to be integrated into the comprehensive and complicated methods of negotiations than they were in the 1950s and 1960s when conditions were almost archaic. Nevertheless, this improvement is merely an expression of the decreasing functional capabilities of this institution, which can only insufficiently adjust to changing conditions.

CENTRAL ISSUES OF INTERNATIONAL ECONOMIC RELATIONS: INTERNATIONAL PAYMENTS

In the financial and monetary field, substantial differences between the less developed countries and the state trading countries are to be noted in their relations with international economic organizations and institutions.

Since 1960, the CMEA countries have consistently run hard currency deficits in their trade with the OECD nations. CMEA's hard currency indebtedness has been estimated at approximately $40 billion at the end of 1976. (8) These debts, translated into debt per capita ratios, work out to about $130 at the end of 1975 for total CMEA, with the Soviet ratio being approximately $60, and the Eastern European ratio about $260 (see Table 7.1). Surprisingly, the per capita indebtedness of the less developed countries compares favorably with this. Their ratio was about $100 at the end of 1975. However, if foreign indebtedness is compared with the Gross National Product (GNP), the picture changes dramatically. This ratio works out to roughly 25% for the less developed countries, whereas the figure for the CMEA nations is about 5%.

It is not necessary to discuss here the causes for the indebtedness of the less developed countries. However, in order to get a clearer picture of the crucial problems of the state trading countries' monetary system, some causes for their consistent hard currency deficits in trade with the West will be discussed briefly.

Hard currency earnings are limited by the fact that the share of manufactured products (SITC 5-8) in CMEA exports to the West is about 40%, whereas imports are more than 80%. This lack of competitiveness with manufactured products is due mainly to lack of innovation, reliability, and marketing. (9) Existing Western import restrictions do not play a decisive role in this respect. These deficiencies, in turn, can be attributed to internal, systemic factors of the CMEA countries, although due to differences in economic systems, these arguments do not apply to all CMEA countries to the same extent.

Inefficient systems of success indicators, distribution according to plan, and tautness in plans cause a lack of competition in domestic markets and intra-CMEA trade and result in sellers markets, thereby preventing unplanned exchanges of commodities ("commodity inconvertibility"). Hence, intra-CMEA trade flows are negotiated on a bilateral level. In trade with the West, these factors prevent a more flexible adjustment of the amount of imports to exports and vice versa.

Commodity inconvertibility and the divergent price formation systems within CMEA prevent prices and exchange rates from fulfilling any real allocational function and make CMEA currencies inconvertible. Exchange rate changes cannot, therefore, be used as a tool for achieving an equilibrium in the balance of payments.

The use of convertible currencies and world prices in East-West trade eases some of these problems and has, therefore, led to their increased application in intra-CMEA trade as well. (10) Other attempts to overcome the CMEA currency problems through internal measures have not been very successful so far. Economic and price reforms have not been carried far enough to boost technological

Table 7.1. Foreign Indebtedness of Less Developed and CMEA Countries: 1975

Countries	Per Capita Indebtedness: (US $)	Share of Indebtedness in GNP (%)
Low income countries (per capita income less than $265)	30	21
Medium income countries	200	28
OPEC countries	200	20
LDC total	100	25
Soviet Union	56	2
Eastern European countries	260	11
CMEA total[a]	130	5

a) Without CMEA banks

Sources: Finanzierung und Entwicklung 14 no. 4 (1977): 23; Friedrich Levcik and Jan Stankovsky, "Kredite des Westens und Osterreichs an Osteuropa und die UdSSR," Report no. 28 (Vienna (Wien): Wiener Institut fur Internationale Wirtschaftsvergleiche, June 1977); and computations from World Bank Atlas (Washington, D.C., 1977, pp. 10-30.

progress and efficiency; programs and measures for making the Transferable Rule (TR) more functionable have not succeeded (e.g., intra-CMEA trade is still bilateral); the less developed countries hesitate to accept the TR as a basis for a multilateral system of payments with the CMEA; (11) and Western enterprises are hardly making use of the offer to keep TR accounts with Eastern banks.

Consequently, even though some CMEA countries are quite resourceful in their attempts to get hard currencies from abroad and from their citizens, the basic problems remain. Only Hungary, due to its relatively radical reforms, might be in a position to reach a partial convertibility of its national currency in the forseeable future, e.g., along the lines which Yugoslavia followed.

To be sure, neither the creation of an East-West development bank under the auspices of the United Nations Economic Commission for Europe nor membership of CMEA countries in the IMF would solve the problem. However, further growth of East-West trade and multilateralization of intra-CMEA trade could be promoted thereby. Currently, Romania is the only CMEA member of IMF. (12) Romania's application was accepted on the basis of Article XIV of the IMF statutes, which allow economically weak members to restrict current transactions during a transition period. This article makes no distinction with respect to the motives underlying the payment restrictions. It is doubtful, however, whether Article XIV could be applied to other more highly developed CMEA countries as well. Especially for Czechoslavakia, which, just as Hungary and Poland, is reported to negotiate with the IMF on accession, this may turn out to be a problem. (13)

Even though the collapse of the Bretton Woods System and the uncertain future of the international monetary system may have diminished the incentives to join the IMF, there are a number of reasons why an accession of CMEA countries should be considered. First, it should be easier to take into account the specific requirements of Socialist countries while discussing the contours of a new monetary system as opposed to the modification of an already existing one. Further growth of East-West economic and political relations could be promoted by an arrangement acceptable to both systems. Second, demands of the less developed countries in a new monetary system, e.g., more stable exchange rates and stabilization of export earnings, meet with the interests of the state trading countries. Third, the economic situation within CMEA has changed insofar as the terms of trade of the Eastern European countries vis-a-vis the Soviet Union have worsened considerably. Moreover, these countries have to secure their raw material supplies more and more from outside CMEA, which makes them more dependent on international monetary arrangements and facilities. However, chances for a universal monetary system, including the state trading countries, appear to be rather slim. The East proposed that a monetary institution be put under the aegis of the United Nations and that all countries that wish to participate could join. Distributional and redistributional functions are to play the central role. (14)

In contrast to that, the West proposes that the IMF should increasingly evolve into an international central bank, empowering it as a lender of last resort in crisis situations. Wide participation by many countries is expected to impede the decision making process, and the key role should, therefore, be left to smaller groups of countries which collaborate together. (15)

It is doubtful whether these two conceptions can be combined in a new system that is multipolar in character, i.e., which permits diversifications according to the interests of participating countries and groups of countries. Such a system could constitute a worldwide framework where special arrangements could be made on a regional level. However, it has to be kept in mind that questions of price formation and the determination of the role of money touch upon the very root of the political economy of Socialism and its underlying ideology.

ISSUE-ORIENTED AND REGIONAL DEVELOPMENTS: APPROACHES AND SOLUTIONS

Since the problem of a new world economic order has moved into the foreground of the international agenda, we are confronted with suggestions coming from diverse sources. A closer examination of the proposals coming from the West and East shows that they concentrate on regulating the relations with the less developed countries. They have in common also a recognition that the realization of a comprehensive global approach, such as the creation of an International Trade Organization, has become less important especially as far as the West is concerned. At the global level, mainly concrete problems of international economic relations, such as food, energy, oceans and environment, are dealt with in negotiations between blocs or groups of countries (EEC, CMEA, OECD, OPEC, Group of 77, etc.). This setting facilitates the management and solution of problems at the regional level. This can be illustrated through the following two examples:

Just as in earlier "Triangle Papers," (16) the Trilateral Commission's recently published report concentrates on management problems of transnational relations and on international interdependence. (17) To attain better worldwide cooperation, "countries should work out modes for international cooperation that are practical and effective for each of the particular problems they face" (18) and consider the following principles:

- Piecemeal functionalism, i.e., separation of the issue in order to hasten the progress on solutions and to make them more durable.

- Rule making with decentralization, i.e., minimizing the extent and complexity of cooperation required in order to design the international regime as a framework of rules, standards, and procedures and to decentralize decision making and operational management.

- Flexible participation. As wide participation may impede action on important issues and produce solutions too complex or too compromised to be effective, greater progress can be made when smaller groups of countries collaborate together.

- Evolutionary change. Collaboration among nations must allow for changes in institutional relationships as objective circumstances change, so that effective decision making and management may continue.

As essential areas for the realization of these principles, international monetary arrangements, pollution of the environment, national social and industrial policies, and peaceful use of nuclear energy are mentioned. These areas are not covered in a report of Trilateral Commission on East-West relations. There, a list of most promising areas for negotiations include trade policy, food, oceans, and nuclear exports and nonproliferation. (19) This discrepancy is due to the considerable difference between basic interests and the possible solutions of existing problems in relations among the triangular countries on the one hand and between East and West on the other.

Proposals from the Eastern countries regarding their position in the world economic system have been rare. However, references can be gathered from some statements given by the Eastern European countries and the Soviet Union within the past years. (20) At this point it becomes evident that the Eastern concepts link the remodeling of international economic relations to the problems of the armament race, disarmament, and the consolidation of security, and progress in economic relations is said to depend on detente. The statement, however, that "progress in remodeling the international economic relations (is) in itself a contribution to the deepening and expansion on detente" (21) leads to the conclusion that the nature of linkage between political and economic questions is not altogether clear. The following principles can be abstracted from Eastern European and

Soviet statements although they refer mainly to the Soviet viewpoint since there are substantial differences within CMEA as far as goals and instruments are concerned.

- Priority of bilateral arrangements, i.e., long-term trade and payments agreements, as well as agreements on economic and technical cooperation.

- Controlled multilateralization, i.e., a gradual supplementation of bilateral relations by forms of multilateral cooperation on the basis of possibilities which tie in with the statute and mechanism of the CMEA's activities (e.g., multilateral settlements on the basis of the transferable ruble).

- Development of economic relations in accordance with the principle of mutual interest, so that only parties involved in drawing up contracts and other agreements are actually affected.

From both conceptions one could draw the conclusion that developments, which have already been forseeable for several years, have been subsequently legitimized through corresponding proposals. The formal similarities in the way of piecemeal functionalism and flexible participation, however, cannot hide the fact that the intended institutional frameworks diverge substantially. While the Western proposals, such as those of the Trilateral Commission, aim more at bringing affected and selected countries together under pragmatic viewpoints, increasing the system's functioning ability, and controlling possible regional and/or issue related conflicts, the Eastern side seems to follow a twin strategy. Initially, there were indications that in order to remove their relative economic isolation and to manage their foreign trade problems, the Soviet Union and Eastern European countries were considering solely solutions at the global level under the auspices of the United Nations. (22) However, the agreement on "basket" two of the CSCE, which provides for a strengthening of the UN-ECE, and the presentation of a draft agreement between the CMEA and the EEC in February 1976 indicate that the Eastern European countries under the leadership of the Soviet Union are increasingly trying for regional solutions to their foreign economic problems.

Since the signing of the CSCE Final Act, the Eastern activities within the framework of the ECE have been remarkably intensified, e.g., by proposing to hold the All-European conferences on transportation, energy, and environment. (23) Nevertheless, it does not seem that these proposals have been taken up at the recently concluded Belgrade meeting of the CSCE.

The CMEA countries' conception of coming to terms with the EEC about trade and credit questions reaches farther than their notions about the ECE. (24) The European community's reservations are known. They draw attention to the unequal material competencies of the EEC and the CMEA. The EEC wants, on the one hand, to avoid the strengthening of Soviet dominance in the CMEA, and on the other hand, it wants to avoid the possibility that the CMEA's extensive economic goals would be carried out without agreement over "cooperation in humanitarian and other areas" as stated in basket three of the CSCE. Hence, substantial negotiation results are not to be expected for the near future. It is, however, doubtful whether the community's proposal of November 1976 to negotiate further technical problems such as standardization, the preparation of statistics, economic prognoses, etc. in framework agreements between CMEA and EEC corresponds to actual internal developments within CMEA. Real developments are indicating an increasing trend towards supranational structures within CMEA, which result in a growing economic and political dominance of the Soviet Union in the integration process and in turn in a reduced margin of sovereignty of the Eastern European countries. Further retardation of the negotiations with the CMEA could jeopardize the proclaimed goals.

The fact that the Eastern and Western nations considered have turned towards more regional or issue oriented solutions to their foreign economic problems becomes clearer when one realizes the role the OECD has begun to play in recent years within global economic conflicts. Negotiations between Western industrialized and oil exporting countries have become institutionalized through the International Energy Agency (IEA). It seems worthwhile to consider the use of this pattern for negotiations with state trading countries as well.

Formation of such a committee could promote the exchange of information and the development of joint strategies among OECD countries vis-a-vis CMEA. Above all, the codification of policy norms for OECD members could be addressed. The OECD members have agreed on uniform credit lending conditions vis-a-vis less developed and state trading countries. The establishment of and compliance with this agreement has turned out to be very troublesome. Even though its future is uncertain, it seemed to be a first step in the right direction.

Also, it is conceivable that problems of East-West economic relations could be discussed and managed by the CIEC. The Soviet Union and Eastern European countries aim at developing their own relations with the Third World and try to avoid being forced to do so by the economic superiority of the Western industrial nations. The East-South relationship is already problematic enough, because the less developed countries are requesting substantial concessions from the state trading countries (25) and are not content any more with declarations of solidarity from the East.

Although until now the state trading countries have refused to participate in North-South dialogues, precisely those economic demands of the less developed countries which become increasingly hard to resist could, in effect, support the practice of regional or issue oriented management. In the nongovernmental field, there are already examples of tripartite cooperation, and they could be supplemented with more general regulations. (26)

CONCLUSIONS

In order to maintain the benefits of international trade and cooperation, it seems necessary that some sort of institutional framework be preserved at the global level. Without rules governing the conduct of foreign economic policy, there will be a growing temptation for governments to take unilateral actions that would increase political friction among countries. In view of the structural changes in the economic situation, the diffusion of power among countries, and the plurality of their interests, such a framework will have to be looser than the Bretton Woods-GATT Systems. The implementation of a revised system requires that nonindustrialized and Socialist countries as well find it acceptable and attractive. Otherwise, some governments might come to the conclusion that they are better off outside the system or that they can contribute to the destruction of the system by taking a free ride.

The lack of consensus on issues of global economic management, even among the industrialized countries, makes it unlikely that comprehensive programs like a "new Bretton Woods" can be agreed upon, and some believe this disagreement regarding constitutional basis is likely to lead to an increase in politicization of international economic relations. (27) More likely, improvements, if any, will be made on an incremental basis, i.e., pragmatic, organizational adjustments to altered conditions without the formulation of an overall concept; for example, the changes in the functions and instruments of the IMF during the last few years point into this direction.

A pluralistic international order in which no single nation or smaller group of nations plays a predominant role requires management of the difficult problem of reconciling demands for a more egalitarian international order with the inegalitarian distribution of power and wealth in the world. The formulation of the rules would not only require consideration of this problem, but also would have to take into account the economic systems of the Socialist countries as well. Within such an institutional framework, closer cooperation with stricter rules could then develop on a multipolar and/or regional level. From this point of view and in the interest of global economic stability, it seems desirable to seek greater participation of the Socialist countries in the reorganization of the international economic organizations.

NOTES

1. In this context, we will broadly analyze international governmental organizations as a continuation of studies which have been presented at earlier dates. Max Baumer and Hanns-Dieter Jacobsen, "CMEA and the World Economy--Institutional Concepts," in East European Economies Post-Helsinki ed. J.P. Hardt (Washington, D.C.: Joint Economic Committee, United States Congress, 1977), pp. 999-1018. "Die KSZE und die Beziehungen Zwischen EG und RGW" in Grunbuch zu den Folgewirkungen der KSZE. J. Delbruch, N. Ropers, G. Zellentin (Cologne: Verlag Wissenschaft und Politik, 1977), pp. 341-56. "International Organizations and East-West Economic Relations in The EEC and Eastern Europe, ed. A. Shlaim and G. Yannopoulos (Cambridge: Cambridge University Press, 1978),

2. For a more detailed analysis of these developments see Baumer and Jacobsen, "CMEA And the World Economy."

3. Art. XXXVI of the GATT states: "The developed contracting parties do not expect reciprocity for commitments made by them in trade negotiations."

4. Compare Baumer and Jacobsen, "CMEA and the World Economy," p. 1011 with R. Baban, "State Trading and the GATT," Journal of World Trade Law 11, no. 4 (1977): 346-51.

5. O. Long, "The Protectionist Threat of World Trade Relations," Intereconomics 12, no. 11/12, (1977): 284. The number of these quantitative restrictions is difficult to designate; one reason is

that GATT or other international organizations are not informed of a part of newly introduced restrictions.

6. Compare Hasenpflug, Nicht-tarifare Handelshemmnisse (Hamburg: Verlag Weltarchiv, 1977), pp. 18,19.

7. Compare L. Quambusch, Nicht-tarifare Handelshemmnisse. Ein Beitrag zu ihrer Systematisierung, Anwendung und Beseitigung (Cologne: Institut fur Wirtschaftspolitik an der Universitat Cologne, 1977), p. 332.

8. F. Muller, Die Verschuldung des RGW gegenuber dem Westen, (Ebenhausen bei Munchen: Stiftung Wissenschaft und Politik, SWP-AZ 2148 1977), p. 45.

9. F.D. Holzman, "CMEA's Hard Currency Deficits and Ruble Convertibility" (Paper prepared for the conference of the International Economic Association on "Economic Relations Between Different Economic Systems," Dresden, June 29-July 3, 1976), pp. 2-4.

10. H.D. Jacobsen, "Operation and Importance of the COMECON Banks and the Request of Credits," COMECON - Progress and Prospects (Brussels: NATO Directorate of Economic Affairs, 1977), pp. 177-86.

11. Compare "Report of the Intergovernmental Group of Exports to Study a Multilateral System of Payments Between Socialist Countries of Eastern Europe and Developing Countries" (Geneva: UNCTAD Document TD-B-663, December 14, 1977).

12. For details of Romania's accession to IMF see Baumer and Jacobsen, "CMEA and the World Economy," p. 1013.

13. Vereinigte Wirtshaftsdienste/Europa, no. 46/78, March 7, 1978, p. 0/2.

14. J. Fekete, "Monetary and Financial Problems in East-West" (Workshop on East-West European Economic Interaction, Vienna Institute for Comparative Economic Studies and Institute for World Economics of the Hungarian Academy of Sciences, Budapest, October 16-20, 1977), p. 20.

15. R.N. Cooper, K. Kaiser, and N. Kosaka, "Towards a Renovated International System," Triangle Paper, no. 14 (New York: 1977), p. VIII; and O. Emminger, On The Way To A New International Monetary Order (Washington, D.C.: American Enterprise Institute for Public Policy Research, 1976), p. 20..

16. C.I. Bergsten, G. Berthoin, and K. Mushakoji, "The Reform of International Institutions," Triangle Paper, no. 11 (New York: 1976); E. Ortona, J.R. Schaetzel, and N. Ushiba, "The Problems of International Consultations," Triangle Paper, no. 12 (New York: 1976); C. Hosoya, H. Owen, and A. Shonfield, "Collaboration with Communist Countries in Managing Global Problems," Triangle Paper, no. 13 (New York: 1977).

17. Cooper, Kaiser, Kosaka, "A Renovated International System."

18. Ibid., p. VIII.

19. Hosoya, Owen, and Shonfield, "Collaboration with Communist Countries," pp. 3-17.

20. Compare the Joint Statement of the Socialist Countries at UNCTAD IV in Nairobi, May 28, 1976 Europa Archiv 32, no. 10 (1977): D 249 - D 259; Statement of the Soviet Government on the Reorganization of International Economic Relations, October 4, 1976, ibid., pp. D 263 - D 268; J. Bognar, The Fight for a New System of International Relations: Trends in the World Economy no. 21 (Budapest: Hungarian Scientific Council for World Economy 1977).

21. Statement of the Soviet Government, Europa, p. D 268 (translated from German).

22. Compare the Soviet proposals to UNCTAD I in 1964 and the GATT accession wave of the Eastern European countries at the end of the 1960s and beginning of the 1970s. That this goal has not been entirely given up is to be seen in a declaration of the Soviet Foreign Trade Minister Patolichev who did not want to exclude that UNCTAD may become an international trade organization which has competence over GATT problems. (Aussenhandel (Moscow), No. 7, 1976, p. 8).

23. Baumer and Jacobsen, "CMEA and the World Economy," pp. 1009-10.

24. Compare the CMEA draft for a treaty with the EEC of February 1976; an unofficial translation was published in Vereinigte Wirtschaftsdienste (VWD), no. 36, February 21, 1976, pp. I/7. A detailed analysis of the respective goals and tactical positions is to be found in Baumer and Jacobsen, "Die KSZE und die Entwicklung der Besiehungen zwischen EG und RGW," pp. 341-56.

25. See, for example, Manila Declaration and Program, 77/MM (III)/49, February 7, 1976, Section 8; UNCTAD IV, Resolution 95 (IV), June 16, 1976.

26. Compare UNCTAD's Tripartite Industrial Cooperation Study by the UNCTAD Secretariat, TAD SEM 1/2 (Geneva: UNCTAD, November 25, 1975); K. Bolz, "The Prospects of Tripartite Cooperation," Intereconomics 11, no. 11 (1976): 308.

27. F. Hirsch and M. Doyle, "Politicization in the World Economy: Necessary conditions for an International Economic Order" in Alternatives to Monetary Disorder, ed. F. Hirsch, N. Doyle, and E. Morse (New York: 1980's Project-Council on Foreign Relations, 1977), pp. 11-64.

8 Legal and Organizational Factors in the Participation of Western Multinationals in East-West Trade and Industrial Cooperation
David Winter

INTRODUCTION

This chapter will discuss the factors of an organizational and legal nature which arise through the participation of large multinational Western companies in East-West trade, whether the trade be of a traditional form or of a more advanced form such as that of industrial cooperation. This paper is presented against a background of past and current experiences as a legal advisor in the field of East-West trade and while this has obvious advantages as it represents a view based on actual experience, nevertheless it has certain disadvantages in that for reasons of confidentiality, individual case studies cannot be presented.

The "Guidelines for Multinational Enterprises" (Annex to the Declaration of June 21, 1976 by the governments of the OECD member countries on International Investment and Multinational Enterprises) states in Section 8 that multinational enterprises, "usually comprise companies or other entities whose ownership is private, state or mixed, established in different countries and so linked that one or more of them may be able to exercise a significant influence over the activities of others and, in particular, to share knowledge and resources with the others." (1) This is a perfectly acceptable statement, and a definition adopted and used for the purpose of this paper shares the notions expressed by the said definition. This paper defines a large multinational Western company as a corporate entity situated in a market economy country, which through its branches or subsidiary companies, whether direct, indirect, or associated companies, conducts operations usually in the industrial sector in more than one country and typically in several countries.

VARIOUS FORMS OF EAST-WEST ECONOMIC RELATIONS

East-West trade means commercial intercourse between various countries of the world and the East European member countries of the Council for Mutual Economic Assistance (CMEA). The various forms which that trade takes can be divided for all practical purposes into the following:

1. There is the simple purchase and sale of products between East and West.

2. There is the sale and leasing of light and heavy equipment by the West to the East and vice versa.

3. There is a sale by the West to the East and vice versa of equipment together with certain associated technology, whether transmitted by way of documentation and/or training. A typical example of this would be the sale by the West to the East of equipment with associated technology and training with the ultimate intent of the contractual arrangements to establish an industry in whole or in part or more commonly, the modernization of an industry in Eastern Europe.

4. There is a sale by the West to the East and vice versa of technology by way of straightforward licensing agreements which often involve, by reason of the technology purchased by Eastern Europe, the purchase of equipment by Eastern Europe from the West or the use of equivalent equipment purchased from within Eastern Europe.

The foregoing forms of trade are of a traditional nature, and the following forms, although owing their origin to the foregoing, represent to a greater or lesser degree the newer forms of East-West trade.

1. There are joint ventures whereby, for example, in Hungary a Western firm can take an equity interest in an enterprise established in East Europe through various methods; these are what may be called "pure" joint ventures.

LEGAL AND ORGANIZATIONAL FACTORS 113

2. There are forms of industrial cooperation, which are contractual arrangements in the very forefront of East-West trade at the present time and for that reason warrant a further enumeration of the forms this trade can take. A useful analysis of these agreements can be found in the United Nations' "Guide on Drawing Up International Contracts on Industrial Cooperation," which refers to an equally useful statement of the position in the "Analytical Report on Industrial Cooperation among ECE Countries" also published by the United Nations. (2) The former guide correctly states that industrial cooperation agreements mean arrangements going beyond the normal or straightforward sale or purchase of goods and which involve a long-term arrangement between the parties. This Guide enumerates the following transactions as industrial cooperation agreements:

   a. The transfer of technology and technical experience.

   b. Cooperation in the field of production, including in the field of specialist production.

   c. Cooperation in developing natural resources.

   d. Joint marketing either in the countries of the contractual parties or in third markets of the products of the industrial cooperation.

3. There is compensation trading or compensation cooperation, to which the Soviet Union is paying particularly great attention at the present time. For example, in the report given by L. Brezhnev, the General Secretary of the CPSU Central Committee, to the Twenty-Fifth Party Congress, this form of cooperation on a compensation basis was regarded as a new form of external economic links beyond normal trade, and further the report stressed that this type of trade would produce the greatest return for the Soviet Union. The forms which this cooperation can take are numerous and allow flexibility; a particular instance is referred to later in this paper.

4. Barter trade whereby a Western supplier of products is paid by the Eastern Europeans by way of certain commodities.

5. Counter trade or counter purchase is playing a particularly important role and for some large multinational Western companies is of considerable value and significance.

6. Buy back, which is a form of compensation trading, is also in the very forefront of East-West trade.

The above-listed forms of East-West trade show the very rich and varied characteristics currently taken by trade, which are of significance not only in purely economic terms but also of very great intellectual interest since they involve a real and genuine cooperation between East and West by reason of the essential nature of the forms of the trade particularly in relation to the developing and more advanced forms of the trade.

Trade Arrangements

To end the enumeration of the forms of the trade and "to give them life," it is worth noting a selection, and it is only a selection, of the following types of trade arrangements recently concluded: (3)

1. An agreement between Czechoslovakia and Laos regarding geological and mining cooperation.

2. A sale by an American company to the Soviet Union of combined drilling rigs.

3. The sale by a United Kingdom company to the Soviet Union of certain material testing machines for use in research establishments.

Later information lists certain specialization and cooperation contracts: in Bulgaria, a general agreement on commercial and industrial cooperation between Bulgarian economic organizations and Air France; in the German Democratic Republic, a French agreement involving a cooperative program for engineering, motorcar, electrical, and chemical industries in 1977; in 1978 an Austrian agreement in the chemical industry between Chemie Linz AG whereby Chemie Linz supplies chemicals, plant protection chemicals, and fertilizers to the German Democratic Republic against potash under a 4-year contract; in Hungary, an agreement with Montedison in pharmaceuticals' research with mutual deliveries of chemicals and cooperation in the production of man made fibers; in Poland an agreement relating to

LEGAL AND ORGANIZATIONAL FACTORS 115

special grinding appliances between the Swedish firm Malcus and "Metalexport"; in Romania the establishment of a mixed oil development company in Ecuador and the establishment by Auto-Dacia of Romania and Citroen of an enterprise to produce in Romania cars under Citroen specifications to be marketed at home and abroad; and finally in the Soviet Union a cooperation agreement with NSN Danone Gervais for scientific and technological cooperation in relation to soft drinks and food production. (4)

On April 14, 1978, many other instances were cited: a machine contract relating to corn processing machines between a United Kingdom company and a Hungarian enterprise; a reference to a 1974/1983 cooperation agreement with CSEPEL Automobile Works and Mogurt whereby Volvo, the Swedish company, will take Hungarian made Laplander cross-country vehicles, of which the chassis and body assemblies will be manufactured in Hungary, while Volvo is to provide engines and certain other parts; a contract between the Soviet Union and a United Kingdom company for the supply by the English of flash welding equipment; and finally an agreement whereby in the Soviet Union Borsig is to build to carbon dioxide liquefaction plants of which Davy Power Gas of the United Kingdom has been named as the main subcontractor. (5)

The foregoing, together with other following instances, are only examples of the very many transactions being effected with all the countries of Eastern Europe and are cited in order to give practical examples of the forms of East-West trade.

In addition to the trade per se, a great deal more is happening in the field of East-West trade. For example, there are many meetings at government, business, and scientific levels between West and East, such as the recent Anglo-Soviet Trade Seminar organized over a weekend at which there was a top Soviet team represented by the Soviet Deputy Chairman of the State Committee for Science and Technology to meet leading British industrialists and government officials. There are also many missions to Eastern Europe, trade fairs, and symposia arranged by Western firms there. Of the last two types of events, there are indeed an enormous number which deal with a vast range of industrial products, such as electronic equipment, building technology, food packaging, medical products, textiles and clothing, automated equipment, and so on.

THE LARGE MULTINATIONAL COMPANIES AS THE MOST SUITABLE PARTNERS

The foregoing general and broad description of East-West trade and what follows in this section of this paper are vital to understanding the essential role of the large multinational western company in the field of East-West trade.

What are the potential advantages of trade which results in companies engaging in it? A detailed answer would require a substantial departure from the subject matter of this paper, and it is proposed, therefore, to take a narrow, but exceptionally important, part of East-West trade to illustrate the kind of broad answer that could be given to such a question. The narrow part of the trade to which reference has just been made is in the field of technology transfer or licensing, and here, without distinguishing between the position in the West and in Eastern Europe, one can state that licensing or technology transfer offers the following advantages:

1. The rapid assimilation of industrial techniques where such techniques are needed.

2. The provision of employment.

3. A lesser financial investment and a lesser commitment to the use of currency in the industry concerned than would be involved in reaching the same level of industrial standards without outside assistance provided by way of the transfer of technology.

4. The possibility of the opening up of third markets.

5. The benefits that are not easily calculated, which arise naturally out of the licensing transaction, for example, knowledge of marketing.

This recital of advantages of a narrow but critical part of East-West trade will indicate the broader answer which could be given for East-West trade in general with particular reference to the new and developing forms of that trade.

The characteristics and types of East-West trade discussed previously form a necessary background to the essential thesis of this paper: that with an extremely important exception, and an exception which cannot and must not be either overlooked or underestimated,

LEGAL AND ORGANIZATIONAL FACTORS 117

for large scale East-West projects and for the developing new forms of East-West trade, on the whole, the most suitable current partners for the enterprises of Eastern Europe are in fact the large multinational Western companies, primarily because of organizational factors.

It was hypothesized that existing statistics to support this thesis and published details of contracts that could be found in various journals to support this thesis, and the statistics and published articles do support the postulated thesis. Before supporting the conclusion reached, it is critical to deal with what has been characterized above as, "the extremely important exception." The exception, based on many personal experiences with large multinational Western companies, points to those Western companies with highly specialized products or technology or both which they are able to supply to Eastern Europe. Numerous examples could be cited where small and medium sized companies have most successfully competed in Eastern Europe and won valuable orders, even against the fierce competition of large multinational Western companies, because these small and medium sized companies are in the very forefront of the fields in which they operate. Additionally, these companies can offer a very direct and personal service and contact at the highest level to the enterprises of Eastern Europe, and these factors directly affect the value of those companies to the enterprises of Eastern Europe and touch upon critical questions such as those of ultimate responsibility. It is believed that these companies will continue to have a long-term future in East-West trade.

Bearing in mind the domination of the large multinational Western company in East-West trade and industrial cooperation, one might ask why the importance of the exception has been stressed, and the answer is simple. The exception to the general rule is not one of a few examples only; the exceptions are numerous. An examination of current cooperation programs, contracts, and past listings will show these exceptions exist, and furthermore, the published details are only the tip of the iceberg. Having stated the exception, to reiterate it, it is believed that from a general perspective, the more natural partners on the whole for the developing forms of East-West trade with particular reference to the large industrial cooperative projects are the large multinational Western companies. As a preamble to that conclusion, there is an overemphasis on the peculiarities and difficulties of East-West trade, and this overemphasis is harmful to the trade. It would be idle to suppose or state that there are no problems arising out of East-West trade, but experience shows that dealing with international transactions in general, not only in East-West trade, there are very few examples where international trade is easy, and to this extent East-West trade is no exception. It is always invidious and it would be unwise to cite examples of this, but one can say with certainty that rarely is trade with any area of the world outside one's own domestic market easy, and why should one suppose then that trade with Eastern Europe should be easy. Perhaps a fundamental reason for the difficulties encountered in East-West trade by some Western firms, whether small, medium, or large, is a lack of understanding on the part of many of them of: the economic system of CMEA; the psychology of the people of the various countries of Eastern Europe; their cultural and ethnic differences; and a patience and rigidity of mind towards the problems of East-West trade, which do not accord with the necessary requirement of flexibility that is essential if one wishes to be successful in East-West trade. Specifically, not that many Western firms really understand in depth the real structure of CMEA, for example, the role that the State's Monopoly of Foreign Trade plays or the planning system of the various countries of Eastern Europe.

THREE FUNDAMENTAL FACTORS

The reason that it is believed that East-West trade is basically for the large multinational Western company can be related to three fundamental factors:

1. Financial resources.
2. Time available and required personnel.
3. Technological resources.

The latter two are organized factors.

The historical stability of the large multinational Western company is not required as a fact to support the conclusion, but undoubtedly could be called on to support the conclusion since it is a matter of some significance to the enterprises of Eastern Europe in many cases.

Why are the listed factors important? First, the question of a company's financial resources and their importance must be examined. One has to look at the method of getting into and then trading in Eastern Europe and then to refer back to the forms of East-West trade as enumerated earlier in this paper. With certain exceptions, it undoubtedly does take time to break into the markets of Eastern Europe, and the reasons for this are numerous and hardly need stating. The net result however, is that in many cases Western firms have to engage in lengthy procedures for the introduction of those firms to the East

LEGAL AND ORGANIZATIONAL FACTORS 119

European market, and this lengthy procedure involves financial expenditure. Time is money, and time involves personnel and an adequate organizational structure. It may take a long time before one gets to the stage of negotiating the contract itself: one may have to make numerous visits to Eastern Europe; in appropriate cases one may have to arrange symposia; one may have to take part in trade fairs and go on trade missions; one may not find it easy to reach the end user in Eastern Europe; and one may have many meetings with research institutes and the other important organizations in Eastern Europe before reaching the end user. Because one is often competing with many other companies, the Western companies cannot fall behind in the race, and this, together with steps that need to be taken and which have just been set out, can involve a great deal of time and expenditure of money. All this is costly both in terms of actual disbursements on travel, accommodations, and subsistance, but also in terms of costing time and the use of key personnel. These are generalizations, and the time and the difficulty involved in reaching the end user and other organizations in Eastern Europe to make oneself and one's product known, depends very much on the product, the country, and the Western company involved.

The second factor (the first organizational one) is linked intimately to the first factor, and because the first two factors are linked, the second one, which could be subdivided, contains two elements also closely linked.

The third factor of technological resources is partially organizational and partially purely of a technological nature. As to the former, this has been touched upon earlier in this paper; the latter should need no comment since the technological resources of a large multinational Western company will normally exceed those of small companies, although again the smaller Western company may allocate considerable funds and personnel to a specialized product, possibly more than the larger company in relation to that product.

THE PROCESS OF INTRODUCING A WESTERN COMPANY

It is worth making the cautionary point, which is truer of the large multinational Western company than of the smaller or medium company, that there is not always the total support for a commitment to East-West trade in the larger company that one finds in the smaller or medium company. In the latter case, the "man on the road" might be a member of the board of directors of the company in question or for that matter the owner of the company. In a hierarchical large-scale

Western company, one has very often as a proponent of East-West trade to argue forcibly for the continuation of Eastern European negotiations, particularly when in some Western countries the political ups and downs of East-West political relations might make some boards of directors think one way or another about the advisability of proceeding with a particular transaction. This sometimes causes delays in East-West negotiations, and these delays, which often stem purely from the Western side, cost money.

A large multinational Western company also needs a central organizational framework for conducting that company's East-West trade. This might, for example, be more conveniently based in Western Europe, but the organizational setup should oversee and coordinate all Eastern European aspects of that company's trade and form a continuing base and link for the Eastern European operations of the company in question. This specialized organization, which experience leads one to believe is most important, also involves a financial commitment in some cases of some substance. Reverting, however, to the theme of time, personnel, and the question of the length of negotiations, in particular in relation to the large projects of East-West trade, there is the peculiar point that these projects which are so exciting and offer such excellent opportunities for cooperation in human and commercial terms are the very ones which are more difficult to negotiate both in terms of financial and organizational commitments. It is after all obvious that it would take less time to sell a particular machine tool to Eastern Europe than to engage in and set up a large-scale project involving the supply of plant and technology with elements of buy back and perhaps of cooperation in third countries.

Given all these factors, it would be less than honest to state that some companies consider that there may well be easier markets than Eastern Europe, but however correct that view may be in some instances, in other instances it is believed that such a view is incorrect and may well be very shortsighted. Such a view also does not sufficiently consider the broad and immediate advantages of East-West trade, such as the creation of job opportunities in the West, the compensation to Western companies in respect of past expenditures for research and development, and the technological flowback from Eastern Europe.

As part of the process of introducing a Western company to Eastern Europe, sometimes framework or cooperation agreements are signed with organizations in Eastern Europe, for example a Ministry or a State Committee, and these agreements contemplate the development of trading relationships and set up an organizational framework for their development. Typically, they may involve the creation of a committee of representatives on each side which will meet regularly and exchange information, and depending on the stage at which such an agreement is signed, they may or may not be referred to in the framework agreement which concretely establishes the future relationships between the parties or other parties in the countries concerned.

It is thought that this type of agreement is by its very nature more suitable for the large multinational Western company than for the smaller or medium size company, which may require for financial reasons instant results. A review of the parties to those agreements is available and clearly supports the conclusion advanced by this paper. Whether these agreements are advisable or inadvisable, suitable or unsuitable, valuable or valueless is not the purpose of this paper, but nevertheless it can be stated that for those companies commited to the concept of East-West trade and long term cooperation with Eastern Europe, such agreements can be very helpful. These agreements involve a permanent organizational commitment on both sides to ensure this, and they do not become a "dead letter." A team permanently or semipermanently assigned to implement the agreement is critical, and it would be a rare small or medium sized company which would have the financial and personnel resources to be able to do this.

CONTRACT NEGOTIATION

After penetrating Eastern Europe either by visits, participation in international or specialized fairs, or the arranging for symposia, one then starts the process of contract negotiation. Here again it would be inaccurate to state that the normal course of events is for contracts to be speedily concluded.

It must be stated there are exceptions to these rules, but these exceptions are not common, and negotiating contracts in Eastern Europe, particularly those of the more sophisticated type, do take time. It must be stressed, however, that they take time not only because of the organizational and economic nature of Eastern Europe, but also very often because of the procedures adopted by Western firms.

The contract process is lengthy and here again, as with the negotiating process, time is money, although these procedures can be shortened in many cases by Western firms taking more trouble to understand the real requirements of Eastern Europe in general and their future partners in particular. It goes without saying that, as indicated earlier, anyone dealing in Eastern Europe should have a real understanding of the East European economic systems, of the responsibilities of the East European officials involved, and of the need for real flexibility. Although these comments relate to the contractual aspects of the transaction, they apply equally to the technical side of any transaction in that there is an equivalent need to understand the real technical requirements of the East Europeans and the responsibilities of the East European technicians. As a general rule, it is possible that a large multinational Western company with its organizational and economic resources, the sources of information available to it, and its financial backing is more likely, or in an ideal world should certainly be able, to better understand East European needs than the smaller and medium sized company. In this connection one might go further and speculate that in certain respects the organizational procedures and the internal framework of some large-scale multinational Western companies are in certain aspects not too different from those of certain sections of industry in Eastern Europe; this should make the Western company more sympathetic and understanding of the position and problems of its East European partner.

The negotiating of the contract does demand special skills and an allocation of manpower on the Western side and equally requires the Western company to have available for its negotiations technical and commercial experts sufficient in number to match the Eastern European counterparts. Thus, for example, the Eastern Europeans through their monopoly of foreign trade and the economic systems in their countries are likely to have at meetings technical experts from institutes, ministries, and end-user factories, and there is very little doubt that in many cases the experts put forward by the countries of Eastern Europe will have a very deep knowledge of their own experts. In addition, the commercial negotiators for the Eastern European parties will often be of a very high standard and extremely skilled in the commercial side of matters, for example in the field of pricing, knowledge of costs of Western raw materials, inflationary tendencies, the position relative to international credits, and the like. It is increasingly common also that the East Europeans will have available legal assistance of a high standard relative to the matters in question. All these technical, commercial, and legal experts must be matched by the Western negotiators in terms of providing personnel. It is not cheap to travel internationally, and here again the cost of "fielding" a negotiating team of adequate technical, commercial, and legal strength is not cheap, particularly since contractual negotiations can be protracted and the distance from home base often requires frequent references and visits back to the Western country by the Western negotiators; meetings are, for example, quite often

LEGAL AND ORGANIZATIONAL FACTORS 123

postponed during visits to Eastern Europe in order for Western firms to supply the necessary information required by their Eastern European counterparts. One should bear in mind that, as indicated earlier, such negotiations are in many cases conducted against the background of fierce competition from other Western firms.

The negotiators from Western firms need to be of a high standard and able to answer all questions from their Eastern European counterparts, and these negotiators, whether technical, commercial or legal must be flexible and understanding of Eastern European requirements.

THE NATURAL COMPLEXITY OF ARRANGEMENTS

These generalities should be taken into account when considering the natural complexity of many of the trade arrangements under development, and here again enumerated and described forms of East-West trade, particularly in the field of cooperation and compensation arrangements, should be noted.

As well as these negotiations, the Western firm has to make financial arrangements, and for that matter so does the Eastern European enterprise, in relation to long-term credits, for example, and the availability of long-term credits at favorable rates of interest may be a critical factor that adds a further complication to the negotiation and conclusion of substantial contractual arrangements.

As an actual example of the complexities of a substantial deal and what must be taken into account in relation to the same, an article appeared in the monthly magazine published by the Ministry of Foreign Trade of the Soviet Union. (6) This article describes, among other matters, the project for prospecting the Sakhalin Island Shelf for oil and the development of oil deposits in that region. It refers to the general agreement on cooperation in developing the resources of the Sakhalin Island Shelf between the Soviet Union and Japanese enterprises. It sets out the obligations on the Soviet side, given that certain works will be profitable and states that certain drilling operations and other works will be carried out with the participation of the Japanese parties. There certain external gas and oil transport facilities would be designed and built, and once development had been started, the Russians would export certain products to Japan. The Japanese are stated to be able to provide credits and ensure the delivery of machines, equipment, materials, technical documentation, consumer goods, and certain services, as well as grant to the Russians a commercial credit in the amount of 100 million dollars with a provision for the extension of further credit. If profitable oil fields are found, work will be carried out in relation to equipping them and further credits will be involved for the purchase of machinery, equipment, materials, and services.

It is quite clear that the supporting contractual documentation for large-scale projects will be of a highly complex nature and require considerable long-term planning by both the Western and Eastern European parties, particularly when one is projecting a long way into the future the delivery of raw materials and anticipating pricing problems and similar matters. The said article, although related particularly to the fuel industry, is a fascinating and interesting description by a Soviet author of compensation projects and agreements and has particular value in view of the very great interest of the Soviet Union in this particular form of East-West trade.

Again it is quite clear that for practical purposes, only the large multinational Western companies could engage in these large-scale projects, and they are the only suitable partners for Eastern Europe because of their manpower, technological, and economic resources.

THE LICENSING OF TECHNOLOGY

However, even if one considers commercial and contractual arrangements of a size and complexity less than the grand projects of East-West trade, negotiating and concluding contracts can still take time and skills, which in many cases are only to be found in the large multinational Western companies. As an illustration of this, an example of a Western company licensing an Eastern European company for the production of a particular type of equipment can be cited. It may well be that the Western company has considerable licensing experience, but it is more than likely to have previously licensed only on a royalty basis with minimum annual royalties and a good knowledge of what its license is likely to produce, based upon the licensor's analysis of the market which the licensee hopes to exploit. If one translates that experience into Eastern Europe, it is probable that the Eastern Europeans will only pay a lump sum for the licensed technology and this will involve an assessment by the licensor of the Eastern Europeans' likely production based upon the Western company's own knowledge, the information given to it by the Eastern Europeans, and other available statistics. The commercial aspects of the license agreement, therefore, will involve a rather expert assessment by the Western firm of the potential to the licensee of the transfer of the technological processes. The license agreement itself, although in many respects standard in form, if one considers international legal practice, is likely to have certain special peculiarities, which will involve the assessment by the Western licensor of its commercial obligations with particular reference to the translation of those obligations into risk or financial terms. For example, it is likely that the Eastern European licensee will require a guarantee of performance; in other words, what the licensor will be required to guarantee is that its technology will work in Eastern Europe with consequential financial penalties for failure, and the Eastern Europeans may well require that if the failure is great enough, the license agreement will be canceled, the documentation will be returned by the licensee to the licensor, and the licensor will return to the licensee the moneys already paid for the license, possibly with interest on the same, and with possible additional financial penalties. This form of agreement is one which the Western firm would not normally find in licensing agreements that it has negotiated with countries other than those of Eastern Europe, and this requires an assessment by the Western licensor of its responsibilities quantified in technological and financial terms, which is a highly skilled task involving expertise. It is more likely that such an assessment and the skills required in making such an assessment will more easily be found in large multinational Western companies than in small or medium sized companies, although again experience shows that many small or medium sized companies are well able, particularly in specialist fields, to make such an assessment.

The author has taken the licensing of technology as an example because it is something to which currently so much attention is given by both the West and Eastern Europe, but it must be obvious from this paper so far that, a fortiori, the particular considerations given thus far to contractual arrangements must also apply to other forms of East-West trade currently in vogue such as counter trade. Counter trade involves the requirement by a Western company to analyze carefully its obligations in relation to the supply of goods to Eastern Europe, but equally involves an evaluation of the Western company's obligations to counter purchase from Eastern Europe. There is no reason at all why the smaller or medium sized company cannot enter into counter trade arrangements. Nevertheless, such arrangements are easier for large multinational Western companies to contemplate and carry out because it is possible that through the multinationals' network of subsidiary or associated companies or branches that it could itself make use of the counter purchase goods in house, whereas the small or medium sized company has to make use of the many specialist firms to be found in centers of counter trade; for example, London or Vienna in Europe.

Yet again in relation to the extremely fruitful possibilities of third market cooperation, it is more likely that a large multinational Western company could be of more use to its Eastern European partner than a smaller or medium sized company because of the availability of manpower, whether technical or commercial, and financial resources.

THE ROLE OF SMALL AND MEDIUM SIZED COMPANIES

Perhaps if one was forced to summarize or make basically only one point, it could be said that it is more likely that a large multinational Western company would be able to make a serious long-term commitment to the development of Eastern European trade than a smaller or medium sized company with its more limited manpower and financial resources, and it is possible that the more fruitful role on the whole for the smaller and medium sized company in the field of East-West trade lies in acting as a subcontractor to the large multinational Western company. However, a major, and not enough explored, possibility for the smaller and medium sized company in East-West trade is to tender for the larger projects of East-West trade by way of joint associations or consortia so that these companies can match in terms of scale (from the total consortia's point of view) the financial and manpower resources of the large multinational competitor. This solution is particularly appropriate for those companies from smaller Western countries where there is not the tradition in any particular field of the large multinational company, and this could also be a more acceptable solution for those Eastern European countries which prefer, for one reason or another, not to deal with a large multinational Western company. It is believed that not enough use is made by the smaller and medium sized Western companies of the device of working together in consortia in the field of East-West trade, although the reasons for this are obvious, i.e., psychological, economic, and purely legal reasons. Nevertheless, in this way the smaller and medium sized company can fulfill a more substantial role in the development of East-West trade beyond that which it is currently fulfilling, which is primarily supplying specialized or sophisticated technology and equipment to Eastern Europe. There are, of course, other ways whereby the smaller and medium sized Western company can make its presence felt in Eastern Europe to a greater extent than its resources might apparently allow, for example, by the use of agents, but the advantages and disadvantages of such an arrangement will not be discussed herein. It is also almost certainly true that it is beyond the reach of most smaller and medium sized Western companies to maintain official offices in Eastern Europe because of the costs of maintenance.

ADVANTAGES AND DISADVANTAGES OF SIZE

In many cases, the large multinational Western company is likely to be a more natural trading partner for Eastern Europe because through its network of associated and subsidiary companies and branches, it is almost certain to have some products, technology, and services which are useful to the Eastern Europeans; therefore, it has an inherent flexibility in matching the changing needs of Eastern Europe. If the highly specialized smaller or medium sized Western company with a particular product and technology is considered, then that is all it has to offer, and either there is a market for it or there is not. If a typical large multinational Western company is considered, then it would be very surprising indeed if somewhere there was not among its various entities one or more which had technology, products, or services useful somewhere in the industrial sector of Eastern Europe. However, the latter statement must be qualified in that if consideration is not only given to the commercial aspects of a transaction in terms of the immediate exchange of money for global technology, services, or products, then there is perhaps not too much of a difference between the large multinational Western company and the smaller and medium sized Western company, particularly in specialized fields, because there is no reason why there should not be an exchange of information and research between the smaller company and its East European counterpart equal to that between the large multinational Western company and its East European counterpart.

Having directed, and it is hoped supported, the conclusion earlier adduced, there are certain disadvantages inherent in the participation of large multinational Western companies in East-West trade, because some of these companies tend to be rather cumbersome in their management structure with particular reference to the need for quick management decisions; in some Western countries they are peculiarly susceptible to governmental influence and the opinions of their shareholder, and in some cases they might be regarded by their Eastern European partners as simply too large, which would result in an uncomfortable alliance.

Having stated these disadvantages, they lead to directly to the opposite position referred to previously and to a matter which is of vital and critical importance, i.e., that the smaller and medium sized

Western company offers a personal service to Eastern Europeans and there is no doubt at all that this personal service, the personal contacts which that company can offer at a high level, and the personal understanding which is bound to arise between smaller organizations, are of the most essential significance; not only can the smaller and medium sized Western company compete on an equal scale with its large multinational competitor, but in many cases its smallness gives it an advantage over the large multinational company. The large multinational company can, of course, equally gain such an advantage by operating in East-West trade in appropriate cases through a smaller entity, but experience has shown that sometimes this can result in the worst of all possible worlds for the large multinational company, because the smaller entity is very often subject to the procedures and general principles under which its large parent operates, which can inhibit its actions.

CONCLUSION

In summary it is assumed that the conclusion as to the role of the large multinational Western company in East-West trade is a correct one, while it is accepted there are no doubt many arguments to oppose such conclusion. Given that the conclusion is correct, however, then it is felt that there results from such conclusion certain inevitable consequences. Undoubtedly in some limited cases large multinational Western companies will influence and perhaps even dominate their Eastern European counterparts not only because of size, technological, and financial resources, but also by the very fact of cooperating with the Eastern European enterprise in the evaluation and decision of critical factors which arise continuously in the implementation of a contract, whether the contract be medium sized or a large-scale project. It is not for this paper to state whether such influence is a good or a bad thing, but it is felt that it is an inevitable result that a large multinational Western company will bring to certain contractual arrangements an inevitable influence, particularly where there is an imbalance between the parties. Scientific studies as to this will remain for the future until such data, particularly the large-scale projects have been concluded, and it could be that the paper's view in this connection is wrong, especially since there remains to be seen the form which such influence will take. A field of interest where undoubtedly research would be of great interest would be the role and influence exercised by the large multinational Western company in the

LEGAL AND ORGANIZATIONAL FACTORS

field of finance, typically banks, but again it is felt that a digression in relation to this would be outside the scope of this paper.

In an ideal world, perhaps the large multinational Western company would only have as its Eastern European partner, the larger Eastern European enterprises, and the totality of enterprises with which the large multinational Western company deals (end users, research institutes, other organizations, and their associated ministries), while the smaller and medium sized companies would only work with the smaller enterprises of Eastern Europe. This is, however, quite impractical and no doubt an impossible state of affairs to attain, and it is highly arguable whether an attempt to attain it should be made. Perhaps the correct approach is the pragmatic approach, and whether in a model world "such and such" should be the position, the fact is that East-West trade does work within its current organizational and institutional framework, but whether this will continue to be the case is another matter. It might well be the present organizational and institutional framework will not continue to be suitable for the current and developing forms of East-West trade. Although the enterprises of Eastern Europe have been, to a certain degree, dependent on the West for some technology and the provision of large-scale credits, nevertheless, with the existing forms of East-West trade and those which will undoubtedly develop in future, many Western companies will increasingly depend on Eastern Europe for raw materials as an example, so that it is possible that what in some cases is an imbalance in the partnership between Western companies and Eastern European enterprises will to a degree disappear because of the future mutual interdependence of Western firms and Eastern European enterprises, particularly in the field of industrial cooperation. Furthermore, the development of antitrust legislation in Western Europe, for example, via the Common Market, and general antitrust legislation may well put a limit on the role of the large multinational Western company in the future.

Nevertheless and in summary, considerable persuasion would be needed to change the basic view of this paper, i.e., that in general terms large multinational Western companies are the more natural partners of Eastern European enterprises, particularly with reference to large projects, because of their financial resources; flexibility commercially through their international network of associated and subsidiary companies and branches; technological resources, expertise, and commitment to future technical development; experience in commercial and legal matters; current and historical stability (financial or otherwise); and ability to think on a large scale. Nevertheless, as also stated earlier, smaller and medium sized companies have a vital and continuing role to play through their personal commitment to

East-West trade, enormous expertise in certain specialized technological fields, potential ability to form consortia to take part in larger projects of East-West trade, and ability to adapt themselves to the changing forms of their trade. In this way, although through a looser organizational and legal framework than the one through which the large multinational Western company operates, the smaller and medium sized firms can and could increasingly in the future match the resources of large multinational Western companies, while still preserving the special advantages which they enjoy and which have been stated previously.

NOTES

1. Organization for Economic Cooperation and Development, Guidelines for Multinational Enterprises, Paris: OECD, 1976.

2. United Nations Economic Commission for Europe, Analytical Report on Industrial Co-operation Among ECE Countries, Geneva: United Nations, 1973; United Nations Economic Commission for Europe, Practical Measures to Remove Obstacles to Intra-Regional Trade and to Promote and Diversify Trade. Addendum: Long-term Agreements on Economic Cooperation and Trade, Geneva: United Nations, 1975.

3. The Press Bulletin of the Moscow Narodny Bank, London, 5 April 1978.

4. The Press Bulletin of the Moscow Narodny Bank, London, 12 April 1978.

5. The London Chamber of Commerce and Industry, Bulletin of Current Commercial Intelligence, 14 April 1978.

6. S. Ponomaryov, "Compensation-based Co-operation between the USSR and the Capitalist Countries in the Fuel Industry," Foreign Trade, Moscow, April 1978.

9 Organizational Problems of Multinational Corporations in East-West Trade
G. Peter Lauter

INTRODUCTION

Multinational corporations play a key role in East-West trade. Their size, control over sophisticated technology, vast financial resources, and worldwide marketing systems are but a few of the characteristics that make these corporations sought after trading partners in the East. On the other hand, in their constant search for new markets and low cost production sites with an educated and nonstriking labor force, many multinational corporations consider the Socialist economies to be among the more promising regions of the world. These views, their implications, and the current problems plaguing East-West trade, such as the size of the Eastern debt and the growing protectionism in the West, have been adequately explored. (1) However, the question as to what type of organizational problems multinational corporations engaged in East-West trade have to face and how they respond to these problems have not yet received any attention. (2)

It is the purpose of this paper to present a discussion of selected organizational problems faced by American and European multinational corporations engaged in East-West trade and to provide an analysis of their organizational responses to such problems, based on data from personal, independent investigations and selected data from a comprehensive corporate strategy study. (3) More specifically, the paper deals with those organizational problems and responses which developed partially as a result of the rapid growth of East-West trade during the first half of the 1970s and partially as a consequence of the counter trade demands made by the Socialist economies during the last two to three years.

The topic merits consideration, because corporate strategies are implemented through organizational structures. Furthermore, the changing of organizational structures in large corporate systems is a costly and risky undertaking and it is done only if management can assume that the long-term benefits obtained through the changes are, at least, equal to the costs incurred. Thus, an investigation of organizational problems generated by the changing East-West trade environment and an analysis of the organizational responses to such problems can provide some insight into the commitment of American and European multinationals to such trade.

THE ORGANIZATION OF MULTINATIONAL CORPORATIONS

Multinational corporations are large, complex structures. Their organizational patterns are maintained and corporate strategies are implemented through a continuous differentiation and integration of organizational tasks (international division, the worldwide product division, the worldwide functional, and the national subsidiary patterns). (4) Differentiation means specialization both in terms of organizational arrangements and managerial attitudes. Integration refers to the use of organizational devices that are needed to achieve a unity of effort in all responses to the continually changing environment. The process of differentiation creates conflicts; the process of integration is designed to reduce such conflicts to a level where the organization can achieve its objectives efficiently and effectively.

Continuous organizational differentiation and integration are difficult undertakings. They are impeded by inertia, vested interest, and the inability to properly evaluate environmental changes and to clearly measure organizational costs and benefits. Nevertheless, differentiation and integration must continually be done because the changes in the environment, together with the new complexities that arise from organizational responses to the changes, gradually reduce the effectiveness of organizational structures.

As multinational corporations expand into new regions of the world and as their sales increase in both the old and new markets, established organizational patterns often get blurred. Such mixed organizational patterns may function quite well for a long time. Sooner or later, however, the cost of effective integration may force management to review and change its organization.

BASIC ORGANIZATIONAL PATTERNS AND EAST-WEST TRADE DEVELOPMENTS

The basic organizational structures of American and European multinationals involved in East-West trade represent complex systems developed over a number of years. Typically, an American corporation trading with the East is also engaged in the manufacture and marketing of its products on the North American continent, in Latin America, the Far East, Asia, and Western Europe. In contrast, European multinationals tend to serve more limited markets; their engagements are chiefly in Europe and to a lesser extent, in the Middle East, Latin America, and the Far East.

The basic organizational patterns of the United States corporations reflect this difference. Their structures range from the international division (worldwide regional combination through the international division) to a worldwide product division combination, through the almost pure form of worldwide regional arrangement. European multinationals prefer the national subsidiary pattern, although some also conduct trade with the Socialist economies directly from corporate headquarters or through product divisions.

American multinationals are based on highly differentiated and decentralized organizational patterns. This is necessitated by their worldwide engagement, strong marketing orientation, the distance of corporate headquarters from the Socialist markets, and their evolutionary history. The more limited global engagement of European multinationals permit a less differentiated and more centralized organizational approach.

The basic organizational patterns followed by American corporations deserve a few additional observations. Direct marketing activities are usually conducted through the previously discussed, highly differentiated multilayered structures. In the majority of multinationals, however, industrial cooperation projects are handled by specially assembled management teams at corporate headquarters. The large scale and protocol frameworks of such projects explain the more centralized decision making approach.

The basic organizational structures of multinationals also include Eastern European (EE) departments of varying sizes, usually attached to the European regional headquarters or established in Vienna. The functions of these units and their relationships to the rest of the corporate systems, however, is not always clear and tends to change over time.

European multinational corporations also maintain special EE units usually attached to headquarters. The functions and organizational relationships of these departments are usually better defined than in American corporations, although they are not without uncertainties. However, since in most cases such departments have direct access to top management, such uncertainties are potentially less damaging than in American multinationals.

As long as the East-West trade volumes of both American and European multinationals were modest and as long as trade was not complicated by counter trade demands, these basic structures tended to perform in a satisfactory manner. The almost three and one-half increase in the total volume of trade between 1970-75 and the emergence of counter trade demands by the Socialist governments during 1975-76 substantially altered the East-West trade environment. (5) The composition of trade also changed. More sophisticated and broader product lines were introduced, and the number of industrial cooperation projects grew from about 300 in 1970 to almost 1,200 in 1975-76. (6)

Furthermore, more complex financing schemes emerged, and competition became intense. Socialist trade officials obtained better information, and the managers of some multinationals began complaining about "whipsawing" and other tough Socialist negotiating strategies. (7)

With the emergence of counter trade, conditions became even more complex and competition more severe. Initially, the managers of multinationals considered counter trade a nuisance that could be ignored and it was only during 1976-77 that they learned to appreciate the nature and cost of the organizational problems it caused.

ORGANIZATIONAL PROBLEMS

During 1970 to 1975, the most difficult volume generated problems were experienced by those American multinationals that approached the Socialist markets through worldwide product divisions. The substantial increase in demand for the products of the various divisions resulted in divisional marketing representatives calling on foreign trade organizations in an independent and uncoordinated fashion. This often caused consternation among the Socialist trade officials who did not quite understand why representatives of the same corporate system tried to obtain deals under differing conditions. They also found it aggravating that it was not always clear what divisional representative had to be contacted for a given product. Finally, the officials, who value longstanding personal contacts, found it disconcerting that they could not develop close working relationships with a limited number of clearly identifiable corporate representatives.

Interorganizationally, such a high degree of differentiation led to the inevitable duplication of functional expertise. Every division had its own technical, financial, and marketing experts who developed divisional strategies. While in most of the world such highly differentiated approaches are necessary to deal with diverse markets, in the centralized Socialist economies the better the experts served divisional interests, the more problems they created for the corporate system as a whole.

American multinationals organized on a regional basis and European multinationals operating through the national subsidiary pattern or directly from headquarters experienced less disruptive problems. Their marketing staffs could meet increased demand in a less confusing manner. On the other hand, the absence of product specialists frequently raised problems, because the regional representatives (territorial or country specialists) could not always deal with the sophisticated technical questions asked by the Socialist buyers and end users.

The emergence of strong Socialist counter trade demands during 1975-76 affected all multinationals regardless of organizational patterns or nationality. The severity of the problems differed, however. Counter trade demands caused major organizational problems in corporations that were organized in a worldwide product division basis, that engaged in the direct marketing of products not on the import priority lists of those Socialist economies which had strict counter trade policies that excluded the possibility of linkages, and that had products which could not be used internally. Linkages made it possible for multinationals to meet counter trade demands through acceptance of products from a foreign trade organization or industry other than the one to which the sale was made.

A number of American and European multinationals experienced such conditions. They were in the chemical and machinery industries, traded heavily with Romania and Bulgaria, and frequently had to accept semifinished or finished industrial products to satisfy counter trade demands. The organizational patterns of the product division made it difficult to develop and implement uniform ways of dealing with such demands. This resulted in the acceptance by various product divisions of differing counter trade conditions. Many of the products thus obtained had to be sold through European counter trade houses which charged high subsidies (special charges imposed by counter trade houses in addition to the usual commission, which are negotiable in many instances, but always passed on to the final buyer).

The least affected by counter trade demands were those multinationals which were organized on a regional or national subsidiary basis, manufactured and marketed high technology products on the import priority lists, and traded primarily with Socialist economies that had liberal counter trade policies that permitted, among other things, linkages.

This group included both American and European multinationals in the computer, machinery, and transportation equipment industries. They traded mostly with the Soviet Union (which is interested chiefly in long-term industrial cooperation buy-back projects), Poland, Czechoslovakia, and in some cases, with the German Democratic Republic. Hungary is special, since if a product is on the import list, no counter trade demands are made, but if it is not on the list, counter trade demands are likely to be 100% or even more. Most of these corporations were engaged in some form of industrial cooperation and were thus given the time and opportunity to establish linkages between foreign trade organizations and industries and to carefully choose the products. A number of multinationals used the selected counter trade products (components) internally; i.e., they included them in the final products manufactured by one of the subsidiaries for the European markets. Others had no great difficulties marketing the chosen finished products through subsidiaries in the developing countries.

Most multinationals, however, were not facing either of the previously described extreme set of conditions: they were engaged in both direct marketing and industrial cooperation projects; their product lines included items on and off the import priority lists; they traded with almost all Socialist countries; and the counter trade products they had to accept ranged from internally usable to marketable through unmarketable low quality items. The resulting wide range of problems made generalizations impossible, although some interesting industrial differences could be noted. Both American and European corporations in the chemical and pharmaceutical industries (most of them organized along product division lines) were subject to strong counter trade demands in most countries. This problem was compounded by the fact that a number of Eastern European chemical and pharmaceutical companies, some of which the multinationals helped to build, were about to enter into or expand in the world markets. The severity of the organizational problems which this created varied from corporation to corporation and ranged from the manageable to the almost grotesque. The experience of one European multinational illustrates the point well. It took the management of this corporate system a full year to find out that the alleged competitor, who through the acceptance of unfavorable counter trade deals continually undercut the negotiating position of one of its divisions, was in fact another corporate division.

As a result of the increased volume of trade during the early 1970s and the Socialist counter trade demands over the last few years, the highly differentiated basic organizational patterns of multinational corporations came under strain. The integrating devices and the various kinds of EE departments established during the low-volume, relatively straightforward East-West trade era, could no longer effectively cope with the problems generated by the rapidly changing environment. Although national and industrial differences were present, all multinationals experienced, to varying degrees, serious organizational problems.

ORGANIZATIONAL RESPONSES

Simultaneously, with the emergence of organizational problems, multinationals were searching for new, more effective, integrating devices. They needed organizational means that would have made it possible to develop unified negotiating positions in order to link deals obtained by divisions or subsidiaries and to arrange for a coordinated approach to counter trade demands. In other words, managers were searching for integrating devices that would have made it possible to approach the Socialist markets under the umbrella of a more consistent and comprehensive corporate strategy, however, without any substantial change in the basic corporate structures.

American multinationals were much more reluctant than Europeans to even attempt to adjust basic corporate structures. The nature of East-West trade involvement made no difference. American multinationals engaged chiefly in industrial cooperation were as reluctant as corporations more involved in direct marketing. The most frequent organizational response of American multinationals was an increase in the staff of the EE departments attached to regional headquarters or established independently in Vienna. In some instances, such an increase in size was combined with a redefinition of organizational relationships; they were clarified and simplified. In a few multinationals, this meant that the EE departments reported directly to top management in the United States instead of having to go through regional headquarters. In a limited number of corporations the new position of an East-West trade director was created in the United States to coordinate corporate activities. However, in most cases the position of these directors in the corporate hierarchy was not clearly defined. Their influence over product divisions, regional headquarters, or subsidiaries had to be exercised through the vice presidents of the international divisions. While this is a typical organizational arrangement, experience shows that unless such trade directors have considerable informal authority, their influence may never emerge.

A few American corporations, engaged chiefly in direct marketing, not only increased the size of their Vienna offices but also turned them into profitable centers. Thus, the staff of these offices engaged in both direct marketing to the Socialist economies and in order allocation (an integrative function). The profit centers bought the products at transfer prices and charged the divisions or subsidiaries for any services rendered.

American corporations in the chemical and computer-electronics industries showed the most systematic organizational responses. In both industries the EE departments were established in Vienna as profitable centers or as units that reported directly to American headquarters. Their marketing forces were composed of both product and territorial (country) specialists and were supported by local offices and/or agents in the Socialist markets. The more systematic responses of chemical multinationals could be explained through the increased competition from other Western corporations, the changing demand of Socialist buyers who asked for more specialty as opposed to standard products which were produced domestically, the strong counter trade demands, and the emergence of a number of Socialist competitors in the world markets.

The organizational responses of American computer-electronics corporations could not be explained in the same manner, because their competitive positions in both East and West were not in danger. As the developers, manufacturers, and marketers of the most advanced technology, they were recognized industrial leaders. Their responses could better be explained by the relatively short life cycles of their products and by the forward looking and dynamic managerial attitudes which made them industrial leaders in the first place.

As a group, American multinational corporations responded in a more limited and opportunistic fashion than Europeans. This could be explained, first of all, through their more limited engagement in East-West trade -- only a few obtained more than 1% of their worldwide sales in the Socialist markets -- through the high degree of organizational differentiation and decentralization characteristic of marketing oriented large American corporate systems, and through the more reserved views American managers had had about the future growth of East-West trade.

Although as a group, European multinationals responded in a more systematic and comprehensive fashion, there were some interesting exceptions. Some corporations took the position that any organizational response to counter trade demands would be a strategic error, because it would be seen by the Socialist side as a legitimization of an unacceptable trading practice.

European multinationals were organized mostly on a national subsidiary basis, although the chemical industry had a number of product-division-based corporations. The special EE departments were usually attached to corporate headquarters in the country of domicile. Consequently, the first organizational response to changing trading conditions in most European corporations was an increase in the staff and the number of functions performed by these departments. These initial moves were quite similar to the organizational responses of American multinationals. There was, however, a major difference; the EE departments of European corporations were not in Vienna or at regional headquarters, but at corporate headquarters. Consequently, their staff had direct and quick access to top management.

Integrating Devices

A more complex integrating device, the so-called Eastern European Business Committee, was developed by a number of product-division-based European multinationals in the chemical and pharmaceutical industries. These committees included representatives of each product division and the special corporate level departments, such as the office of licensing. It was their responsibility to integrate all corporate activities in the Socialist economies and in particular, to make it possible for the organization to counter balance the centralized bargaining power of the Socialist negotiators. While the committees were expected to monitor implementation, they did not have the authority to direct divisional activities and had to influence divisional managers through top corporate management.

In each of these multinationals the committees were supported by independent administrative staffs that took care of the day-to-day collection, analysis, and communication of needed information. In addition, special corporate level counter trade, industrial cooperation, market research, and other organizational units were also involved in the integration efforts.

The most comprehensive integrating device was developed by the management of a large European chemical corporate system. This multinational group was comprised of a large number of product divisions and subsidiaries producing and marketing over 25,000 products. It was engaged all over the globe and obtained more than 5% of its annual sales in the Socialist markets.

Its key integrating device was a large EE department attached to corporate headquarters in Western Europe. The staff of this department performed an active role, not only in advising and coordinating but also in developing an overall corporate strategy for the Socialist markets. It was represented on the board of directors by a director who specialized in East-West trade. The staff performed its coordinating and strategy development functions through the continuous collection, evaluation, and reporting of East-West trade information obtained from the product divisions, corporate offices throughout the Socialist economies, and independent sources. It continually monitored corporate activities, reformulated them, or developed new corporate policies whenever necessary.

The influential position of the department was not without its problems. Divisional management occasionally resented the functional authority that it had gradually obtained over counter trade, financing, industrial cooperation, trade fairs, and other divisional activities. Nevertheless, because of the strong support it had from the board of directors, it could exercise its special role in a very effective manner. To illustrate the point, through the department's carefully developed and coordinated corporate counter trade strategy, more than 90% of all products accepted by the different divisions and subsidiaries could be internally utilized.

More Effective European Results

The major reason for the more systematic and comprehensive organizational responses of European multinationals was their historically conditioned higher degree of involvement in the Eastern European region. In addition, their more limited global engagements and consequently, less complicated basic organizational patterns made it possible to introduce more effective integrating devices than American corporations could. The reasons for the more effective organizational response of European chemical corporations, as opposed to other European multinationals, were the same as in the case of the American chemical group. Increased competition in both East and West, changing buying habits in the East, and strong counter trade demands made it imperative for the chemical multinationals to develop and implement more effective integrating devices. The response of the large European chemical group could additionally be explained by the forward looking attitude of its top management.

CONCLUSIONS

It is the basic proposition of this paper that since corporate strategies are implemented through organizational structures, the organizational responses of multinational corporations to organizational problems caused by recent East-West trade developments are an indication of how these corporations view their involvement in such trade.

Based on the evidence presented, it can be argued that although national and industrial differences were present, as a group with a few notable exceptions, American and European multinationals appeared to be taking a hesitant, short-term view of their East-West trade participation.

The integrating devices developed and employed, such as the special departments, committees, and new corporate coordinating positions, were sufficient to deal only with the organizational problems caused by increased volume. Better exchange of information, more coordinated order allocation (sourcing), and the development of more unified marketing approaches involved matters that could be handled in a routine fashion in the short run.

The resolution of the problems caused by counter trade was another matter. These problems were of a nonroutine nature and involved long-term organizational considerations. The previously mentioned special departments, committees, and coordinating positions that were expected to also handle such problems did not have enough authority to develop and enforce corporation wide counter trade strategies. Only the management of the European chemical group recognized the need to develop, approve, and enforce such strategies at the highest level of corporate management. In most other corporations the prevailing view seemed to be that counter trade was only a temporary phenomenon, an unfortunate aberration which if ignored would go away, or what was even better, would soon be eliminated through political pressures and negotiations.

Most corporations were reluctant to recognize that given the state of the world economy and the outlook for East-West trade, counter trade is not likely to disappear within the foreseeable future and that because of their worldwide diversified manufacturing and marketing engagements, they are the most obvious targets for counter trade demands, not only by the Socialist but also by the developing economies. Only the large European chemical group and the few European corporations that did not want to legitimize counter trade have, in their own ways, decided to take a clear position. They have understood that the effective resolution of the problems calls for more than halfway measures; it demands a substantial investment of organizational resources and a long-term corporate counter trade strategy, or reduced participation in East-West trade.

This is not to say that there is a single best integrating device that would enable all multinationals to effectively deal with the problems. Organizational structures are influenced, among other forces, by size, technology, the nature of growth strategies, the scope and length of international engagements, and the corporate history. It could also be argued that in corporations that are subject to a wide variety of counter trade conditions, as was the case with the majority of multinationals investigated, no corporation wide organizational integrating devices (organizational arrangements and thus, counter trade strategies) can be developed. The unwillingness of most multinationals to systematically respond to the organizational problems, however, was not the result of the previously mentioned differences or any inability. Their unwillingness was rather the result of a decision not to formally include counter trade considerations in longterm corporate strategies.

The continued need of the Socialist governments to insist on some form of counter trade and the unwillingness of most multinationals investigated to formalize counter trade considerations through organizational arrangements and corporate strategies is a harbinger of future conflicts. It, of course, could be argued that if counter trade is the price for trading with the Socialist economies, that sooner or later for competitive reasons, most multinationals will reconsider their positions. There is an element of truth in this argument. A number of corporations, as shown in this paper, have already done so (industrial differences). However, the number willing to do so in the future is open to question.

The observed national differences are relevant in this respect. The development of effective integrating devices to deal with counter trade problems requires substantial reorganization of corporate structures on a regional basis. For globally organized multinationals, this, however, is not possible without also affecting the entire worldwide corporate system. This was one of the major reasons for the more limited and opportunistic organizational responses of American multinationals.

In summary, the prospect of continual counter trade demands by the Socialist economies, combined with the unwillingness of numerous multinational corporations to include such considerations in long-term corporate strategies, raises a number of questions about the future involvement of these corporations in East-West trade.

NOTES

1. See, for example, J. Wilczynski, *The Multinationals and East-West Relations: Toward Transideological Collaboration* (Boulder, Colo.: Westview Press, 1976); R. Portes, "East Europe's Debt to the West: Interdependence Is a Two-Way Street," *Foreign Affairs* 55 (July 1977): 751-82; and K. Ravasz, "The East-West Trade Situation," *The New Hungarian Quarterly* 18 (Summer 1977): 213-19.

2. The most recent comprehensive annotated bibliography on East-West trade, for example, lists only one entry dealing with organizational issues. See Paul Marer et al., *An Annotated and Cross-Referenced Bibliography of East-West Commerce* (Bloomington: International Development Institute, Indiana University, 1977).

3. For the comprehensive study, see *Corporate Strategy, Planning, Organization and Personnel Practices for Eastern Europe* (Geneva: Business International S.A., 1977).

4. For a discussion of the concepts of differentiation and integration, see Paul R. Lawrence and Jay W. Lorsch, *Organization and Environment: Managing Differentiation and Integration* (Boston: Division of Research, Graduate School of Business Administration, Harvard University, 1967).

5. *Figyelo* 22, no. 6 (February 8, 1978): p. 8.

6. Ibid.

7. "Whipsawing" became a controversial issue mostly in the United States. Views on the existence and/or severity of the problem still differ. See, for example, *U.S. - U.S.S.R. Trade and the Whipsaw Controversy* (Washington, D.C.: Department of Commerce, Domestic and International Business Administration, Bureau of East-West Trade, 1977).

10 Western Multinational Corporations in Eastern Europe and CMEA Integration*
Paul Marer

INTRODUCTION AND THE MAIN THEME

The main topic of this paper is the relationship between CMEA integration and East-West commerce. Are the two competitive, complementary, or independent? The consensus of Western opinion is that they tend to be competitive. Indeed, there is a basis for holding this view, especially when one focuses primarily on the short-term movement of trade flows involving energy and primary products.

The consensus of the Western view can be stated as follows: the more a CMEA country turns to buy from the West, the more this signals the unavailability of goods from its CMEA partners in adequate quantities and quality. More importantly, the larger a CMEA country imports from the West, the more it needs to sell to the West its primary products and best quality manufactures for convertible currency (CC), to pay for these imports, and to service its debts. These goods are thus becoming less available for sale to the CMEA, and since the volume and share of trade with one's regional partners has much to do with economic integration, this reorientation must be at the expense of CMEA integration. Generally, the greater the pressure to import from the West and the greater the CC debt which must be serviced by increasing exports, the greater the pressure to

---

* The author acknowledges with thanks the comments of his conference discussant, Egon Neuberger, some of which have been incorporated in this revised version, and the help of John Garland for looking up references and for comments.

"reorient" the most desirable goods to the West--often the same goods that are also in great demand on the CMEA market. The main focus is on Soviet oil and raw material exports to EE. It is pointed out that the Soviet Union is increasingly less able or willing to supply the increased quantities of such goods needed by Eastern Europe (EE).

To be sure, there is also another side to this simplified analysis of the Western "consensus" view, and it goes something like this: the larger the debt of a CMEA country, the greater the constraint it faces in further increasing its imports from the West. This constraint is reinforced by the growing difficulties all CMEA countries face today trying to expand their manufactured exports to the West. Hence, they are forced to reconsider the desirability and feasibility of strengthening their links with the West; they must "re-reorient" their trade toward the CMEA. Some would argue further that the greater the CC indebtedness of an EE country, the more it becomes dependent, not on the West but on the Soviet Union, through an explicit or implicit reliance on the Russian "credit umbrella" (this might be more the view of Western lenders than of the EE countries themselves); i.e., counting on the Soviet Union as a lender of last resort to help some of them avoid having to reschedule their debt. (1) This increased dependence of the EE countries on the Soviet Union for trade and for last resort finance is tantamount to greater economic integration with the Soviet Union and with the rest of the CMEA.

These kinds of views tend to be reflected with particular emphasis in the writings of those who assign prime importance to short-term changes in a CMEA country's trade shares. "Last year 50 percent of CMEA country X's imports came from the West versus only 40 percent five years ago, ergo, country X is moving away from integration with the CMEA." Now, one cannot deny that correctly calculated trade shares are important indicators and that large changes in the share of trade conducted with one or another bloc of countries can be significant. It may indicate the shifting of resources and priorities away from one group of countries and toward another group. A mechanical focus on trade shares is overly simplistic, however, and the implications drawn from it can be mistaken.

The theme that will be developed in this paper is that the relationship between CMEA integration and East-West commerce can be both competitive and complementary, but rarely independent. Greater emphasis is placed on the complementary aspects, which are somewhat less obvious; these aspects are particularly important in East-West industrial cooperation (IC) as compared with simple trade. And since the focus here is on Western multinational corporations (MNCs), which play a significant, possibly even a dominant role in East-West IC, an emphasis on complementary aspects is appropriate.

The following section attempts to define CMEA integration by presenting alternative views from the East and West on the topic. The main point is that integration, however defined, can be viewed either as a state of affairs or as a process. The distinction is important because in seeking to find the relationship between the activities of Western MNCs in EE and CMEA integration, one must focus on the process of integration rather than on the state of things as they are today. The section concludes with observations on the pitfalls and shortcomings of so-called trade share analysis.

The next section focuses on East-West IC, its definition, and the extent of American and other Western involvement in this activity up to now. It also discusses how MNCs are viewed by the CMEA countries, and then examines the other side of the coin: do Western MNCs view the CMEA as a group? What views do MNCs hold regarding the effect of CMEA integration programs on their strategy and operations in the Soviet Union and EE?

The last section develops the main theme of the paper, the relationship between the process of CMEA integration and the East-West commerce in its various forms. It concludes that there is no inherent conflict between a strong MNC presence in the CMEA countries and the CMEA integration process, but to exploit the opportunities, it will be largely up to the CMEA countries to make certain policy decisions and to move forward with institutional reforms.

ECONOMIC INTEGRATION: CONCEPTUAL PROBLEMS OF DEFINITION AND MEASUREMENT

There is consensus in Western scholarship on three things: (a) economic integration refers basically to division of labor, to specialization; (b) it involves mobility of goods, or factors, or both; and (c) one component is economic discrimination in favor of members of a group as compared with nonmembers, but there is no consensus on the definitional content of these components. (2)

Economic Integration

Integration can be understood either as a process or as a state of affairs reached, which has been brought about by that process. But what is the substance of integration, and what are its essential criteria? By what statistical indicator or qualitative change that can be specified in advance can one deduce whether there is a process at work or a state attained?

Integration can refer to legal and institutional relationships within a region in which economic transactions take place or it can refer to the market relationships among goods and factors within the region. It seems that integration in the CMEA can be defined principally in terms of the institutional linkages among the members, although market relationships also exist to some extent. By contrast, integration among market economies, such as the European Economic Community (EEC), can be defined principally in terms of market relationships, although these must be supported by newly created regional institutions. These institutions become more important if economic integration among nations is to evolve successfully toward economic union, such as that which exists among the states in the United States. As far as market economics are concerned, Balassa's distinction among trade integration, factor integration, policy integration, and total integration is a good one if interpreted as stages rather than alternatives. (3) For nonmarket economy (NME) countries, it is unclear whether the same stages would describe the integration process. A search for a single definition of integration that can be applied to market and MNEs is perhaps inappropriate.

Let us turn to some of the best known Soviet economists and see how they define integration among the CMEA states. Maximova, one of the leading Soviet specialists on the topic, offers the following definition:

> First, integration is a process of the development of stable and deep ties, and of the division of labor between national economies, that is accompanied by the mutual complementing and adjustment of individual enterprises, branches and economic areas of various countries, and leads to the formation of international economic complexes initially (by) . . . groups of countries close to each other on the level of economic development. . . . Second . . . the state machinery of individual countries and international institutions have an active role to play. (4)

As to how it can be achieved, Maximova points out that planning and the market both must play a role:

> While paying particular attention to the coordination of plans and joint production, scientific and technical activity, the CMEA member countries also attach much importance to commodity and money relations, to the development of trade, to the

improvement of the price system, and to the monetary-financial and credit relations. (5)

Another leading Soviet economist, Bogomolov, gives a similar definition and also stresses that both planning and market must play a role. On the one hand:

> . . . . joint planning activity provides the basis for . . . enlarging the scale of production, . . . developing a common infrastructure, . . . giving greater depth to international specialization and cooperation in production. Joint planning includes mutual consultations on basic aspects of economic policy, joint forecasting of development in the key industries, and coordination of five-year national economic plans. . . . Recently, (in some line of production) . . . joint planning covers research and development projects, investments to enlarge production, loading and specialization of industrial facilities and deliveries of the products involved. (6)

But on the other hand:

> . . . it would be wrong to regard integration through planning as being incompatible with the market and socialist commodity and money relations. Economic planning under socialism implies a development of commodity and money relations both within individual socialist countries and between them. (7)

Specialization

But what is to be the content and criteria for specialization through planning, and what role should "Socialist commodity and money relations" play in bringing about integration? To raise this is not to try to be difficult; many of the same questions are also being raised, in a different institutional context to be sure, regarding further integration among market economy countries, such as the EEC. But as Haberler and Hardt pointed out in commenting on Bogomolov, because the great bulk of production and trade decisions in the West are made by private business, a reduction of trade barriers is already a big step toward integration, whereas the same cannot be said for integration among NMEs, where both the planning and the market aspects of the process of integration must be designed and implemented by the participating states themselves. (8) A critical aspect, which is particularly important in centrally planned economies where visible planners rather than the invisible market make the decisions, is the willingness of partner countries to abandon the protection of industries producing commodities subject to specialization agreements.

McMillan argues convincingly that the Soviet position strongly favors integration through joint planning, not only because it views this as efficient, but also because this would place limits on the extent of domestic reforms that can be undertaken by member states, which is another instrument for exercising economic and thereby political control over the East Europe region. (9) A further important aspect from the Soviet point of view is the politically motivated desire to set up a centralized Eastern economic bloc as a counterweight to the Common Market, just as the Warsaw Pact is viewed as a counterweight to NATO and vice versa.

Integration Among CMEA Countries

In briefly reviewing the literature, one finds that the writings of experts are not terribly helpful in pinpointing what exactly is meant by integration among the CMEA countries, except that their definition also focuses on the same kinds of things we focus on, namely, increased division of labor and increased specialization, but they stress that joint planning and international economic complexes must play a major but not clearly defined role in facilitating the integration process.

Given this state of affairs, it is not surprising that those in the West as well as in the CMEA, who wish to measure the degree of integration in the CMEA or compare the EEC and the CMEA, focus on trade flows and use changes in (a) trade to national income ratios and (b) trade shares with members of the bloc versus trade shares with nonmembers as their indicators. These, after all, are the most frequently used indicators of integration among market economies. Balassa, for example, suggests:

> Under the assumption that the historical relationship of imports to the GNP would have remained unchanged in the absence of integration, . . . a rise in the ratio of the growth rate of total imports to GNP be taken to represent trade creation, and a decrease in the corresponding ratio for extra-area imports to represent trade diversion. (10)

Independently of the theoretical weakness of this measure even for market economies, the use of trade shares is fraught with special difficulties calculated for NMEs for the following reasons:

1. The CMEA countries trade at one set of prices, usually current world market, with the West and at another set of prices, historical world market, with each other; at times, the differences between the two price sets can be very substantial. Since most CMEA countries do not publish indices of trade volume by region, we are forced to rely on value data. But trade shares, based on value data that combine trade flows with nonuniform prices, can be quite a bit off the mark; moreover, large price changes in one trade flow, e.g., East-West during 1973-74, can cause large swings in trade shares based on value data, changes that would not be reflected, or reflected only to a much smaller degree, in the real trade structure. (11)

2. As Haberler first pointed out more than ten years ago, the requirement of bilateral balancing of trade prompts CMEA countries to import and then to re-export a significant volume of goods. Such trade does not contribute to increased international specialization, although it gets around the constraints imposed by bilateralism, but such flows are included in all CMEA countries' trade data (12) Moreover, even regular trade is said to contain a certain percentage of what might be called uneconomic exchange, such as the need to import and use domestically certain "tied" goods so that a foreign market for one's own "soft" manufactures may thereby be created. Such tendencies are brought about by forces unique to centrally planned economies with nonconvertible currencies, tendencies which Alan Brown dubbed "trade proclivity." (13)

These examples suggest that more trade within the bloc does not automatically mean more gain, more integration, or even greater economic dependence, just as less trade should not necessarily signal a loss, less integration, and greater economic independence. This view is underscored by Levcik and Stankovsky, who point out that the share of intrabloc trade was at its highest during the peak of the Cold War in the 1950s, but one could hardly speak of economic integration in the CMEA. (14)

Trade Creation and Diversion

There is at least one further point which applies to market and to NME countries. Trade creation and diversion, which are essential concepts in measuring integration, are static concepts. Upon reaching a certain stage of development, economic growth will lead, through a high income elasticity of demand for high-technology products, to imports from countries that can supply those products. If such countries happen to be located outside the bloc, then over an extended period of time, (a) the effects of trade diversion in reducing trade with the outside world can be masked by a high income elasticity of demand for the products of the outside world, or (b) the favorable effects of trade creation can be masked by a low income elasticity of demand for the products of the countries in a regional grouping. (15) This, I suspect, describes at least in part what has been happening in the CMEA countries since the early 1970s. Now, whether the unavailability of high technology (broadly defined) products, as well as many other products, can be ascribed to the shortcomings of the CMEA integration process up to now or principally to other factors is debatable; the issue will not be discussed because it is not central to the argument in this paper.

A good measure of the success of regional integration would probably be the absence of duplicated industries producing the same product in different countries if the benefits of specialization, e.g., economies of scale, indicate that a duplication of effort is wasteful. This suggests that to discern the effects of integration over time, one should look at both changes in production and trade patterns rather than changes in trade flows and shares over time.

There is neither the time in this paper, nor the ready availability of information on changes in production and trade patterns over time, for all CMEA countries and on a comparable basis, to attempt to undertake an empirical analysis. But we know that as far as the involvement of MNCs in the CMEA is concerned, a growing share of their activity during the 1970s consist of what might loosely be called "industrial cooperation" and that the relative importance of such activities in the total East-West economic picture will almost certainly continue to rise. Hence, in trying to analyze the relationship between the MNCs activity in the CMEA countries and CMEA integration, it is not inappropriate to focus briefly on East-West industrial cooperation, to which we next turn.

MULTINATIONAL CORPORATIONS AND EAST-WEST INDUSTRIAL COOPERATION

There is no internationally accepted definition of industrial cooperation (IC) beyond the convention that it must encompass more than simple, arm's length, import-export transactions. (16) Each Eastern country employs its own definition; most Western countries, including the United States, do not maintain official records on IC. After critically assessing a large number of Eastern and Western definitions, McMillan conceptualizes IC as "arrangements whereby individual producers, based in East and West, agree to pool some tangible or intangible assets and jointly to coordinate their use in the mutual pursuit of complementary objectives. (17)

We agree with this conceptualization, but our definition would encompass a broader range of transactions than those included by McMillan or the Economic Commission for Europe (ECE) and would include all types of licensing and turnkey contracts; the ECE records only those for which the Eastern partner pays with resultant products. This reflects a focus on technology transfer issues and the practical consideration that information on payment arrangements is not always available.

According to the narrower ECE definition, since the early 1960s there have reputedly been about 2,000 IC agreements. They appeal to Western firms because they can be vehicles for entering the CMEA market; the CMEA countries, especially the Soviet Union, are a relatively untapped source of raw materials; their costs are lower; and there are no strikes. Industrial cooperation also offers economies of scale and opportunities for specialization, but most of all it gives access to a new market. In return, the CMEA countries get advanced Western technology and know-how, foreign capital, and easier access to Western markets. The Soviet Union is mostly interested on compensation, or buy-back projects; the EE countries prefer co-production, specialization, and now also joint ventures.

American IC

Prior to 1970, American business relations with these countries were by and large limited to exports and imports, small in volume, and often transacted through subsidiaries in Western Europe. However, when detente brought an improvement in political relations, many American companies began to negotiate in the Soviet Union and Eastern Europe (EE).

American executives found that the market potential was large and prospects for long-run profits encouraging if a company could establish a foothold. However, in many cases the CMEA countries did not want to become regular customers for American consumer and industrial products, but preferred to obtain modern technology as well as managerial and marketing know-how under IC agreements. This approach is prompted in part by these countries' development strategy, a key aspect of which is a narrowing of the East-West technological gap, and in part by their acute shortage of hard currency, which they hope can be alleviated by IC with the West. American companies also found that political and ideological considerations foreclosed the possibility of penetrating the CMEA market through wholly owned subsidiaries, as they had done earlier in Western Europe. With resistance to exports for economic reasons and the prohibition of subsidiaries for political reasons, those American companies willing to enter IC often had the best chance of penetrating the CMEA market.

What is the attitude of policy makers in the CMEA countries toward multinational corporations (MNCs)? Somewhat ambivalent, it appears, a posture well articulated by Hungary's former Deputy Minister of Foreign Trade:

> For us socialist economists and economic leaders, examination of the activities of MNCs still depends on mainly insufficient information. We have no detailed knowledge and, therefore, cannot formulate a comprehensive opinion about them. There can be no doubt, however, that in the course of the evolution of the economic integration of socialist countries there will emerge enterprises in whose activities several socialist countries will be interested. (18)

Soviet and EE economists take the view that MNCs are a fact of life and that they have to deal with them. They believe that their countries can take advantage of the strengths of MNCs in technology, management, marketing, and also their production scheduling expertise, as well as longer term planning, while ensuring that they do not suffer any of the unwanted consequences. They see great benefits for their countries by calling in MNCs to carry out specific tasks and thereby extend the CMEA division of labor. An important strength of MNCs that they admire is ability to cross national boundaries in a way that state monopolies cannot.

Beginning in 1976 when the American corporations involved in approximately 600 actual and prospective IC agreements (according to our broad definition and including the activities of their foreign affiliates) were classified by two categories of American firms, including those in Fortune's 1975 list of the 500 largest firms, and all others, it was found that approximately three out of four agreements or projects completed or underway involved Fortune 500 firms; in almost all cases they were MNCs. The reason for this strong participation by the giants of American industry can be explained by the preference of Soviet and EE decision makers and by the high costs and risks, but also potentially high payoffs, of entering a Socialist market. Soviet and EE planners have stated repeatedly their desire to harness the know-how and resources of the world's technologically leading corporations that are financially strong and have far flung marketing-distribution networks. Soviet planners are particularly impressed by the large-scale projects possible with American firms.

Conversely, risks for an American company are high because of the uncertainties, costs, and delays in negotiating an IC agreement and because the cost of implementation, especially in areas involving transfer, can be higher than the cost of similar projects in market economy countries. Large firms can more readily afford such costs and may view possible cost overruns as a long-term investment in acquiring experience and getting a permanent foothold in a region where competitors may already be established. Moreover, the revealed pattern is consistent with the dominant international economic role of large American multinationals in other parts of the world.

CMEA Countries IC

CMEA countries have no common, agreed upon strategy regarding East-West IC. (19) Each CMEA country makes decisions in this regard on the basis of its own interest. To be sure, there is some joint borrowing on the Eurodollar market via the International Investment Bank and joint purchases, for example to import steel pipes for the Orenburg gas pipeline. This enables these countries to take advantage of economies of scale of borrowing and buying, which lower costs somewhat, but it still falls considerably short of having a common policy on IC. There is no joint institution set up whose task it is to coordinate the IC activity of member countries with Western enterprises. (20) From the point of view of a Western firm, there is no CMEA equivalent of the EEC. First of all, the CMEA has no institution such as the EEC Commission, which interprets and enforces EEC rules and regulates certain conditions under which member countries may enter into trade and industrial cooperation agreements with outsiders, e.g., regarding such issues as granting tariff preferences on goods imported under IC agreements. More importantly, there is no comparison with the EEC in the sense that if a company once gains a foothold inside the region, it automatically gains improved access to the markets of other CMEA countries. Access to the rest of the CMEA markets can be obtained only indirectly, by working through whatever agreements, mechanisms, or channels each country relies upon to get linked up with the economies of the other CMEA countries.

American Perspective on East-West IC

There is a counterpart to these observations on the Western side also. One of the interesting findings of our study of the American perspective on East-West IC is an apparent lack of a global strategy for many

American MNCs regarding how their current and prospective future operations in the CMEA can fit into the global strategy of the corporation, although there are important exceptions. This may be explained in part by the unfamiliarity many Western corporations still have with the operations of the CMEA economies, especially their decision processes regarding foreign commerce, and the somewhat uncertain and fluctuating environment that still characterizes East-West commerce, which makes forecasting long-term trends particularly difficult. Many American and other Western companies also apparently have no clearly formulated policy objectives when they begin their explorations of the Soviet and EE markets. Their marketing and IC strategies in this region often seem opportunistic, i.e., a response to the attitudes they find, information and advice they happen to get in particular situations and in particular countries. This is also no doubt a reflection of the fact that not only does the CMEA lack a common policy regarding cooperation with Western firms, but the policies of the individual CMEA countries, if they have a clearly defined one, are often difficult to fathom.

To be sure, a growing number of firms monitor developments regarding CMEA integration, particularly the large investment projects and the important bilateral and multilateral specialization agreements, with a view toward identifying business opportunities and in a few cases gaining a better understanding of prospective long-run developments and trends. But the consensus of American and other Western firms is that for the time being the economic situation and policies of each CMEA country are more important than any bloc-wide development.

Summary

Whatever relationship may be found between the activities of MNCs in the Soviet Union and EE and integration among the CMEA countries does not derive from institutions deliberately established or policies purposefully conceived to facilitate such a linkage. At the present time, no such institutions or policies apparently exist on either side.

MULTINATIONAL CORPORATIONS AND CMEA INTEGRATION

Since the adoption of the Comprehensive Program in 1971 by the CMEA countries, there has been some progress toward the coordination of national production and investment plans. The CMEA wide coordination of national plans is confined to those aspects of production; investments, including the so-called joint projects; and trade that require foreign sourcing for or marketing of production. It generally encompasses the main economic branches, selected commodity groups, and investment in infrastructure, most notably in transport.

Specialization Agreements

The record with respect to specialization agreements is mixed. While specialization agreements have become important for such products as machine tools; ball bearings; and trucks, buses, and cars, their number has been limited by (a) lack of direct contact among firms, which reduces information flows and tends to exclude some promising forms of cooperation; (b) desire by enterprises and ministries to avoid potentially disruptive dependence on suppliers from other countries; and (c) absence of scarcity prices, making it difficult to evaluate gains from specialization. As a result, there are relatively few intrabranch specialization agreements, i.e., those that partition the production process by a division of labor in parts, components, and accessories. (21) Hence, in deciding how actively and how far to pursue specialization agreements with CMEA, each country follows a "limited regret" strategy, to use Egon Neuberger's felicitous phrase.

The difficulty of implementing specialization agreements can be shown by reference to the machinery sector. Between 1956 and 1973, the various CMEA standing commissions made 5,300 specialization proposals. However, these recommendations did not exert a significant influence over the development of the machinery industries and export structures of the member countries. Pecsi indicates:

> This reflects one of the basic problems in the work of the CMEA: how to reconcile the interest of particular branches with macroeconomic considerations. That is, the branch committees came up with lots of recommendations but without analyzing how their implementation would affect the development of the entire economy, its structure, and mutual trade. In each country such questions are considered principally in the context of foreign trade planning, which in turn is constrained by existing machinery production patterns and the fixed, inflexible export-import structure within the CMEA that derives from strict bilateral balancing. (22)

In spite of the difficulties, notable progress has been made in a few sectors such as transport, and some countries have been able to

WESTERN MULTINATIONAL CORPORATIONS 157

achieve excellent results in the case of certain products. There seems to be a pattern which suggests that success with respect to specialization in the machinery sector is more likely in those branches and in the case of those products which are able to make use of advanced Western technology on a continuous basis. The reason for this is as follows. Suppose a CMEA country offers to specialize in a particular industrial branch or product. If the branch's technical level is low and it lacks a tradition of exports, the other countries will object. The other countries cannot, of course, stop any country from developing any branch, except that if the other countries do not agree with the specialization proposal, any one of them may veto the granting of a loan by the International Investment Bank. If the branch subsequently is able to produce high quality goods that are in demand, the fact that it was not assigned to specialize will not hinder its ability to export, just as the fact that a country has the CMEA specialization assignment is no guarantee that it will have an assured CMEA market if other countries decide not to discontinue or newly produce the same goods or if the quality of the exports leaves too much to be desired. First, a CMEA country cannot expect to be assigned large-scale production and be relied on for delivery to other countries of complicated machinery, such as buses, motor cars, or their components, unless the country can give reasonable and concrete assurance that it will be able to do the job. Second, having been given the assignment on paper will mean little unless it is able to produce, deliver, and service on a continuous basis acceptable quality machinery and products and sell them at a reasonable price. Third, to be able to produce high quality products, especially in the machinery sector, often requires the importation of Western components, licenses, and technical know-how, sometimes on a temporary and sometimes on a permanent basis. (23) Fourth, the more a CMEA country succeeds in producing high quality manufactures, the more it will be able to penetrate Western and hard currency Third World markets with the same product, but this may require some additional cooperation with Western firms in order to acquire not only technical but also marketing and perhaps financial and service facilities and expertise.

Case Study

Let us illustrate how this works by the example of a case study, that of the production of buses in Hungary. (24) Motor public transport, mainly the production of buses, is one of seven high priority branches in the country. Today this branch produces 25% of Hungary's machinery output and almost one-third of machinery exports. During the 1971-75 plan period, the main enterprises producing buses (Ikarus,

CSPEL Motor Co., Raba Wagon and Motor Co., and Electric Components for Motor Cars Co.) increased their output threefold, and production continues to expand during the current five-year plan. Ikarus is slated to produce 60,000 buses during the current plan, or approximately 12,000 units per year, as compared with 8,000 per year during the previous plan. With this capacity, Hungary apparently is able to produce buses on a scale that makes it competitive in Europe, since in 1974 the English Bedford produced 33,600 units and the German Mercedes 13,700 buses.

This scale of production in Hungary is made possible first and foremost by contractual access to the CMEA market, a successful example of specialization in finished products as well as components and parts. Although Hungary had a prewar tradition of producing buses--this is often the case for branches that have the most successful specialization agreements with the CMEA and the most promising IC agreements with Western partners--before it could become a successful large-scale supplier of buses to the CMEA during the 1960s, for a long time it imported many of the basic materials, components, and licenses from such Western countries as Germany, the United Kingdom, Italy, and Finland.

The main market for Hungarian buses is the Soviet Union and the GDR. In 1976, Hungary exported to Russia 6,000 buses under long-term agreements and an additional 700 units as part of Hungary's contribution to the building of the Orenburg pipeline. More than 1,400 units were shipped to the GDR and 650 units to the other CMEA countries. At the same time, nearly 1,300 buses were sold to Western countries and 1,600 units added to the domestic market. The Soviet Union ships to Hungary the midsection of large buses, and the GDR supplies some of the machinery complexes used in producing the buses. Hungary's Raba factory in turn supplies chassis not only to Ikarus, but the same product in even larger quantities to several other CMEA countries. Further specialization agreements in this sector are also in effect with the GDR and Bulgaria and the Soviet Union. For example, Hungary supplies the Soviet Volga Motor car factory, which produces the Zhiguli passenger car, certain parts and components, such as the dash board, window wiper units, starters, door handles, locks, radios, and so on. Similar specialization agreements are in effect also with Poland's Fiat. Hungary does not produce passenger cars, but imports them from other CMEA countries; in 1976 Hungary imported a total of 80,000 units: more than 30,000 each from Russia and the German Democratic Republic, 10,000 from Czechoslovakia, 5,000 from Poland, and 1,000 from Romania.

Establishing large-scale production of buses and various motor car components within the framework of CMEA cooperation has recently made it possible for Hungary to begin exporting buses also to Western markets and to do so economically. Economic production has two aspects: first, producing modern, high-quality products that have a chance to penetrate Western markets at a price that is not unduly low and thus is not likely to elicit a charge of dumping; second, producing on a scale and with advanced methods so that costs will not be unduly high; i.e., the cost of producing a dollar or ruble of export revenue is reasonable. But ability to penetrate and service the Western markets, i.e., to have old customers continue to put in new orders and to acquire new customers, requires the Hungarian enterprises to keep abreast of and utilize product and technological innovations just about the same time that these innovations become standard features in the products of their Western competitors. For example, the Raba Company purchased and adapted General Motors (GM) technology for the production of axles so successfully that today it is able to supply rear axles to a GM plant in Britain while also supplying similar products to Ikarus and to the CMEA. We understand that recently both Volvo and two American firms had entered into negotiations for buying the complete finished product, i.e., Hungarian buses, and one of the American firms is attempting to market them in California.

Quality Requirements of the Soviet Union

At the same time, there is also continuous pressure from Hungary's CMEA partners for receiving buses of high quality, i.e., "world standard class." So the requirements of both the capitalist and the CMEA markets are forcing the Hungarian enterprises to pay continuous attention to quality, performance, and service. Since one hears so much about the poor quality, not only of the manufactures produced but also traded on the CMEA market, is the case of the Hungarian buses not really an exception? The tentative answer is both yes and no. An exception if we look at past history, perhaps less of an exception if we look at the current situation, and possibly increasingly the rule rather than an exception if we look to the future.

For several years, more and more has been heard about the increased quality standard all CMEA countries have begun to insist upon for their manufactures imports from the CMEA. Especially important in this regard are the import-absorption norms of the Soviet market. An expansion of Soviet trade and industrial cooperation with Western countries are factors in the Soviets insisting more and more firmly on being supplied with machinery that is reasonably up to Western quality and standards. While this requirement is far from universal in the CMEA today—if it were, there would have to be a drastic drop in mutual deliveries—it is a tendency that must be taken into account when one considers the relationship between the process of CMEA integration and East-West trade and industrial cooperation (IC). While such tendencies are probably stronger in the high priority machinery sectors than in the consumer sector, for example, even the latter branch may not be immune from such pressures. To be sure, in the consumer sector one would expect that a CMEA country would find competition tougher in those CMEA countries that are relatively well supplied with quality domestic and Western products (e.g., the GDR and Hungary) than in those countries where there are big shortages and the quality of many consumer goods is low (e.g., Romania, Bulgaria, Poland, and the Soviet Union). But pressures for improved quality of consumer goods exerted on CMEA suppliers by Western competition may be felt even on the Soviet market. As an illustration, in one district in Moscow there is a coin laundry with American washing machines while in another district there is a coin laundry with washing machines from a CMEA country. People stand in line waiting to use the American machinery while there is no waiting in the other laundry, principally because of the difference between the quality of the service provided. (25)

It seems that the Soviet Union in particular clearly has an interest, and the bargaining clout, to insist on improving the quality requirements of the manufactures it buys from EE.

First, this is a way to mitigate somewhat the economic pressures it feels from its declining economic growth rate on the one hand and from its growing indebtedness to the West on the other. The growth pressure is forcing it to seek improved productivity as a source of growth; in that context, improving the quality of machinery, both domestically produced as well as the imports from CMEA, has a role. The balance of payments pressure, in turn, causes it to seek to replace when possible Western machinery with imports from the CMEA countries. This is probably not yet a realistic possibility on a significant scale, but examples can be found. If Poland, for example, co-produces with Western firms large earth moving machinery and equipment, as we understand it does, and the Soviet Union has a huge unmet need for such machinery and buys substantial quantities from the West, which it does, there is no reason why a good earth moving machine imported from Poland cannot be viewed as a substitute for Western machinery and possibly even paid for in part with hard currency.

Second, improving the quality requirements on imports from the CMEA may be one approach to deal with the dilemma of Soviet energy and raw material exports to EE. For political as well as for economic reasons, the Soviet Union apparently does not wish to reduce such exports to EE; in fact, it must deal with pressures exerted on it by all EE countries to continue to increase such exports. The Soviet Union can link the rate of growth of its energy and raw material exports to individual EE countries, in part due to the improvement in the quality of each country's manufactured exports to Russia. Such type of linkage is nothing new of course in the CMEA; since the early 1950s the tendency in bilateral relations to exchange so-called hard goods only against other hard goods of similar value has been practiced by all countries. Until the late 1960s, this rule was operational mainly in trade among the EE countries, however, while the Soviet Union had become a larger and larger net supplier of hard goods to EE.

Eastern European Viewpoint

Let's look at the question from the point of view of the countries of EE.

The more an EE country finds that the amount of energy, raw materials, and possibly even hard currency (HC) it can obtain from the Soviets depends on the quality (hardness) of the manufactures it supplies to Russia, the more it will be in its interest to seek out specialization opportunities in the Soviet Union. It is believed that at least some EE countries today are exploring opportunities to help the Soviet Union to "save" HC and in the process help themselves also. The kinds of opportunities of which they might try to take advantage logically would seem to be of the following types.

1. Replacing or supplementing Soviet imports from the West. Such opportunities might be found principally by the GDR and Czechoslovakia as the two most advanced technological countries. As our earlier examples showed, Poland might also be successful with its good quality mining and construction machinery. Many EE economists believe that significant quantities of machinery currently imported from the West by the CMEA countries could be bought from CMEA sources but for lack of information about possible suppliers and lack of user incentive to seek them out. This is another cost CMEA countries are inadvertently paying for overcentralization of decision making and for insulating the users of the equipment from the producers in other countries.

2. Joining with a Western partner in supplying the Soviet market, either outright or as a partner in Western-Soviet IC projects, i.e.,

a new kind of tripartite industrial cooperation involving a Western MNC, an EE subcontractor, and a Soviet buyer.

3. Joining the Soviet Union as a partner in supplying the Western or hard currency Third World markets with manufactures, again either outright or as subcontractors on large projects. Since the Soviets would earn hard currency, the EE partners could logically also be expected to be paid in HC or its commodity equivalent.

4. Making it possible for the Soviet Union to export machinery, etc., to Western or Third World countries for hard currency by replacing such exports to meet Soviet domestic demand. No practical examples are known, but hypothetically speaking the following scenario may not be unrealistic. A machinery factory located on the Eastern side of the Ural mountains has been shipping its output to domestic users located in the Western part of Russia. The producer has an opportunity to sell its output, for example, to Japan (maybe after a license or co-production agreement is signed with a Japanese firm) for hard currency but would have to satisfy domestic demand as a constraint. Is it not conceivable that if an opportunity were provided for an EE producer to supply the Soviet domestic market and to be paid at least in part in hard currency an EE producer would find this an attractive proposition? It would seem that the more decision independence, the more frequent contacts firms have with their counterparts in the other CMEA countries, and the more financial incentives, the more inclined they would be to explore such opportunities.

However, can any of these options be considered realistic as long as settlements in intrabloc trade are made rigidly and bilaterally in so-called transferable rubles (TR)?

Nonconvertibility of the TR into goods is a key defect of the CMEA financial system. The basic cause lies not in the financial system itself but in the nature of central planning, the CMEA pricing system, and the bilateral trade and settlement constraint which is an inevitable accompaniment of the existing arrangements. Convertibility of the TR into goods within the CMEA would mean that the owner of TR resources may use them on demand to purchase goods from other CMEA countries, but the allocation of goods in the CMEA countries is based on plans and directives, not financial instruments. (26)

CMEA Integration

This is why the question raised on p. 148, after giving Maximova's and Bogomolov's definitions of CMEA integration, is so important, i.e., what is to be the content and criteria for specialization through planning, and what role should "Socialist commodity and money relations" play in bringing about integration?

It seems that the position of those who argue that a road toward CMEA integration—in the sense by which Maximova and Bogomolov define it: "division of labor between national economies, accompanied by the mutual complementing and adjustment of individual enterprise, branches . . ."—must lie in the strengthening of commodity and money relations is logical and convincing.

The use of prices reflecting resource scarcities clarifies the available choices and reduces uncertainly with regard to possible gains and losses from specialization agreements. As was pointed out at the 1974 Budapest meeting of the International Economic Association, one does not have to accept the Western theory of value to agree that it is desirable to know real opportunity costs; i.e., how much of commodity x does a country have to export to be able to import commodity y, from whatever source? Once a country had decided to import a certain product rather than produce domestically, all it needs to know is its quoted prices abroad. For the importer it does not matter how prices in the exporting countries are determined, although it does matter for the exporting countries; quoted prices permit one to calculate which foreign country demands the lowest real sacrifice in exports for a given quantity of imports. (27)

Then, to be able to take advantage of economic opportunities to export and import, it is also essential that enterprises be properly motivated and guided and that the constraint of bilateralism, especially structural bilateralism, be reduced or eliminated. Under the present system of economic organization and management found in most EE countries, the managers of firms are often not very eager to enter into IC with Western partners as long as they can more comfortably supply the less demanding CMEA market. This problem highlights the need for coherent systemic change as Neuberger's comments stressed in this volume:

> (a) some movement toward decentralization in the decision-making structure, (b) improvement in the information structure internally and inter-state, mainly by moving toward prices reflecting resource scarcities, and (c) motivation of enterprises to take advantage of possibilities created by integration; integration increases the set of feasible acts but unless incentives are created under manipulative planning or alternative feasible acts are excluded under administrative planning, the specialization agreements will not be implemented. (28)

Convertible Currency (CC)

The limitations within the CMEA for finding and taking advantage of specialization opportunities are still substantial. These limitations gradually have given rise over the years to a convertible currency (CC) financial subsystem within the CMEA, in which a certain portion of trade is valued at current world market prices and is settled in CCs. My own calculations, based on Hungarian statistics, show that in 1975 about 13% of Hungary's exports to Socialist (CMEA plus other CPE) countries and approximately 7% of its imports from the same group were settled in CCs. (29) Brainard estimates the share of CC trade as percentage of intra-CMEA trade during the mid-1970s at between 5% and 10% in value terms. (30) Although my estimate for Hungary was somewhat higher, apparently there are significant differences among pairs of CMEA countries in the use of CC in mutual trade. (31) To be sure, settling a portion of intrabloc trade in CC is no substitute for multilateralism, as Levcik pointed out in his comments in this volume, as long as such transactions continue to be bilaterally balanced.

The rise of a CC subsystem since about 1970 reflects several things. As the world market prices of certain commodities rose sharply after 1973 while intrabloc prices in the CMEA remained unchanged for a time, it became uneconomical for the suppliers of such goods to sell them to the CMEA countries, but they were obligated to do so under long-term agreements or contracts. Hence, so-called above-quota deliveries would often be made only against CCs and current world market prices were charged. Another factor was the rising share of Western components (inputs, technology, and investment resources) acquired for CC and incorporated in products supplied to other CMEA countries, normally for TR. More and more, countries have sought to receive a certain percentage of the value of such export in CC.

In assessing prospects for CMEA integration with the help of IC with MNCs, the financial aspects are crucial. Given the large CC debts of all CMEA countries, EE countries are less and less able to enter into IC agreements with a Western partner which involves an outflow of CC—which may be a one-shot burden to buy the technology or a continuous burden if component imports are necessary—but do not envisage an inflow of CC, only of TR.

Is there a way of overcoming this obstacle short of proposing that the TR or the national currencies of the CMEA countries become convertible, which most exports would agree is not a realistic possibility for the time being? Perhaps a workable approach, because it has already been introduced, is to settle a growing share of intra-CMEA commerce in hard currency. Brainard's analysis of the CMEA financial mechanism shows that a dual financial structure is already in place and that the CC subsystem plays a positive role in CMEA integration:

> The CC financial subsystem appears to operate with considerable success; possibilities which exist for the two CMEA banks to develop activities in CC are being utilized and some of these activities support progress toward integration. The shortcomings of the TR subsystem stand in sharp contract . . . (and are) a major barrier to CMEA integration. . . . Here we encounter a basic contradiction in the conception of CMEA integration. The goal of multilateral trading and the benefits which would derive from it conflict with the self-interest of each country's policy-makers in preserving the present system of trading the pricing. . . . Without basic changes in pricing and trading, CMEA cooperation will continue to be based essentially on a system of barter, with only limited monetary elements present. Under these conditions, CMEA joint planning and coordination, which is viewed as a key element of the current stage of integration, will be complicated by the difficulties of determining mutual long-term advantage. Thus, there will likely be continued reliance on administrative or scientific-technical rather than economic criteria in CMEA decision making. But the stability and usefulness of long-term cooperation agreements depends on the maintenance of the mutual interest of the parties. This will be difficult to achieve without effective economic calculus and incentives. (32)

Summary

Integration is essentially a dynamic process, whereby countries hope to diminish the obstacles to growth that derive from inefficiency. Whether integration comes through market forces, through planning, or more likely through some combination of market and planning, it must stand the test of competition, failing which inter- and intrabranch specialization decisions will be lagging and investment resources will be misdirected.

Technological developments, or what the Soviet and EE economists often call "the scientific and technological revolution," inexorably make large-scale production economic. This leads to the need to sell not only on the domestic market but also in foreign countries. This imperative has been most effectively recognized and implemented by MNCs, which for a variety of reasons decided, or in some cases were forced, to set up or share production facilities outside their own country. But this requires the coordination of activities and operations in many countries. Well-founded and spurious criticisms of their activities notwithstanding, the MNCs have achieved such coordination to a remarkable degree. Since such transnational coordination is what economists favoring regional integration claim to want, MNC activity can be both a precursor and an important component of regional integration even in the CMEA countries.

The conclusion of this paper is that there is no inherent conflict between a strong MNC presence via IC agreements in the CMEA countries and the process of CMEA integration. The experience up to now is adequate to show that this position has merit, but is quite limited as compared with future possibilities. It seems that the decision regarding the creation and exploitation of opportunities, as well as giving it direction and speed, lies largely in the initiatives the CMEA countries might decide to take.

NOTES

1. An excellent article discussing the status and ramifications of East Europe's CC debt is Richard Portes, "East Europe's Debt to the West: Interdependence is a Two-Way Street," Foreign Affairs, 55, no. 4, (1977).

2. Fritz Machlup, A History of Thought on Economic Integration (New York: Columbia University Press, 1976), p. 14.

3. Bela Balassa, "European Integration; Problems and Issues," American Economic Review, Papers and Proceedings, May 1963.

4. Margarita Maximova, "Comments." In Economic Integration--Worldwide, Regional, Sectoral, Proceedings of the Fourth Congress of the International Economic Association, Budapest, Hungary, 1974, F. Machlup, ed. (London: Macmillan Press, 1976), p. 33.

5. Ibid., p. 35.

6. Oleg T. Bogomolov, "Integration by Market Forces and through Planning," in Machlup, Ed., Economic Integration, p. 310.

7. Ibid., p. 310.

8. Gottfried Haberler and John P. Hardt, "Comments," in ibid., p. 318.

9. Carl H. McMillan, "Some Thoughts on the Relationship Between Regional Integration in Eastern Europe and East-West Economic Relations." In <u>Internationale Wirtschaft: Vergleich und Independenz</u> F. Levcik Ed., (Vienna: Institute of Comparative Economic Studies, 1978).

10. Balassa, "European Integration"; see also Bela Balassa, "Types of Economic Integration," in <u>Economic Integration</u>, Machlup, Ed.

11. For a more detailed discussion of the issues and empirical calculations, see Paul Marer, <u>Postwar Pricing and Price Patterns in Socialist Foreign Trade (1946-71)</u> (Bloomington: International Development Research Center Report no. 1, 1972).

12. Gottfried Haberler, "Theoretical Reflections on the Trade of Socialist Economics." In <u>International Trade and Central Planning</u>, A. Brown and E. Newberger, Eds. (Berkeley: University of California Press, 1968), p. 44.

13. Alan A. Brown, "Towards a Theory of Centrally Planned Foreign Trade," in ibid.

14. F. Levcik and J. Stankovsky, <u>Industrielle Kooperation zwischen Ost und West</u> (Vienna: Springer-Verlag, 1977), p. 115.

15. Richard Lipsey, "Comments," in <u>Economic Integration</u>, Machlup, Ed., p. 38.

16. This section is based largely on the experience of American corporations, and makes use of findings of a survey of American firms, conducted in behalf of the United States Department of Commerce, which the author coordinated. The permission of the Bureau of East-West Trade of the United States Department of Commerce to publish the findings is gratefully acknowledged. For a statistical picture of American participation in East-West IC agreements, see Paul Marer and Joseph C. Miller, "U.S. Participation in East-West Industrial Cooperation Agreements," <u>Journal of International Business Studies</u> (Fall-Winter, 1977).

17. Carl H. McMillan, "East-West Industrial Cooperation," In East European Economies Post Helsinki: A Compendium of Papers Submitted to the Joint Economic Committee, U.S. Congress (Washington, D.C.: U.S. Government Printing Office, August 25, 1977); pp. 1177-78.

18. Peter Veress, "Opening Statement for Group Discussion," in Economic Integration, Machlup, Ed., p. 159.

19. Kalman Pecsi, A KGST termelesi integracio Kozgazdasagi Kerdesei (Economic Issues of CMEA Production Integration) (Budapest: K & J Publishers, 1977), p. 345.

20. Some years ago the Soviet Union proposed the establishment of a central CMEA office to coordinate the purchase of Western licenses in order to avoid duplication, but apparently the practice in this field is limited to voluntary purchase consultations. The CMEA's Committee on Scientific Technological Cooperation is informed that a license has been purchased, but the Committee exerts little influence on the decisions by individual countries regarding license acquisition.

21. Balassa, "Types of Economic Integration," in Economic Integration, Machlup, Ed., p. 26.

22. Pecsi, A KGST termelesi, p. 113.

23. McMillan reports that there have been instances of EE countries vying to acquire Western technology to obtain official designation as the supplier of a commodity under a CMEA specialization agreement. See McMillan, "Some Thoughts on the Relationship."

24. Based on Pecsi, A KGST termelesi, passim.

25. Pecsi, A KGST termelesi, p. 340.

26. Lawrence J. Brainard, "The CMEA Financial System and Integration." In East European Integration and East-West Trade. P. Marer and J.M. Montias, Eds., forthcoming.

27. Lipsey, in Economic Integration, Machlup, Ed., p. 40.

28. For a pioneering discussion of an approach to analyzing economic systems which takes all three aspects simultaneously into account,

see Egon Neuberger and William J. Duffy, Comparative Economic Systems: A Decision-Making Approach (Boston: Allyn and Bacon, 1976).

29. Paul Marer, "Economic Performance, Strategy, and Prospects in Eastern Europe," in East European Economics Post Helsinki, p. 566.

30. Brainard, "The CMEA Financial System."

31. Although in 1975 about 20% of Hungarian-Romanian trade was settled in CC, the corresponding shares in Hungarian-Czechoslovak trade were insignificant. The share of CCs in Hungary's trade with the Soviet Union, Poland, and the GDR was in between. See Brainard, ibid.

32. Brainard, "The CMEA Financial System."

11 Comments
Egon Neuberger,
Sylvain P. Wickham,
and Angela M. Conning

The three previous papers by Winter, Lauter, and Marer present an interesting combination of issues and important contrasts. They are at three levels of aggregation: Winter discusses the nuts and bolts of negotiation; Lauter presents an analysis of different organizational structures; and Marer identifies the role of multinational corporations (MNCs) in CMEA integration. Each paper asks an important question or presents an interesting hypothesis: Winter believes that the multinationals make the best partners for CMEA countries; Lauter holds that the degree of differentiation and integration are determined by the complexity of the environment; and Marer asks if East-West trade and CMEA integration are substitutes or complements.

THE MULTINATIONALS

In connection with Winter's paper, it is argued that Eastern Europe (EE) is primarily interested in dealing with the world leader in technology, and secondarily with the largest companies; thus, I would make Winter's exception the major point. Since multinationals are generally also technological leaders, they combine both desiderata. However, as Winter points out, when they are not on the technological frontiers, then a smaller company can carve a niche for itself in the EE markets.

This argument has dealt with the demand by EE for the multinationals' trade. There is also a supply side, i.e., the multinationals' ability and willingness to trade with EE. Their size and financial resources give them an advantage in the more complex, longer lasting, and often larger trade deals in EE.

ORGANIZATIONAL THEORY AND THE ECONOMIC APPROACH

The Winter paper does not lend itself to analysis by means of my DIM (decision-making, information, motivation approach), but the Lauter and Marer papers are appropriate subjects. Lauter's paper is in the spirit or organizational theory and, therefore, provides a very good analysis of the decision making structure, touches upon the information structure, and basically ignores the motivation structure. Marer's paper is the economic approach and is somewhat more balanced in dealing with all three aspects.

Lauter's major conceptual tools are differentiation and integration. Differentiation deals with the issue of decentralization in the decision making structure and the type of decentralization that is most appropriate. Since complete centralization of decision making is impossible due to problems in the information and motivation structures, multinationals must decentralize in some manner. Lauter deals mainly with the problem of selecting the criterion for partitioning the decision making structure according to regional, functional, or commodity lines, and the advantages and disadvantages of each approach; this is done very well. Lauter pays less attention to the question of whether the decentralization should be administrative (corporate headquarters limit the feasible acts faced by lower echelons) or manipulative (they structure incentives in such a way as to make lower level executives act in accordance with their wishes).

Integration deals with the mechanisms for achieving coordination of decisions by organizing the decision making process. However, a crucial factor in coordination is the content, type, and direction of information flows, i.e., the essential features of the information structure. Lauter deals with this only when mentioning profit centers and transfer prices.

Marer and Lauter agree that most MNCs have no coherent strategy for dealing with CMEA and provide some cogent reasons for this, particularly the small size of the EE market for most of these firms. Since EE is more important to West European based MNCs than American based ones, it is not surprising that some West European firms have developed specific strategies. This was particularly true of six chemical and pharmaceutical firms that set up an EE Business Committee as an integrating coordination device.

Lauter's analysis of differences between American and Western European MNCs, among MNCs in different industries, and the need for centralized coordination within an MNC faced with EE demands for counter trade were particularly enlightening.

WHIPSAWING

Whipsawing is an interesting issue; as I wrote in a study done for the National Planning Association:

> Because the Ministry of Foreign Trade is the sole buyer for the total Soviet market, it can create competition among different sellers and engage in "whipsawing," that is playing off one seller against the other in order to force down the price. For example, when the Soviet Union requested bids from various Western companies on an air traffic control system, the officials of the Ministry of Foreign Trade informed each of the bidders of the bids received from others, thereby encouraging them to offer a lower bid. Reportedly, IBM was told that it should reduce its bid to the $80 million range if it wanted to compete; at the same time, Raytheon was told that it was not competitive with the French. On the other hand, the chairman of the East-West Trade Advisory Committee of the Department of Commerce indicated that in the five years his company had conducted business in Eastern Europe, it had never experienced whipsawing. (1)

EE COLLABORATION WITH MNCS

I found Marer's analysis very stimulating and his thesis that EE collaboration with MNC's can be complementary, as well as substitutable for CMEA integration, very enlightening.

Marer's discussion of the role that planning and "Socialist commodity and money relations" play in CMEA integration highlights the need for coherent systemic change: a) some movement toward decentralization in the decision making structure; b) improvement in the information structure internally and interstate, mainly by moving toward prices reflecting resource scarcities; and c) motivation of enterprises to take advantage of possibilities created by integration. Integration increases the set of feasible acts, but unless incentives are created under manipulative planning or alternative feasible acts are excluded under administrative planning, the specialization agreements will not be implemented.

Movement of goods and factors across international borders are key aspects of integration. The efficacy of implicit versus explicit barriers and supports to such movements should be discussed. Also the use of administrative versus manipulative mechanisms as barriers or supports. Marer's argument on the quality of output is a necessary condition for successful integration, but not a sufficient condition. Integration also requires the willingness of partner countries to abandon the protection of the industries producing these commodities.

I agree with Marer's stress on the fact that integration means a change in the commodity and geographical composition of trade, and not necessarily on changes in the volume of trade, although there generally is an increase in the volume when countries integrate their economies. Industrial cooperation should be viewed in the same light as integration for these purposes. Marer's discussion of trade creation and diversion as static concepts, and of the fact that changing income elasticities can mask them, was enlightening.

The attempt to use convertible currency trade to improve the informational and motivational aspects of intra-CMEA trade is a fascinating subject that could use more analysis. Finally, I agree with Marer's emphasis on the impact of increased quality demands within EE on East-West trade and industrial cooperation, but I would have liked to see more analysis of the impact of systemic reforms on these important international issues.

Egon Neuberger

My comments on the papers by Lauter and Marer will be organized according to subject. (2)

EAST-WEST BARGAINING VERSUS INTRA-WEST MARKETING

Large Western firms, particularly in the United States, appear to suffer from inertia when faced with East-West trading patterns, according to P. Lauter. I would like to suggest an interpretation which is more favorable to American management, based on the contrast between the prolonged bargaining characteristics of large East-West contracts and the marketing approach first developed inside the United States and formalized for the rest of the world by prominent American business school experts after the war.

The marketing approach, as received on the other side of the Atlantic, along with other American contributions, systematizes selling as a veritable "Discourse on Commercial Method" and results in three axioms.

1. A carefully elaborated range of strictly standardized products, with the exclusion of any selling to order: The marketing system encourages a nominal respect for the client in that individual bargaining with any client is ruled out.

2. Centralized and peremptory decisions on sales offers and prices on the part of the director of marketing: A minimal margin of freedom and negotiation is left to salesmen, commercial intermediaries, and merchants, all of whom are considered highly untrustworthy. Hence retail prices are imposed by the manufacturer.

In France, the postwar generation of marketing managers, who were trained in American methods, had nothing but contempt for old-fashioned bargaining over prices in the marketplace.

3. Low pressure selling: If the potential client, attracted on contact with the sales network by the publicity barrage, does not immediately declare his intention to purchase, there is no need to insist; he will not go far. If your marketing organization is good, you will catch him at the next corner, at your own terms, without any concessions as to price, which after all may increase distribution costs.

The more extreme a large Western firm has been in strictly applying the logic of marketing, as are American companies, the more the prolonged bilateral bargaining involved in East-West contracts appears commercially regressive. They see it as bureaucratic and diplomatic guerilla warfare, which it is difficult to reconcile with the practices of a large standardized organization.

In France, we are now coming to the conclusion that in the search for Eastern markets we must often employ specialized technical and commercial intermediaries who are familiar with Eastern bureaucracies, or international firms of consulting engineers, whose members will forget the Western and American adage that "time is money" and will be willing to patrol, on seemingly endless missions, the large hotels of Moscow or Warsaw and the antechambers of outlying head offices. Training in journalism, economics, diplomacy, or the military is probably more of an asset in achieving commercial success in the East than training in marketing, which has now become classical, on both sides of the Atlantic and which is adapted only to Western business dealings.

As illustrated in East-West relations, the marketing approach, despite all its proven merits, does not exhaust the range of appropriate commercial activity when confronted by different social systems.

THE ROLE OF WESTERN INDUSTRIALISTS IN CMEA INTEGRATION

Paul Marer provides information which is essentially insights into the unique nature of the process of Eastern integration and also our influence on this process, that is paradoxically considerable and generally underestimated.

CMEA integration remains based on and restricted by the bilateralism which proceeds from the very principles of "Command Economy," as analyzed by Peter Wiles. This bilateralism applies to relations between partners in the Eastern bloc almost as strictly as it does to their relations with us. In Western thought, any standard definition of economic integration involves a reference, whether explicit or not, to multilateralization, an idea which is only just beginning to appear on the horizon in the East. A particular reason for this is the refusal, generally attributed to the Soviets, to let the transferable ruble become a convertible currency, even to a limited extent, between partners.

Thus, CMEA integration must be carried out under such constricting and technically difficult conditions that an opening up towards the West, despite the obvious gulf between different social systems, has in recent years tempted every state in the East as an easy way out of the occasional bottleneck in national development.

Thus, also, while the transferable ruble remains the generally accepted unit of account between CMEA partners, convertible Western currencies have progressively developed into the obligatory means of payment between CMEA partners for the sale of hard commodities (those which are immediately exportable to the West). Even the Soviet Union has accepted this on several occasions, e.g., for exceptional purchases of Hungarian foodstuffs. Should the Soviets continue to reject convertibility for the transferable ruble, e.g., pointing out the past difficulties for internal British development by transferable sterling accounts, the American dollar might well become before 1990 the principal means of payment between Eastern partners, as it was in 1950 between Western European trading partners.

The intensification of intra-CMEA relations, periodically announced, and which became suddenly quite obvious in 1977 for the first time in years, is in part involuntary and stems especially from the numerous barriers recently affecting the ongoing development of East-West industrial cooperation in France. Although the smaller countries of Eastern Europe make the most adaptable partners, if the whole of their outside market must be found in the West, they can be disappointed. This is particularly due to the unexpected competition from new Third World industrialists, who have recently appeared to many French firms as more interesting, more expeditious, and less costly than Eastern partners. This has led to the idea put forward by international organizations in Geneva of so-called tripartite cooperation, that is East-West cooperation turning toward the South.

This idea is politically attractive and was well received in France, but it has proved very disappointing in practice, since the Third World countries have no confidence in the East's ability to deliver and demand that Western partners be exclusively responsible for the whole of the operation, even if they have to subcontract in the East at their own risk. On the other hand, the possibility suggested by Paul Marer, i.e., cooperation between West and Eastern European partners turning toward the Soviet Union with guarantees as to the profitability of the operation in currency and with a minimal triangular pattern, seems to be a way to remove many of the present barriers, if the two CMEA partners concerned agree to it, something which will not always be easy to achieve. This type of arrangement resembles certain trade negotiations presently being carried on by French industrialists in the area of Hungarian and Bulgarian agricultural products.

            Sylvain P. Wickham

My remarks naturally will relate mainly to the experience of British industry and to CBI members, but I think many of the points will be familiar to other Western organizations as well.

The serious papers by Marer, Lauter, Winter, and Baumer and Jacobsen describe in some detail the international institutional framework against which we set East-West relations. The various intergovernmental joint commissions have also been mentioned, and as someone who has had direct experience at such meetings, I would like to emphasize that these meetings and bilateral discussions can only create the framework within which individual companies are able to pursue their contacts. The expansion of East-West trade depends on the individual companies both from the West and from Eastern Europe, and certainly in the United Kingdom it is up to the company itself to decide whether a project for economic, trade, or industrial links with Eastern Europe is advantageous or not. The Confederation of British Industry (CBI), as with similar organizations on the private enterprise side, has close links with individual organizations in Eastern European chambers of commerce, industrial ministries, and with industry itself. Protocols have been signed, specialist delegations exchanged, training programs agreed, and so on. Such contacts are maintained to strengthen our links, not only with the representatives of government but also industrial enterprises. Our members find such links particularly useful in helping to establish contact with the end users.

I would now like to consider three topics which have only been touched upon in the papers: industrial cooperation, compensation trading, and cooperation in third markets. These three concepts are critical to any undertaking of East-West trade today, and any expansion of East-West trade will depend very much on the development in these three areas.

INDUSTRIAL COOPERATION

It may be helpful to identify exactly what is meant by industrial cooperation. It is an easy phrase which trips off the tongue lightly but can mean different things to different people not only between East and West but also to individual United Kingdom companies. Its purpose is more easy to identify, i.e., to promote long-term relationships between Western companies and East European industry.

East European industry, having now reached world standards in so many fields, wishes to fulfill their development plans by their own contributions of equipment, know-how, and labor. If for technological reasons, to save time, or to overcome a temporary shortage a Western company is asked to assist, Eastern European industry still wishes to contribute as much as possible. The hard currency cost of any project is thereby reduced. To succeed, industrial cooperation must be of mutual benefit to both countries and to all partners. Such cooperation may take several forms: subcontracting whereby components are incorporated in a joint product; co-production where certain items in a product line are made by both partners and then usually jointly marketed; payment by end product of the equipment supplied, i.e., when the Western partner supplies equipment and receives payment in the product of that plant or equipment; joint marketing; joint research and development; and joint ventures which are now possible with some of the Eastern European countries. Under these types are, of course, many variations, but undoubtedly there will be increasing pressure by Eastern European industry to cooperate with Western companies rather than buy from them in the years ahead.

The implication of this may be far more widespread for industry in the West than is appreciated today. For example, end product payment in the chemical industry may lead to an increase in supply of particular chemicals from Eastern Europe which could seriously affect both capacity and price in the Western world. There is also increasing pressure, so far resisted by the Western European countries, for any products coming to the West under industrial cooperation agreements to be exempted from any restrictions (e.g., quotas) or to receive more favorable tariff rates. In the EEC at present, on some aspects of this problem members react differently, and some member countries treat such matters on a bilateral basis.

COMPENSATION TRADING

Today an obligation for compensation trading enters into an increasing proportion of contracts. Under this the supplier of plant or equipment has to guarantee that he will purchase a fixed percentage of the price of the original contract in goods from the Eastern European country. The proportion can vary from relatively small cost (5-10%) to the entire cost of the project (100%). Such stipulations pose great problems for Western suppliers. There are many products or raw materials which Western companies would be only too pleased to buy from the Soviet Union or Eastern Europe. Regrettably, these are seldom offered. instead a rather rigid approach demands that products from the same enterprise or foreign trading cooperation are purchased. Although the West appreciates that the foreign trading organization which purchases from the West wishes to receive the credit, not to mention the hard currency from a sale to the West, it makes the purchase extremely difficult, and a more flexible approach whereby goods from a number of Foreign Trading Corporations could be offered would be helpful.

Other goods offered are not competitive price wise; the difference may be as much as 40%. No Western company in any country can afford to buy components or equipment at such inflated prices. Lack of capacity too is a problem. Given the long-term planning arrangements in Eastern Europe, production is usually committed for many months if not years ahead. To meet compensation trading commitments, extra capacity has to be found, which is not always possible particularly as such production outside plans already commands hard currency payments within CMEA.

Continuity of supply is another hurdle. Repeat orders appear to be impossible to guarantee. Delivery dates sometimes are not met, and quality control is hard to establish. I have heard it said that compensation trading is a scheme for unloading second rate products on Western markets. Certainly there is a tendency for Eastern European goods that are competitive both technically and commercially in the Western market not to be involved in such a transaction. We appreciate that the development of East-West trade depends on the ability of the Eastern European to sell more in Western markets, and in recent years the cards have certainly been against them due to Western recession; increased prices for fuel and raw materials, which divert potential hard currency exports to other areas; and so on. But when it is asked why British industry does not do better in Eastern European Markets, it is said that British industry should be more aggressive, more competitive, particularly price wise, with better delivery terms etc. Surely some of these remarks have a wider application, and the countries of Eastern Europe will have to learn better marketing techniques to increase their exports and reduce their reliance on Western partners to do their marketing for them.

COOPERATION IN THIRD MARKETS

Finally I would like to consider cooperation in Third World markets. Undoubtedly, Eastern European companies have better access in some of the markets of the world and are able to assist not only British industry but also Western industry in these countries. Eastern European costs are sometimes lower and transportation costs reduced. Often they have a large labor force there, e.g., the 2,000 Romanians in Libya, which can be of great use to Western countries undertaking projects there, because Westerners may find it difficult to convince their labor force of the advantages of "dry states." Sometimes Eastern European industry is not able to offer all the technology required by the Third World customer: some purchasers, in fact, appear to request Western participation in such projects.

In theory the potential for such cooperation seems unending. In practice it develops slowly. Finance, credit and management all present considerable problems. New firms, however, can be brought into East-West Trade in this area, which is a vital consideration if East-West trade and East-West economic relations are to develop further.

Angela M. Conning

NOTES

1. Egon Neuberger and Juan Lara, The Foreign Trade Practices of Centrally Planned Economies and Their Impact on U.S. International Competitiveness (Washington, D.C.: National Planning Association, 1977), pp. 10, 11

2. Translated from French by Sinclair Robinson, Carleton University, Department of French.

III

The Choice of Partners: The Experiences of Some Selected Countries

Introduction

After examining in the preceding sections various aspects of the changing context in which the choice of partners in East-West relations occurs, we turn in the remaining chapters to an analysis of the determinants of choice. Chapters included in this part examine the factors, political as well as economic, influencing the trade-partner composition of selected Socialist countries. A pioneering work on the Soviet Union, applying rigorous theoretical and empirical analysis is presented by a British economist. The experience of Hungary and Czechoslovakia is discussed by prominent economists from those countries. Another British economist offers some comments on several small, and less well known centrally planned Socialist economies: Albania, Mongolia, North Korea, and Vietnam. The commentary in the final chapter contains a detailed discussion of the paper dealing with the Soviet Union and its methodology by an American economist; some observations on the Hungarian case by a French economist; and brief comments by an Austrian economist on all three chapters, but with special attention to the case of Czechoslovakia.

12 The Trade-Partner Composition of Soviet Trade with the West*
Philip Hanson

INTRODUCTION

The comparative performance of different Western countries as exporters to the Soviet Union and Eastern Europe is a subject on which one hears a variety of interesting observations from businessmen and officials. However, there is only one systematic study of the subject printed in English. (1) This paper is a first attempt at such a study for Soviet imports from the West. It is confined to the conventional "major 14" OECD countries, (2) to their exports to the Soviet Union, to the period 1960-76, and to sales of machinery and transport equipment (Standard International Trade Classification (SITC) section 7) only.

The focus is on country shares in the total of these 14 countries' SITC 7 exports to the Soviet Union. Two kinds of analyses are attempted: first, the formulation and statistical testing of some hypotheses about factors affecting all 14 countries' shares in a given period of time (a cross section analysis); second, a more historical examina-

---

* The author is indebted to Morris Bornstein, John Hardt, Madoo Kanbur, Allen Lenz, Paul Marer, and Peter Wiles for comments and suggestions made in earlier, informal discussions of this topic. Hedija Kravalis and Allen Lenz of the United States Department of Commerce very kindly provided a computer printout of 1971-76 market shares data at the four and five digit levels for subgroups of SITC section 7. It has been possible in this revised version to take into account only a few of the very helpful, constructive criticisms made at Montebello by Tom Wolf (see "Comments" by Wolf in Chapter 16).

tion of changes over time in the shares of two countries (the United Kingdom and the Federal Republic of Germany).

Throughout, political as well as economic factors that might affect a country's performance have been considered. This does not mean that the impossible task of separating "political" from "economic" influences and measuring their separate impacts has been attempted. It means simply that certain possible influences with a substantial political content, such as the CoCom embargo and the general state of bilateral relations between two countries are brought into the analysis. Such factors affect both Eastern and Western actions in East-West commerce. In other words, the Soviet Union's choice among Western trade-partners and the Western countries' readiness to be chosen will be discussed.

On both sides there will be economic considerations: on the one hand, the pursuit by Soviet Gosplan and Ministry of Foreign Trade (MFT) officials of the most cost effective means of national plan fulfillment and the pursuit by Foreign Trade Organization (FTO) officials of their own (bonus-determined?) objectives; on the other hand, export promotion by Western governments on balance of payments and employment grounds and the pursuit of profits by Western firms. On both sides the pursuit of these goals may be constrained by deliberate acts of government policy intended to achieve diplomatic or strategic objectives. Equally, the pursuit of these economic aims may be affected in a far less conscious manner by a variety of background influences, such as traditional trading practices, cultural affinities, ideologically colored perceptions of trade-partner countries, and the like.

The aim of this paper is to assess in a quantitative way the importance of at least some of these influences. A comparison of the 14 OECD countries' market shares in the Soviet Union with their shares in other trade provides a convenient starting point. There is some similarity of approach, therefore, with other studies of East-West trade focusing on market shares; these have been mainly concerned, however, with the very different problem of estimating the effects of American extension of MFN tariff treatment to exports from those CMEA countries which do not have American MFN status. (3)

Focusing on sales of machinery and transport equipment has two advantages. First, it reduces the variety of Western exports under consideration to a section of the Standard International Trade Classification, in which all the 14 selected OECD countries have significant volumes of exports and in which differences in natural resource endowments are not a major source of variation that has to be allowed for in comparing performance. Second, problems of allowing for time lags are reduced. Most deliveries of machinery and transport equipment follow the signing of the relevant contracts at least by several months, often by a year, and sometimes by well over a year. A CIA series of reported machinery orders placed in the West in 1972-76 suggests an average time lag of about a year. (4) No doubt, there is a wide dispersion about this average, but the average time lag is certainly longer and the dispersion about the average is probably relatively smaller than for total trade. It should be somewhat easier, therefore, to trace the effects of specific events on a time series of SITC 7 exports than on a time series of total exports.

INFLUENCES ON MARKET SHARES

In any one period the share taken by a particular Western nation in Soviet purchases of Western machinery might be expected to be influenced by the following factors.
 1. The general competitiveness of that country's suppliers.
 2. Soviet import priority fit, i.e., the extent to which the Western country's suppliers specialize in the particular kinds of machinery which may be thought of as being on the Soviet hard currency shopping list. (5)
 3. Distance, which affects both transport and transactions costs.
 4. The extent to which potential suppliers are affected by the Western strategic embargo.
 5. The availability and if it is available, the terms of official credit support by the government of the exporting country.
 6. Political affinity, i.e., the prevailing climate of opinion in the exporting country about East-West contacts and the presence or absence in the exporting country of major political groups or social movements which Soviet policy makers might wish to encourage.
 7. The current state of bilateral intergovernmental relations.

None of these factors is easily identified and measured, and some can be represented quantitatively only by a proxy measure. The choice of measures used here has been determined in part by data availability and by limitations on the time available for data processing; it could certainly be improved. The choice of operational definitions and measures needs, in any case, to be explained.

General Competitiveness

The 14 OECD countries' total annual SITC 7 exports provide the starting point. For 1960-75 these are divided into sales to the Soviet Union and sales to the rest of the world (RW), and each country's percentage share in each of these totals is calculated (Soviet share and RW share, for short). The annual Soviet and RW shares data are given in Table 12.1. The Soviet share is the dependent variable to be explained, and the RW share is used as a measure of the independent variable, "general competitiveness." This, of course, reflects economic as well as price and product competitiveness. In running cross section regressions for average 1960-70 and average 1971-75 data, RW shares adjusted to exclude Canadian SITC 7 exports to the United States have been used. These adjusted shares are illustrated in Figures 12.1 and and 12.2. (6)

Soviet Import-Priority Fit

If one particular OECD country is a major shipbuilding nation, in the sense that exports of ships account for a substantial proportion of its total SITC 7 exports, while another OECD country is not, these countries' Soviet shares may be influenced by the extent to which Russia is ordering vessels from Western yards. This import-priority-fit aspect of competitiveness will not be captured by the RW share.

To allow for this one needs to compare the commodity composition of total Soviet SITC 7 imports from the 14 OECD countries with that of each of these countries' total SITC 7 sales worldwide. This needs to be done at least at the four digit level, since it is apparent from studies of so-called "intraindustry" trade that a great deal of the national specialization that develops in Western international trade in manufactures is in subgroups of the three digit commodity groups. Comparison at the five digit level would be better still.

All that has been attempted here is a trial calculation for one year, an exercise rendered a great deal less laborious than it would otherwise have been by the very considerable assistance of the United States Department of Commerce computer printout referred to in the acknowledgements. What has been done, for the year 1976 only, is a calculation of what each country's share of the Soviet market would have been if total OECD-14 SITC 7 exports to Russia in each four digit subgroup had been divided among the 14 countries in the same proportions as their total sales of each four digit subgroup to the world as a whole, i.e., where subscript i denotes the i th country and j the j th 4-digit product sub-group, X denotes exports to the world and XS exports to the USSR (of SITC 7 goods),

$$\sum_j \frac{X_{ij}}{\sum_i X_{ij}} XS_j / \sum_j SX_j$$

TABLE 12.1 - Shares in 14 Countries' SITC Exports to the Soviet Union and the Rest of the World, 1960-75 (Percentage)

	United States		Canada		Japan	
	To USSR (a)	To Rest of World (b)	To USSR (a)	To Rest of World (b)	To USSR (a)	To Rest of World (b)
1960	6.15	30.23	.01	1.86	5.63	3.97
1961	4.35	28.46	.08	1.98	6.63	4.27
1962	0.90	29.00	.35	2.11	18.49	4.1
1963	0.29	27.16	.02	2.14	19.30	4.7
1964	1.00	27.56	.25	2.79	23.63	5.4
1965	1.39	26.27	1.75	3.10	16.37	6.7
1966	1.04	25.71	.05	4.44	22.33	7.4
1967	2.50	26.42	.04	5.95	10.70	7.9
1968	2.35	26.19	.11	7.00	7.25	8.84
1969	4.68	25.10	.30	7.39	7.84	9.36
1970	4.94	23.48	.15	7.07	11.40	10.17
1971	7.50	21.97	.44	6.87	13.95	11.86
1972	5.53	20.46	.74	6.62	17.46	12.89
1973	13.02	20.30	.18	5.80	10.69	13.17
1974	10.76	22.31	.16	5.11	11.03	14.72
1975	13.20	22.64	.79	4.73	13.46	13.47
	a<b	16	a<b	16	a<b	5
	a>b	0	a>b	0	a>b	11

	Federal Republic of Germany		France		Italy		United Kingdom	
	To USSR (a)	To Rest of World (b)	To USSR (a)	To Rest of World (b)	To USSR (a)	To Rest of World (b)	To USSR (a)	To Rest of World (b)
1960	26.64	21.22	18.23	7.14	5.60	4.35	18.00	18.35
1961	29.79	22.23	14.86	6.81	7.56	4.89	19.72	17.68
1962	15.53	21.95	16.18	6.90	7.62	5.07	13.09	16.65
1963	20.35	22.38	6.85	7.08	12.32	5.08	15.57	16.60
1964	26.30	21.83	6.53	6.70	7.84	5.34	8.85	14.95
1965	21.72	21.49	7.35	6.86	8.63	5.63	13.74	14.46
1966	20.84	21.24	8.03	6.85	7.72	5.86	18.91	13.89
1967	18.09	20.40	17.15	6.78	10.91	6.10	16.64	12.07
1968	18.12	20.37	23.82	6.48	11.24	6.23	20.20	11.03
1969	22.50	20.24	16.20	6.84	19.57	6.03	12.67	10.72
1970	18.12	20.71	15.66	7.53	19.20	6.18	11.19	10.29
1971	20.11	20.76	16.46	7.66	16.64	5.93	9.98	10.57
1972	32.70	21.02	10.44	8.07	11.39	6.20	8.50	9.52
1973	36.65	22.71	10.68	8.27	9.84	5.55	6.60	8.52
1974	36.28	21.87	13.85	7.25	8.23	5.61	3.29	8.31
1975	32.57	20.30	13.85	8.34	9.41	5.93	5.07	9.06
	a<b	7	a<b	2	a<b	0	a<b	10
	a>b	9	a>b	14	a>b	16	a>b	6

(Continued)

Table 12.1 (continued)

	BLEU		Netherlands		Denmark		Norway	
	To USSR (a)	To Rest of World (b)	To USSR (a)	To Rest of World (b)	To USSR (a)	To Rest of World (b)	To USSR (a)	To rest of World (b)
1960	.68	2.12	1.72	3.26	4.21	.74	.01	.38
1961	1.89	2.32	1.84	3.13	.57	1.14	.18	.45
1962	1.80	2.54	3.37	3.19	4.73	1.12	.14	.43
1963	.43	2.78	1.48	3.45	6.98	1.22	.14	.50
1964	1.41	3.05	.29	3.95	3.52	1.21	.06	.55
1965	1.28	3.36	4.95	3.50	5.46	1.23	.08	.64
1966	.33	3.07	2.58	3.33	5.01	1.16	.08	.60
1967	.70	2.87	7.56	3.05	3.29	1.17	.11	.81
1968	.45	2.85	2.40	2.99	2.58	1.07	.33	.82
1969	1.16	3.13	2.05	3.10	1.70	1.16	.06	.81
1970	.97	3.24	.45	3.03	2.32	1.13	.14	.75
1971	.61	3.11	1.01	3.10	2.04	1.06	.14	.67
1972	.46	3.55	.61	3.30	1.58	1.08	.27	.90
1973	.73	3.50	.72	3.26	1.28	1.19	.19	1.07
1974	1.06	3.06	2.52	2.81	.95	1.24	.30	1.08
1975	1.04	3.29	1.54	2.90	.18	1.27	.49	1.16
	a<b	16	a<b	13	a<b	3	a<b	16
	a>b	0	a>b	3	a>b	13	a>b	0

	Sweden		Switzerland		Austria	
	To USSR (a)	To Rest of World (b)	To USSR (a)	To Rest of World (b)	To USSR (a)	To Rest of World (b)
1960	4.92	3.30	2.85	2.36	5.37	.72
1961	5.38	3.41	2.07	2.47	5.10	.76
1962	11.65	3.56	1.43	2.49	4.73	.82
1963	5.72	3.67	2.65	2.43	7.89	.78
1964	12.88	3.51	1.62	2.32	5.81	.79
1965	7.19	3.58	3.01	2.32	7.08	.79
1966	3.70	3.46	3.85	2.24	5.54	.73
1967	5.12	3.47	3.57	2.19	3.61	.77
1968	4.12	3.24	2.93	2.17	4.10	.73
1969	5.88	3.17	2.63	2.16	2.77	.79
1970	7.79	3.46	4.14	2.09	3.51	.86
1971	3.98	3.52	4.17	2.07	2.97	.86
1972	2.47	3.44	4.35	2.01	3.49	.93
1973	2.73	3.58	4.56	2.20	2.11	.90
1974	3.99	3.52	3.97	2.14	3.62	.98
1975	3.21	3.69	3.00	2.24	2.19	1.03
	a<b	3	a<b	3	a<b	0
	a>b	13	a>b	13	a>b	16

Source: OECD, *Statistics of Foreign Trade*, Series B and C, (Paris: OECD) except data for Japan, 1960-63 from Japan External Trade Organization, *Foreign Trade of Japan 1963*, Tokyo: 1963.

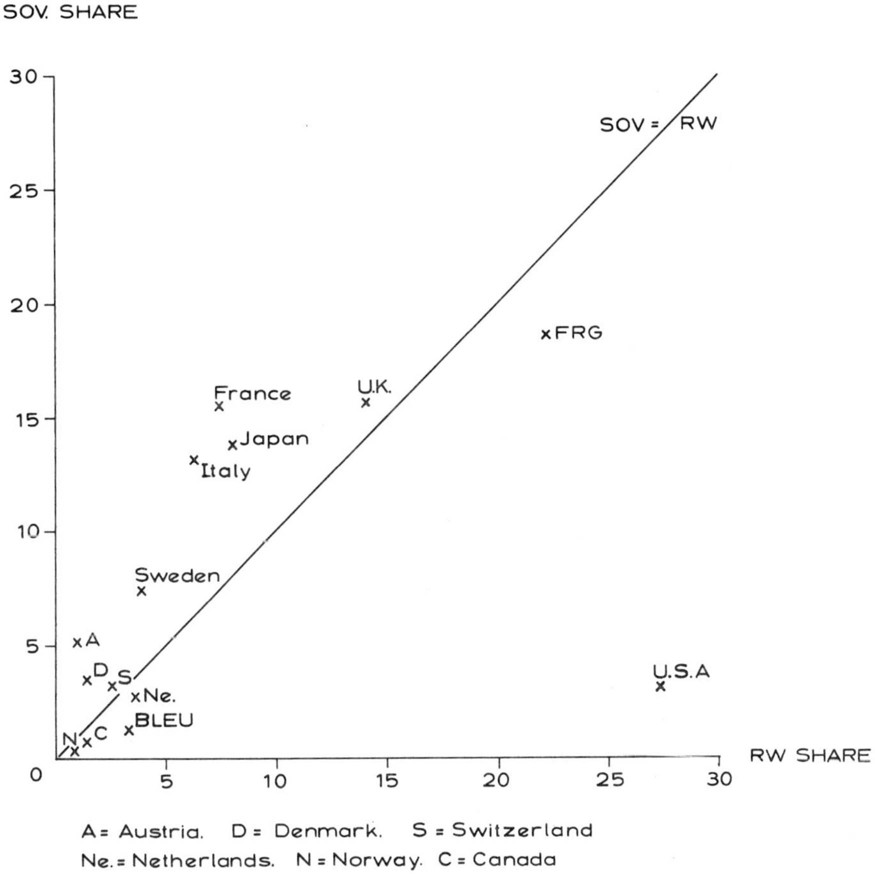

Fig. 12.1. 14 OECD countries' percentage shares in the total SITC 7 exports to the Soviet Union (SOV) and to the rest of World (RW), 1960-1970.

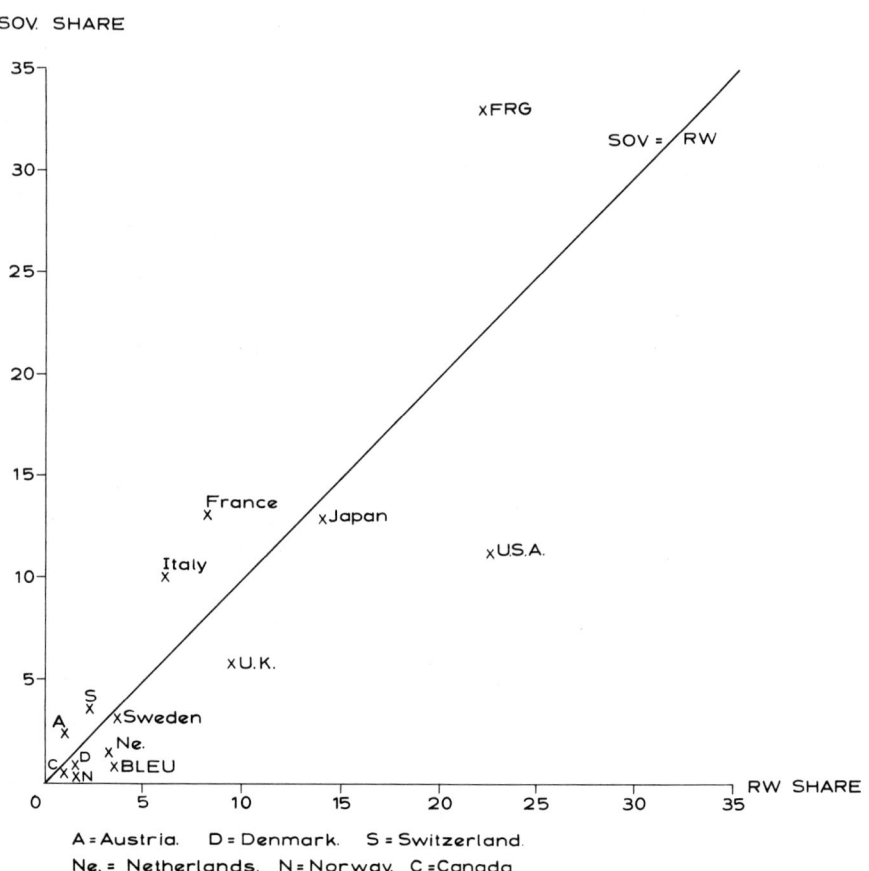

Fig. 12.2. 14 OECD countries' percentage shares in their total SITC 7 exports to the Soviet Union (SOV) and to the rest of World (RW), 1971-1975.

SOVIET TRADE WITH THE WEST

This yields what may be called "standardized Soviet shares" (see Table 12.2). These reflect, in principle at least, both general competitiveness and Soviet import priority fit. Their divergence from actual Soviet shares should reflect the influence of factors other than these two. Their divergence from the RW shares should show the importance of Soviet import priority fit. How far the standardized Soviet shares (Table 12.2) fall short of capturing the full distinctiveness of the Soviet shopping list is unknown; certainly the range of functions and specifications of machinery even within a five digit SITC category can be considerable.

Even this incomplete allowance for Soviet import priority fit makes a considerable difference, as Table 12.2 shows. That there can be a substantial difference between a country's actual world share and its standardized Soviet share is hardly surprising, though, this sum relevant magnitudes are considered. In 1976 the Soviet market accounted for only 1.8% of total 14 OECD exports of machinery and transport equipment: $4.3 out of $233.7 billion. Even at the two digit level, there was a big difference in the composition of Soviet and world sales. Non electric machinery (SITC 71) made up 76% of sales to Russia and not quite 40% of sales worldwide. The Soviet market, therefore, accounted for 3.5% of the 14 OECD sales of non electric machinery.

Distance

In the present context, the influence of distance is a more problematic consideration that it might at first appear. First, machinery has a higher value-to-weight ratio than most other traded items and a correspondingly low proportion of transport costs in c.i.f. value at the importer's border. For example, Marer cites transport cost percentages of around 0.3 for Hungarian machinery imports from all sources in 1976-75. (7) Second, the buying of most kinds of machinery is characterized by very great attention to product specification, reliability, after sales servicing, and so on, with fine differences in price typically being a small element in buyers' comparison of overall cost effectiveness. On these grounds one might question whether distance should be expected to exert a perceptible influence on market shares.

However, the transport of the product is not the only distance factor involved. The negotiation of machinery sales tends to involve relatively complex and lengthy negotiations compared with other kinds of trade, and the buyer in many cases needs to send inspectors to test equipment at the seller's plant before it is shipped. There may also be quite extensive travel involved for personnel being trained to operate an unfamiliar machine. Ease and convenience of personal communi-

TABLE 12.2 - Actual and Standardized Shares of 14 OECD Countries in Their Total SITC 7 Exports to the Soviet Union and to the World in 1976 (Percentage)

	Actual Soviet Shares	Standardized Soviet Shares	Actual World Shares
United States	14.2	20.1	21.2
Canada	.8	2.6	5.2
Japan	16.0	10.6	15.4
Federal Republic of Germany	32.8	26.1	20.8
France	9.6	8.4	9.0
Italy	8.4	6.6	5.4
United Kingdom	4.8	8.5	7.8
BLEU	.4	2.5	3.5
Netherlands	1.5	3.1	3.3
Denmark	1.0	1.4	1.1
Norway	.4	.8	0.9
Austria	2.6	1.5	1.0
Sweden	3.9	3.5	3.5
Switzerland	3.6	4.2	2.1

Source: Derived from a United States Department of Commerce Bureau of East-West Trade (BEWT) computer printout of SITC 7 exports and percentage market shares at the 4 digit level, based on Western trade returns. Note: The actual Soviet shares in this table may not be precisely comparable with those for earlier years in Table 12.1, since the BEWT printout for 1971-75 gives percentage shares that in several cases differ slightly from those in Table 12.1.

cation between buyer and seller is, therefore, likely to be important. Accordingly, some consideration of distance is desirable.

Mileage, however, is a less appropriate indicator of ease of communication than it would be of transport costs. Therefore, the logarithm of time zone differences in hours between Moscow and the capital city of the exporting country has been used, although it is a very imprecise measure. (8) This gives distance measures of .903 for the United States and Canada, .778 for Japan, .477 for the United Kingdom, and .301 for the other European countries.

The Western Strategic Embargo

Many different views have been aired about the effectiveness of the embargo, and there are several aspects of it that one might try to bring into the analysis. I have incorporated merely the simple matter of CoCom membership or non-membership, assigning a dummy variable of 0 to member nations and 1 to nonmembers, the latter of which consist of Austria, Sweden, and Switzerland out of the 14 countries considered.

The CoCom variable might be expected to exert an influence on Soviet shares insofar as producers in non-CoCom countries supplied the Soviet Union with embargoed items; while the embargo was effectively applied in CoCom countries, with relatively few exceptions and evasions with respect to direct sales to the Soviet Union; and/or the prohibitions on re-export to the Soviet Union were more readily evaded in non-CoCom than in CoCom countries. (9) One might also consider the possibility that CoCom nonmembership is a proxy for something that Soviet policy makers might wish on foreign policy grounds to reward, viz., neutrality.

Official Credit Support

Variations in the mechanisms and terms of official credit support among the 14 OECD countries are considerable and complicated. One simple distinction that has been brought into the analysis of the 1960-70 cross section data is between the one country which did not make official credit support (OCS) available for exports to the Soviet Union, although it did for most other markets, and the others. Thus an OCS dummy variable of 0 is assigned to the United States and 1 to the others. This is obviously a crude measure of the influence of OCS and may best be thought of as an indicator of more general American versus OECD differences in East-West trade policies, with the United States administrations of the 1960s generally adhering to more "arm's length" arrangements.

For 1971-75, when American Eximbank credits were available for exports to Russia over part of the period, this variable is dropped. In the analysis of the 1976 data, on the other hand, an attempt has been made to introduce the influence of differing degrees of attractiveness of the terms of the various countries' OCS. The rationale for doing this is the hypothesis that Soviet import decisions are especially sensitive to credit terms so that, other things equal, an exporting country whose OCS terms are more attractive than those of its competitors will tend to perform especially well in the Soviet market. The OCS variable introduced here is an interest rate for an officially supported eight-year supplier's credit, including blending where OCS covers less than 85% of the value of the transaction, in each country in late 1975 or early 1976. The interest rates are either the sole rate quoted or the mid point of a range quoted in an OECD survey of member states' OCS. (10) The interest rates used are listed in Table 12.3.

The interest rates derivable from this OECD source are not given on a precisely uniform basis for all the countries. Even if they were strictly comparable, they would be only one element in the overall competitiveness of OCS terms and not necessarily a reliable guide to the latter, even so far as rank ordering is concerned. On the whole, though, they do in fact seem to correspond fairly well with the conventional wisdom about ranking by comparative overall competitiveness, at least for the largest exporters. There has been too little public discussion of the OCS terms of most of the smaller countries to know what to expect about them.

In one case (Italy) where the figures in the OECD source did not correspond with the conventional wisdom, a little bit of what the econometric model builders euphemistically refer to as "analyst intervention" was permitted (see Table 12.3). In the case of the United States, of course, Eximbank support for exports to the Soviet Union was no longer available by late 1975, but an American figure is included nonetheless. It happens to be among the higher interest rates, and there is at least a slender case for including the United States on the grounds that some of the 1976 deliveries were under contracts financed at a time when Eximbank credit was still obtainable.

In general, it must be admitted that the data for the OCS competitiveness variable are poor, but a separate study would be needed to improve on them, and they are used here in the belief that they probably correspond tolerably well to overall competitiveness of OCS terms, at least in rank ordering.

TABLE 12.3 - Representative Interest Rates on an Eight-Year, Official Supplier's Credit in 14 OECD Countries in late 1975 (Percentage)

United States	9.45
Canada (March 1976)	9.95
Japan	8.50 (a)
Federal Republic of Germany	8.20
France (May 1976)	8.61
Italy	8.50 (b)
United Kingdom	8.33
Belgium	9.50
Netherlands	9.63
Denmark	10.61 (c)
Norway	8.80
Austria	8.42
Sweden	9.38
Switzerland	9.00

Source: OECD, The Export Credit Financing System in OECD Member Countries (Paris: OECD, 1976).

Notes: (a) Source quotes 8.10%, plus banking charges.

(b) Source quotes 9.30%, with 50% mediocredits participation, but press reports suggest that about 8.5% was attainable with the maximum (85%) mediocredits participation.

(c) But 8.13% for ships, and "downpayment requirements can be waived."

Political Affinity

The root idea here is that some national "political cultures" (11) in the various Western countries differ considerably with respect to the prevailing set of views and attitudes towards the Soviet Union. This is reflected in the climate of business and government policy discussion of East-West trade.

Political cultures might be considered a factor affecting the degree of attention, flexibility, and energy which the national business community and the national government are prepared to devote to East-West trade.

This hypothesis can best be clarified by an example: viz., a report on East-West trade policy adopted by the French <u>Conseil Economique et Social</u> in June 1976. (12) Any British or American specialist reading this will be struck by the difference in tone and content from corresponding policy discussions in London and Washington. Foreign policy and strategic issues are scarcely alluded to; no time is spent on wondering whether detente is a one way or two way street. Instead, the key problem is briskly defined at the outset as that of maximizing the French share of the traffic.

How might this difference among Western countries be represented statistically? One possible way of doing this is indicated by the French example justed quoted. It seems plausible to suggest that this sort of policy making stance would be in part a reflection of a country's predominant political culture. Thus, so-called cold war attitudes and considerations might be expected to affect East-West trade policies less in a country such as France, where a favorable response to such stimulus-words as "Marxism," "Communism," or "Moscow" is less unusual and more respectable than it is in British or American society. No doubt business executives and government officials who share this response are relatively few in all the 14 OECD countries under consideration. The contention is simply that they are relatively less scarce in some countries than in others and that this makes a difference to East-West trade.

One possible proxy measure of such differences in political cultures, and hence of attitudes towards East-West trade, would be electoral support for the Communist Party (CP). This need not nowadays imply a clearly Moscow oriented CP, but in much of our period it has implied this. CP electoral support (percentage of votes at national elections), therefore, is used as a proxy measure of political affinity (see Table 12.4).

Conceivably, political affinity represented in this way could also be a consideration in Soviet decision making. Might not Soviet decision makers have some tendency to prefer to trade with Western coun-

TABLE 12.4 - Communist Party (CP) Shares in Votes at General Elections or Equivalent, at Dates Close to 1965, 1970, and 1975.

	Date	Percentage CP Vote
IN OR CLOSE TO 1965		
France(a)	1967	22.5
Italy(b)	1963	25.3
United Kingdom(b)	1964	0.1
Belgium(b)	1961	3.1
Netherlands(b)	1963	2.8
Denmark(c)	1965	0.1
Norway(c)	1965	1.4
Sweden(d)	1964	5.2
Austria(b)	1962	3.0
Japan(e)	1963	4.0
IN OR CLOSE TO 1970		
France(a)	1968	20.0 (First Ballot for National Assembly)
Italy(f)	1968	21.9 (Chamber of Deputies)
United Kingdom(g)	1970	0.1
Federal Republic of Germany(h)	1972	0.3
Belgium(f)	1968	3.3
Netherlands(h)	1972	4.8
Denmark(h)	1971	1.4
Norway(c)	1969	1
Sweden(d)	1970	4.8
Austria(g)	1970	1.4
Finland(a)	1970	16.6
Japan(i)	1969	6.8
United States, Canada, and Switzerland: as for 1965 figures.		
IN OR CLOSE TO 1975		
France(h)	1973	21.4 (First Ballot for National Assembly)
Italy(h)	1976	34.4
United Kingdom(h)	1974 (October)	0.1
Federal Republic of Germany(j)	1972	0.3
Belgium(h)	1974	3.2
Netherlands(h)	1972	4.8
Denmark(h)	1973	3.6
Norway(c)	1973	(1.3)(k)
Sweden(h)	1975	6.7
Austria(h)	1974	1.2
Finland(h)	1972	17.0
Japan(h)	1975	10.4
United States, Canada, and Switzerland: as for 1965 and 1970.		

Sources: (a) John H. Hodgson, "Finnish Communism and Electoral Politics," *Problems of Communism* 22 (January-February 1974): 3. (b) *Europa Yearbook* 1965, London: Europa Publishers, 1966. (c) Trond Gilberg, "Patterns of Nordic Communism," *Problems of Communism* 24, no. 3, (May-June 1975): 22. (d) Daniel Tarchys, "The Unique Role of the Swedish CP," Problems of Communism 23, no.3 (May-June 1974). (e) P.F. Langer, "The New Posture of the CPJ," *Problems of Communism* 20, no. 1-2 (January-April 1971): 16. (f) *Europa Yearbook 1970*, 1. (g) *Europa Yearbook 1971*, 1. (h) *Europa Yearbook 1977*, 1. (i) *Europa Yearbook 1970*, 2. *Europa Yearbook 1977*. (j) *Europa Yearbook 1976*, 1. (k) Gallup Poll measures of electoral support. The Norwegian CP has fought recent elections in an electoral alliance: Gilberg, op. cit., p.30.
Note: In 1965 the Communist Party (CP) was still illegal in West Germany; in the United States, Canada and Switzerland there was either no CP as such or one with negligible electoral support. In all these cases CP electoral support was assigned a figure of 0.1 percent.

tries with strong Communist parties, either because the latter are perceived as more progressive or on more deliberately formulated foreign-policy grounds? This seems at least a possibility worth considering.

The use of CP electoral support as a proxy, therefore, is intended to capture political affinity in a sense which encompasses possible influences on both Western and Soviet decision making. It provides no way of separating the hypothesized influence of the Western trade partner's political culture from that of Soviet favoritism. In general, the limitations of this measure, particularly for the era of Euro-Communism, will be apparent.

The political affinity factor is envisaged here as a fairly persistent, long-run influence unlikely to alter rapidly. This is what chiefly distinguishes it from the bilateral relations variable. Thus, the tradition of the Franco-Russian special relationship, which predates the Bolshevik Revolution, for example, could also be subsumed under the heading of political affinity.

The State of Bilateral Intergovernmental Relations

The notion here is of a diplomatic state of play which can fluctuate quite sharply against a background of a given, longer-run degree of political affinity for a variety of reasons. Obvious examples would be the British government's expulsion of 105 Soviet officials from London in 1971 and the Japanese retention for some time of the Soviet "Foxbat" aircraft after the pilot landed it in Japan in 1976. No attempt has been made to bring this variable into the statistical analysis, which is mainly of cross section, not time series, data. It is considered, however, in the brief historical case studies.

It should be noted that there are certain possible influences which have not been considered at all. These include traditional cultural links and trading practices (13) and what might be called "institutional affinity," e.g., the presence or absence of a well oiled government machine for promoting East-West trade, the extent of government involvement in industry, and the like. There has also been no attempt to consider price competitiveness. This is expected to be incorporated in the RW share as an indicator of competitiveness and size; also, price comparisons are especially unreliable in the case of such highly differentiated products as those in the SITC section 7.

The next section reviews some results of regression and other quantitative analyses employing the variables described above.

QUANTITATIVE EVIDENCE

It is apparent from Table 12.1 that some countries in 1960-75 tended to do better in the Soviet market then elsewhere, i.e., to have Soviet shares greater than their RW shares. For others, the situation was reversed, and for some the ranking of their Soviet and RW shares showed no consistent ordering. This observation provides a starting point.

The countries that showed a statistically significant tendency (chi-square test; five % level) for the Soviet share to be the larger were the following (numbers of years when Soviet share exceeded RW share appears in parenthesis): Italy (16), Austria (16), France (16), Sweden (13), Switzerland (13), and Denmark (13).

Conversely, the following showed a statistically significant tendency in the opposite direction: the United States (0), Canada (0), BLEU (0), Norway (0), and Netherlands (3).

In the case of the remaining countries (Federal Republic of Germany, the United Kingdom, and Japan), the null hypothesis that the Soviet share was as likely as not to exceed the RW share could not be rejected at the five % level.

In attempting to test hypotheses about the relationship between these two shares, a number of regressions have been run. Regressions on cross section data for individual years and on time series data for individual countries yielded results that in some cases were quite good statistically. (14) On further reflection, though, cross section analyses of shares over periods of several years appear to be more promising.

Regressions using national time series of market shares are uninformative because for most of the countries the more interesting of the independent variables, i.e., those other than RW shares, do not change much, if at all, over time. And the difficulty with cross section data for individual years is that for the smaller countries, at least in the earlier years, the Soviet shares are composed of such tiny flows (e.g., less than $10,000 for Norway in 1960) that they are highly vulnerable to influences, which would be random disturbances. Thus, the delivery of one medium sized ship by Norway in 1960 would have changed Norway's Soviet share dramatically - from nil to 0.2%.

Therefore, attention is focused here on cross section regressions: (a) for shares in the whole period 1960-70, (b) for shares in 1971-75, and (c) introducing an OCS variable for 1976 since data for several years are not available. The periods 1960-70 and 1971-75 were chosen to represent predetente and detente eras. The distinction is made (a) because detente did not affect Soviet relations with all 14 countries in equal degrees, but was heavily concentrated on Soviet-American relations; and (b) the use of different periods enables the stability of the coefficients over time to be considered, which provides some indication of the predictive value of the equations estimated.

Figures 12.1 and 12.2 illustrate the Soviet and RW shares in the first two periods. Figure 12.1, like Table 12.1, encourages the notion that either CoCom nonmembership or a high degree of political affinity might be a sufficient condition for a country to have a Soviet share that is high relative to its RW share. However, the presence of Denmark and the United Kingdom to the left of the SOV = RW line in Figure 12.1 goes against the notion that the possession of at least one of these attributes might be a necessary condition for a relatively high RW share.

Figure 12.2 is less encouraging to the CoCom and political affinity hypotheses, since Sweden and the Federal Republic of Germany now appear on the "wrong" side of the SOV = RW line. The influence of closer Soviet-American relations is strongly indicated by the movement of the United States from a Figure 12.1 position way out to the right of the SOV = RW line to a Figure 12.2 position much closer to it.

If the Soviet share is treated as the dependent variable, there is no obvious reason to treat the relationship between the independent variable as other than additive, in other words, to envisage a country's share in the Soviet market as corresponding to its RW share adjusted additively by the other independent variables.

The equation fitted to the 1960-70 data was therefore:

1) $\quad$ Soviet share $= b_1$ (RW share) $= b_2$ (distance) $+ b_3$ (CoCom membership) $+ b_4$ (OCS availability) $+ b_5$ (political affinity).

The political affinity measure in this case is percentage CP votes at a date close to 1965 (see Table 12.4). The independent variables are so defined that b_2 is the only coefficient one would expect to be negative. The regression is run without a constant term, since the Soviet and RW share figures are both percentages, the differences between them sum to zero, and they should be accounted for by the independent variables other than the RW share.

Equation 2), fitted to the 1971-75 data, is the same as equation 1) except that the OCS availability variable is omitted (see "Influences on Market Shares"). Here the CP electoral support figures used as a proxy for political affinity are for dates close to 1973, except that in four cases the arithmetic means of two election results are used, as follows: Japan 1969 and 1975, Italy 1968 and 1976, Sweden 1970 and 1975, Austria 1970 and 1974.

Equation 3 uses the same variables as equation 1 for 1976 data except that the measure of OCS terms, discussed in the previous section and listed in Table 12.3, is used instead of OCS availability.

SOVIET TRADE WITH THE WEST

Equation 4 resembles 3 except that standardized Soviet shares (see previous section and Table 12.2) replace RW shares.

A more direct approach to the assessment of influences other than general competitiveness was also tried. In these regressions the equations fitted were as follows.

1960-70

5) $\dfrac{\text{Soviet share}}{\text{RW share}} = 1 + b_1 \text{(distance)} + b_2 \text{(CoCom)} + b_3 \text{(OCS)}$ availability $+ b_4$ (political affinity)

1971-75

6) $\dfrac{\text{Soviet share}}{\text{RW share}} = 1 + b_1 \text{(distance)} + b_2 \text{(CoCom)} + b_3 \text{(political)}$ affinity)

1976

7) $\dfrac{\text{Soviet share}}{\text{Standardized Soviet Share}} = 1 + b_1 \text{(distance)} + b_2 \text{(CoCom)} + b_3$ (OCS terms) $+ b_4$ (political affinity)

In equations 5-7, the rationale of introducing a constant term constrained to equal one is simply that the independent variables are being introduced in an attempt to account for deviations from unity in the ratio of a country's Soviet share to its RW or standardized Soviet share. This should be a more sensitive test of the influence of the independent variables other than general competitiveness. The results of estimating these equations are shown in Table 12.5.

RW Share

Where the Soviet share is the dependent variable, the R^2's, adjusted for degrees of freedom, are quite high. The RW share performs fairly well as an explanatory variable, with t statistics indicating significance at the .05 level and coefficients reasonably stable in the equations for periods after 1970, though markedly different in 1960-70. For 1976, however, where the standardized Soviet share is introduced instead, the latter performs marginally better than the RW share, as one would expect. For this reason the share ratio regression for 1976 (equation 7) uses the standardized share as the denominator, not the RW share.

TABLE 12.5 - Accounting for 14 OECD Countries' Percent Shares in Their Total SITC 7 Exports to the Soviet Union, 1960-76

some regression results (t statistics in brackets)

Dependent Variable	Standardized Soviet Share	RW Share	Distance	CoCom	OCS Availability	OCS Terms 1975-76	Political Affinity	DW	R^{-2}
1. Soviet share 1960-70.		0.5556 (3.2602)(a)	-7.5551 (-1.4553)	-0.9237 (-0.2936)(a)	6.1969 (2.3781)		0.2627 (1.6233)	1.8046	0.7792
2. Soviet share 1971-75.		1.1639 (6.2128)(a)	-7.3406 (-1.7918)(a)	2.1304 (0.7533)			0.2070 (1.5248)	2.0267(b)	0.8397
3. Soviet share 1976		1.4418 (8.8628)(a)	-14.626 (-2.8924)(a)	2.1252 (0.8722)		0.2633 (0.9512)	(0.0451) (0.4583)	2.0221(b)	0.9138
4. Soviet share 1976	1.1833 (9.1926)(a)		-3.5317 (-.8034)	1.2225 (0.5226)		-0.0774 (-0.2853)	0.1011 (1.0671)	1.7514(b)	0.9193
5. Soviet/RW share ratio 1960-70			-0.7010 (-0.5722)	1.9255 (2.0719)(a)	0.2537 (0.3305)		0.0448 (0.9377)	1.9801	0.3054
6. Soviet/RW share ratio 1971-75			-0.6182 (-1.9274)(a)	0.7581 (2.4255)(a)			0.0257 (1.6948)	0.07837	0.3572
7. Soviet/ standardized Soviet share rates, 1976			0.4080 (0.8266)	0.6361 (2.3481)(a)		-.0660 (-2.0993)(a)	0.0246 (2.2110)(a)	2.1381	0.3584

Notes: (a) Significant at the 5% level.
(b) The test is inconclusive with respect to autocorrelation (2-tail, 5% level).

Distance

The distance variable, which is used in all seven equations, generally has the right sign and appears significant in several of the regressions. Confidence in it, however, is reduced by the variability of its regression coefficients over different time periods and its loss of statistical significance once the influence of Soviet import priority fit is introduced (equations 4 and 7); and in equation 7 the sign actually goes the "wrong" way. This result may well reflect the inadequacies of the measure of distance used rather than anything more substantial.

Independent Variables

The other independent variables come out poorly in the first four equations where the Soviet share is the dependent variable. However, it is worth noting that in equations 1 and 2 the political affinity variable is significant at the .10 level and in equation 4 at the .20 level, while the CoCom variable is also significant at the .20 level in equation 4. The OCS availability measure, which merely distinguishes the United States from the other 13 OECD countries in 1960-70, works well in equation 1 but poorly in equation 5, where the variations to be accounted for are those in the ratios of Soviet to RW shares in 1960-70. In general the first four equations do little more than strengthen the not very interesting hypothesis that general competitiveness will be a major influence on performance in the Soviet market, while doing little to support the more interesting hypotheses about other influences.

Share-Ratio Regressions

Instinctively, however, one might expect the share-ratio regressions (equations 5-7) to provide a more sensitive measure of these other influences. Now, the $\bar{R}^2$'s in these equations are relatively low; in other words, it appears that a great deal of the variation in ratios is accounted for by influences other than those introduced here. However the CoCom variable now shows up as significant throughout, though of apparently lesser power after 1970 than before. This constitutes some evidence for the CoCom hypothesis. Other things equal, a non-CoCom OECD country will tend to do relatively better as a machinery exporter in the Soviet market compared with the rest of the world than an OECD country that is a member of CoCom. The apparent decline in the importance of this factor between the 1960s and the 1970s could well be associated with a milder application of the embargo. This is sometimes said to have obtained in the detente period, in the sense that licenses to export items in the industrial list were granted more readily than before.

Similarly, the political affinity hypothesis derives some modest support from equations 5-7. True, it is only in equation 7 that the political affinity measure is significant at the .05 level. However, its regression coefficients are fairly stable over time, and they are significant at the .20 level in 1960-70 and at the .10 level in 1971-75.

The OCS terms variable performs well in equation 7, poorly in 4 and perversely in 3. Since the share ratio equations should provide a fairly sensitive measure of the various influences on what might be called "relative performance in the Soviet market," the notion that OCS terms are of special importance in the Soviet market should certainly not be rejected.

All these cross section regressions should be considered with the variability of individual countries' bilateral relations in mind. This possibly important influence has been omitted here for reasons set out later, but some instances of these bilateral relations are reviewed in the next section. In other words, evidence will be examined of a rather different kind that would tend to support or refute the view that part of the unexplained variance in equations 5-7 can be attributed to differences between the 14 countries with respect to the state of their short/medium-term bilateral intergovernmental relations with the Soviet Union.

CHANGES OVER TIME IN THE BRITISH AND GERMAN MARKET SHARES

We noted previously that the state of bilateral intergovernmental relations was a factor that seemed likely to influence a Western country's share of the Soviet market. It is not, however, an influence that can readily be incorporated in a cross-section analysis among countries and was, therefore, omitted from the discussion on quantitative evidence.

The problem is the lack of comparability among Western countries of their varying diplomatic states of play vis-a-vis the Soviet Union. Thus, we might characterize Anglo-Soviet relations as normal in 1970, bad in 1971-72, good in 1975, and normal in 1977, but this would provide a rank ordering of different short-run states of play which was neither cardinally nor ordinally commensurable with similar characterizations of Franco-Soviet bilateral relations.

Variations over time in the state of bilateral relations nonetheless manifestly do occur and could be an important influence on Soviet shares. Indeed they might provide at least a partial explanation of the shortcomings of the cross-section regressions, particularly the instability of some of the regression coefficients over different time periods.

In other words, "politics," in the sense of "political affinity" and "state of bilateral relations" combined, might be quite a substantial influence on Soviet shares, as indeed on country shares in other national markets. The problem in assessing this is that it appears to be impossible to combine these two variables in any quantitative way. It seems best, therefore, to consider changes in bilateral relations by means of historical case studies and to restrict oneself to qualitative conclusions.

Soviet-Western Trade

So far as recent developments in Soviet trade with the West are concerned, the most conspicuous example of a major change in bilateral relations is the Soviet-American detente of 1972-74. This was reflected, of course, for a short time not just in the provision of Eximbank support for American exports to Russia, but also in changes in the United States Government's stance over export licensing and in both institutional and informal changes in government backup for East-West trade generally. The results of these changes are well-known, as are the limits placed on them so far. Some indication of the results in machinery trade is provided by the contrast between the American positions in Figures 12.1 and 12.2.

West Germany and the United Kingdom provide two rather less obvious cases. These are two countries in our sample of 14 whose Soviet shares in 1960-75 were neither consistently above nor consistently below their RW shares (see "Influences on Market Shares"). The third such country was Japan, but the Japanese case is considered in another publication. (15)

West Germany

In the case of West Germany, there is a dramatic upward shift in the West German share of Soviet imports after 1971 (see Figure 12.3). Previously, despite a long period in which there was no formal intergovernmental trade agreement between Bonn and Moscow, West Germany's Soviet share had fluctuated around its RW share. This might perhaps be interpreted as reflecting a canceling-out of the favorable factors of geographical proximity and traditional trading

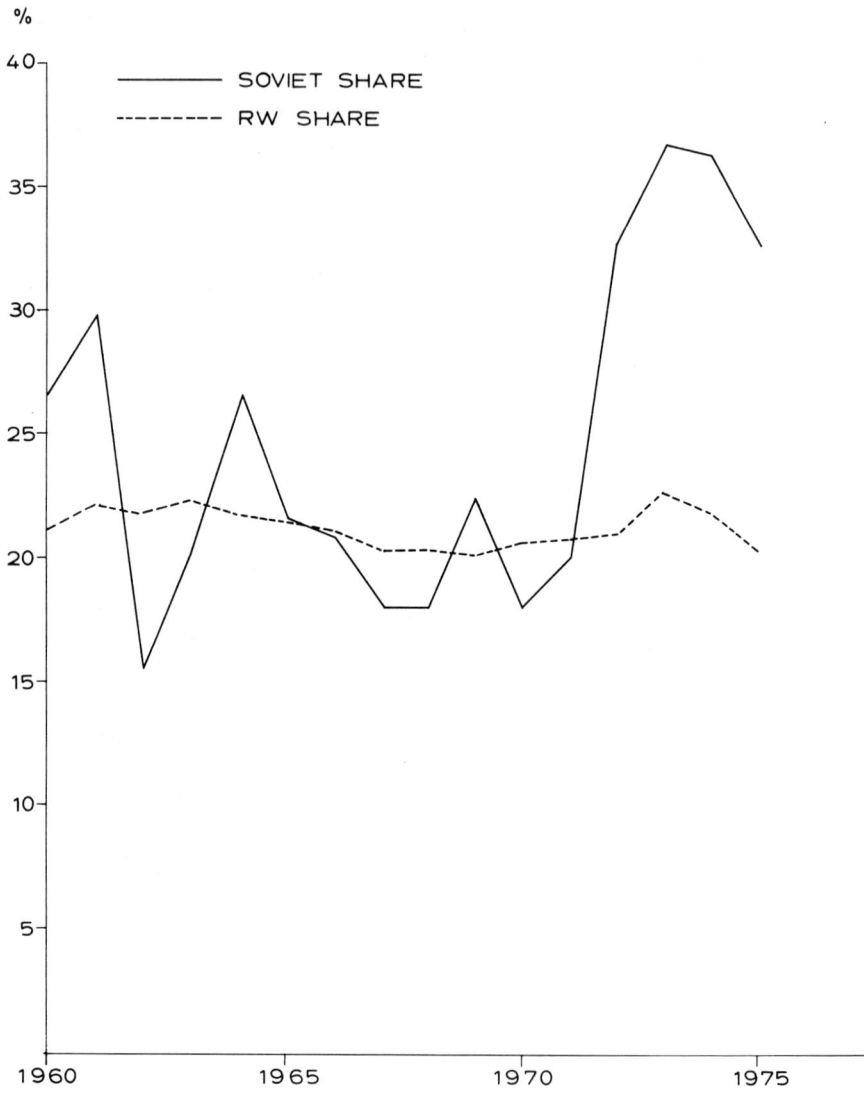

Figure 12.3. Federal Republic of Germany's shares in 14 OECD countries; SITC 7 exports to the Soviet Union and to the rest of the world, 1950-1975 (percent).

links by the unfavorable factors of the deep-seated Russian resentment and suspicion of Germany after World War II and the near absence of formal intergovernmental contacts.

If this is so, the subsequent dramatic increase in the Soviet share might be explained by the Ostpolitik, the Berlin agreement, and the general establishment of Soviet-West German governmental relations. One must, however, assume a lag between the operation of influences favorable to the signing of contracts and the manifestation in the trade returns of those influences in increased deliveries. Whether the abrupt upward shift in 1972 is too early, in the light of this, to reflect the developing Ostpolitik, is a question for someone better informed about West German-Soviet relations to answer.

It can at least be noted that the Ostopolitik, usually dated from the accession to power of Brandt's Social Democrats in 1969, was preceded by an initial thaw in East-West German relations, including a West German-East German trade agreement in 1968, and that the agreement recognizing the present East German, West German, and Polish frontiers was signed in August 1970. (16) Allowing at least six months for changes in Soviet policies and attitudes towards West Germany to result in an increased German share in Soviet machinery, to get import contracts signed, and permit an average lag of a year from contract signature to delivery (see "Influences on Market Shares"), we come to early 1972, which fits the trade figures. The later normalization of Soviet-German relations and a number of economic and cultural agreements signed in May 1973 (17) would then have to be regarded as a formal endorsement of a new situation, with little effect on machinery import choices.

It is true that Italian Tolyatti related deliveries were leveling off at this time, so that other suppliers' shares in total had to rise somewhat, but it is equally true that the American share was also rising at this time in the course of the Nixon-Brezhnev detente moves.

On the whole, it seems highly likely that a marked improvement in Soviet-German relations led to the observed sharp increase in West Germany's Soviet share. How this came about is another question. One might conceive of deliberate encouragement by Soviet policy makers to the Soviet MFT and FTO's to favor West German firms by way of reward and stimulus to a further evolution of the Ostpolitik. Equally, one might conceive simply of the fading away of an atmosphere of disapproval of deals with West German firms, of more active informal encouragement by the Bonn government of West German firms pursuing Soviet orders, a combination of some of these factors, or all of these influences.

The United Kingdom

In the case of the United Kingdom there is a positive correlation between the Soviet share and the tenure of office by the Labor Party (1964-70 and 1974 onwards), which is so remarkable and so remarkably lacking in time lags that it must be at least partly spurious. Over the period 1960-75 as a whole the general decline in the British share of world markets emerges clearly. Broadly speaking, the British share of the Soviet market follows it down, but fluctuates widely about it. It is possible that the relatively high British Soviet share for most of the 1960s is connected with its specific UK capabilities in chemical plants of particular kinds sought in the earlier stages of the Soviet chemical drive. This is a question which might possibly be answered by calculating standardized Soviet shares (see "Influences on Market Shares") for each year of the period. There certainly were a number of large chemical plant sales to the Soviets by British firms in this period, and chemical plants constituted a large share of total Soviet imports of Western machinery.

Some people with extensive experience in Anglo-Soviet trade consider that British firms were especially favored in the 1950s because there was still a traditionally strong orientation towards the United Kingdom on the part of Soviet foreign trade officials. More of their commodity dealing than at present was through the London markets, and their training had focused on British business methods and terminology. If this was an initially strong but declining influence on the Soviet choice of machinery suppliers in our period, however, one would expect the British Soviet share to exhibit a trend starting above the RW share in 1960 and thereafter approaching the latter as it followed it down. This is not in fact what Figure 12.4 reveals.

The clearest evidence of political factors in Figure 12.4 is the fall of the Soviet share relative to the RW share in 1972-74. This is almost certainly the result mainly of the freezing of Anglo-Soviet relations after the British explusion of Soviet officials from London in 1971. Apparently, this did not prevent tying up some deals that were very close to completion, but it became extremely difficult for a time for British businessmen to initiate new negotiations or develop negotiations that were at an early stage. Business relations may have been restored to near normality before the Conservative government that had taken the explusion decision left office in February 1974, but this did not show up in actual deliveries until 1975. That, at least, is a crude summary of developments in which there were many further nuances.

In the case of Soviet-British trade, as far as Soviet machinery imports are concerned, it looks as though the long-run decline in the

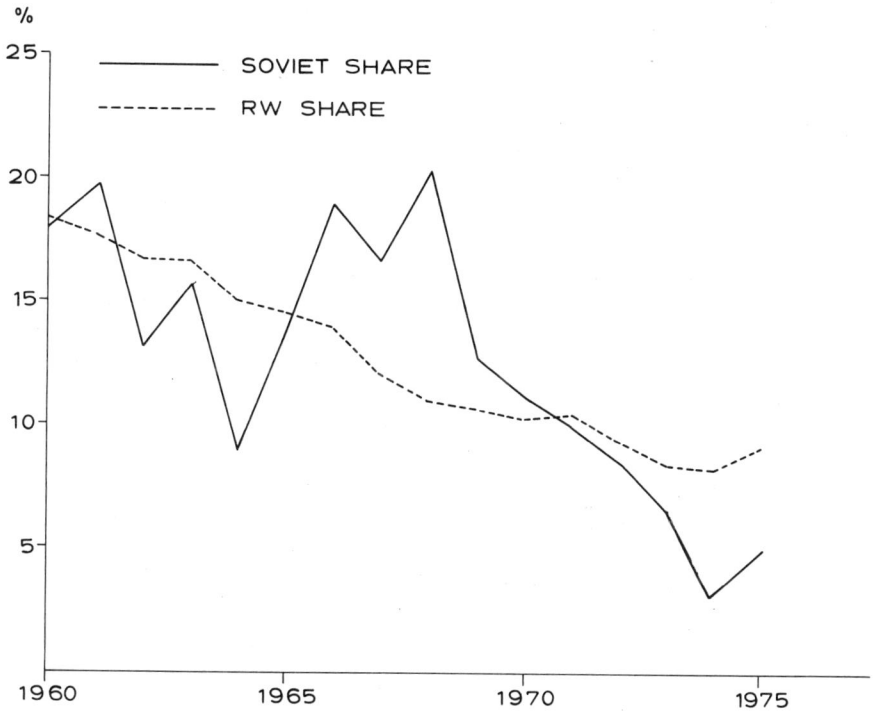

Figure 12.4. United Kingdom's shares in 14 OECD countries' SITC 7 exports to the Soviet Union and to the rest of the world, 1960-1975 (percent).

British share of the Soviet market is powerfully explained by the underlying decline in British competitiveness which has affected its trade share in the rest of the world. In the mid-to-late 1960s this process was partly obscured by other factors favorable to the British share of the Soviet market, possibly to do with specific Soviet product mix requirements. On the other hand, a particularly severe flare-up in bilateral political relations in 1971 seems to have superimposed on the long-run trend a sharp additional short-term fall in Britain's Soviet share. Here the initial move came from the British government which expelled the Soviet officials, but the effect on trade was the result of the Soviet response. Perhaps such a response, in a centrally administered society, can be akin to a conditioned reflex and need not be thought of as a carefully deliberated act of policy. In the present instance, there probably was a calculated retaliatory response which included instructions from top policy makers to freeze contacts with British firms as well as with the British government. But one can easily conceive of a more reflexive kind of response: high-level meetings under intergovernmental framework agreements (e.g., Joint Commission meetings) are called off as a routine expression of affronted dignity; and without receiving specific instructions, people lower down the hierarchy (including MFT and FTO officials) interpret these actions as a signal to themselves to minimize contact with nationals of the offending country.

In a Western nation, the more deliberate kind of commercial retaliation arising from diplomatic affront can occur through formal government measures on trade and credit and through informal government "suasion." It is likely to be less effective, one would imagine, than equivalent action by the Soviet authorities. If Soviet policy makers are better able to control the balance of payments than their Western counterparts, (18) it might reasonably be argued that their direct, administrative control over imports should also make them better able than Western policy makers to cut imports from a particular country. It also seems reasonable, furthermore, to expect the reflexive kind of retaliatory response described previously to be more noticeable in Soviet than in Western trading behavior, since Western businessmen have far less reason to take their cues "from above" than do Soviet officials working in a single Party-State hierarchy.

Summary

Altogether, the experience of the United States, West Germany, and Britain in trading with the Soviet Union in the 1970s shows that variations in the state of bilateral intergovernmental relations can be a substantial influence on a Western country's share of the Soviet market. It does not follow that all such variations influence market shares; the cases we have looked at are all of major changes in bilateral relations, although not necessarily lasting. It may well be that lesser fluctuations in the temperature of mutual political relationships have little or no effect on trade.

The initiative for a change in diplomatic relations may come from the Soviet or the Western side, or it may be impossible to allocate. Given such a change, there are channels on both the Soviet and the Western side whereby its effects can be transmitted to trade. There are some reasons, however, for thinking that these shock effects can travel more powerfully through the Soviet system than through a Western system.

CONCLUSIONS

How well a Western country performs in selling to the Soviet Union, at least in machinery exports, is evidently very strongly influenced by its size and general competitiveness as an exporting nation. The cases of the United States and latterly, West Germany, however, show that other factors can have a substantial influence also.

The other factors considered in this paper are far from providing a good explanation of deviations of a country's Soviet share from its RW share. The attempts made here, using various proxy measures and dummy variables, however do suggest that a Western country's relative performance in the Soviet market will tend to be better:

1. the more closely the exporting country's specialization or "product profile" at the SITC four digit (subgroup) level, corresponds to Soviet import priorities;
2. if the exporter is not in CoCom;
3. the more favorable, relative to those of other supplier nations, are the exporter's OCS terms;
4. the greater the long-run political affinity of the exporting country with the Soviet Union, as indicated by the strength of electoral support in the former for the Communist Party;
5. if bilateral relations with the Soviet government have markedly improved, rather than markedly deteriorated, just before the start of the period in which contracts were signed (with respect to currently observed export deliveries).

The proposition that increasing distance from Moscow will affect Soviet shares negatively has not been upheld, though the weakness here may be more in our "distance" measure than in the proposition in a more general form.

Statistically, the evidence for item 4 is rather weak; the evidence for item 5 is of a qualitative, case study kind. Overall, the regressions run for 1960-76 probably do not have more than a very modest predictive value, except with respect to the RW and standardized Soviet share variables. They do, however, indicate that influences of a more or less political nature are, as one might expect, of some importance.

Further elaboration of some of these measures and alternative specifications of possible relationships might yield somewhat stronger results. Probably, though, the best way of obtaining further insight into these relationships is through a detailed review of the case histories of different Western countries' trade and other relations with the Soviet Union.

NOTES

1. Thomas A. Wolf, "US-West German Competition in Exporting Manufactured Products to Eastern Europe and the Soviet Union," Jahrbuch der Wirtschaft Osteuropas, Band 7 (Munich: Gunter Olzog, 1978), pp. 431-59. Wolf's study was published as the first draft of the present paper was being completed. As the title indicates, its focus is somewhat different from that adopted here. Nevertheless, there is some overlap, and some of Wolf's methods (e.g., the use of a "Western reference market") might be usefully applied to the present topic. The conclusions of the two studies, insofar as they impinge on one another, do not seem to be in conflict.

2. USA, Canada, Japan, France, FRG, Italy, UK, BLEU, Netherlands, Denmark, Norway, Sweden, Switzerland and Austria. Finland is also a major Western exporter to the Soviet Union, but is omitted here on the grounds that its special relationship with Russia, especially the bilateral-settlements basis of Fenno-Soviet trade and payments, sets it apart from the 14 OECD countries.

3. See, for example, Helen Raffel, Marc Rubin, and Robert Teal, "The MFN Impact on US Imports from Eastern Europe." In US Congress Joint Economic Committee, East European Economies Post-Helsinki (Washington: US Government Printing Office, 1977), pp. 1396-1428; and the papers by A. Elias and M. E. Searing, by J. E. Jelacic and by T. A. Wolf cited therein on p. 1398.

4. Central Intelligence Agency, USSR: Hard Currency Trade and Payments, 1977-78, ER 77-10035 U, (Washington, D.C., March 1977), p. 13.

5. There appears to be a "hard currency shopping list" rather than an individual currency shopping list drawn up for financial settlements purposes. Both the logic of the convertible currency settlement and the evidence of Soviet coefficients of reciprocity in total merchandise trade with individual countries indicate this. In 1975 the unweighted arithmetic mean of reciprocity coefficients, calculated from the Soviet trade returns, was 0.333 for trade with the OECD 14, compared with 0.038 for Soviet trade with the European CMEA countries. The difference in reciprocity

ex post does not of course preclude the possibility that some ex ante bilaterialism pressures also operate in Soviet hard currency trade; i.e., that there may be some attempt by Soviet planners to keep surpluses and deficits with individual hard currency trade partners, or groups of trade partners, within certain limits, as well as to aim at a certain overall hard currency current-account surplus or deficit.

6. The argument for excluding Canadian exports to the United States is that they are a high percentage of total Canadian SITC 7 exports and their inclusion gives a misleading impression of Canadian "general competitiveness" outside North America. Both transport costs and the particularly high degree of transnational integration of parent and subsidiary companies are involved, of a kind that is unusual in international trade as in agreements, e.g., on production sharing in the motor industry. It is arbitrary, no doubt, to make this adjustment and not make others, but it is at any rate a very conspicuous special case. Shares in a selected reference market might be preferable here to RW shares, but a reference market that was appropriate on geographical grounds might be less appropriate than the "rest of the world" if, e.g. its mix of machinery imports differed greatly from both the Soviet mix and the RW mix.

7. Appendix D of Paul Marer, "Towards a Solution of the Mirror Statistics Puzzle in East-West Commerce." In Internationale Wirtschaft: Vergleich und Interdependenz, F. Levcik (Ed.), in press.

8. British summer time and its counterparts have been ignored and the proximity of Tokyo to Nakhodka has been treated as uninteresting compared with the remoteness of Tokyo from Moscow. The coastal trade with Japan conducted by Dalintorg from Hakhodka includes very little machinery. See K. C. Davis, "Soviet-Japanese Trade and Commercial Relations (1956-1973): A Study in Soviet Commercial Policy" (Ph.D. diss., University of Birmingham, 1976).

9. Strictly speaking, one should note that this last source of difference might not show up in trade data for Austria and Switzerland, since these two countries report special, not general, trade; i.e., they exclude re-exports. It is hardly likely, though, that anyone engaged in evading re-export prohibitions would show customs documents in which the item in question was shown as a re-export, not as a re-export at any rate to the Soviet Union.

10. OECD, The Export Credit Financing System in OECD Member Countries (Paris: OECD, 1976).

11. The concept of political culture is discussed in a number of writings; one clear and succinct account is in Robert C. Tucker, "Culture, Political Culture and Communist Society," Political Science Quarterly 88, no. 2 (June 1973): 173-91. All political scientists, it should be noted, adapt the same operational definition of this term.

12. Journal Officiel de la Republique Francaise, October 22 1976.

13. For example, a British official has suggested to me that it might be of some importance to the British share of the Soviet market that in the early post-World War II period the English language and British trading practice were the major "Western" elements in the training of Soviet foreign trade officials at the Academy of Foreign Trade. There may, therefore, be at least one vintage of MFT officials, who at least in the start of their careers were more attuned to dealing with British than with other suppliers. If this is so, they appear to have adapted to German trading practice very rapidly.

14. Cross section results for 1965 and with Finland added for 1970 and 1975 are reported in Hanson, USSR: Production structure, Demand Structure and Foreign Trade (Koln: Bundesinstitut fur Ostwissenschaftliche und Internationale Studien, 1978).

15. K. C. Davis and D. Ghosh, "Effects of Politics on International Trade: Soviet-Japanese Trade, a Case-Study," (University of Birmingham, Faculty of Commerce and Social Science Discussion Paper Series B, no. 37, 1976) sought to account for changes in Japan's share of all Soviet nongrain imports from the West during 1957-71, by inter alia regressing that share on time, Soviet national income, an index of Japanese export prices divided by an index of other Western export prices, and dummy variables for "normal," "tension," and "detente" years in Soviet-Japanese relations. Coefficients for the dummy variables were not significant. The appropriateness of the choice of other variables, however, is open to question.

16. See "Calendar of Political Events, October 1964 to June 1977." In The Soviet Union Since the Fall of Krushchev, 2nd ed. Archie Brown and Michael Kaser, Eds. (London: Macmillan, 1978), p. 334.

17. Ibid., p. 336.

18. See P. J. D. Wiles, Communist International Economics (Oxford: Blackwell, 1968). For a discussion of mid-1970s evidence of the limits to the ability of Soviet and Eastern European planners to control the balance of payments, see L. J. Brainard, "Financing Eastern Europe's Trade Gaps the Euromarket Connection," Euromoney, January 1976, pp. 16-18.

13 Choice of Partners in International Economic Relations: The Hungarian Experience
Mihaly Simai

INTRODUCTION

The selection of foreign trade partners of states has been seldom based in the past on deliberate policy decisions and even less on the results of scientific research, but the "captive market" problem is excluded since it represents special cases. Economic relations and especially traditional foreign trade have developed in the sphere of firms. The choice of partners, however, even on the enterprise level was influenced by several objective conditions including general or specific decisions on international economic policies by states.
 As economic growth became more organized and economic policies more intensively influenced decisions also on international economic relations, the formerly spontaneous micro economic processes were more and more effected by macro economic decisions on the national and international level as well as in given countries. The set of international economic relations of a state, even in this respect, could not be defined as a result of recognized national interests based on comparative advantages or disadvantages. In the choice of partners and traditions, different historical conditions were mixed with new factors which emerged in the process of economic growth, and they were also influenced by economic and political changes. The centrally planned economies from this point of view did not represent exceptional cases. Neither were the centrally planned Socialist countries unique in the sense that international economic policy, occasionally of crucial importance, has become a significant part of the state's economic policies. More or less similar questions emerged everywhere so that even under the umbrella of

the "most favored nation clause," in certain cases the state had to stimulate or hinder the development of economic relations with some countries and also had to decide how international economic policy should be defined concerning one or the other partner state.

Economic integration pushed these issues to the forefront especially in connection with such questions as which type of states could integrate most easily and whether the relationship between the member and third countries should be more or less intensive within the framework of a given system.

In the case of Hungary, as for all the countries of the world, the analysis of the factors determining the choice of partners is also a rather complex task due to the following factors.

1. The factors which have determined the importance of one or another country in the more recent history of her international economic relations and which lead to changes in country shares in exports and imports cannot be singled out and measured individually.

2. Such categories which often measured market growth, export performance, etc., are aggregates of interrelated factors.

3. The changes could be better understood in a more general context, not only in an East-West context. It is necessary to formulate the factors in more general terms and to put the countries and factors into comparative perspective so one can also place East-West relations properly.

In 1976, Hungary's trade turnover with the industrially advanced capitalist countries corresponded to a proportion of her GNP which was roughly equal to the share of entire foreign trade in the GNP for 1938. True, the share of foreign trade has greatly increased since then.

In pre-World War II Hungary the share of highly advanced capitalist countries was more than 70% in her foreign trade; thus, between 1934 and 1938 about 60 to 65% of the imported consumer goods and 90% of the capital goods have come from the capitalist countries of Europe. This pattern reflected the political and economic realities of those times. The Eastern European countries, including Hungary, remained more or less backward and as semi or underdeveloped agricultural countries with a rather narrow industrial basis. The most important source of the changes in partners was the political landslide in Europe after the World War II, which has brought about tremendous shifts in social, economic, political, and cultural aspects alike. This can be seen from Tables 13.1 and 13.2.

From these tables, in which the most important trading partners of Hungary are included, one can draw also some rather interesting but not necessarily surprising conclusions:

TABLE 13.1 - Main Trading Partners of Hungary and Their Shares in Total Exports and Imports

1. Exports (%)

	1938		1950		1960		1970		1976	
1.	Germany	27.4	U.S.S.R.	28.9	U.S.S.R.	29.3	U.S.S.R.	31.4	U.S.S.R.	30.2
2.	Austria	18.3	Czechoslovakia	10.6	G.D.R.	11.5	G.D.R.	9.7	G.D.R.	9.1
3.	Italy	8.5	Poland	8.2	Czechoslovakia	10.7	Czechoslovakia	8.7	F.R.G.	8.0
4.	United Kingdom	8.1	Roumania	7.7	Poland	5.2	Poland	6.0	Czechoslovakia	7.5
5.	Czechoslovakia	4.1	G.D.R.	7.4	F.R.G.	6.0	F.R.G.	6.0	Poland	4.4
6.	Roumania	4.0	F.R.G.	7.4	Yugoslavia	4.3	Italy	5.7	Italy	4.0
7.	Switzerland	3.7	Austria	5.1	Austria	3.7	Austria	2.8	Austria	3.7
8.	Yugoslavia	3.0	Switzerland	3.7	Roumania	3.0	Switzerland	2.6	Roumania	2.7
9.	United States	2.4	Italy	3.4	Roumania	2.4	Yugoslavia	2.5	Yugoslavia	2.7
10.	France	1.9	Netherland	2.1	Switzerland	2.3	Roumania	2.3	Switzerland	2.3
11.	Sweden	1.9	Bulgaria	1.9	United Kingdom	2.0	Bulgaria	1.2	France	1.9
12.	Argentina	1.9	Argentina	1.9	France	1.6	United Kingdom	1.1	Iraq	1.7
13.	Netherland	1.6	Turkey	1.8	Bulgaria	1.4	Netherland	1.1	Bulgaria	1.4
14.	Egypt	1.4	Belgium	1.4	Netherland	1.3	France	1.1	United Kingdom	1.3
15.	Poland	1.0	Egypt	1.2	Argentina	1.2	India	1.0	Netherland	1.1
Total 1-15.		85.9		92.7		85.0		85.9		82.5

2. Imports (%)

	1938		1950		1960		1970		1976	
1.	Germany	30.1	U.S.S.R.	24.5	U.S.S.R.	31.0	U.S.S.R.	33.2	U.S.S.R.	27.5
2.	Austria	11.5	Czechoslovakia	10.3	Czechoslovakia	11.5	G.D.R.	10.4	F.R.G.	9.6
3.	Roumania	9.8	Poland	9.9	G.D.R.	10.3	Czechoslovakia	7.9	G.D.R.	8.8
4.	Czechoslovakia	6.7	F.R.G.	9.9	F.R.G.	5.7	Poland	5.8	Czechoslovakia	6.4
5.	United Kingdom	6.3	Roumania	7.0	Poland	5.1	F.R.G.	5.3	Austria	4.8
6.	Italy	6.3	Austria	5.6	Roumania	4.3	Italy	3.8	Poland	4.4
7.	United States	5.3	Switzerland	3.9	Austria	3.5	Austria	3.3	Italy	4.0
8.	Yugoslavia	4.5	Belgium	3.6	United Kingdom	3.2	Roumania	2.8	Switzerland	2.5
9.	Netherland	3.7	Argentina	3.5	Italy	2.7	Yugoslavia	2.3	Roumania	2.3
10.	Switzerland	2.5	United Kingdom	3.5	France	2.6	United Kingdom	2.2	France	2.3
11.	Egypt	1.5	Italy	2.9	Yugoslavia	2.1	Bulgaria	2.0	United Kingdom	2.0
12.	France	1.5	Netherland	2.7	Switzerland	1.3	France	2.0	USA	2.0
13.	Poland	1.4	G.D.R.	2.6	Bulgaria	1.3	USA	1.5	Yugoslavia	1.7
14.	Greece	1.2	Bulgaria	2.0	Sweden	1.3	Netherland	1.3	Netherland	1.6
15.	Belgium	1.1	United States	1.8	Netherland	1.3	Switzerland	1.1	Iraq	1.4
Total 1-15.		93.4		93.8		87.2		82.9		81.3

Source: **Magyar Statisztikai Zsebkonyv** [Hungarian Statistical Yearbooks], 1970, 1974, 1977. Statisztikai Kiado, 1970, 1974, 1977.

TABLE 13.2 - The Ranking of the First 15 Trading Partners of Hungary in 1976 and in Selected Earlier Years

Exports

Country	1976	1970	1960	1950	1938
Soviet Union	1	1	1	1	0
GDR	2	2	2	5	1
Federal Republic of Germany	3	5	5	6	1
Czechoslovakia	4	3	3	2	5
Poland	5	4	4	3	15
Italy	6	6	9	9	3
Austria	7	7	7	7	2
Romania	8	10	8	4	6
Yugoslavia	9	9	6	0	8
Switzerland	10	8	10	8	7
France	11	14	12	0	10
Iraq	12	0	0	0	0
Bulgaria	13	11	13	11	0
United Kingdom	14	12	11	0	4
Netherland	15	13	14	10	13

Imports

Country	1976	1970	1960	1950	1938
Soviet Union	1	1	1	1	0
Federal Republic of Germany	2	5	4	4	1
GDR	3	2	3	13	1
Czechoslovakia	4	3	2	2	4
Austria	5	7	7	6	2
Poland	6	4	5	3	13
Italy	7	6	9	11	6
Switzerland	8	15	12	7	10
Romania	9	8	6	5	3
France	10	12	10	0	12
United Kingdom	11	10	8	10	5
United States	12	13	0	15	7
Yugoslavia	13	9	11	0	8
Netherland	14	14	15	12	9
Iraq	15	0	0	0	0

Note: 0 indicates that in the given year the respective country was not among the first 15 partners.

Source: <u>Magyar Statisztikai Zsebkonyv</u> [Hungarian Statistical Yearbooks], 1970, 1974, 1977. Statisztikai Kiado, 1970 1974, 1977.

THE HUNGARIAN EXPERIENCE 223

1. From among the 15 countries, which were the main export markets of Hungary in 1938, almost 40 years later only 3 were missing. One major partner (the Soviet Union) and one smaller partner (Iraq) entered into the list. One could, of course, register major changes like the establishment and role of the two German states. In the case of import sources, beyond the changes in shares which occurred also in the export markets among the first five-six countries, the list remained even more stable.

2. In the period between 1950-76 the relative stability of most of the countries is also clearly indicated by the tables, as far as their ranking is concerned. A declining concentration of the top five countries on the list regarding their shares in exports and import is also reflected by the figures.

3. The ranking of the partners changes with a greater intensity among the lowest five-six countries. After 1950 the entry of new countries and the elimination of certain partners from among the top 15 were also mostly in this lower group.

THE GEOECONOMIC FACTOR

From the tables it is also evident that geoeconomic conditions played a great role in the choice of partners, not only in the past when relations developed most spontaneously but also recently. Among these conditions, the natural endowment of the given countries was also decisive and important.

The People's Republic of Hungary is poorly endowed with raw materials and efficient sources of energy. At the same time, the output of her processing industries, which have developed during the last 30 years by about 700%, requires a significant amount of raw material imports. As a consequence, the role of those partners which could secure the necessary raw materials and especially fuel under the most favorable conditions has become extremely important. First of all, it was important that the products of her processing industries or agriculture could be favorably exchanged for raw materials. The direct purchases and barters proved to be more advantageous for many years than the raw material purchases from intermediary countries. Second, raw material deliveries should be secured based on long-term agreements. Third, those sources are preferred which could be coordinated with the geographical position of the country and the possibilities of the given transport system. Raw material cooperation with the Soviet Union has, therefore, been favorable in the past decades because most of the mentioned conditions were present and most of the problems which have arisen could have been solved in a mutually satisfactory way. Despite the changing conditions, the Soviet Union will be the most important source of raw materials for Hungary in the years to come.

Agriculture

The role of geoeconomic conditions also facilitated the development of agriculture as an important export source. The Hungarian People's Republic has favorable possibilities for the effective development of agriculture and especially food production. Hungary is able to produce significant export surpluses, and from certain products could achieve double or more internal consumption. It is evident that the role of agricultural export markets was also an important essential element in choosing partners already in the medieval period, e.g., Italy.

At present, the following countries could be considered as natural markets for agricultural exports: the Socialists countries (the Soviet Union, Democratic Republic of Germany, and Czechoslovakia); and the developed Western countries (the Federal Republic of Germany, United Kingdom, Austria, the Scandinaivan countries, and Italy). The agricultural Common Market, therefore, isolated some of the natural markets from Hungary.

Geographical and Historical Factors

Traditionally the location of markets is also one element among geoeconomic conditions, which closely connects geographical factors with historical ones. In the past the magnitude of transport costs and the backwardness of communication systems rather limited the extension of possible export markets or import sources beyond Europe. Today this factor plays a more limited role than in the past. It is, however, not entirely negligible especially when the vicinity is supported by other positive factors or the greater distance is aggravated by some other negative factors as well. For instance the geographical distance between the United States and the People's Republic of Hungary is further "deepened" by the American administrative restrictions such as high tariffs, and so on. The closeness of the Austrian and German markets is at the same time promoted by other structural factors.

The interrelated role of geographical and historical factors was mainly responsible for the fact that in our trade with the industrially advanced Western countries the most important partners have been some of the developed capitalist countries of Western Europe.

The size of the country is a geographical factor but at the same time an economic factor. Smaller countries are seldom able to satisfy the economic needs of each other. The structure of output, the technological conditions (development potentials), relatively small internal markets, etc., are all responsible for the limited possibilities of economic relations among smaller countries under the traditional conditions of market mechanism. They could efficiently help each other only in the case of a deliberately organized and intensive division of labor and if they could bridge their structural gaps and problems, thus sharing the benefits from the economy of scale. This, however, is not typical of their relations in the world economy. That is one of the reasons why the bigger powers are playing a major economic role in the given areas.

Markets of bigger countries have more absorbing capacities; they could react more flexibly to the export offers of smaller states. Their wider structure of production renders at the same time the possibilities to satisfy the multiple need of smaller countries. The specialization of smaller countries, for instance, to mass produce components for bigger countries, could promote the economic advantages of scale in such fields where final products could not be manufactured. Furthermore, smaller countries are also capable of specialization for such end products which could be placed on the bigger country's, or even more countries' market(s). In the Hungarian-Soviet relations, the Hungarian bus production and export (59% of the output is sold on Soviet markets), and the cooperation in car component are partial examples of such possibilities. A few cooperation schemes with Western partners, like the "rear axis" and other components for large vehicles with American truck manufacturing firms, are similar examples.

Bigger countries can help the smaller ones also with long-term arrangements reflecting the changing needs of output and imports (which influence the production and export of the smaller country) and they may give direct assistance in the adjustment of the smaller country to the new conditions. Favorable conditions are provided in certain areas for the smaller countries in the Socialist system of cooperation by the coordination of plans.

Within the CMEA, the Soviet economy plays an important structural balancing role for the smaller countries in many branches.

THE ROLE OF SOCIOPOLITICAL FACTORS

Economic and social traditions play a significant role in the choice of partners as well. These include: (a) the accumulated experiences of cooperation, (b) the mutual information flows of the given economies, and (c) the traditional goodwill on the level of firms.

Experiences

It is also evident that the mutual positive experiences of the previous period greatly influence the intensity and the existence of more developed forms of relations, e.g., the change from the simple barter trade to industrial cooperation. That is why most of the East-West industrial cooperation agreements of Hungary have been concluded with West German firms which have the longest foreign trade traditions in the region.

Human factors are part of the traditions as well, such as the orientation of engineers in technology, knowledge of the language of the experts, tourism, or the popularity of consumer goods from certain other countries, etc. The traditional reputation of Hungarian food products within the Federal Republic of Germany, Austria, the United Kingdom, and other Western European countries causes an important source of demand for Hungarian food export. International migration has also had some effect on creating market activity. In the United States, Canada, Brazil, and Australia a special kind of market has been created for Hungarian consumer goods within the population of Hungarian origin.

Political Factors

An important and controversial issue is to what extent political factors could be singled out under normal conditions (peaceful environment) in the choice of partners. The concrete analysis proves that political factors are extremely complex and cannot be reduced to some simplified formula.

There are of course certain fundamentals. Identical sociopolitical systems, similar interests, and institutions have undoubted influence on firms and governments as well. It is also well known that the atmosphere of the cold war, with distrust and hostility had a negative influence on the relationship between Hungary and the developed Western countries.

THE HUNGARIAN EXPERIENCE 227

Due to the cold war, relations with the advanced capitalist countries decreased to a minimum during the 1949-53 period. Thus, there was no other choice for the European Socialist countries, again including Hungary, but to provide and reinforce the external resources of economic growth in that area where the identical social system could create the most favorable conditions for the corresponding external economic relations. Nevertheless, Hungary's economic connections with the industrially developed countries were maintained even during the darkest years of the cold war period, if only at a very low level. Based on mutual interests, trade relations proved to be feasible even under those circumstances, although their maintenance demanded considerable efforts against the stragegic embargo and political pressure, also exerted by the Western partners of the Socialist countries. True, this foreign trade hardly exceeded the scope of a primitive barter deal for several years. It was simply impossible that the more advanced forms of economic cooperation gradually accepted all over the world, such as specialization and cooperation built on deliberate long-term agreements, would be possible between Hungary and the industrially advanced capitalist countries.

In the sixties with the development and advance of the detente policy, there have been new possibilities and conditions created in the field of economic relations between Hungary and the industrially developed western countries. The restrictive role played by politics, then later the importance of the improved political preconditions in the intensification of economic cooperations, verified that Hungarian relations with the industrially advanced capitalist countries were much more sensitive to politics than any other similar relation; foreign trade and foreign policy are not completely independent from one another within the same systems either, of course. Political factors in this context will continue to exert an influence on the economic relations in the future as well.

Quite naturally, however, such high sensitivity to politics may affect the development of relations, not only in an adverse but also in a favorable direction. If both parties realize that a reinforcement of the economic basis of the detente in conformity with the principle of mutual advantages is important and expedient, political decisions may obviously promote the settlement of unsolved economic problems, although an opposite possibility cannot be excluded either. Until forces acting against detente and the improvement of such relations do exist and exert an effect on world politics, there is always a risk that restrictive factors of a political character may hinder the development of economic relations.

Socialist Countries

In connection with these political factors, our Western partners often criticize that the state and economic institutions of the Socialist countries limit economic cooperation with the capitalist world.

But these institutions, built up by Socialist countries including Hungary, have not been established in a vacuum. They have been brought about by the given historical stiuation, as well as the economic objectives and conditions prevailing at a given time, and they had to function under given internal and external conditions.

With the economic development and transformation of the existing conditions, these institutions are naturally changing, and their functions in the choice of partners are similarly modified. In Hungary, for example, the government monopoly of foreign trade manifests itself quite differently today than 20 or 25 years ago. Hungarian institutions have to accomplish entirely new different duties than previously and in a completely different way than two-three decades earlier. In the early fifties, for example, Hungary's foreign trade organization reflected not only political motivations, but it was influenced also by the fact that Hungary did not attribute sufficient importance to international economic cooperation as a factor of growth. It is similarly obvious, however, that in the fifties the Western countries, too, have limited their economic relations with Hungary because of political reasons and that they have built up a wide range of national and international institutions for this purpose. The institutions of the Socialist countries had to defend their countries accordingly, and they will protect the national economy in the future as well if similar problems emerge. But this was a natural reaction, just like the attitude of the government institutions of the developed and developing capitalist countries in similar situations. However, under normal conditions the institutions of the Socialist countries have no such duties; in the choice of partners their political role may become more limited or even neutral, so economic forces and considerations may become dominant elements.

East-West Partnership

The institutional differences in the choice of partners are blamed occasionally in the Western literature for other reasons as well. The East-West partnership is often described as a relation between a giant organization of a Socialist country - sometimes even Hungarian firms are characterized with these terms - and a defenseless Western midget company, wherein the Socialist state enterprise has naturally a unilateral advantage. Sometimes, these descriptions discourage smaller firms from entering into meaningful relations with Socialist countries. However, a Socialist enterprise is certainly not a giant as compared to the defenseless Western dwarf. On the one hand, the Western partners of the Socialist countries are, in the majority of the cases, really industrial giants with global dimensions, a capital power, and production value exceeding those of a whole Socialist country; this is certainly the case with Hungary. On the other hand, since the conditions of a cooperation will always be developed by bargaining and since the partners have given alternatives, no smaller firm is taking greater risk by developing East-West relations than it would generally.

The planned character of a Socialist economy also means that international economic relations should be preferably developed on a long-term basis. Hungary desires to increase her economic security, therefore, since a considerable part of her national income (almost 50%) is directly affected by international economic relations. However, this endeavor is not against the interest of Hungary's Western partners either, but it is rather favorable from their viewpoint as well. The possibility for establishing longer term, more stable relations with Western partners also plays a considerable role in the choice of partners.

During the Cold War when East-West relations had been at their lowest level, Hungary's relations with the highly developed capitalist countries could not be regarded as suitable for stable planning; they influenced the choice of partners accordingly. In the seventies, on the other hand, the Socialist countries did not attempt to mitigate or eliminate the adverse effects of the recession in the capitalist economy by restricting relations and this was correct. On the contrary, by extending these relations they placed considerable orders, and with these orders they helped to a given extent in some of the industrial branches of certain countries. Those, by the way, who attack the institutions of the Socialist planned economy for creating problems of East-West relations, do forget easily that even in the present situation the administrative discrimination against the Socialist countries is still the strongest in the industrially advanced capitalist countries.

LEVEL AND STRUCTURE OF DEVELOPMENT AND THE RATE OF MARKET GROWTH

Among the more complex economic factors in the choice of partners, the role of differences in development level is often considered as one of the most important. This is very closely related to the differences in factor proportions and technological levels within the developmental level to which modern trade theories attach a crucial role.

Hungarian Relations with Other Countries

The establishment and development of relations between Hungary and the more developed countries also is chiefly stimulated by the possibilities of importing more developed technology, know-how, products, or eventually capital, and exporting such articles where the comparative position is favorable. There are indirect favorable effects for the less developed partner country as well. Higher requirements in the market of the more developed country stimulate better qualities in production and utilization of organizational and other experiences in the field of productivity. The demonstration effect of the relations with a more developed market could make consumption more efficient and more rational. The given country, however, has to pay eventually a rather high price for these advantages. The costs of learning, gaining good will, and proving the quality of the products are often forgotten by trade theorists.

Hungarian-Canadian relations, for example, prove what the potential reserves of factors are which could provide good conditions between the more developed Canada and Hungary with her developed structure of qualified manpower, industry, and science in certain areas. The comprehensive use of these possibilities, rooted in the level differences in the establishment and development of relations, however, require other conditions as well, such as competitive prices, favorable financing traditions of cooperation, etc.

Stabilizing or further improving these relations also requires additional mutual efforts from both partners in these cases, and the necessary efforts will surpass the results at the beginning. A country on a lower level is otherwise forced to make greater sacrifices. Later, however, the efforts may be generally compensated if an adequate atmosphere and the necessary good will could be created. The partners in these enterprises could be brought together, and consumers on both sides could get used to each other's goods and consumption habits.

Structural Interrelations

The role of development level differences in the choice of partners is closely connected to structural interrelations as well. It is evident that the competitive or complementary character of economic structure influences the affinity and thus trade relations. Defining the competitive or complementary structures in a dynamic, growing economy is difficult. The modern industrial branches, products, and components often are parallel in most of the industrial states. There are some developed countries as well where certain branches of industry do not exist and supply their need from imports. Many modern, highly research oriented, intensive branches, for example, could not be developed in smaller countries. Some states deliberately restrain from developing certain branches of product groups because the optimal size of production is too large for them. In Hungary, for example, there is no aviation industry and no development of personal cars, etc. Hungary deliberately has been trying to develop the complementary character of the structure of production through cooperation agreements with states which have the necessary conditions. Consequently the "microsphere" plays a decisive role regarding structural interrelations even in cases when international coordination of plans otherwise provide the preconditions through which the partners could consider each other's long-term needs in transforming the patterns of their production.

Changes in Structure

Changes in the commodity structure of our turnover with the advanced capitalist countries have been relatively slow during the 1960-76 period. In our exports the share of agricultural and food products decreased between 1960 and 1976 from 48 to 39%, while that of the industrial consumer goods increased from 16 to 20%, the ratio of materials and components grew from 29 to 34%, and that of the machines and other investment items from 4 to 6%. As compared to 1938, however, these changes are rather remarkable since that time almost two thirds of the total Hungarian exports to the industrially developed countries consisted of agricultural items, food, and food industry products.

Changes in the Hungarian production and export structures were much more far-reaching than those in the structure of our exports directed to the industrially advanced capitalist countries. The differences were due partly to economic and partly to commercial policy reasons.

First, under the conditions within the CMEA framework where the development level differences among the countries involved have not been that great, the circumstances were much more favorable for Hungary to carry on export much more suitable for her industrial production structure and to make use of her comparative advantages or position. In addition, exports to this area were much better supported by cooperation and specialization agreements than those aimed at the highly industrialized capitalist countries.

Secondly, the competitive position of Hungary did not increase sufficiently. In certain cases Hungary could not continually deliver products at the high quality level (e.g., machines and equipment) that was demanded by the Western markets. Sometimes Hungary did not produce sufficient quantities of these items or did not follow the changes in demand fast enough.

Finally, the export structure differences in relation to the Socialist and the industrially advanced capitalist countries, respectively, are also due to discriminations imposed on Hungary by the latter, to the less favorable conditions Hungary still has to face, and to the lack of insufficient manifestation of good will, which, however, is of utmost importance in foreign trade.

Hungary's New Export Oriented Trade Strategy

Hungary's new export oriented foreign trade strategy aimed at increased production of commodities efficiently marketable everywhere under identical conditions in the years to come may favorably affect both the quantity and quality of exportable products. But even if Hungary accomplishes the objectives set by this new foreign trade strategy, it will have to reckon with a situation where conditions other than economic, therefore, are related i.e., political and administrative decisions instead of quantity, quality, and price, might have an unfavorable effect on efforts in the market of the industrially developed Western countries.

The composition and problems with Hungarian imports have also been interrelated with the present stage of the development level and structure to a great extent.

For 1960-1976 imports from the industrially advanced countries, the first place was occupied by the category of materials and components, although the share of this category has decreased somewhat during this 15-year period, from 76% in 1960 to 63% by 1976; the latter has remained more or less constant ever since 1965. The share of consumer goods varied between 3 and 7% of the total, whereas the ratio of agricultural and food industry products increased from 8 to 13%. Although increasing slightly, the share of machines and equipment did not change much either (from 13 to 15% in the 1960-1965 period to 16-17% on the average between 1970 and 1976).

In the recent years a so-called stages approach to specialization connected to the development level and to the related structure has raised certain interest in the economic literature. Its main point is that a given development level is connected with a definitive capital stock, manpower composition, or expertise level, and the individual states on these bases could participate in the world market as exporters or importers. The more developed countries could accordingly give up some sectors, productive components, or products which are characterizing lower development level while modernizing their production. States on the lower level of development could take over those sectors from the more developed countries without a considerable amount of adaptation costs; thus, their export could be "automatically" secured because they are substituting the previous export of the states on higher level.

It is, of course, a correct observation that more advanced developing countries compete with developed states in certain fields by creating capital intensive import-substituting industries and labor intensive export sectors. Higher costs and losses are also due to the "artificial" stimulation of labor intensive exports. (1)

In the case of Hungary, to a certain extent, similar problems can also emerge in the choice of partners. It would be a great mistake, however, to consider the development level and the related comparative advantages as absolute factors for the choice of partners. Eventually, it is not at all unlikely that Hungary can take certain products which are also suitable for export from more developed countries within the framework of organized cooperation agreements, because for the given products there is still a demand on developed markets. The overemphasis of this approach, however, could make the chances of a state basically hopeless to implement a structural breakthrough in areas where the best conditions are provided towards the most developed world level and their relative position within the system of international relations would be forever frozen.

The dynamics of economic development supposes that the states do not leave their economies any more to spontaneous forces of the market but deliberately consider changes, objectives, and subjective possibilities.

One should not argue much about the role of the rate of market growth in the selection of partners. Rapidly expanding markets attract the firms of other countries, especially in those cases when other factors are also favorable. In the sixties and the early part of seventies, for example, in the Hungarian-West German relations about 50% of the turnover increase was due to the expansion of that market at a rate relatively faster than that in the other areas and to the fact that Hungarian foreign trade organizations are able to meet the increasing demand and have been in a position to maintain or even increase the ratio of Hungarian exports.

THE NEW CONDITIONS AND THE ROLE OF MORE ADVANCED FORMS

The role of different factors in the choice of partners in the coming decades will not necessarily follow the old patterns. First of all, while traditions, the vicinity of markets, etc. will still remain important, the structural factors will play a much greater role than in past decades. Trade will grow in those cases faster when mutual structural adjustments can take place with the respective countries and structural difficulties may cut traditional ties.

Industrial Cooperation

One form of structural adjustment is industrial cooperation. Hungarian enterprises might conclude agreements with their Western partners on the basis of transferring the production of certain items or product categories to Hungary, in those cases when the takeover would not mean the degradation of Hungary's industrial base, and for products which will still be in considerable demand in Western markets. The Hungarian enterprises might, at the same time, participate in new up-to-date branches as well by component deliveries, subcontracting, etc. and by building up research and development cooperations. As a result of these changes in Hungary's economic relations in the next 10 or 15 years, the importance of individual, industrially developed, capitalist countries will depend upon how extensive new forms such as joint ventures, industrial-technological cooperation, or cooperation in third markets, etc., will be, all of which could integrate the interests and definite objectives of the partners concerned.

The importance of relative market growth differences may also increase in the future, since those markets which will grow at a slower rate may not only be less attractive but more protectionist as well.

New Factors

If the more rapidly growing markets in the Western world will be chiefly outside Europe, the role of some traditional factors may be reduced, creating changes in the regional trade patterns for Hungary. These factors cannot and will not bring rapid and major changes, however, in the list of partners among the top 15 countries. Certain country's shares may change in both exports and imports, however.

Among the future, although not necessarily new, factors in the choice of partners, the degree of balancing in the mutual deliveries may also play a greater role in the world economy where a "selective protectionism" or "organized free trade" will be more important in the years to come. This means that administrative (commercial policy) instruments may play a greater role in both stimulating or discouraging the relations between certain countries of the West and Hungary. If common ground will not be found with the members of the European Economic Community and the respective countries will not adjust their international economic policies, trade between Hungary and the industrially advanced Western countries, other than Common Market members, may increase much faster than in the past, despite the role of historical and geoeconomic factors.

NOTE

1. See Bela Balassa, Stages Approach to Comparative Advantage. World Bank Staff Working Paper No. 256, May 1977, pp. 24-25.

14 Traditional and Nontraditional Trade: The Case of Czechoslovakia

Jaroslav Nykryn

INTRODUCTION

As stated at the first United Nations Conference on Trade and Development in Geneva in 1964, Czechoslovakia is a traditional trading country and its economy has a distinct outward looking character because of its highly developed industry and its comparatively limited raw material base. (1)

In terms of the per capita turnover of foreign trade, Czechoslovakia's foreign trade volume has been always roughly amost three times larger than the world average. The share of foreign trade in the volume of national income in the first postwar period was steadily 20-25% a year and has grown to 35-37% in the years 1975-77. (2) During the period 1971-75 of the fifth five-year plan and through the years 1976-77 of the sixth five-year plan, the volume of foreign trade grew yearly by 8-11% on the average.

Table 14.1 presents statistics on absolute value of trade and its commodity and geographic structure in some selected years.

The rate of growth of Czechoslovakian foreign trade, its growing share in the formation of the GNP in the period of the preceding and the present five-year plans, as well as distinct structural changes of exports and imports give certain evidence for the inclusion of Czechoslovakia in the network of international economic relations. Nevertheless, when comparing the small size of the economy with other European advanced countries, it is clear that the Czechoslovakian economy still does not exploit sufficiently all the opportunities of the international division of labor, both in East-West and North-South relations. It is, therefore, not only a matter of good intentions,

THE CASE OF CZECHOSLOVAKIA

TABLE 14.1. Czechoslovakian Foreign Trade

	Value of Trade (Millions Devisa Czechoslovakian Crowns)				
Turnover	10,328	18,535	39,463	108,133	121,440
Exports	5,422	9,988	19,764	52,137	58,240
Imports	4,907	8,537	19,699	55,996	63,200
Balance	515	1,451	65	-3,859	4,960
	The Structure of Trade According to Major Commodity Groups: CMEA Trade Classification (Percentages)				
EXPORTS					
Machinery, equipment, tools	20.3	43.6	48.5	50.1	51.3
Fuels, raw materials	40.9	39.2	30.4	28.7	27.9
Animals for breeding	0	0	0.2	0.1	0.1
Foodstuffs, including materials	5.5	6.1	4.4	3.5	3.2
Nonfoodstuffs, consumption goods	33.3	11.1	16.5	17.6	17.5
IMPORTS					
Machinery, equipment, tools	6.2	13.3	29.9	36.6	39.0
Fuels, raw materials	55.3	53.6	48.9	46.5	45.2
Animals for breeding	0.1	0	0.1	0.1	0.1
Foodstuffs, including materials	34.7	29.0	15.9	10.2	9.7
Nonfoodstuffs, consumption goods	3.7	4.1	5.2	6.6	6.0
	The Geographic Structure (Percentages)				
TOTAL TURNOVER	100	100	100	100	100
Socialist countries' total	39.7	70.2	73.2	72.0	71.6
CMEA	32.5	63.7	68.1	67.7	67.5
nonmembers of CMEA	7.2	6.5	5.1	4.3	4.1
Advanced capitalist countries	45.6	16.4	17.9	21.7	21.1
Developing countries	14.7	13.4	8.8	6.3	7.3

Source: Zakladni statisticke udaje o cs. zahranicnim obchode [Main statistical data on Czechoslovak foreign trade], Economic Information, no. 111/1977. (Prague: Research Institute for Foreign Trade, November 1977) pp. 9-17.

but also a matter of objective necessity that Czechoslovakian authorities support all efforts aimed at the promotion of trade and other economic relations and seek to utilize the potential benefits of the internationalization of production and technical and scientific progress.

CMEA Membership

Czechoslovakia is a member of CMEA, and approximately two thirds of total trade takes place with other CMEA countries, primarily with the Soviet Union. The Socialist economic integration assumes new and increasingly progressive forms of cooperation, especially by:

1. coordination of the national five-year plans, presently for 1976-80, with outlooks for 1985-90, including measures for closer harmonization of the national macroeconomic policies;
2. combined efforts in the field of research, development, and scientific cooperation;
3. specialization of production programs and industrial co-production and steps aimed at joint planning of certain products, industrial standardization, and unification.
4. concluding the five-year trade agreements with three types of quotas, presently for the period 1976-80;
5. collaborating in the field of payments, credits, transport, insurance, services, legal arrangements, and other areas of economic relations.

It should, however, be stressed that the Czechoslovakian trade policy and commercial methods, together with the steadily growing volume of trade with many Western partners, demonstrate that the economic collaboration within the framework of the CMEA is no obstacle to a wide and profound cooperation and trade relations with third countries. One of the most promising opportunities for an expansion of new economic relations with many non-Socialist countries could and should be the utilization of the nontraditional trade.

Trade Patterns with Western Countries

The development of trade relations with the advanced Western countries is illustrated by Table 14.2. The German Federal Republic is the traditional leading trade partner among all Western countries. The mutual exchange of goods and services rose from 917 million Cz. crowns in 1960 to 5.946 million in 1976, i.e. more than six times.

THE CASE OF CZECHOSLOVAKIA

TABLE 14.2. Share of 11 Selected Countries in Czechoslovakian Trade Turnover in Percent, All Advanced Countries Taken as 100 Percent

	1960	1970	1976
German Federal Republic	19.1	28.5	25.3
Austria	9.7	10.6	12.7
Great Britain	13.9	10.3	8.2
Switzerland	8.0	9.2	7.6
United States	2.7	3.0	7.2
France	4.4	6.3	6.5
Italy	6.2	8.9	5.9
The Netherlands	5.7	5.8	5.8
Belgium-Luxembourg	5.2	2.8	4.3
Sweden	3.0	4.1	3.3
Denmark	2.1	2.1	2.0
Canada	2.2	2.4	1.8

Source: *Facts on Foreign Trade* (Prague: Chamber of Commerce, 1960, 1970, 1976).

Austria is in the second position: the trade volume in 1960 was 466 million, in 1976 exactly 2.986 million, and it grew more than six times too. The figures for the remaining countries (in millions) are: Great Britain 664 and 2.122 (more than 3 times); Switzerland, up to 1975 including Lichtenstein was 383 and 1.707 (almost 4 times); the United States was 129 and 936 (7 times); France was 213 and 1.491 (7 times); Italy was 297 and 1.460 (more than 4 times); The Netherlands was 271 and 1.366 (5 times); Belgium-Luxembourg, up to 1975, then Belgium only was 251 and 690 (2.7 times); Sweden was 144 and 744 (more than 5 times); Denmark was 101 and 402 (4 times); and Canada was 106 and 412 (4 times).

MAIN FEATURES OF THE NONTRADITIONAL TRADE

Nontraditional trade begins to play an increasingly important role inside the complex structure of economic collaboration of the member states of CMEA. It is difficult to recognize exactly the shares of both types of trade, the traditional and the nontraditional, in the total volume of the exchange goods and services in these relations, as the two types of trade develop simultaneously, but the general trend of a steady replacement of the older type by the new one is quite obvious. The same tendencies appear in economic relations between the industrially advanced countries of the West. Only in relations between the Socialist and the non-Socialist countries, inexactly called East-West relations, does the new type of trade seems to have difficulties finding its way and its place.

At this time, two rather theoretical comments might be useful: first, what factors have an impact on the development of the nontraditional trade; second, what is the essence of this trade?

Factors that Affect Nontraditional Trade

Taken very generally there are four main objective factors which have a decisive impact on the rise and expansion of the nontraditional forms of international trade: 1) the steady acceleration of the internationalization of production; 2) further development of science and technology with their growing sophistication; 3) the expansion of international integration processes; and 4) a relatively positive development of international political relations.

These four elementary factors are interrelated. Not only industry, science, technology, integration, and international politics influence trade, but vice versa, trade creates new opportunities for a better utilization of the productive forces and should be encouraged. These objective factors, of course, have always had a strong impact on the national economy of Czechoslovakia, its foreign trade, and other elements of its external economic relations. Whereas significant progress has been achieved in Czechoslovakian relations with the member states of CMEA, although even here important opportunities have not been exploited sufficiently as yet, the level of trade relations with the West and the South, including the possibilities of nontraditional trade, is lower than it could and should be.

Features of Nontraditional Trade

The essence of the nontraditional trade might be characterized by several main features: 1) it originates in the sphere of material production, research, and development; 2) it is represented by deliveries of goods deriving from production for a priori known final consumers; 3) it is the result of the encounter of specific offer and specific demand, prevailingly for most types of the means of production, i.e., capital or investment goods in the broader sense, including many kinds of material services; 4) it is based on different types of legal agreements which cover the respective obligations of the partners as to sales and purchases; and 5) it has multiple effects on the volume and structure of international economic relations; these effects are individually much stronger than in the case of traditional trade.

It is not always easy to speak of pure types of nontraditional trade. They might be quite difficult to distinguish from traditional trade and from certain transgressive forms, but theoretically and methodologically we have to discern the classical, the transgressive, and the nontraditional types of trade developing simultaneously and interdependently. The identification of these three types might cause trouble for statisticians of national and international trade should they care to identify them at all. The problem is that the outer form of nontraditional trade and its incidental transgressive alternatives are identical with the classical form and alternatives. All the questions of an eventual formal identification of the three types of trade are at present not so important as the innermost nucleus and the practical aspects of these types.

Briefly, nontraditional trade can be described by five main features.

First, it emerges from material production, including the spheres of research and development. Research and development form an integral part of what is called the sphere of material production and most adequately represent direct links in the process of the transformation of science into a productive force. Nontraditional trade, contrary to traditional trade, is the result of decisions made a priori in production in anticipation of the market demand, not in response to it like classical trade.

Second, nontraditional trade is represented by acts of international exchange in which the goods delivered emerge from production for consumers known beforehand. In its most absolute form it is an exchange between the original producer in one country and the producer of final goods in another country. Direct methods of exports and imports make in these cases the exclusion of intermediaries an advantage for both partners. Objects of the respective agreements are prevailingly different kinds of means of production, raw materials, intermediate products, machinery, equipment, etc. Nontraditional trade is not quite possible in case of consumer goods. Millions of types of these products never pass directly from producer to the final (personal) consumer. Not even the most intricate planning is able to designate the final consumer in advance.

Third, nontraditional trade arises where specific offers meet with specific demand and vice versa. This paper will not go into details of how specific demand might be created, since there are different theories how all this happens, (3) but this question will be discussed in a different manner later in this chapter.

Fourth, nontraditional trade is usually based on much more complex and broader types of agreements than the traditional ones, for which more or less simple sales contracts are typical, but under all circumstances, any specific type of agreements (deliveries of complete technological units, industrial co-production, joint tenders, etc.) must contain firm obligations of the partners to sell and buy within the broader agreements. In other words, broader agreements must contain sales and purchasing obligations.

Fifth, nontraditional trade has individual stronger impact and multiple effects on the volume and structure of international economic relations when compared with the traditional trade. There are, of course, always exceptions to the rule, but international contracts such as Soviet agreements with American, German, of French firms on exploitation of natural resources, which are based on the compensation principle, belong to the biggest international transactions. Nontraditional trade often creates further opportunities for new transactions.

THE CASE OF CZECHOSLOVAKIA 243

NON TRADITIONAL TRADE WITH CMEA COUNTRIES

Czechoslovakia cooperates with the CMEA countries in many different fields: in science and technology, research and development, production specialization and industrial cooperation, joint projects of the Orenburg type, payments and credits, etc., and, of course, in trade. (4)

But one of the most remarkable changes in the economic relations of Czechoslovakia with CMEA countries, which at the same time takes place in all member states of CMEA, is the switch from simple forms of traditional trade to more sophisticated forms of nontraditional trade, based on the coordination of the five-year plans and other forms of joint planned efforts. Simple trade is no longer the decisive base for economic cooperation inside CMEA.

For the sake of comparison it might be useful to mention the fact that during the period 1976-77 alone at least 116 new agreements on specialization and industrial cooperation and 84 agreements on scientific and technical collaborations were concluded. Most of these new agreements, together with those valid since earlier dates, simultaneously developed from the nontraditional exchange of goods and services.

The center country in Czechoslovakia's economic relations with the CMEA countries is the Soviet Union. Nontraditional trade plays an increasingly important role in the mutual relations. Besides machinery and equipment, Czechoslovakia imports large quantities of important raw materials from the Soviet Union. During 1976-77 the Soviet deliveries represented 99.9% of the total imports of natural gas, 92.6% of all imported crude oil, 83.5% of ferrous metals, 58.2% percent of cotton, etc. Because of the direct flow of these commodities from the original producer to the Czechoslovakian producer of final goods, the contractual nature of that trade, and other typical parameters, these imports may be classified as types of nontraditional imports.

Types of Commodity Groups

The five-year trade agreements with all member states of CMEA for the period 1976-80 contain three types of commodity groups.

The first group of commodities chiefly covers economically essential goods, such as raw materials, special machinery, equipment and foodstuffs, which are subject to firm quantitative and qualitative quotas in the trade agreements and in their yearly protocols. These quotas are more or less fixed in advance and represent firm obligations to sell and buy. Not all deliveries within these quotas may come automatically under the heading of nontraditional trade, but many of them belong to that trade, for example, when they originate in agreements on specialization and co-production.

The second group covers somewhat less important commodities, such as different types of industrial consumer goods, foodstuffs, etc. Export and import quotas for these goods also represent firm obligations of the trading partners to sell and buy during the five-year or the yearly period, but the quotas are fixed only in terms of value without further technical specification. Only some of these goods might come under the heading of nontraditional trade, given the necessary parameters mentioned earlier.

The third group of goods, which might be classified as nonessentials belongs mainly to the simple types of traditional trade. No quotas and no firm obligations to sell and buy are made in advance, which is usual in these cases. In most relations with the CMEA countries their share in the total volume of exchange is small and usually does not reach the level of 10%.

Interrelation between Trade Agreements and Other Collaborative Efforts

The interrelation between the trade agreements and other types of collaboration with the CMEA countries is obvious. Nontraditional trade finds its way into the network of economic integration. It has already become typical in most cases of production specialization and industrial co-production.

It is being developed in certain international joint investment projects aimed at the exploitation of national resources which take place not only in the different fields of the extracting industry but also in the transforming industries and in the infrastructure, including cases, such as the Drushba pipeline for crude oil, the Orenburg gas pipeline, the Joint Electricity System, the Joint Truck System in railway transport, etc., not to mention other specific cases like the Intercosmos Program. All these cases require deliveries which by no means correspond to parameters of the simple traditional trade.

NONTRADITIONAL TRADE WITH THE WEST AND THE SOUTH

Economic relations between the East and the West have been described in many books and discussed in many international meetings. (5) This is not, however, the case so far as North-South relations are concerned.

In relations with the West and the South, Czechoslovaika wishes to establish economic collaboration, not only in the field of the traditional trade but also in other types of economic relations, such as industrial cooperation, scientific and technical collaboration, refining processes, deliveries of complete plants and technological units, etc., from which nontraditional trade may originate. Collaboration in these types of economic relations forms the economic base of peaceful coexistence. Prerequisites for an objectively useful expansion of these relations are the adoption of well-known principles of equal treatment, mutual benefits, and nondiscrimination.

Irrespective of the known difficulties in foreign markets, the volume of Czechoslovakian trade with the industrially advanced Western and developing countries rose during 1976-77 roughly by 20%, as compared with figures mentioned earlier in this paper. A very small share, difficult to quantify, belongs into the category of nontraditional trade.

The East-West and the North-South economic relations could and should be encouraged to participate in more sophisticated trade as the result of deeper forms of collaboration. The trend towards all elements of international economic relations, from which nontraditional trade may originate, should be supported nationally and internationally not only between the industrially advanced countries but also between the industrialized and the developing countries. This support is very important as national economies depend more upon being effectively and efficiently included in the network of international division of labor. This applies to all small and medium sized economies who wish to participate with other countries, including the outward looking economy of Czechoslovakia. Nontraditional trade should gradually become an increasingly important agent of the intensification of the Czechoslovak productive forces.

In the case of Czechoslovakia not all opportunities for the expansion of nontraditional trade have been utilized so far, and this situation exists not necessarily because of that country's fault. There are many types of transactions which can stimulate the expansion of nontraditional trade between Czechoslovakia and the West and the South, and it may be useful to discuss them now in some detail.

Cooperation Deliveries

Cooperation deliveries belong generally to the most dynamic forms of nontraditional trade. The Czechoslovakian economy in this area in the West and South relations still has considerable unutilized opportunities, and of course, the same opportunities exist in Czechoslovakia for foreign partners. It is true that Czechoslovakia has at present a great number of specific interstate long-term agreements on economic, industrial, and scientific cooperation with non-Socialist countries (all nine members of EEC and with many of the most important trade partners among the developing countries), but these formal commercial and political prerequisites alone do not lead and have not led automatically to concrete inter-firm cooperation contracts.

Any agreements on industrial cooperation, especially agreements on industrial co-production, must contain deliveries of components, one way or two way deliveries, and in this way specific demand meets specific offer.

There are many reasons why Czechoslovakia supports the expansion of cooperation deals and the nontraditional trade which they generate:

1. The flow of cooperation components inside the respective agreements leads to higher volumes of mutual trade in general.
2. Industrial co-production as the basis for industrial co-operation has the well-known specialization effect of raising the productivity of labor and decreasing production costs per product unit because of exploitation of bigger product series.
3. Co-production enables the economization of costs for R & D if an agreement on collaboration in this field is part of the broader contracts.
4. Nontraditional trade inside the cooperation contracts may bring about the required modernization of production capacities and higher standards of the final products.
5. The "assortment" function of cooperation is important also since it might help to solve the disadvantages of too broad assortments. This function of international cooperation must be underlined in the case of Czechoslovakia, especially in the machine building industry.
6. The possibility to help to solve the problem of insufficient labor which had been exploited to maximum years ago, is equally important for Czechoslovakia.
7. Cooperation may not only expand trade in general, but also may help to overcome certain commercial policy barriers (import quotas, tariffs, legal and administrative obstacles,

etc.) which Czechoslovakian exports meet in certain Western countries.

Nontraditional trade originating from these agreements is also considered to be of value to the Western firms who seek to find new markets for their products in the markets of the CMEA countries. Deliveries of components may be followed by products outside cooperation agreements which may pave the way for them. Other reasons include the possibility to reduce unemployment in certain countries and branches of industry. It might be of some interest to say that among certain measures now underway in Czechoslovakia, which are aimed at obtaining greater support for cooperation deals with foreign firms, a new role for the Czechoslovakian production enterprises in the direct negotiations with producers outside the country is in sight within the framework of the state monopoly of foreign trade. (6)

Because of the technological parity of the Czechoslovakian industry in relation to Western firms, it is clear that better possibilities for the expansion of nontraditional trade are given in these relations rather than in relations with the developing countries.

Processing Operations

Processing operations may serve as another example of a base for nontraditional trade, both the so-called active and passive ones. This very old element of international economic relations might be much better utilized than at present, not only in relations with Western firms but also with the developing countries. Czechoslovakia considers processing operations as a good tool for trade expansion.

Deliveries of Made-To-Order Goods

Deliveries of made-to-order goods form a firm base for the development of the nontraditional trade in cases of machines, individual equipment, and the like, although not in cases of consumer goods. Production of certain of these goods for example according to the technical and technological documentation of the buyer, may lead to a very substantial volume of nontraditional trade. The value of machinery made-to-order goods might be very high, not to mention the possibility of the advance production of certain individually made machines for the consumer, or of complete integrated systems of product lines. Trade operations of this type may take place between the industrialized and the developing countries. Under certain circumstances the volume of this trade could be considerably raised.

Production and Profit Sharing

Production sharing and in certain alternatives also profit sharing could be named as other examples of possibilities to expand nontraditional trade, especially in the North-South relations.

Production sharing is in fact a way of financing certain activities mostly in the developing countries, for example extracting and refining raw materials (ferrous and nonferrous metals, wood, ores, etc.). Some authors call this type of deal two-way cooperations. (7) In fact Northern firms deliver credit, technology, engineers, know-how, and management skills to domestic Southern firms, which supply the land, resources, buildings, and unskilled labor. The credit granted to start the respective activity is then repaid to the North by deliveries of products resulting from the project. In other words, production sharing is nothing else than a form of credit and repayment.

Czechoslovakia also starts certain projects for production sharing, out of which the deliveries of crude or refined raw materials emerge. These deliveries are planned for use in Czechoslovakian factories. They definitely belong in the category of nontraditional trade.

Considerably different in conditions, although the same in their substance, are the so-called cooperation agreements based on the compensation principle, as effectuated especially by the Soviet Union in East-West relations.

Exports of Technological Units

The export of complete technological units takes place typically in the North-South direction and might be closely linked with nontraditional trade. These exports have three main forms:

1. Exports of components to be used in building the respective technological unit in the given developing country.
2. Exports of the "turn-key" type, which are only slightly different from the first one.
3. Entrepreneurial deliveries of technological units are the newest known form, and they are recommended and asked for by governments of the developing countries. The domestic investor not only wants foreign machines, know-how, etc., but also asks his partner from the industrialized country to take

over together with the investor all risks of production and marketing of the goods produced for a certain period; the average seems to be five years. This deal may contain agreements from which nontraditional trade can emerge.

Czechoslovakia takes this development into consideration and is willing to cooperate in this way with all developing countries which so desire.

Other examples of deals in international economic relations from which the nontraditional trade emerges could be cited, but the examples mentioned might be quite sufficient for the clarification of the problem.

HOW TO SUPPORT NONTRADITIONAL TRADE

In the first place it seems useful to recognize the essence of this trade. In this sense it is felt that "there is nothing more practical than a good theory." In reality, economists and other theoreticians should try to explain in their countries the values of nontraditional trade. The same should happen in international economic organizations such as the Economic Commission of the United Nations Organization (UNO).

Steps to Promote International Economic Relations

In the second place, certain steps seem to be necessary in order to promote more efficiently those elements of international economic relations which are more up to date and which form in many cases the best base for nontraditional trade. We have in mind: (1) international specialization of production and industrial co-production; (2) refining operations and deliveries of goods made to order; (3) production sharing and other types of deals mentioned above; (4) joint projects and joint ventures; (5) entrepreneurial deliveries of complete technological units, besides more obsolete forms of these deliveries; (6) subcontracting; (7) three-partite cooperation in the East-West and in the North-South relations; and (8) direct cooperation in the field of R & D, including cross-licensing and trade in the field of know-how.

Current Measures

In Czechoslovakia, especially since October 1975, certain measures are underway to promote economic and industrial cooperation, coproduction, scientific and technical collaboration, joint ventures, production sharing, and other relatively new elements of our external economic relations, both with the West and the South. Without being too specific we may mention certain steps and means which are important.

<u>Planning.</u> Deals in industrial cooperation, for example, have an average validity of 6-8 years, with possible exceptions. The periods of validity of the cooperation agreements are, therefore, longer than the typical five-year planning schemes, and it is necessary to harmonize and to include cooperations into the system of the five-year plans in an effective way.

<u>Economic incentives.</u> The level and the structure of internal prices, price preferences, etc., which are determined, for example, for export operations of the nontraditional type, emerge from newly introduced, highly sophisticated production capacities or from old, but modernized factories because of utilization of collaboration in R & D.

<u>Exchange policy.</u> To promote cooperation in the broadest sense and to encourage our producers in these deals, certain bonuses may be granted in foreign exchange, specific accounts in foreign exchange may be introduced, etc.

<u>Organizations.</u> Certain measures in the organization of the state monopoly of foreign trade may be introduced; for example, a new organization, "Intergeo," exists since 1977 and is aimed at collaboration with partners in the developing countries in the form of production sharing for the exploitation of their natural resources. Direct trade representation of Western firms in Czechoslovakia is possible since 1975 according to a decree of the minister for foreign trade, etc.

<u>Legal instruments.</u> All the new measures call for adequate legal arrangements in the field of education, personnel, and in other respects.

Additional Improvements Necessary for International Economic Relations

Improvements are also needed in international relations. Steps are necessary to improve the commercial policy conditions, first of all in East-West relations. It is necessary to remove all obstacles to the expansion of all types of trade with countries of different social systems.

The expansion of nontraditional trade requires some further improvements:

<u>Contractual instruments.</u> The existing agreements are utilized only insufficiently. The mixed commissions and the groups of experts do not seem to be active enough, and sometimes initiative on both sides is missing, etc.

<u>Autonomous instruments.</u> These instruments include granting customs preferences to trade emerging from deeper economic collaboration; removing differentiated tariffs; abolishing sometimes unnecessary administrative, if not bureaucratic, practices and improving the legal procedures; using economic and other incentives to promote this trade; and removing all remnants of discriminatory treatment.

<u>Information.</u> Information as to the existence of opportunities for collaboration should be improved.

We are convinced, of course, that mutual understanding is the most important prerequisite in the promotion of a useful expansion of the nontraditional trade based on many different types of deeper economic collaboration in East-West and North-South relations, although understanding by itself is only the starting point. Realistic thinking, as well as economic and commercial considerations come next. The evaluation of what has been done already and what could be done at present and in the future follows in subsequent chapters. Theory might just help a little bit.

NOTES

1. For more details see Czechoslovakia and the UN Conference on Trade and Development (Prague: Rapid, Foreign Trade Publicity Corporation, 1964) pp. 148-155.

2. Facts on Foreign Trade (Prague: Chamber of Commerce) 1971-77.

3. For one of them see J. K. Galbraith, The New Industrial State (Boston: H. Mifflin Co., 1967) pp. 16, 200-5.

4. Comprehensive Programme of the Socialist Economic Integration (Prague: Svoboda, 1971).

5. A Research Note on Industrial Co-operation as a Factor in the Growth of East-West European Trade (Geneva: Economic Bulletin for Europe, Vol. 21, No. 1, 1971) pp. 67-88; J. Wilczynski, The Economics and Politics of East-West Trade (London: Macmillan, 1969); Analytical Report on Industrial Co-operation among ECE Countries, (Geneva: United Nations) 1973; C. T. Saunders, ed., East-West Cooperation in Business: Inter-firm Studies (Vienna, New York: The Vienna Institute for Comparative Economic Studies, 1977); J. Nykryn and K. Stepan, La Cooperation economique des pays de l'Est avec la Suisse (Geneva: Institut universitaire de hautes etudes internationales, 1977).

6. See a Czechoslovakian publication of the author of this paper: J. Nykryn., Vyrobni podnik ve vnejsich ekonomickych vztazich, (Production Enterprise in External Economic Relations) (Prague: SNTL - State Publishing Agency for Technical Literature, 1977).

7. For example, A. Adahl, IIIrd East-West Round Table on East West Industrial Cooperation (Brussels: ELEC, 1969).

15 Factors Influencing Trade with the West: Albania, Mongolia, North Korea, and Vietnam

Adi Schnytzer

INTRODUCTION

The expansion of trade between the Eastern European members of CMEA and the developed capitalist world, witnessed over the past decade, has had its motivation, from the Eastern point of view, in the desire of the CMEA economies to foster intensive economic growth with the aid of advanced Western technology. In this paper, it is argued that for small Socialist economies situated either outside Eastern Europe or those sharing no borders with a CMEA economy, the determination of the level of trade with the West has been influenced at least as much by their government's view of the Sino-Soviet split and by ideological considerations as by questions of technology. The recent experience of the economies of Albania, North Korea, Vietnam, and Mongolia is used to illustrate this hypothesis. It is also suggested that the choice of Western trading partners has been influenced primarily by geographical and historical factors.

ALBANIA

In the wake of the split with the Soviet Union in 1961, Albania began trading at modest levels with the West. Prior to 1961, when the Soviet Union was supplying the economy with lavish aid, the Albanian leadership had deemed it unecessary to import technology from the West. Under cold war circumstances it was extremely unlikely that developed capitalist economies would be willing to provide Albania with easy credit arrangements because the Albanian economy could not begin to produce export manufactured goods of sufficient quality and quantity to finance the level of imports necessary to maintain a high rate of growth.

On the other hand, modest trade with the West has been encouraged since China became Albania's major financial donor. This has been due largely to China's inability to provide Albania with all her capital requirements. At the same time, the rapid growth of the Albanian economy has been accompanied by the production of a greater variety of exportables than in the past. Thus, while imports from developed capitalist economies remained stable at $19 million between 1965 and 1970, Albanian exports rose from $2 million to $9 million (see Table 15.1).

Albanian hostility towards detente and the magnitude of Chinese aid during the sixties ensured that trade with the West would not rise significantly as it had done elsewhere in Eastern Europe. However, while the magnitude of Chinese aid since 1971 has remained high, its distribution over the period has been sufficiently uneven to interfere with the fulfillment of the 1971-75 plan. A detailed consideration of the performance of the Albanian economy since 1971 will provide an insight into the significance of trade with the West since that time.

Albania's Economy: 1971 to Present

The Sixth Congress of the Albania Labor Party (PLA) approved a target of around 11.6 billion leks for the value of global industrial production in 1975, an increase of 61-66% over 1970. (1) The increase in group A production was to be 78-83%, while consumer goods production would rise by 40-44%. (2) Statistics published in 1974 suggest that these fifth five-year plan targets would probably be met. At 9,608 million leks, global industrial production in 1973 (3) was slightly higher than the 9,533 million leks which would have been achieved had the average annual rate of 10.3%, foreshadowed in the plan, (4) been maintained over the 1971-73 period. Further, the increase in output was in approximate accordance with the planned split between group A and group B production, the former having increased by 40% over 1970 and the latter by 29%. (5)

However, from the beginning of 1974 it seems clear the Albanian authorities felt that the industrial output targets of the fifth five-year plan might be beyond the economy's grasp. The 1974 annual plan called for an increase of 8% in global industrial production, (6) while the rate achieved was 7.3% (7) The 1975 plan was even more pessimistic, calling for an increase of only 4.4% over the 1974 total. (8)

TABLE 15.1 - Albanian Trade with Market Economies
(millions of dollars)

	Imports	Exports
1973 (Quarters)		
I	7	6
II	12	6
III	15	7
IV	10	12
1974 (Quarters)		
I	12	9
II	26	15
III	22	19
IV	21	17
1975 (Quarters)		
I	26	15
II	30	18
III	15	19
IV	15	20
1976 (Quarters)		
I	9	10
II	11	14
III	10	8

Source: M.C. Kaser, "Trade and Aid in the Albanian Economy," Joint Economic Committee, United States Congress, East European Economies Post-Helsinki, (Washington, D.C.: U.S. Government Printing Office, 1977), p. 1329.

In any event, even this modest target was not reached; global industrial output increased by only 4% over the year. (9)

Thus, for the five-year plan period as a whole, global industrial production had risen by 52% according to Mehmet Shehu's report (10) to the Seventh Congress of the PLA, while the annual data suggest an increase of 51%. Given the degree of rounding off involved in the preparation of the data for publication, this discrepancy does not appear to be significant. The changing structure of production does, however, represent an important problem, for whereas the increase in the production of industrial consumer goods was 45% (11) and thus exceeded the plan target of 40-44%, the value of group A production was only 57% greater than it had been in 1970, against the 78-83% that was planned. (12) Thus, over the last two years of the plan period, 1974 and 1975, the rate of growth of group B production exceeded that of group A, with rates for the period at 12.4% and 12.1%, respectively.

A distinct change in the nature of Albania's industrial development at some stage in 1973 or 1974 is also indicated by the increases in labor productivity and the capital-labor ratio registered by Albanian industry during the fifth five-year plan. Thus, between 1970 and 1973 the incremental capital-labor ratio rose by 17.4% against an increase of 18.1% in labor productivity. (13) In other words, industrial capital productivity had risen for the first time. Although the increase was less than 1%, the fact that the decrease experienced during the fourth five-year plan was halted suggests that some of the labor misallocation problems besetting the earlier period had been solved. Further, the increase in experts and skilled workers forthcoming over time could only contribute positively to production efficiency.

In the 1974-75 period capital productivity again fell and industrial labor productivity rose by only 2.4% as against a 6.5% increase in the incremental capital-labor ratio. Finally, it should be noted that whereas the share of heavy industrial output in the total rose between 1970 and 1973, its share may have fallen between 1973 and 1975. This is suggested by the increase in the share of food and light industrial output, from 48.4% in 1973 to 49.3% in 1975. (14) The share had been 51.4% in 1970. (15)

Reasons for Economic Change

The absence of any official Albanian analysis of the change in industrial development experienced halfway through the fifth five-year plan--its existence is not even acknowledged--renders an explanation difficult. However, on the basis of the available evidence some tentative conclusions are possible. In the first place, Kaser has suggested that there may have been a reduction in Chinese aid in 1975. (16) If this were the case, the downward revision in the five-year plan implied by the low 1974 target for global industrial production may be explained by the PLA's possible anticipation of the reduction in aid. Mehmet Shehu's statement, (17) at the Seventh Congress of the PLA, that the failure of the industrial plan was in part due to a failure to complete the construction of important projects on time, is consistent with this line of argument.

However, the economic outcomes of the 1974-75 period remain to be explained in terms of the PLA's development strategy. In other words, on the basis of the PLA's reaction to the reduction in Soviet aid in 1961, it might be predicted that resources would have been reallocated away from other sectors so that heavy industry could have a greater opportunity to fulfill its plans, the lack of foreign capital notwithstanding. On the other hand, the success of the light and food industries, coupled with the relatively modest increase in the industrial labor force between 1973 and 1975, suggests that a decisive change in industrial development policy took place at some time in 1973. Further evidence of this change is provided by statistics on Albania's trade with the developed capitalist economies over the relevant period (see Table 15.2).

The doubling of turnover in the second quarter of 1974 and the return to 1973 levels in the first quarter of 1976 (even below in volume terms) suggests a modification of Albania's trade policy. Further, although the planned increases in exports in 1973 and 1974 were only 5.4% and 11% respectively, the value of exports actually rose by 15% in 1973 and by 17% in 1974. (18) Thus, if there was a reduction in the level of capital imports from China in the 1974-75 period, and the evidence is not concrete, the PLA clearly responded with an export drive to the developed capitalist economies, possibly designed to pay for capital imports. On the domestic front, it was evidently decided that other sectors should not be permitted to suffer losses from reallocations to heavy industry. The overall failure of the third five-year plan may have been influential in determining this temporary shift away from the Stalinist model.

That the policy shift was only temporary was made clear when the minister of trade, the minister of industry and mining, and the chairman of the state planning commission were all dismissed at some time towards the end of 1975, i.e., when Albania's trade turnover with the West was beginning to drop. A possible reason for these dismissals emerges if it is assumed that there were sharp differences in the PLA leadership over the nature of the response to an aid reduction in 1973. It is likely, given the consistent attempts to maintain Stalinist development policies since the very early days of the PLA's rule, that some members of the leadership would have argued

TABLE 15.2 - Albanian Trade with the EEC (millions of European Units of Account (EUA)

	1972	1973	1974	1975	1976(a)	Jan.-June 1977 (a)
EEC exports to Albania	14	14	29	33	27	21
EEC imports from Albania	9	10	22	22	24	16

Source: *Monthly External Trade Bulletin* [hereafter METB] (Brussels: Stat. Office of the European Committees)

NOTE: European Units of Account are defined in Commission Decision No. 3289/75/ECSC of December 18, 1975 (O.J. No. L. 327 of 19.12.1975, p. 4).

(a) Preliminary data

for a continuation of the current policy even in the face of anticipated
difficulties. In any event, this faction was overruled, and although
an 8% planned increase in global industrial production in 1974 represented a setback to the five-year plan, the deficit might still have
been recovered in 1975 if the switch in foreign trade had yielded the
desired capital imports to make the recovery possible.

The continued success of light industry in 1974 and the sharp
increase in exports suggest that the low target for industrial production in 1975 was due either to an inability to obtain the desired capital
imports from the West or to a further reduction in Chinese aid, which
had not been anticipated in 1973. Kaser's figures (19) suggest that
the latter explanation is more plausible, calculating that China provided Albania with $75 million credit in 1974 while Albania ran a surplus of $24 million with China in 1975. Whatever the reason, the fifth
five-year plan could no longer be met; the policy of temporary moderation had failed, and its advocates suffered the political consequences.

The accusations leveled at the dismissed ministers at the PLA's
Seventh Congress in November 1976 are not inconsistent with the
above hypothesis. Thus, Shehu accused (20) former Chairman of the
State Planning Commission Kellezi, former Minister of Industry and
Mining Theodhosi, "and others in the economic sector" of sabotaging
the oil industry, while Hoxha in his report (21) blamed those
purged for the failure to complete certain construction projects, as
well as shortfalls in the five-year plans of the oil, chromium, copper,
coal, bread grain, and industrial crop sectors. Referring to the oil
industry, (22) Hoxha charged Kellezi and Theodhosi with using "refined methods to disorient exploration" and mismanage the industry,
with preventing the exploitation of new sources of oil and gas, and
with using "barbaric" methods for the exploitation of existing wells.

There has been no official indication as to whether or not China
has been supplying aid to Albania since 1975. However, it is clear
that relations between the two countries are strained.

In July, an editorial in Zeri i popullit criticized some of China's
underlying foreign policy, although China was not mentioned by name. (23)
In particular, it was argued that the United States and the Soviet
Union were equally dangerous superpowers and that the Third World
could not be considered as a shield against their power. Later in
July, reports from Belgrade suggested that the Albanian government
had asked Chinese experts to leave Albania, while official sources in
both Tirana and Peking denied the reports. (24) On the other hand,
the Chinese press attacked what it called "splitism" in Albania.
From the viewpoint of economic aid, there was a significant report
broadcast by Radio Tirana on July 26, which contended that the
Albanian government had asked the Soviet government for credits to

assist in the construction of the metallurgy complex at Elbasan in 1960 and that they had been refused. The likely validity of this contention is supported by the fact that Romania's request to the Soviet Union for a steel plant at Galati was also turned down at the same time. (25) Moreover, the Czech government had said earlier that it could supply all of Albania's steel requirements if it received Albanian iron-nickel ores. (26) The report went on to add that the Albanians were thus forced to build the complex relying on their own resources and that this had been successfully achieved up to now; that the project could not have been undertaken without Chinese aid was not mentioned. In fact, the Chinese were not thanked for aid at all. A confidential memorandum by the Chinese foreign minister for domestic briefing, dated July 30, is reported as having listed the issues in dispute with Albania but also to have stated that the Chinese would not make the matter public. (27) Both countries broke their silence about each other in April 1978; the publication of innocuous news items suggested that some accommodation had been reached.

Trade with Western Capitalist Countries

If the PLA leadership decides that Albania should maintain a balance of foreign trade, it is possible that a large part of that trade will be with the developed capitalist economies of Western Europe. The agreement signed between the Albanian and Greek governments to open a Tirana-Athens air link may have been a first step in this direction. (28) However, should Albania's pattern of trade alter in this direction, and Albania's increased volume of trade with the EEC in the first half of 1977 indicates that it might, and should China lose status in the Albanian press of a Socialist economy, any future Albanian requirement for foreign credit would pose the PLA constitutional problems, for article 28 of the constitution states:

> The granting of concessions to, and the creation of foreign economic and financial companies and other institutions or ones formed jointly with bourgeois and revisionist capitalist monopolies and states as well as obtaining credits from them are prohibited in the People's Socialist Republic of Albania. (29)

As Kaser has pointed out, "no government in the world has ever asked its legislature constitutionally to disbar it from raising an external loan." (30)

Albania's major trading partner in the West is Italy. As the data in Table 15.3 show, the Italian economy has been the largest

TABLE 15.3 - West German and Italian Trade with Albania
(millions of EUA)

	1972	1973	1974	1975	1976(a)	Jan.-June 1977
Italian exports to Albania	8	8	11	13	12	7
Italian imports from Albania	7	8	14	13	12	9
West German exports to Albania	4	2	10	10	5	8

Source: METB

(a) Preliminary data

TABLE 15.4 - Mongolian Trade with Developed Capitalist Countries
(millions of dollars)

	1973	1974	1975	1976
Mongolian exports	2.3	2.1	1.6	3.7
Mongolian imports	3.0	3.9	3.7	4
Percentage of total trade turnover	1.4	1.4	1.1	1.4

Source: CMEA Statistical Yearbooks. The following exchange rates were used to convert trade rubles into dollars: ITR = $1.36 (1973), ITR = $1.33 (1974), ITR = $1.33 (1975), ITR = $1.33 (1976). See M.C. Kaser, International Currency Review, 9, no. 2, p. 117 and 7, no. 2, p. 47.

importer of Albanian goods throughout the seventies by a fair margin and was marginally ahead of West Germany in sales to Albania. However, it is interesting to note that the sudden increase in Albanian imports in 1974, 1975, and the first half of 1977 is reflected most starkly in the West German figures, supporting the hypothesis that Albanian leadership is using trade with the West as a means of obtaining the capital goods which China is no longer delivering.

The reasons for the significant trade ties between Albania and Italy are largely historical. Prior to World War II, Albania was virtually an Italian colony and postcolonial relationships tend to be reflected in higher levels of trade than would otherwise be expected.

MONGOLIA

In 1921 Outer Mongolia gained its independence from China with the aid of Soviet troops. By 1929 the majority of Chinese traders had been driven out of the country and a Soviet foreign trade monopoly was established. (31) Virtually the whole of Mongolia's foreign trade was conducted with the Soviet Union between 1931 and 1951, after which the country began to trade with China and other Socialist economies. By 1957 this non-Soviet trade amounted to 25% of the total. (32) The Chinese government began to provide Mongolia with economic aid in competition with the Soviet Union and in particular, supplied the country with a substantial number of workers; the peak has been variously estimated as lying in the range of 12,000 to 20,000. (33)

Chinese aid continued to flow into its northern neighbor until 1964, when the Mongolian leadership irrevocably committed itself to the Soviet side in the Sino-Soviet dispute. While there is evidence to suggest that several high ranking Mongolian officials were purged in 1965 for taking a pro-China line, (34) it seems unlikely, given the massive quantity of Soviet aid and extent of Soviet military influence in the country, that the Mongolian government could seriously have contemplated a break with the Soviet Union. It has been suggested that by "1965, total aid to Mongolia from all sources, received and promised, amounted to about $900 per capita, making Mongolia the most intensively aided country in the world." (35)

On the occasion of Soviet President Leonid Brezhnev's visit to Ulan Bator to mark the fiftieth anniversary of the Mongolian revolution in 1974, Host President Yumjaagiyn Tsedenbal commented that the Mongols and the Soviets were "always together," "one crew in battle, one brigade in labour." (36) In mid-September 1975, Party Politburo Member and First Deputy Premier Damdinjavyn Maidar remarked that "direct contacts" had been established between 13 ministries and departments in Mongolia and 20 in the Soviet Union. (37) Soviet influence over the development of the Mongolian economy, thus, is all pervasive and apparently very welcome to the present leadership. Under these circumstances it is not surprising that trade with the West has not exceeded two% of total Mongolian foreign trade turnover for many decades, and because it is landlocked by China and the Soviet Union, this has mitigated against any significant expansion in its trade with the West. Some of the relevant data is shown in Table 15.4.

The details of Mongolia's trade with the United Kingdom in 1976 provide some indication of the unimportance of Mongolian links with the West. In that year, Britain imported goods valued at £400,905 as against exports worth only £24,085. (38) Cashmere accounted for 73% of the imports, while the rest was composed of other animal hairs, wool, and tissue paper. (39) British exports were more diversified, but only seven categories exceeded £1,000, and the largest one was filing cabinets worth £3,951. (40)

There is insufficient evidence available to explain the means by which the Mongolian authorities choose Western trading partners, although on the basis of the low level of such trade and its apparently wide spread over categories in the case of Mongolian imports, it seems reasonable to suggest that ad hoc procedures play an important part in the process.

NORTH KOREA

In a speech before a group of Party workers in 1955, President Kim Il Sung outlined his vision for an independent Korea. Fundamental to that vision was a strong Korean economy, able to grow without recourse to excessive levels of economic aid from China or the Soviet Union. Thus was North Korea's national catch-word, chuch'e (lit., national identity), born. (41) Sharing a common border with both China and the Soviet Union placed North Korea in a delicate situation with the advent of the Sino-Soviet split. P'yongyang attempted to maintain reasonable relations with both countries during the 'sixties, swinging first one way and then the other. (42)

As the figures in Table 15.5 indicate, North Korea's evenhanded policy extended to foreign trade; levels of exports to and imports from China and the Soviet Union remained almost equal throughout the midsixties. It is also significant to note that Japan was by far North Korea's most important trading partner in the West, although the volume of trade involved was moderate. Thus, even when trade with the West was relatively unimportant for the North Korean economy,

TABLE 15.5 - North Korean Trade, 1960 and 1964-67
(millions of dollars)

	1960	1964	1965	1966	1967
Exports to:					
Soviet Union	75	81	82	92	108
China	n.a.	81	82	92	88
Other Communist countries	n.a.	21	21	26	26
Japan	0	20	15	23	30
Other non-Communist countries	6	3	8	11	9
Total	n.a.	206	208	244	260
Imports from:					
Soviet Union	39	83	90	86	110
China	n.a.	82	89	86	81
Other Communist countries	n.a.	20	20	21	21
Japan	1	11	17	5	6
Other non-Communist countries	4	7	17	21	21
Total	n.a.	204	233	219	240

NOTE: The figures for trade with China have been calculated as differences. Any discrepancies in the summation are due to rounding.

n.a. = not applicable

Source: R.S. Shinn, Area Handbook for South Korea (Washington, D.C. 1969), p. 373

the major trading partner was, as in the Albanian case, the former colonial power. The geographical proximity of the two countries has undoubtedly also been an important factor stimulating trade, while Japan's comparative advantage in raw materials and the production of labor intensive commodities suggest that both countries would benefit from trade.

There were, however, several impediments to the further expansion of North Korean trade with Japan in the sixties. The Japanese government's recognition of South Korea in 1965 was accomplished by means of an ambiguously worded treaty, which to P'yongyang and many opposition politicians in Japan implied that Tokyo was recognizing the Seoul government as the legitimate government of all Korea. Consequently, North Korea accused Japan of being "a militarist trailing behind U.S. imperialism," (43) and Korean imports from Japan fell sharply in 1966. The increase in exports over the same period is probably accounted for by P'yongyang's assessment that foreign exchange earnings may offset the disutility arising from Japanese political insensitivity. Further, the aid being provided by North Korea's neighbors made a search for Western financial donors unnecessary, if official statistics on the country's development are to be believed.

Thus, the targets of the first five-year plan of 1957-61 were reportedly fulfilled in two and a half years. (44) As a consequence, an engineering industry, which would hopefully provide the basis for an independent economy, was established. The year 1960 was designated as a year of "shock absorption," during which the economy would be prepared for the more ambitious seven-year plan of 1961-67. (45) According to this plan, global industrial output was to increase at a rate of 18% per annum over the period. (46) In the event, in October 1966, it was announced that the plan would be extended for a further three years; the annual growth of industrial production for the six years 1961-66 having averaged only 14.3%. (47) This is nonetheless an impressive growth rate when compared with other Socialist economies.

On the other hand, the slowdown of the late sixties was of concern to the North Korean leadership, and it was decided the country's development strategy would have to be modified. The absence of reliable data on North Korea's economic development since the late sixties makes the outline of a precise scenario impossible. However, it is clear that the North Korean leadership decided that an expansion of trade relations with the West would allow the economy to resume its former rapid rate of growth. It has been suggested (48) that the tension of the Sino-Soviet dispute led North Korea to search for an independent foreign policy with better relations with the West in order to minimize the threat of invasion from the south. Whatever the validity of this assertion, it is clear that the P'yongyang government made continued efforts to improve relations with Japan, if not to gain recognition. These efforts have focused largely on gaining the support of left-wing elements in Japan.

In an attempt to obtain the foreign capital necessary to meet the targets of 1971-76 six-year plan, the North Korean Committee for the Promotion of International Trade negotiated its first trade agreement with representatives of a non-Communist country. The Japanese government, however, was not the signatory to the agreement; rather, it was the Dietman's League for the Promotion of Japan-North Korea Relations. The five-year agreement, which was signed by P'yongyang in 1972, made the following stipulations. (49)

1. Mutual trade between Japan and North Korea should increase to about $450-500 million by 1976.

2. Japan would make available deferred payment conditions to North Korea for a period exceeding 8 years on the latter's purchase of machinery.

3. Commodity fairs would be held in each other's capitals.

4. The Japanese mission would try to facilitate the entry of trade and technical representatives from North Korea into Japan.

5. Trade representatives from each of the signatory countries would be permitted to operate in the other's country.

Table 15.6 shows the impact of the agreement on Japanese-North Korean trade. In 1974, the year of peak trading, Japanese heavy industrial and chemical products accounted for more than 70% of Korean imports. (50) In terms of the importance of the trade flow, it should be noted that by 1974 Japan had become North Korea's second largest trading partner (the Soviet Union was first), and this trade amounted to less than one per cent of Japan's total trade. (51)

Since 1972 North Korea's balance of trade has become increasingly unfavorable, the deficit rising as the volume of trade increases. It has been suggested that increases in the world price of oil, a decline in the price of North Korean exports, and excessive imports from Japan and elsewhere for the ambitious six-year plan have all contributed to the worsening situation. (52) Further, North Korea's apparent inability to finance the deficit has led to defaults. Thus, as of October 1976, North Korea's total debt to Japan was $260 million of which $70 million was in arrears. (53) North Korea has asked Japanese creditors for a two-year moratorium on deferred payments and on payments with usance with a 7.5% interest rate, which the Japanese countered by requesting 10.45%, and they were apparently unhappy about the North Korean request. (54) The rescheduling of a number of foreign debts was agreed upon in 1977, and China offered to provide credit to assist the North Koreans.

TABLE 15.6 - North Korean Trade with Japan (millions of dollars)

	1969	1970	1971	1972	1973	1974	1975	1976
Japanese exports to North Korea	24	23	29	93	100	252	180	96
Japanese imports from North Korea	32	34	30	38	72	109	65	72

Source: Japan External Trade Organization [hereafter JETRO].

TABLE 15.7 - North Korean Trade with EEC (millions of EUA)

	1972	1973	1974	1975	1976(a)	Jan.-June 1977(a)
EEC exports to North Korea	20	89	194	113	64	37
EEC imports from North Korea	27	31	65	88	59	23

Source: METB.
(a) Preliminary data

This credit problem, however, led to a drop in the volume of trade between Japan and North Korea after 1975, as Table 15.6 indicates. Further, the North Koreans have refused to allow the establishment of a Japanese trade mission by P'yongyang, as stipulated by 1972 agreements, on the strange grounds that the Japanese government is unfriendly to North Korea. It is not inconceivable that P'yongyang's procrastination on debt problems and the clumsy handling of the implementation of the 1972 agreement will lose North Korea considerable support from left wing groups in Japan and that chuch'e will be seriously endangered.

North Korea's trade with the European Economic Community (EEC) since 1972 is shown in Table 15.7, and the data reflect a pattern of trade similar to that with Japan. Again, the year of peak turnover is 1974, and the drop since 1975 may probably also be attributed to debt problems. It may, however, be significant that while trade was almost balanced in 1976, the excess of Korean imports over exports grew considerably in the first half of 1977.

VIETNAM

The Vietnamese economy prepared for its transition to a peacetime five-year plan with the announcement by the Vietnam Workers' Party Central Committee at its Twenty-Second Plenum in January-February 1974 of a two-year economic reconstruction and rehabilitation plan. (55) Preparations for the transition also included a significant foreign aid agreement drive.

Relations with Russia and China

A senior government and party delegation led by First Party Secretary Le Duan visited Moscow toward the end of October 1975 and came away with two major aid agreements, which apparently would not only underwrite the forthcoming five-year plan, but also would assist in the reunification of the country. The two parties pledged to coordinate "economic development plans," and it has been suggested that Vietnam was offered a special role in CMEA. (56) On his visit to Peking a month earlier Le Duan had secured a long-term, interest free loan and a protocol on the supply of general goods for 1976. (57) In August an economic delegation led by Le Thanh Bghi had secured Chinese agreement on aid for 1976 and an agreement on long-term economic cooperation amounting to approximately $400 million. (58)

In October Vietnam received a $27.6 million grant from Japan, of which it was expected that more than half would be made available in 1976. Aid agreements were also secured with Scandinavia and Australia ($A 5 million). (59)

Relations with Western Countries

North Vietnam's trade with the EEC and Japan is shown in Tables 15.8 and 15.9, respectively. As can be seen from the data in the tables, Vietnamese trade with the West increased significantly during the course of the two-year plan. However, it was not until December 1976 that the Vietnamese leadership made clear its intention to significantly expand trade relations with the West in the future. On that occasion, at the First Party Congress since 1960, emphasis was placed on the country's need to attract and use foreign aid and investment in fostering development. (60) Le Duan noted that the major goal of Vietnam's foreign trade policy would be to ensure that the country gained access to the world's modern technological resources to facilitate its interests and to improve the standard of living of the population. (61)

The most startling indication of the newly unified country's intentions to foster closer links with Western economies came with the promulgation of Decree No. 115/CP on April 18, 1977 by Vietnam's Government Council. The decree was entitled "Regulation on Foreign Investment in the Socialist Republic of Vietnam." (62) In its concessions to foreign capital, the decree went further than any similar regulations issued recently in Eastern Europe. Thus, article S stated:

> The foreign party may invest in Vietnam in the following forms:
> 1. Cooperation in production with sharing of products.
> 2. Joint enterprise or company.
> 3. Private enterprise specializing in the production of commodities exclusively for export purposes. (63)

The condition of the first two types of cooperation do not differ in essence from those established in Eastern Europe, while article 8 of the Regulation details the conditions for foreign private enterprise:

> The private enterprise specializing in the production of commodities for export purposes shall abide by the following conditions:

TABLE 15.8 - North Vietnam's Trade with the EEC (millions of EUA)

	1972	1972	1974	1975	1976[a]	Jan.-June 1977
EEC exports to North Vietnam	1.4	5	12	21	31	34
EEC imports from North Vietnam	1.4	1.3	3	8	7	4

Source: METB.

(a) Preliminary data.

TABLE 15.9 - North Vietnam's Trade with Japan (millions of dollars)

	1964	1966	1967	1968	1969	1970	1971	1972	1973	1974	1975	1976
Japanese exports to North Vietnam	3	6	1-2	2	7	5	4	3	4	20	43	119
Japanese imports from North Vietnam	10	10	7	6	6	6	12	3	8	30	27	40

Source: JETRO, except 1964 figures which are from H.H. Smith, Area Handbook for North Vietnam, (Washington, D.C., 1967), pp. 318-19.

TABLE 15.10 - North Vietnam's Trade with France (millions of EUA)

	1972	1973	1974	1975	1976[a]	Jan.-June 1977
French exports	0	0.4	3	11	20	9
French imports	0.2	0.5	1.4	2	2	1.5

Source: METB.

(a) Preliminary data.

1. The foreign party shall import into Vietnam technical equipment, raw materials, fuel and other materials, etc., needed for the construction and operation of the enterprise with the exception of those which the Vietnam Party can supply in the form of sale and purchase.
2. The operation of the enterprise must in no way be detrimental to the economy of Vietnam.
3. The export of the commodities produced by the enterprise shall be subject to Vietnamese customs control, and foreign currency earnings from such exports shall be deposited with the Foreign Trade Bank of Vietnam.
4. The employees and workers of the enterprise shall be of Vietnamese nationality except for cases stipulated in Article 12 of the present regulation. (A subsection of this article states that foreign technical personnel may be employed "for those services which Vietnam is not prepared to provide, after obtaining approval to this effect from the Ministry of Foreign Trade of the Socialist Republic of Vietnam.") (64) The salaries and wages of these Vietnamese employees and workers shall be paid in foreign currency.
5. The enterprise is a juridical person constituted in accordance with Vietnamese law and must have its statutes registered with the Socialist Republic of Vietnam. (65)

In another subsection of Article 12 it is stated that a private enterprise will be permitted to import its production requirements free of duty, will be exempted from export duties on its products, and will be able "to enter into direct transaction with economic organizations of other countries, in accordance with the regulations on foreign trade and foreign exchange control in force in Vietnam." (66)

According to Article 15 foreign private enterprises will be required to pay income tax at a rate of 30% of tax bearing profits "to be collected at a fixed rate either on business turnover or per unit of product." (67) The regulations also provide for payment to the investor in the investment currency and "within an appropriate period of time"; in the event that the enterprise should be nationalized, it is stated that under these circumstances "a reasonable price agreed upon by the two sides" would be paid. (68) Whereas the above formulation is unlikely to inspire confidence in a Western investor, it has been rumored that the Vietnamese government has indicated it will give assurances that joint ventures will not be nationalized for at least ten years. The same undertaking would presumably also apply to private enterprises. It is too early at this stage to draw conclusions on the likely future extent of foreign investment in Vietnam.

Summary

Most probably for geographical reasons, Vietnam's major trading partner since the Vietnam War has been Japan. France, the former colonial power, has been the country's major partner in the EEC, although it is interesting to note that whereas Italy has been the largest purchaser of Albanian goods in the EEC and has maintained an approximate balance of trade with Albania throughout the seventies, France has been the largest seller of goods to Vietnam, but has kept imports from the latter at a very low level (see Table 15.10).

CONCLUSIONS

On the basis of the foregoing discussion, it seems reasonable to draw conclusions regarding two important questions: (a) what determines the extent to which a small, developing, socialist economy will trade with the West; and (b) what are the factors influencing the choice of major trading partners?

The experience of the four countries considered in this paper suggests that decisions to expand the level of trade with the West have not been motivated to any great degree by differences in available technology between the West and the more developed Socialist economies. Rather, the evidence suggests that the particular country's stand with respect to the Sino-Soviet dispute has been an important variable. Thus, the Mongolian decision to side wholeheartedly with the Soviet Union has implied that the rate of Mongolia's economic development is and will probably remain closely linked to economic assistance from CMEA economies in general and the Soviet Union in particular.

The Albanian experience reflects the consequences of a decision to side firmly with China. The ideological considerations underlying such a response to the dispute has implied an unwillingness on the part of the Albanian leadership to maintain diplomatic relations with either the Soviet Union or the United States. Given the fact that other developed capitalist and Socialist economies were regarded by Tirana as "lackeys of imperialism," it was unlikely that Albania would expand trade with the West, or for that matter CMEA, while Chinese aid was forthcoming. On the other hand, the absence of such aid in 1975 led to a short lived expansion. Given the scarcity of official statements on the current dispute between Albania and China, it is impossible to predict the likely state of Albanian trade relations with the West in the near future.

The other two countries considered in this paper, North Korea and Vietnam, have both attempted to maintain reasonable relations, trade and otherwise, with the Soviet Union and China. North Korea, sharing a common border with both adversaries in the dispute, evidently considered that total reliance on both could endanger its long-term objective of political and economic independence. Consequently, in the early seventies North Korea launched a massive trade drive with the West, the volume of imports largely exceeding the exports. In any event, the Western economies have proven unwilling to finance North Korea's economic development, Korean leadership has led to a reduction in trade with the West since 1975, and it is unlikely that there there will be any significant increase in the future.

Vietnam's geographical position is not as sensitive as that of North Korea, the former sharing only a border with China. However, while domination from Moscow is largely ruled out, a hegemonic Chinese government might cause Hanoi problems if the Vietnamese economy is weak. Thus, as in the North Korean case, the Vietnamese government sought to expand trade relations with the West as soon as an end to hostilities with the Americans was in sight. Possibly as a result of the Vietnam War, the Vietnamese leadership has been able to obtain Western credit to supplement aid from China and CMEA. Thus, it is to be expected that Vietnam's trade with the West will continue to expand. Vietnam's seemingly liberal invitation to Western investors appears likely to reinforce this trend.

With the exception of the Mongolian case, where the level of trade with the West has been too low to draw any significant conclusions, it may be concluded that a former colonial power will always be a major trading partner of a small Socialist economy. On the other hand, geographically proximate developed capitalist economies also will generally loom large in the Socialist economies' trade figures. Thus, Japan has been North Korea's largest trading partner in the West; it has shared that role with France in Vietnam, and Italy remains Albania's major trading partner in the West.

NOTES

1. Mehmet Shehu, Report on the Fifth Five-Year Plan (1971-75) (Tirana: 1974), p. 51.

2. Ibid., p. 52.

3. 30 vjet Shquiteria socialiste (Tirana: 1974), p. 55.

4. Mehmet Shehu, Report on Fifth Plan, p. 51.

5. 30 vjet, p. 55-6.

6. Probleme ekonomike, no. 1 (1974): 8.

7. Probleme ekonomike, no. 1 (1975): 4.

8. Ibid., p. 112.

9. Ibid., p. 5.

10. Rruga e partise, no. 12 (1976): 11.

11. Ibid., p. 11.

12. Ibid.

13. A. Schnytzer, "Economic Planning and Industrial Policy in the People's Republic of Albania" (Ph.D. dissertation, Oxford, 1978), chapter 4.

14. Rruga e partise, and 30 vjet, p. 65.

15. 30 vjet.

16. M.C. Kaser, "Trade and Aid in the Albanian Economy," Joint Economic Committee, United States Congress, East European Economies Post-Helsinki (Washington, D.C.: U.S. Government Printing Office, 1977), pp. 1325-40.

17. Rruga e partise, p. 15.

18. Probleme ekonomike, no. 1 (1973): 137; no. 1 (1974); 6, 8; and no. 1 (1975): p. 6.

19. Kaser, "Trade and Aid."

20. Rruga e partise, p. 15.

21. E. Hoxha, Report to the Seventh Congress of the PLA (Tirana, 1976), passim.

22. Ibid., p. 39.

23. Zeri i popullit, July 7, 1977.

24. The Times, July 27, 1977.

25. M. C. Kaser, Comecon: Integration Problems of the Planned Economies, 2nd ed. (London: 1967), p. 106.

26. Zeri i popullit, April 30, 1976.

27. H. Hamm, Frankfurter Allgemeine Zeitung, November 1, 1977.

28. The Times, July 19, 1977. Flights began in April 1978.

29. Kushtetuta e Republikes Popullore Socialiste te Shquiperise (Tirana, 1976), pp. 20-21.

30. Kaser, "Trade and Aid."

31. G. G. S. Murphy, Soviet Mongolia (Berkeley: 1966), p. 195.

32. Ibid.

33. T. N. Dupuy, et al., Area Handbook for Mongolia (Washington, D.C., 1970), p. 295.

34. M. C. Kaser, International Currency Review 9, no. 4, (1977): p. 157.

35. T. N. Dupuy, Area Handbook, p. 294.

36. A. J. K. Sanders, Asian Survey, no. 1 (1976): 66.

37. Ibid., pp. 67-8.

38. M. C. Kaser, "Trade and Aid," p. 156.

39. Ibid.

40. Ibid.

41. B.C. Koh, *The Foreign Policy of North Korea* (New York, 1969), pp. 90-1.

42. This process is described in *ibid.*, *passim*.

43. S.K. Ko, *Pacific Affairs* 50, no. 1 (1977): 33.

44. Koh, *The Foreign Policy*, p. 19.

45. Ibid., p. 20.

46. Ibid.

47. Ibid.

48. Ko, *Pacific Affairs*.

49. Ibid., p. 38.

50. Ko, *Pacific Affairs*.

51. Ibid., p. 40.

52. Ibid.

53. Ibid., pp. 40-41.

54. Ibid., p. 41.

55. C.A. Thayer, *Asian Survey* no. 1, (1976): 19.

56. Ibid., p. 21.

57. Ibid.

58. Ibid.

59. Ibid., p. 22.

60. *International Currency Review* 9, no. 1, p. 157.

61. Ibid., p. 158.

62. Mimeographed (London: Embassy of the Socialist Republic of Vietnam, 1977).

63. Ibid., p. 2.

64. Mimeographed (London: Embassy of the Socialist Republic of Vietnam, 1977), p. 3.

65. Ibid., p. 5.

66. Ibid.

67. Ibid., pp. 5-6.

68. Ibid., p. 4.

16 Comments

Thomas A. Wolf,
Agota Gueullette,
and Friedrich Levcik

In his paper "The Trade-Partner Composition of Soviet Trade with the West," Philip Hanson has taken a very creative approach to attempt to explain individual industrialized Western (IW) countries' shares of the Soviet export market for machinery and transport equipment. Hanson's hypothesis is that a given Western country's share of this market is a positive function of its general competitiveness on world markets, the degree to which there is a "fit" between its export structure and Soviet import demand, its willingness to provide official credit support (OCS) for exports, political affinity, and the degree of relaxation in bilateral intergovernmental relations. Market share is hypothesized to be a negative function of economic distance and the degree of support for the Western strategic embargo policy. Each of these factors seems reasonable as an important determinant of individual countries' market-shares in the Soviet Union. As will be explained subsequently, however, Hanson might want to add one more determinant: bilateralism.

Although Hanson's basic hypothesis is quite intuitively appealing, the results of his econometric analysis are not very persuasive, at least with respect to most of the foregoing explanatory variables. Specifically, only the "general competitiveness" and "import fit" variables are consistently statistically significant. Indeed, one might hazard the guess that respecifying his equations 1 to 4 using only general competitiveness as an explanatory variable would explain nearly as much of the variation of Western market shares as the equations containing five or six independent variables. More technically, the adjusted R^2 ($\bar{R}^2$) would probably not change significantly if all other explanatory variables were removed from the individual regressions.

COMMENTS   279

My comments will be limited to pointing out some possible
methodological problems with Hanson's analysis, problems which if
resolved in future work on this subject might result in stronger empirical corroboration of his basic hypothesis. Three methodological
issues will be briefly discussed: (a) selecting an appropriate reference
market within which to measure "general competitiveness"; (b) increasing the degree of discrimination of certain proxy variables; and
(c) introducing bilateralism explicitly into the analysis.

THE APPROPRIATE REFERENCE MARKET

Hanson suggests that the higher a given IW country's export market
share for machinery and equipment in the rest of the world (ROW),
the higher its share should be of Soviet imports from the IW, <u>ceteris
paribus</u>. Furthermore, in an attempt to allow for the fact that (a) the
general relative competitiveness of the IW exporting countries is not
uniform across all machinery and equipment products and (b) the
structure of Soviet import demand is not identical with that of the
ROW, Hanson wisely calculates a "standardized Soviet share" for at
least one year; i.e., he takes into account what has elsewhere been
called "relative complementarity" of trade structures. (1) But while
such a sophisticated approach can only be applauded, it is questionable whether the ROW defined by Hanson as a reference market is
appropriate. There are at least two basic problems with defining
this reference market as the world less the Soviet Union. The first
problem is that such a procedure, which includes the imports of the
target IW exporting countries as part of the reference market, tends
to give a downward bias to the calculated reference market shares
for the larger exporting countries. This point may be illustrated by
the simple numerical example in Table 16.1.

Assume the world consists of four countries: countries A and
B are IW exporters, country C is a "third" Western country, and D
is a centrally planned economy. The rest of the world, to use Hanson's definition, is composed of A, B, and C. Assume that these
countries have a national income of $250 million, $150 million, and
$100 million, respectively. Therefore A, B, and C account for 50,
30, and 20% of ROW income respectively. Further assume for simplicity that each country is equally competitive in all three of these
markets; for example, country A will supply 50% of each market.
For purposes of developing a benchmark against which to measure
the market shares of A and B in country D, we want to define a Western reference market. Observe that combined A and B sales to the

TABLE 16.1 - Hypothetical Rest-of-World (ROW) Trade ($ Millions)

Selling Region	Sales by Region of Purchase				Exports by Region of Purchase			
Column	1 A	2 B	3 C	4 ROW	5 A	6 B	7 C	8 ROW
A	125	75	50	250	-	75	50	125
B	75	45	30	150	75	-	30	105
C	50	30	20	100	50	30	-	80
Total ROW	250	150	100	500	125	105	80	310

ROW, if we use Hanson's definition, are $400 million (see column in Table 16.1). Country A, therefore, accounts for 62.5% of combined A and B sales ($250/$400 million). Combined A and B exports to the ROW are only $230 million however, of which A accounts for $125 million or 54.3% (see column 8). It is the latter type of figure that Hanson is calculating in his study; yet we see that it understates A's true competitive position in the ROW. This bias arises because the sales of A and B on their own markets are excluded when we consider only exports. Because A is the larger market, its market share is reduced when domestic sales are omitted.

There are two basic ways to eliminate this bias. First, we could attempt to collect data on total sales (columns 1-3 of Table 16.1), from which the "true" A share of 62.5% would emerge. As perfectly comparable data on domestic shipments are difficult to obtain at a disaggregated level, another and actually preferred approach would be to redefine the ROW reference market as Country C. Countries A and B shares of combined A and B sales (= exports) to C could then be calculated. Observe from column 7 in the table that C imports from A and B total $80 million, of which $50 million or 62.5% come from A. The point is that this particular bias can be avoided be defining the reference market as a set of "third" countries. By so comprehensively defining the ROW, Hanson has probably underestimated American competitiveness in the West.

All possible bias is not removed, however, simply by calculating export shares on "third" markets. In the real world of international trade, IW countries' export shares will differ substantially across third country markets. Such variation is a result of discriminatory trade barriers or preferences, relative transport costs, the pattern of foreign direct investment, and political and cultural factors. As indicated in a more aggregative study of five major IW countries' export shares for all manufactured products (SITC 5-8), these countries' shares vary considerably even by major world region. (2) Selection of a reference market should be made with a view to coming as close as possible to satisfying the ceteris paribus assumption which we implicitly are making when we make a market share comparison.

Returning to the example of Table 16.1, it would be good to be able to say that region C is a good reference market because A and B have in some sense equal access to that market. If instead, B receives trade preferences in C, then again it would be understating A's "true" competitiveness on the D market if its share of combined A and B exports to C was used without some adjustment. Only if the expected pattern of preference in favor of B on D's market corresponds to that prevailing in C could the ceteris paribus assumption be validly invoked. In Hanson's study, even an upward-biased "standardized Soviet market share" for a given IW exporting country is possible if it happens to have preferential access to, or for other political or cultural reasons, happens to have an abnormally high export share in, those ROW markets which account for a large proportion of ROW imports of those products as particularly significant in the Soviet import structure.

Hanson does explicitly recognize the general problem of selecting an appropriate reference market when he excludes Canadian exports to the United States in order to avoid exaggerating Canadian competitiveness outside of North America. But by the same token he might want to exclude West German exports to Austria, mutual trade among members of the European Community, and for that matter, United States exports to Canada. This approach logically leads, however, to the selection of a "third" region as a reference market. (3)

PROXY VARIABLES

Variables designed to measure directly or indirectly "economic distance" typically are found to be statistically significant determinants of the pattern of trade. It is surprising, therefore, that Hanson's distance variable is not consistently statistically significant across his regression equations. This is particularly surprising given the earlier findings of this writer that even within a "third" country, West European reference market IW exporting countries' market shares appeared to be correlated with relative geographical proximity. (4) Thus, British market shares were highest in Scandanavia and Portugal, France had its highest market shares in the Mediterranean region, Italy in the Eastern Mediterranean, West Germany to the southeast and northeast, and the United States on the "periphery" of Western Europe (Spain, Portugal, and Turkey). Hanson's distance variable (the logarithm of time zone differences in hours between Moscow and the capital city of the exporting IW country) is probably not discriminating enough. It suggests that all continental Western European exporters are equidistant from Moscow; yet the above-mentioned study suggests that being closer, but not significantly closer absolutely, to an export market may give a country a competitive edge, undoubtedly because of a combination of factors including lower sales, transport and service costs, and possibly cultural and language similarities.
A more conventional measure of distance, such as air or rail miles, might increase the explanatory power of this factor in Hanson's analysis.

Hanson observes that "many different views have been aired about the effectiveness" of the Western strategic embargo directed against the CMEA countries. As if reflecting this ambiguity, his dummy variable for the effect of the embargo is statistically significant in only three of his seven regression equations. Again, the weakness of this variable in explaining market shares in the Soviet Union is probably attributable to the lack of capacity of his dummy variable (Cocom membership or not) to measure finely enough existing differences in different countries' export control policies. The United States, for example, has long had a more extensive embargo list than other Cocom countries, i.e., unilateral export controls. There is now substantial empirical evidence that because of this unilateral United States embargo and historic American dominance in products and technologies subject to the multilateral (Cocom) embargo, its exports to the CMEA region have been particularly affected. (5) Consequently, whether or not a country has been a member of Cocom may not be the only question to ask with respect to the relative effect of export controls.

Perhaps the least appealing use of proxy variables is the attempt to measure IW country availability of official credit support (OCS) for exports to the Soviet Union. As Hanson points out, using a dummy variable to measure whether a country made available OCS to the Soviet Union in the 1960–70 period is really only measuring whether the country was not the United States. Differences in OCS among the other thirteen countries are not captured at all. Furthermore, this variable was excluded in the 1971–75 regressions, although it would not be surprising were it to have a roughly equal level of explanatory power for the latter subperiod, despite the availability of OCS from the United States for most of that period.

Hanson's use of the so-called "blended" interest rate for his 1976 cross section analysis is questionable as a reliable indicator of the "softness" of credit terms and OCS availability. These interest rates can change dramatically in a fairly short period of time. (6) These terms also may not accurately reflect the degree of unofficial government support or assurances regarding credit support, a subtle but important point mentioned by Brainard. (7) Furthermore, subsidized interest rates may in fact be offset by higher prices on exports, an undocumented practice often attributed to West German suppliers. (8) Moreover, Brainard has pointed out that in a world of more flexible exchange rates the supposed advantage of a lower interest credit from one supplier country may be more than offset by Soviet expectations of relative appreciation of that country's currency. (9) Finally, it is debatable whether Hanson's rankings of Western countries by blended interest rates as of late 1975 really do "correspond fairly well with the conventional wisdom about ranking by comparative overall competitiveness."

A final point concerns Hanson's handling of detente. In his econometric analysis, Hanson subdivides the period 1960-75 into two subperiods, 1960-70 and 1971-75, representing the pre-detente and detente eras respectively. With the exception of leaving out the dummy variable for "OCS availability" in the latter period, however, the equation specification is identical for the two subperiods. Consequently, it is not clear why a single equation was not estimated for the entire 15-year period, with a dummy variable for detente taking the value zero for 1960-70 and 1.00 between 1971 and 1975. Either way, Hanson implicitly is suggesting that generalized detente has an effect on market shares in general. Why this would be is not clear. One wonders instead whether he simply had in mind that detente would, <u>ceteris paribus,</u> lead to a higher level of exports to the Soviet market for all Western countries.

BILATERALISM

Finally, there is the slippery and very possibly intractable issue of bilateralism. Hanson argues that the Soviets have a "hard currency shopping list," but he does not develop the notion that the Soviet Union or its Western trade partners practice bilateralism of the old fashioned sort, i.e., attempt to affect the size of bilateral trade imbalances. In a footnote he cites a rather high "irreciprocity" coefficient for the Soviet Union in its East-West trade, presumably to justify not attempting to explicitly take into account possible bilateralism. But as several investigators of the mysteries of bilateralism have observed, bilateralism and reciprocity are in general different concepts. (10) Bilateralism is <u>ex ante;</u> the explicit or implicit attempt by governments, in some cases through bilateral clearing agreements, to make bilateral trade more balanced than it otherwise would be. Reciprocity, on the other hand, is an <u>ex post</u> concept; the attempt to measure reciprocity by calculating, using one of several possible indices, how bilaterally balanced a country's trade actually was.

Formal bilateral clearing agreements have, of course, disappeared between the Soviet Union and the 14 Western exporters which are the subject of Hanson's study. Furthermore, bilateral trade has recently been spectacularly unbalanced in many cases, e.g., Soviet-West German trade. Yet this does not preclude the existence of bilateralism. Indeed, the more bilaterally unbalanced this trade, the more likely we are to see increased pressure from at

least one side for greater reciprocity. This may be as true for the
weaker competitors on the Western side who may run deficits with the
Soviets, e.g., the United Kingdom. As for the U.S.S.R., which not
wanting to become too "dependent" upon any one source of imports or
simply attempting to bargain for increased access for its exports on
a given Western market, it may quite consciously attempt to reorient
imports away from certain countries.

It might be interesting to attempt to test for the existence of
Soviet bilateralism within the framework of Hanson's model. Observe
that if Soviet bilateralism exists and is significant, it would only make
trade more reciprocal than otherwise, but not necessarily perfectly
reciprocal. One possibility might be to introduce a lag structure
which would specify that the change in share of the Soviet market in
the current period is in part a negative function of a country's past
bilateral surplus with the Soviets.

The foregoing comments are intended as suggestions for future
work aimed at econometrically explaining the trade partner composition of Soviet and other CMEA country imports from the West. Needless to say, Philip Hanson is to be commended for an imaginative
attempt to bring more rigorous analytical and empirical analysis to
bear on this issue.

Thomas A. Wolf

Simai's paper has a very difficult objective: to infer from trade data
the complex interplay of the factors influencing or even dictating the
choice of a commercial partner. His analysis shows us the importance
of two factors: stability and dynamism.

HUNGARY'S FOREIGN ECONOMIC RELATIONS

The need for stability in foreign economic relations appears in the
Hungarian case for two reasons:

1. The country is poor in raw materials, so that it seeks traditional suppliers with whom links can be renewed. The suppliers
should, of course, be relatively close.

2. Traditional Socialist planning prefers to act upon a terrain
where there is little change. It is possible that the medium-term
fixing of prices within CMEA, which has been operating since the
beginning of the cold war, is not motivated only by the desire to exclude the fluctuations of world prices, but also by the aim of simplifying the planners' task.

The exigencies of stability dictated, and to a lesser extent still dictate, the use of the country's export capacity for the acquisition of necessary imports. Such a policy does not necessarily favor allocative efficiency in foreign trade or the calculation of comparative costs. Moreover, the advantages which relative stability yields are also in conflict with that dynamism to which every economic system, be it Socialist or capitalist, aspires. In fact this dynamism has seemed to be hindered by the planning system and the geoeconomic position of the country.

HUNGARY'S NEW ECONOMIC MECHANISM

By introducing the new economic mechanism the Hungarians wanted to reduce the conflict between stability and dynamism. By giving microeconomics a greater role they aimed at making their economy more efficient. Since profit was introduced as an economic criterion, a certain erosion of the restrictive practices and controls over foreign trade operations has been observed. There has been a certain opening up, or better, a loosening up of the classical Socialist methods.

This phenomenon will be illustrated briefly. The system of compensation, so widely practiced by other Socialist countries, is used very little by Hungary. Indeed Hungary has a very small share in the compensation agreements concluded between East and West.

From 1969 to 1973, Western statistics register not one such compensation agreement with Hungary. In 1974 the value of compensation agreements did not exceed six million dollars. By comparison, in the same years Poland made compensation agreements worth $755.0 million and the Soviet Union about $5.0 billion. Similar figures for 1976-77 are: Hungary $98.5 million, Poland $128.1 million, and the Soviet Union $467.9 million. The cumulative totals for 1969-77 were: Poland $4.0 billion, the Soviet Union $12.0 billion, and Hungary only $190.8 million.

Another point that distinguishes Hungarian behavior from that of other countries is that the average value of individual contracts agreed upon between Hungary and the West is much lower than for other countries. It is $17 million in comparison with $50 million in Bulgaria, $46 million in Romania, $125 million in Poland, $242 million in GDR, and $230 million in the Soviet Union.

Hungary also has a less rigid attitude in its policy on joint ventures. As to the number of such ventures undertaken Hungary is in the second position after Romania, whose liberalism in this respect is well-known. For example in 1974 Hungary signed the following contracts: Siemens, $530,000; Volvo, $1,740,000; Bowmal, $1,000,000.

Another non negligible step towards liberalization concerns the system of state monopoly of foreign trade. Without being abandoned, this principle is now interpreted in such a way that it gives more powers to the state producing enterprises and less to the ministry of foreign trade. Access to foreign markets has become more simple and easy.

A system of multiple rates of exchange has been introduced. To be sure, the distinction remains between the commercial and the noncommercial rates, but a single commercial rate is in force for the so-called "hard" currencies. Some efforts have been made to render the commercial rate more realistic also vis-a-vis Socialist currencies, so the difference between the rate of exchange and the purchasing power parity has narrowed, even though domestic prices have not been linked to world prices. As a result, the difference between the official rate and the black rate has also narrowed.

SUMMARY

Must it be inferred that thanks to the new economic mechanism, Hungary, in contrast to several other Socialist countries, is aiming at multilateralism? Would this be a first step towards the convertibility of the forint, which Hungarians desire so much? However, the tendency towards multilateralism is hindered by the conflict between the macroeconomic control of prices and investment and the calculations of enterprises based on profit.

In any case, the economic reform seems to yield fruits; in making microeconomic calculation a more important factor in the choice of partner, Hungary has not been constrained to allocate so much recourses for the compensation contracts. In this way Hungary has been able to escape the danger of discouraging deals which this form of contract carries with it. Hungary has tried to balance the foreign exchanges arising from such deals by other ways. May it be inferred that, despite a certain permanence in the direction of commercial relations, the dynamism of Hungary's microeconomy is now firmly secured?

Agota Gueullette

HISTORICAL TIES

There is one intriguing common feature observed in the papers of Simai and Schnytzer; both authors show the importance of historically grown ties in foreign trade, which continue for a long time, even under completely changed conditions of the political setup and in the economic and social system. Adi Schnytzer shows this in the case of Albania, where Italy is still by far the most important trading partner of Albania in Europe, just as in the case of North Korea and Vietnam, where Japan is still important as a trading partner.

In the case of Hungary, Migaly Simai's very interesting figures suggest that the same also applies to this Socialist country. Of course, there is one big exception. Before and immediately after World War II, Hungary hardly traded at all with the Soviet Union, but with the development of the economies of the Socialist countries of Eastern Europe and the deepening of the relations within the CMEA on a bilateral basis, the role of the Soviet Union grew considerably. Aside from this one exception, the trading partners of Hungary are still very much the same as they used to be before the war and immediately after the war, viz., the two Germanies (GDR and FRG), Czechoslovakia, Austria, Poland, and Italy. Historic ties and geographical nearness, therefore, seem to be at least as important, if not more so, than the adherence to the same social and economic system or even the size of the partner country.

NONTRADITIONAL TIES

Jaroslav Nykryn's paper on "Traditional and Nontraditional Trade" shows that Czechoslovakia in its foreign trade with the other CMEA members has developed, besides normal traditional forms of trade, also other forms which Nykryn calls nontraditional ties. He maintains that these nontraditional ties, which according to him are more progressive forms of international economic relations, have developed stronger than traditional trade. He also maintains that some of these forms of nontraditional trade could also be applied to mutual advantage in the development of economic relations with industrially advanced Western countries and with the developing countries. This is especially so, according to Nykryn, because nontraditional forms of trade have also grown stronger between the industrialized Western countries.

Internationalization of Production

Nykryn poses the question of what are the determining factors that influence the development of nontraditional trade. He then poses the question of what are the main features, or what he calls the essence, of nontraditional trade. Jaroslan Nykryn mentions four determining factors: the internationalization of production, the development of science and technology, international integration processes, and political detente.

His enumeration is agreed with; however, one could perhaps improve on it by posing the question: what is behind the internationalization of production? In this case, one would very likely start off by listing the technological changes which instigated profound changes in the structure of production and foreign trade in the developed industrialized countries during the last 25 years. These structural changes led in turn to concentration, specialization, and internationalization of production, spurred by the possibility and perhaps even the necessity of reducing fixed costs by increasing the volume of production. Economies of scale might, therefore, be included among the determining factors.

Industrial Cooperation

As to the main features of nontraditional trade, one may argue that most of these features could be covered by the term "industrial cooperation." Of course, this does not apply to all those features which Nykryn enumerated, especially in his list of examples of nontraditional forms in Intra-CMEA trade. Certainly one could not include the bilateral trading agreements of CMEA countries on the basis of quantitative quotas or value quotas among the types of industrial cooperation.

But in this connection the question arises as to whether this is really a more progressive nontraditional form of trading which should be emulated by others. As far as it is known from discussions between Eastern economists, this type of trading is considered a hindrance for achieving a greater degree of convertibility and of increasing multilateral trade between the CMEA countries. Some of these economists maintain that in Intra-CMEA trade one should increase the third group of commodities, where there are no advance quotas or mandatory obligations to sell and buy, as a precondition for getting a greater measure of commodity convertibility. (11) Most authors, including myself, would regard most of the other features and forms listed by Nykryn as specific forms of industrial cooperation. But after all, it is not very important how one labels commercial deals which can not be included in the category of traditional trade.

Professor Nykryn is certainly agreed with that there is very little of this type of trade between the East European countries and the Western industrialized countries or the Eastern European countries and the developing countries. It is good to learn from Nykryn that Czechoslovakia supports the expansion of cooperation deals, thereby nontraditional trade with Western developed countries, and the quite good reasons why this is so. Nevertheless, the statistics show that Czechoslovakia does not belong to those Eastern European countries, which so far had a very prominent place in developing these forms of trade. Certainly other countries, especially Hungary and Poland but also Romania and Bulgaria, have a better record in this respect.

So the question could be posed: why have some Eastern European countries been more successful with nontraditional trade or cooperation deals with the West than others? It is believed that the answer lies in certain institutional preconditions which are met with to a larger or smaller extent in one or the other country. Some of these nontraditional forms of trade necessitate direct contact between the producer and the seller on the one side and on the other side, the purchaser and user – especially for the industrial enterprise receiving intermediate goods and machines. However, only some of the CMEA countries have so far allowed these direct contacts. In Czechoslovakia the bulk of foreign trade is still being carried out by the foreign trade organizations, and the producing enterprises are either not participating at all or are being consulted only at a very late stage. Some of the nontraditional forms of trade, especially of co-production, also necessitate increasing the rights of the enterprises, which must be free to make such business arrangements. If, however, the entire capacity of an enterprise is geared by a directive plan handed down from the central authorities, then there is very little scope for the producing enterprises to make arrangements with business partners on specific forms of nontraditional trade. Therefore, it seems that more is needed than good will for developing industrial cooperation and nontraditional forms of trade. On both sides, in the East and in the West, quite a few institutional, legal, and other hindrances and barriers will have to be removed to enable a breakthrough of these forms of trade. This is also necessary between countries belonging to different socioeconomic systems.

Friedrich Levcik

NOTES

1. T. A. Wolf, "U. S.-West German Competition in Exporting Manufactured Products to Eastern Europe and in the Soviet Union," Jahrbuch der Wirtschaft Osteuropas 7, (1978): 431-56.

2. Ibid.

3. For purposes of analyzing five major IW country export shares in CMEA more generally a "Western reference market" has been defined as a group of third countries within Western Europe to which, for the time period examined, none of the five IW exporters were believed to have any formal preferential access, Ibid.

4. Ibid; that study was more aggregative than Hanson's, however, as it examined manufactures exports as a group (SITC 5-8). Economic distance might be expected to play a more important role in determining the geographical pattern of trade for chemical products and manufactures classified by material (SITC 5, 6) than for machinery and equipment or consumer goods (SITC 7, 8).

5. Ibid. See also T. A. Wolf, "A Note on the Restrictive Effect of Unilateral United States Export Controls," Journal of Political Economy 81, no. 1 (January/February 1973); and J. C. Brada and L. J. Wipf, "The Impact of U. S. Trade Controls on Exports to the Soviet Bloc," Southern Economic Journal 41, no. 1 (July, 1974).

6. See T. A. Wolf, "East-West Trade Credit Policy: A Comparative Analysis." In U. S. Financing of East-West Trade, P. Marer, Ed. (Bloomington: International Development Research Center, Indiana University, 1975), pp. 149-99.

7. L. J. Brainard, "Discussion." In U. S. Financing of East-West Trade P. Marer, Ed. (Bloomington: International Development Research Center, Indiana University, 1975), pp. 199-201.

8. Wolf, "U. S.-West German Competition."

9. Brainard, "Discussion."

10. See F. L. Pryor, The Communist Foreign Trade System (Cambridge, Mass: MIT Press, 1963), chapter VI; P. J. D. Wiles, Communist International Economics (New York: Praeger, 1969) chapter X and Appendix; P. Marer, "Foreign Trade." In Essays on Comparative Socialist Systems, C. Beck and C. Mesa-Lago, Eds. (Pittsburgh: University of Pittsburgh, 1976).

11. S. Polaczek, "The Trade Effects of Exchange rate Policies" and S. Raczkowski's comments on J. Fekete, "Monetary and Financial Problems in East and West." In Money and Finance in East and West, volume 4, East-West European Economic Interaction Workshop Papers (Vienna: Wiener Institute fur Internationale Wirtschaftsvergleiche, 1978).

IV
Factors Affecting the Choice of Partners

Introduction

Having examined the experience of selected countries in the choice of partners in the preceding section, now analyses of the principal, general determinants of choice will be examined. In the first chapter of this part, Professor Peter Wiles addresses himself to the problem of country size. He examines rich and poor small countries with a market system and small countries with a command economy, and analyzes their involvement and gains from international economic relations in general and from joining political-economic blocs in particular. Some insights are offered on whether the small command economy countries benefit by joining CMEA.

    The second chapter, contributed by Professor Zbigniew Kamecki, deals with the balance of payment problems of Eastern European countries, the limitations which these problems impose on the expansion of East-West relations, and their impact on the choice of trading partners. Professor Eugene Zaleski in the third chapter examines the role of advanced technology in the selection of trading partners, with reference to the Soviet policy in this field.

    The fourth chapter presents an exercise by Professors Henri Dunajewski and Christian Arnal which stresses complementarity between any two countries comparing the world economy as a criterion for the choice of trading partners. The contribution deserves attention as an attempt to introduce a statistical method, which may perhaps be refined to bring more useful results.

    In the fifth chapter Professor Detlef Lorenz analyzes similarities among different major groups of countries into which the world economy can be divided, namely the advanced industrial, the less developed, and the centrally planned Socialist countries, with respect to economic relations and finds a number of parallels. He suggests that systemic factors may not be as important as some other factors.

On the other hand, Professor Jan Mujzel, who has contributed the sixth chapter, finds that systemic factors are most important. He discusses recent changes in the system of planning and management in Poland and points out that these changes did not go far enough to ensure the optimum degree of involvement in international economic relations and that further systemic modifications will be necessary to increase rationality of these relations and to enlarge Poland's participation in the international division of labor in general and in East-West relations in particular.

The final chapter presents commentaries on the chapters in this section by Professor Richard Portes, Dr. Allen Lenz, and Professors Agota Guccione, Alan Brown, and Morris Bornstein.

17 The Importance of Country Size: A Question But Not a Subject
Peter J.D. Wiles

A SMALL COUNTRY AND ECONOMIC THEORY

"What is the appropriate size of a country?" asks Schumacher. (1) History, a three syllable word that can be translated "war," has given us a vague answer. Countries have the sizes that they happen to have, and they are very seldom altered without war. Size changes are worse than land reform; the transaction costs are prohibitively high.

The often expressed fears for the viability of a small country have no empirical basis. With a little external and/or internal enterprise, some profitable activity can be found even for the mini-state; with a little decentralization the maxi-state becomes humanly tolerable; and there are very poor and very rich states of all sizes. There are Communist mini-states and capitalist maxi-states, and vice versa. At first glance, country size is irrelevant for economic performance, except in relation to its rate of participation in international trade. It does, however, remain the case that outside the field of economics, "small is beautiful"; the cultural scene in small, but not mini-, countries has more charm for most people because it is less specialized. (2)

Rich or poor, the small country as such has been neglected by international economics. Even Ricardo's example of Portugal, which traded wine for English cloth at the birth of the theory of comparative costs, (3) was effectually a large country. The English wine market was a small one, the posited differences in comparative and in absolute cost were not big, and were assumed not to alter very much. The main adjustment mechanism was gold flows and prices, not costs; so the effect on Portugal would be small. Similarly, modern international economics is written as if countries had a minimum population of 40 million. Except in money matters the outside world is only an interesting complication, but in the real world foreign trade is at once highly beneficial and deeply disturbing to small countries.

In this chapter ancient Ricardian and middle aged neoclassical principles are mixed with more modern considerations, but it says almost nothing that has not been said before somewhere else. It is as well to set out all the main points, for only then can East-West trade between small countries be discussed. However, a consistent and interesting theory of the economics of country size awaits still some inventive genius since the only book with an appropriate title is scarcely in fact about "the small country problem." (4)

DEFINITIONS OF A SMALL COUNTRY

A small country is defined as one having a population under 20 million, a large country as one over 40 million. Between these limits it is dangerous but not wholly wrong to apply our analysis. Small countries typically export over 20% of GNP, whatever their per capita income, and large countries under 20%. (5) Per capita income is not a very important determinant of this percentage in the modern world, and this is no paradox. As I stated elsewhere:

> It is reasonable to suppose that most subsistence economies produce their own subsistence, and do not get it by trade, if only because transport costs are so high. So when incomes first begin to rise trade should increase more rapidly, simply because it was zero before. It is then normal for the country - now out of the "anthropological" stage and properly speaking an underdeveloped country (UDC) - to export a few raw materials and depend on imports for all the sophisticated products it can afford. But after this stage it is not obvious why trade should grow more or less quickly than national income.... [In fact, once past this stage], population and income per head are both indices of the same things: the abilities to produce a variety of objects, to master many techniques and to dispense with foreign materials....
> [But income per head is also an index of the variety of demands.]
> We must, of course, expect trade per head to rise with income head: the latter is obviously a determinant of sorts. But when it comes to the relative growth of the two magnitudes the connection must be purely empirical. (6)

The maximum of 20 million for small and the minimum of 40 million for large are a personal judgment. The result is that only the following 15 countries may be handled with confidence by traditional size-insensitive theory: China, India, the Soviet Union, United States, Indonesia, Japan, Brazil, Bangladesh, Pakistan, Nigeria, Federal Republic of Germany, United Kingdom, Italy, France, and Mexico. They form 71.4% of the world's population and 8.5% of its sovereign states (out of 177 since definitions differ for mini-states; and using the 1975 populations). Those 17 countries with a population of between 40 and 20 million include: Vietnam, Philippines, Siam, Turkey, Egypt, Poland, Spain, South Korea, Iran, Ethiopa, Argentina, Yugoslavia, South Africa, Romania, Canada, Colombia, and Zaire. They form 13.6% of the world's population and 9.0% of its sovereign states. We are thus talking about 15.0% of the world's population 82.5% of its sovereign states; though we are also very interested in the intermediate category.

A wholly different definition of a small country crops up in the Western literature: a country without any influence on this or that international magnitude. A case in point is the country's trade. This is indeed a very important factor, but I would not make it the criterion, or even a criterion. Thus Jamaica with 18.5% of the world's bauxite production and much more of its traded bauxite, and Saudi Arabia, with oil, can influence the prices of their own exports, but they are obviously small countries in terms of population. On the other hand, scarcely any country is a monopsonist. To be able to influence import prices by buying more or less, a country must be both competitive and rich. Therefore, it would be better to say "noncompetitive" or "powerless in the market" than "small." Indeed the word "small" is quite unjustified, since size of population or national income is never mentioned, and one commodity is all that is considered. By using trade as a factor, would Saudi Arabia be considered large and India small?

There are after all both large and small monopolists, depending on the product and the market in question. To confuse product monopoly with size of country is confusing. Of course, there is no objection to the substance of the literature referred to, only to its curious use of language.

Similarly one might define a small country as having no monetary influence, but this would exclude all countries, except the United States and possibly the Federal Republic of Germany, Japan, and Saudi Arabia, or before the war, the United Kingdom, the United States, and France. In particular the growth of the International Monetary Fund (IMF) has rendered even "small large" countries quite unimportant. Before 1914 the City of London was the world's IMF; this paper refers only to foreign countries' liquidity. Regarding the belief that the world's absolute price level is determined by the United States, it can be said that in Communist countries the domestic price level is isolated by the Preisaugleich, while in non-Communist countries there are flexible rates of exchange. The world's absolute price levels are thus to no degree whatsoever dependent on those of any one country, and it is a sad comment upon economists that so manifestly false a doctrine should ever have been even discussed. The <u>relative</u> prices of traded commodities depend, of course, on the strength of particular firms or state countries trading in those commodities; these countries are quite often small.

RICH, SMALL COUNTRIES WITH A MARKET SYSTEM (RSMEs)

In terms of pure comparative costs the rich (over $1,000 of GNP per head in 1970 prices), small country with a market system is likely to benefit very greatly from foreign trade, for the domestic, but perfectly competitive, relative prices of an autarkic country differ in all probability from world prices before trade. And prices of a small country, producing everything for itself, are almost certain to differ more than those of a large, equally autarkic one, since its factor endowment is less likely to resemble the world's factor endowment. Thus, after the small country's economy has been opened, its prices will change a great deal, but world prices will change very little. Therefore, its factors of production will be shifted around a great deal, and its industrial structure will adapt itself better to its factor endowment. But since each such shift is advantageous, the small country gains more than a larger one would have. This is especially true, of course, where mining and agriculture bulk large in exports, i.e., on the whole in poor small countries.

This argument is strengthened by the fact of increasing returns in manufacturing. Once it has an export market, an extremely efficient large firm might locate itself, or have located itself, in a small country as well as in a large one. But even medium sized firms enjoy very substantial economies of scale vis-a-vis small ones. The rich, small country will typically have a large manufacturing sector, and so be substantially independent of its own factor endowment; thus, it is through increasing returns that it mainly benefits from trade.

Small Countries: Economic Considerations

Manufactures, however, yield smaller rents than minerals, crops, and livestock products. A small country that is rich merely because it is industrialized will derive as much advantage as any other small country from not having to produce the many things it imports, but it will derive from its exports no great rent or royalty from the bounty of nature, only an uncertain quasi-rent from the economies of scale in the manufactures in which it happens to have specialized. So the small country that really benefits is the one blessed by nature, not artifice. The notion that it is bad to export raw materials is insane, though it is still better to process them first, thus capturing the value added as well as the rent.

The early literature (notably Robinson) (7) is obsessed by increasing returns and verges on denying the viability of small countries that do not join large communities. But there is no empirical basis for this denial, and the explanation is surely that technical progress is more important than increasing returns. Indeed the latter doctrine, particularly in its "infant industry" variant, is only partly dynamic. It is better to have a small industry, forever stunted by a small home market but rich enough to buy new machines and licenses, than a large industry with a market of satisfactory size that for any reason suffers from technical stagnation.

The big firm in the rich, small country with a market economy (RSME) must make the same R&D effort as other multinationals. The fact that its headquarters is in a small country would seem to mean nothing in this connection; the headquarters must only be reasonably located and the local language not too difficult, or the native employees bilingual. These conditions are frequently met. There is, therefore, no reason why a dominant multinational should not grow in and out of a small, rich country, and in that field the country will be a technological leader.

A rich small country need not do applied military research, or indeed any pure science. It cannot dominate the world militarily, so there is no need to desperately try to keep ahead in every possible weapon. If it is a member of a major alliance, it will receive all the military technology it needs in the opinions of its major ally or the alliance's bureaucracy; if unattached, it has indeed interesting problems. Austria, Japan, and the rich Latin American countries, such as Mexico, and Venezuela - Japan and Mexico are large countries, but were noted because of a shortage of small unattached countries for this analysis - solve these by subtle diplomacy, a low profile, and/or a very great distance from areas of nuclear danger. Sweden, Switzerland, and Yugoslavia, however, spend huge amounts on military R&D, but not on defense as such. For various reasons that are not explained herein, they have rejected the Austrian-Japanese solution. Their small size is then a very serious disadvantage, since their total military expenditure is effective in proportion to that of the potential enemy, not to their own national income.

Furthermore, without great powers, there would be no great wars and ultimate weapons would develop far more slowly. In the military field small powers are a nuisance, great powers a curse. Therefore, in the name of peace, but on no other ground, great powers should be abolished. (8) Other public sector R&D is easily obtainable abroad.

The capacity to issue one's own paper money is a definitional characteristic of a modern sovereign state, however strange this might seem to a visitor from the eighteenth century. In order to use this power for Keynesian purposes, one must be sure it does not disappear in imports; so Keynesian management is extremely difficult, since 20% or more of the national income goes on imports.

Strictly, a market economy (ME) is more concerned with the marginal effects of trade changes and monetary flows with their present average levels. It is upon the change that policy operates, but the values that are marginal in large countries are very perceptible in small ones, and it is, of course, such magnitues that must count in a small market economy (ME). So the small ME is always in danger of being swamped and has a quite particular interest in the international stability of both trade and money flows. Then, too, in general, high average values mean high marginal ones. A country with a participation ratio of 30% must normally have a higher marginal propensity to import (MPI) than one with a participation ratio of 15%. But just as Keynesian expansion is very difficult, Keynesian contraction is very easy: the high MPI puts most of its burden on the foreigner, who hardly notices it, so that the balance of trade is soon corrected while the domestic economy suffers little.

Economic Illustrations

Only two small countries have seriously experimented with an independent domestic employment policy: Sweden and the Netherlands. It is perhaps no accident that in both cases the emphasis has been on factors really not Keynesian at all; i.e., an income policy and other manipulations of the labor market. This has been the case in Sweden and the Netherlands long before it became fashionable in larger countries. The object is to cause labor flows or wage behavior that will maintain full employment in the face of changing international conditions; actual monetary policy is more or less pre-Keynesian. Similarly Canada until recently has been preoccupied with the rate of exchange, a Keynesian weapon to be sure, but not considered in larger countries to be the only one, and one which is compatible with domestic orthodoxy. Moreover, Canada is also now very much committed to income policies.

THE IMPORTANCE OF COUNTRY SIZE 303

Note that Zurich, London's main rival in expertise on foreign exchange, takes exactly the opposite view on hot currency. She tries to keep it out, and especially out of her bank reserves, by what amounts to be a special deterrent: a low rate of interest. London, on the contrary, welcomes it and hopes to avoid untoward domestic effects by finesse, but the United Kingdom has nine times the Swiss population.

Bilateralism

All bilateralism is unsuited to a small country, regardless of wealth or economic system. Whatever it has to offer a larger country in terms of a particular supply, particular demand, or general stability, it is almost inevitably less important to its partner than to itself. The large country is more of a monopolist or monopsonist in such a deal. This objection to small country bilateralism extends to buy-back agreements. The things bought back are likelier to swamp the local market in a small country than in a large country or community, so what is said here does not apply to the small member of a community. However, bilateralism does assure stability, and this condemnation must be qualified by saying that a large number of small deals could benefit a small country, despite their high transaction cost.

Economic warfare is a form of bilateralism. Small states, except for Egypt in relation to the Suez Canal, are incapable of economic warfare, though not of economic imperialism; i.e., they cannot blockade or boycott with any effect, but they can annex and exploit, provided that larger powers let them. (9)

Similarly, when granting foreign aid the small country's government has small hope of influencing the foreign policy of a less developed country (LDC) which is perhaps larger than its own country; indeed, the small country has no particular foreign policy goals in that part of the world, so its aid goes more through the United Nations (see Table 17.1).

In general the drift of this table is clear; RSMEs had fewer axes to grind and went through the United Nations. Belgium was exceptionally low in column 1 because she was still involved in her imperial past. Italy and the Netherlands had shaken this off and so form part of the normal pattern. Canada and Austria, however, were inexplicably "ill-behaved." Neocolonialist France, of course, was very "ill-behaved." In recent years these distractions remain but are much less pronounced.

TABLE 17.1 - Grants and Capital Subscription to Multilateral Agencies (As Percentage of Official Development Assistance)

Country	1966-68	1974-75	Population 1970 (thousand)
United States	6.4	25.9	204,878
Japan	13.1	24.5	104,345
Federal Republic of Germany	13.5	32.4	60,714
United Kingdom	10.6	32.9	55,421
Italy	24.7	80.3	53,661
France	4.5	14.5	50,768
Canada	19.6	30.1	21,324
Netherlands	30.6	36.0	13,032
Australia	n.a	11.8	12,507
Belgium	14.7	29.7	9,656
Sweden	52.8	37.3	8,043
Switzerland	29.4	33.2	6,187
Denmark	48.6	45.3	4,929
Austria	23.0	45.9	7,391
Finland	n.a.	51.2	4,606
Norway	59.4	44.3	3,877

Sources: United Nations Statistical Yearbook (New York: United Nati 1969, 1976); L.P. Pearson, Partners in Development (London: Pall Mal Press, 1969); A. Dhesi, N.E.P. Research Paper, no. 66, University of Birmingham, U.K., May, 1972.

Note: n.a. means not available

Other Factors

State capitalism means a degree of government control, nay actual planning. In the capital city of any small country everyone knows everyone else, and they cannot help meeting socially; this is one of the charms of living in such a capital. Film stars attend parties given by economists. Specialization in the various tasks of government and economic management is impossible; every one is a generalist, and everyone has an overall view. So it is never difficult to put through an agreed new policy. This is the phenomenon of "willy nilly French planning" in small countries; the economie is informally concertee, whatever may be the official arrangements or lack of them. This is as much as saying that there can be no laissez faire in an RSME, since the number of large enterprises is too small, and the intermarriage of elite families is inevitable, where the elite contains both enterprise directors and senior civil servants. Give a cocktail party, and you have to invite them all. But we must at once qualify this statement most sharply; it holds only so far as foreign trade dependence permits.

The admirable lack of specialization has its obverse. In the top posts of any government we need about the same number of very able people: a politician and a civil servant who understand finance, and a similar pair who understand housing, foreign policy, etc. The number of subject specialities is about the same whatever the size of the country, and the difficulty of the problems increases less rapidly than size. However, since, or at least if, the distribution of intelligence is about the same in a small and a large country, the former must have fewer clever people for the same number of jobs. This may not apply if the small country with a market economy (SME) has no large multinationals to manage, for then it can spare top managerial talent for government tasks, but clearly then it suffers instead from not "possessing" its own multinationals.

Below the top level, this ceases to hold. The SME can clearly produce the same ratio of good professors to graduate students or mining engineers to pit-shafts as a larger country, and this kind of expert can always get a suitable education abroad.

SMALL COUNTRIES AND POLITICAL-ECONOMIC BLOCS

We can now turn directly to the question: what is special about the relation of small countries to economic and political-economic blocs?

There are no purely economic blocs. No two countries will form a close economic union without political, military, and ideological affinities. This includes, of course, the case of military conquest and forcible conversion, as has happened to Italy, both halves of Germany, and all other small CMEA members. Moreover, these noneconomic affinities invariably precede the economic union, as is now particularly evident in Vietnam, Greece, Spain, and Portugal.

Capitalistic Blocs Versus Socialist Blocs

Nevertheless such affinities are possible, indeed common, under capitalism without bloc-joining, although under Communism there tends to be either affinity or enmity, as indicated by relations between the Soviet Union, Albania, Yugoslavia, and China. No large capitalist country is outside the EEC except for geographical reasons (e.g., the United States and Japan). These reasons also exclude Canada, Australia, and New Zealand; the CMEA, like the OECD, also knows no geographical limits. Of the other RSMEs, Sweden, Iceland, Switzerland, and Austria have strong traditions of diplomatic and military neutrality, and only Iceland has a substantial Communist Party. So they have not joined, though they might have, because it is an obvious anti-Soviet gesture. Yugoslavia, as a Socialist country albeit with a market, could hardly join a capitalist bloc. Portugal and Greece have applied, but mainly in order to stabilize their new democracies and as they are poor, to qualify for this or that transfer payment. That leaves an extremely small sample of ceteris paribus small countries which had none of these reasons to join or not to join: Norway, Netherlands, Denmark, Belgium, and Eire. We might wish to say that these five have decided pro or con on the basis of the volume of their trade with EEC at the moment (see Table 17.2). But clearly so crude an analysis is not enough. Denmark is less sensitive than Norway about being Scandinavian, her ecology movement is less enthusiastic, etc. Therefore, her decision to join was more a matter of economics, but in part perhaps due to a misapperception of her economic dependency on the nine others. Specifically, her exports to Britain are only 5% of her national income, though not easy to shift, and her memory of the thirties and the disaster of British agricultural protection is very long.

TABLE 17.2 - Exports [c] to EEC as Percentage of National Income

		All exports	Exports to EEC	Nat. income	Exports nat. income %
Netherlands	1958[a]	3500	1500	7800	19
BLEU	1958[a]	3400	1550	8500	18
Eire	1973[b]	1900	1500	5100	34
Norway	1973[b]	4700	2500	15400	16
Denmark	1973[b]	5700	2650	21900	12

(a) These numbers concern the Six (million $)

(b) These numbers concern the Nine (million Europeans)

(c) About 15% has been added for invisible exports.

Implications

Inferred from Maksimova (10) is yet another factor influencing small countries, this time in favor of joining such blocs; they do not thereby lose; they regain control over their external affairs. The ongoing scientific-technical revolution under capitalism allows for private international integration, the growth of multinational corporations, and their mutual agreements. In this new world the "classical" foreign trade of international commodity turnover between firms situated each in one nation, where the importing and the exporting firm within one state are not the same and all transactions are at arm's length, yields place to technical cooperation agreements, international subcontracts, the international product transfer of components within one corporation's ownership, and cartel agreements not to trade. The state loses its "classical" control, by tariffs, quotas, and exchange controls over what crosses or does not cross its border. It does so, not merely on the above technical grounds, but also because the multinational corporation is so big. It is in particular bigger - and here I go beyond what Maksimova says - than the small country. The capitalist government, even in Marxist eyes, is capable of controlling the economy up to a point, but only if it is big enough. Moreover the constitution and actual behavior of the EEC are genuinely democratic as between states; the voice of the small state counts for much more than its share in the population. So public international integration chases private, and the small state thereby regains some of the economic sovereignty it has otherwise totally lost.

Within a bloc the small country suffers no particular economic discrimination or exploitation. Partly it is protected by the constitution of the bloc, partly by the spirit that animates it. This is, as seen, democratic and egalitarian as between states. So the small country gains power, not only over large corporations, but also over large foreign states within and outside its bloc. No wonder the small countries are the most enthusiastic members, not only of blocs but also of international organizations in general.

POOR SMALL COUNTRIES WITH A MARKET SYSTEM (PSMEs)

For the purposes of this particular volume, the poor (under $700 of GNP per head in 1970 prices) small country with a market economy (PSME) will be discussed briefly. Many of the points in the section on RSMEs apply, <u>mutatis mutandis</u>.

The PSME will probably be less industrialized than the RSME, so its static benefits from international trade are due less to economies of scale in manufacturing and more to an unusual factor endowment in the extractive industries. Dynamically, however, manufactures are essential to development and full employment.

The PSME will also gain by importing technology, if it can afford to do so and is not altogether too poor, but so will a much larger country. The small one must merely be more selective. In either case this is the principal gain to be expected from foreign trade.

The PSME will get more aid per capita than its large competitors, simply because there is more diplomatic advantage to the donors for a lesser sum (see Table 17.3).

The following obvious military aid recipients have been deleted from the table:

South Vietnam	23.0	16.5	117 (1965)
Israel	44.2	2.6	1155

We should note that additionally the EEC gives, via the Lome Convention, very considerable aid through the terms of trade, i.e., through price support to selected exports by selected poor countries. These are all PSMEs, except Nigeria. Nothing hinders the inclusion of Bangladesh and her jute in the Lome Convention, except Bangladesh's size.

Communities of poor countries have an uninspiring record. It is not necessary to ask here whether this is due to their political instability, to the insignificance of their mutual trade, or to the little help they can render each other. Such countries spend an inordinate part of the national income and of export earnings on diplomatic representation and the entertainment of guests. Even a rational allocation for such purposes would be large, since diplomatic representation is like war; i.e., the small compete directly with the big. But the factual allocation is far larger than that, because representation is the PSME's only way of asserting its national pride.

SMALL COUNTRIES WITH A COMMAND ECONOMY (SCE)

This portion of the chapter will discuss the small country with a command (administrative) economy (SCE). It matters very little for the analysis whether it is rich or poor. Many points directly discussed previously apply here too.

TABLE 17.3.

Country[a]	Per Capita Aid in U.S.$		1967 Population (Millions)	Per Capita Income in U.S.$ 1967 Unless Otherwise Stated	
	1967	1973-77			
Indonesia	1.0	5.11	107.8	90	(1963)
Nigeria	2.1	1.46	42.4	75	
India	2.4	1.87	501.7	79	
Brazil	2.7	1.44	83.2	252	
Philippines	2.8	4.55	35.5	226	
United Arab Republic	3.7	5.16	30.1	166	
Pakistan	4.2	5.17	54.6[b]	108	
Bangladesh		8.14	64.0[b]		
Peru	5.1	5.47	12.0	222	
Taiwan	5.2	n.a.	12.8	199	
Colombia	5.2	5.07	18.6	285	
Turkey	5.7	n.a.	32.2	276	
Kenya	6.4	8.70	9.6	96	
Morocco	6.9	7.60	13.7	174	(1965)
Congo	7.1	7.11	16.0	167	(1965)
South Korea	7.4	7.72	29.1	117	
Ghana	7.7	6.94	7.9	285	
Algeria	12.3	7.35	12.2	193	(1965)
Senegal	13.9	24.41	3.6	182	
Dominican Republic	14.2	5.69	3.8	220	
Tunisia	18.9	24.95	4.5	181	(1965)
Laos	23.7	17.70	2.7	68	
Jordan	31.9	29.32	2.1	235	
Papua and New Guinea	38.2	96.01	2.2	46	(1963)

(a) Countries which received more than $5 million for the 1963-67 average.

Source: United Nations Statistical Year Book, 1967, 1976; Pearson, Partners; and Dhesi, Research Paper.

THE IMPORTANCE OF COUNTRY SIZE

If a country is small, it can benefit from the specificity of its factor endowment, from increasing returns in manufacturing, and by abandonment of marginal sites from decreasing returns in extractive industry just like a small ME. However, the irrationality of its domestic price structure and/or its quantitative planning may, and in the past have, prevented the optimal use of these opportunities. Note that such defects can actually push the small country with a command economy (SCE) beyond the optimum; i.e., it can "overtrade." (11) The charging of world prices is a long step in the right direction, but the command system does not guarantee a correct adaptation of the internal economy to them. For instance, it is possible for CMEA members to specialize in manufacturing products so as to gain the economies of scale, but each of them (i.e., countries) in the industries where they do not have a comparative advantage. The goods are then duly exchanged at world prices. Or again, quite simply the CMEA as a whole is autarkic, and members are or used to be compelled to specialize in precisely those products with high costs that should have been imported; here too, however, they receive only world prices. True, a comparative disadvantage in some manufacture need not be permanent. It consists mainly of human capital, and this part of the factor endowment is malleable, but only in the long run.

Autarky

The Soviet development pattern of autarky, especially in "heavy" industry is never right unless military considerations dominate. However, these considerations are never right at all for a small country, for such a policy would ruin it so thoroughly that it could never make war even against another small country. In fact autarky is not a nice word in Soviet parlance. The preferred word is "self-standingness" (samostoyatel'nost'), which is slightly different; it implies capacity in each broad category, upon which base a great deal of trade within each such category should take place. This is not a stupid policy, and it was practiced by Stalin with his satellites; i.e., Soviet autarky itself was abandoned. But even "self-standingness" drove Hungary, under Rakosi, deep into debt for foreign machinery while it was trying to establish the Soviet pattern, and then further into debt for foreign raw materials which Hungary processed so inefficiently that it would have been better to import the finished goods. Even "self-standingness" is quite impossible for a small country. The problem can arise for the small ME, e.g., Australia, but is much less likely to do so, since the ideology is so far less autarkic and so much more cost conscious.

Actually, however, as we have seen, the Soviet development pattern demands that we "import in order to be autarkic," indeed that we import quite generally in order to develop. Consequently, even in Stalin's own case there was a deep ambiguity about foreign trade. In Rakosi's case foreign trade increased very rapidly, but ever since Rakoski's fall, it is quite in order to suspect "overtrading."

Foreign Aid

The poor small country with a command economy (PSCE) has, of course, a claim for foreign aid like any other poor country. Politics determines that it will only get aid from a rich country with a command economy (CE), though Vietnam may yet surprise us. Economics allows that this can be either through favorable terms of trade (better than world prices bilaterally bargained) or through formal capital transfer. It is felt that the total is greater than in the capitalist world, but it is very difficult to quanitfy the benefits from the terms of bilateral trade. The main point is that such benefits are a gift, not a loan. Since the Sino-Soviet quarrel there has been no poor, large, Community country - the term, "with a command economy" cannot be used - eligible for such aid. Until 1961 China received extremely little aid per head, and it is tempting to say her size was at least as important as any other cause. Bear in mind, however, that by now personal incomes in Bulgaria and Romania have outstripped those in the Soviet Union so these countries should not qualify as recipients any more. North Korea is far too independent, but there are plenty of PSCEs left in Africa and Southeast Asia, as well as Cuba with her vast sugar subsidy.

CMEA Membership

Does the small CE benefit by joining CMEA? First note the CE's reason for not doing so; it wishes to maintain political independence. Even quite trivial divergences exclude the country or make it hesitate to join, e.g., Yugoslavia and above all North Korea. Indeed it is curious to note that no other tight community of nations includes a very large country. As we know, Stalin intended the CMEA to be a Communist OECD. He did not want an EEC because first, there was none yet to imitate and secondly, he was obsessively opposed to federal unions among his satellites. But it is not in the nature of this monolithic system to rest with a loose association. The CMEA is predictably converging upon the EEC's supranational model, but with the big country inside it. Nevertheless, the principles discussed for

RSMEs apply. The CMEA is at least constitutionally democratic and egalitarian; witness the many Romanian vetoes. By belonging, the poor or rich SCE, within the military sphere of influence of Soviet Union, can tie down the Soviet Gulliver, at least a little with the gossamer threads of legality, and enter into the many transnational organizations that technical progress has imposed upon the modern world. The terms of trade in the annual trade protocol remain bilateral, but here again the CMEA offers a more open and international ambiance for the negotiations. Nor, it seems, was there ever much cause to accuse the Soviet Union of exploitation in this matter, at least insofar as prices were concerned, although Russia did seem to have forced deliveries that were extremely costly so that world prices were not fair. (12)

A defect of CMEA for small countries is that if they spend a great deal of domestic resources developing a particular project or sign an onerous contract with a large capitalist corporation to import the same capacity, they have no automatic access to the rest of the CMEA market. However, it is almost impossible to get other countries' planning agreements before the new product is actually being made either.

Of course, the largest defect is quite simply the threat of supranational planning, i.e., the death rather than the reassertion of national sovereignty. There is much evidence that this is where CMEA is going. Lenin effectually said so in a quotation worth repeating.

> ...the tendency to the creation of a single world economy, to be run by a common plant of the proletariat of all nations, a tendency that has become very clear already under capitalism, necessarily develops further under socialism and must be brought to its conclusion. (13)

Krushchev said so and caused the Romanian quasi-secession. Many Soviet, but not East European, economists have recently and discreetly returned to this theme. (14)

Economic Reform

Finally does the small CE need economic reform or decentralization more or less than the large one? The SCE certainly needs its wholesale prices be more rational, i.e., more in correspondence with relative prices on the world market. But this could easily be to help its planners not its enterprise managers. The sheer complexity of command planning is clearly much reduced by the smallness of a country, and it is not surprising to find North Korea, East Germany, Romania, Bulgaria, Albania, and Cuba very centralized, or Poland distinctly less so. Rather the positions of Soviet Union and Hungary are paradoxical, and must both be put down to abnormal currents within the broad stream of the common ideology.

NOTES

1. E. F. Schumacher, Small is Beautiful (London: Blond and Briggs, 1973), p. 60.

2. The pioneering work here is L. Kohr, The Breakdown of Nations (London: Routledge and Paul, 1957).

3. D. Ricardo, Principles of Political Economy and Taxation, 1st ed. (London: 1817), chapter 7.

4. Kuznets' study does, however, tackle the subject directly, and on rereading it, I find many reassuring coincidences with the present text. Cf. Simon Kuznets, "Economic Growth of Small Nations." In Economic Consequences of the Size of Nations, E.A.G. Robinson, Ed. (London: MacMillan, 1963).

5. The author will defend this proposition at length in a work under preparation. Preliminary solutions to the problem of what exactly are exports at factor cost in a Soviet type economy and preliminary regressions strongly support the words underlined. They apply to all types of economy equally. Other statistical studies lead to same conclusion.

6. P. J. D. Wiles, Communist International Economics (Oxford: Blackwell, 1969), pp. 420-1.

7. Robinson, Economic Consequences.

8. Cf. H. C. Simons, Economic Policy for a Free Society (Chicago: University of Chicago Press, 1948), p. 21. This book hints many times at the natural affinity of Chicago economics with a preference for small countries, but the school seems not to have followed up this initiative.

9. Egypt could still control the Suez Canal if she was a small country; cf. Wiles, Communist International, p. 467.

10. M. M. Maksimova, Osnovnye Problemy Imperialisticheskoi Integratsii, (Moscow: 1971). For a brief English summary, see John Pinder in The EEC and Eastern Europe. Avi Shlaim, Ed. (Cambridge: Cambridge University Press, 1978).

11. Wiles, <u>Communist International</u>, pp. 428-34. Sometimes in an ME, subsidies can have the same effect. Thus British egg growers imported feed in order to export subsidized eggs in 1956. The export prices of eggs did not cover the marginal cost of imported feed.

12. Cf. Wiles, <u>Communist International</u>, pp. 248-50. Thus the East German planning chief Erich Apel killed himself in December 1965 because he objected to the excessive export of a costly chemical plant to the Soviet Union.

13. V. I. Lenin, Original Draft of the Theses on the National and Colonial Question, June 5, 1920.

14. P. J. D. Wiles and A. Smith in <u>The EEC and Eastern Europe</u>, Shlaim, Ed., p. 134.

18 Balance of Payments Constraints on Socialist Countries: Their Impact on the Choice of Trade Partners[*]

Zbigniew Kamecki

INTRODUCTION

The economic development of the Socialist countries of Eastern Europe (SCEE) from their very beginning to the present day has very often, if not always, been associated with certain difficulties in equilibrating balances of payments, and particularly those in convertible currencies. The intensity of these difficulties has varied according to time and country, but even if they decreased, they usually remained an important factor, restricting increases in SCEE imports and more generally rates of economic growth in these countires. (1)

While recognizing the continuity of this phenomenon up to the present, it should be stressed, however, that it would not seem to be a permanent feature of the socialist economy, nor is it so, incidentally, in market economy countries. It has existed until now for several reasons connected with the current stage of SCEE economic development, these countries' economic policies, and specific circumstances prevailing on the markets of the hard currency countries. If the situation changes in the future, particularly, if SCEE economic growth becomes more export oriented than previously, these countires' balance-of-payments difficulties vis-a-vis convertible currency countries may well disappear.

---

[*] Although a staff member of the United Nations Economic Commission for the European Secretariat, the views expressed in this chapter are personal ones and are not necessarily those in the United Nations Secretariat.

However, if the latter situation really occurs, it will not occur so fast. In the near future at least, for a number of reasons, the balance of payments constraints on the SCEE will probably be maintained, and the only question is how strong or how weak they will be. It is believed that these constraints would not be approached from the point of view of SCEE ability to ensure servicing and repayment of indebtedness towards the West. It is felt that such a question will not arise, since in SCEE history there has been no case when they stopped paying their debts, since they attached the highest importance to the maintenance of a good reputation as debt payers and they will probably need during a certain period some additional credits from the West. Under these circumstances, a repayment of Western credits remains a priority in using those convertible currencies which the SCEE have at their disposal. If some sacrifices are needed because of the balance of payments pressures, they will probably concern SCEE imports and indirectly, the rates of economic growth, their patterns, and the domestic market equilibrium of these countries.

DIFFICULTIES IN MEASURING BALANCE OF PAYMENTS CONSTRAINTS ON THE SCEE

Although it is generally recognized that these constraints exist, unfortunately it is not known how to measure them; an assessment of the degree of SCEE balance of payments difficulties is incomparably more difficult than those in market economy countries. In the latter, first of all, there are relevant statistics, at least in principle. Under these circumstances, conclusions may easily be drawn by using, for example, the International Monetary Fund's (IMF's) balance of payments classification or the distinction made by J. Meade between so-called "autonomous" payments with foreign countries and "accommodating" ones. (2)

When assessing the analogous situation in the SCEE, the first difficulty encountered is a lack of relevant statistics on balances of payments. (3) Some recent estimations have been made, particularly by the Economic Commission for the Europe Secretariat, (4) but they necessarily display only a very general and partial orientation. Indeed, these estimations, open for discussion as are all estimations, cover only SCEE transactions with OECD countries, and thus exclude intra-SCEE transactions in convertible currencies as well as those taking place with developing countries.

However, and this point should be stressed, even if relevant statistics on SCEE balance of payments were available, an assessment of the degree of difficulties in equilibrating these balances would be difficult. The reason, simply, is that one has to deal here with a case of a centrally planned economy, where the State controls not only economic relations with foreign countries, but other factors as well which influence the former, particularly rates of economic growth, patterns of domestic production, distribution of national income, etc. Mutual adjustment of all these has a planned character and is conducted, in principle, ex ante, i.e., already at the stage of elaboration of national economic plans when the relevant foreign trade plan and plans of production, investment, employment, wages, market supplies, etc., are mutually coordinated. The second stage of the mutual adjustment of various sectoral plans takes place during their implementation. If the implementation of plans concerning domestic production, investment, consumption, and others deviate from what has been envisaged for some reason, then the foreign trade and balance of payments plans have to be properly adjusted and vice versa. Of course, this does not mean that power of the state to make these adjustments is unlimited, but generally speaking, it is quite considerable, particularly in the longer run, and especially in those countries where the planning and management system is relatively centralized. (5)

In these circumstances, one can easily imagine a situation in which the deficit in the balance of payments is increasing, but it does not necessarily indicate an increase in the constraints imposed by this deficit. On the other hand, even when the deficit of the balance of payments is decreasing, balance of payments constraints might be more acute than before. For example, in Poland during the second half of the 1960s the basic balance of payments with non-Socialist countries was almost equilibrated, while in the 1970s and particularly in 1974, 1975, and 1976, there was a large deficit. In the latter period, however, industrial ministries, amalgamations, and enterprises were incomparably freer to import Western goods than in the 1960s or in 1977 when the balance of payments situation formally was better. In other words, what J. Meade said about a so-called apparent balance-of-payments equilibrium (6) has full application in this instance.

This is why all estimations based on figures concerning trade deficits or amounts of credits received by the SCEE from abroad may very often be misleading. In particular, as far as credits from Western countries are concerned, this may be not so much a reflection of difficulties in SCEE balance of payments, as was the case in the 1970s, but rather a result of these countries' conscious choice with regard to their economic and social development strategy. The purpose of these credits was not so much to equilibrate SCEE balance of payments, but first of all, to finance the development and modernization of these countries' production potential. The great majority of these credits were of a long-term nature so they had to be considered as autonomous transactions, which by analogy with market economy countries had to be included in so-called basic balances. Only short-term financial credits could be treated as equilibrating transactions which, together with changes in foreign exchange reserves, reflected the degree of the balance of payments disequilibrium. Unfortunately, data on the net amount of the latter credits received by the SCEE in Western countries are lacking, and data on changes in SCEE deposits maintained in Western banks are not entirely conclusive since these changes are influenced, <u>inter alia,</u> by movements of credits.

In these circumstances, it is practically impossible to find a unique and comprehensive measure for assessing the degree of SCEE balance of payments difficulties. A number of factors, in addition to data on SCEE trade, credits received, and overall indebtedness with regard to relations with hard currency countries, should be taken into account when attempting such an assessment. Among these factors, the intensity of direct controls over imports financed in convertible currencies, or rather changes in this intensity, is particularly informative. Additional information may also be derived from comparisons between the rates of growth concerning global imports and national income, imports of engineering goods and investments, imports of raw materials and intermediate goods (7) with industrial production, imports of consumer goods (8) and the personal incomes of a country's population. The existence of some bottlenecks in the SCEE domestic market, particularly in its more important sectors, may also be interpreted as a reflection of the balance of payments pressures because if these pressures had not existed, the state could easily permit some increase of imports and/or decrease of exports of relevant goods in order to improve the domestic market equilibrium.

MAIN REASONS FOR BALANCE OF PAYMENTS CONSTRAINTS ON SCEE

Since the intensity of balance of payments difficulties varies according to time and country, in order to describe fully the background of this phenomenon, the situation in each of the SCEE should be analyzed in detail, but an analysis of this kind is beyond the scope of this paper. Only the main reasons for SCEE balance of payments difficulties with regard to convertible currency countries are discussed, i.e., internal, external, and mixed.

Internal Reasons

Passing from more general to more specific reasons, one has to mention first of all, the impact of the relatively high rate of the SCEE economic growth on their balance of payments. This high rate of growth - in 1960-75, for example, the Soviet Union and Eastern Europe together amounted to an average of 6.7% per year (9) - has meant at the same time a high rate of growth of internal demand. This demand, growing so quickly, has exerted a continuous pressure on SCEE imports and on the other hand, has led to some absorption of exportable goods.

Absorption of Exports

This question of absorption of exports is worth stressing. It is recalled, in this connection, that since the very beginning and even now the share of industrial goods in SCEE exports to convertible currency countries has remained and remains relatively low, and these are traditional exports, i.e., some agricultural products, raw materials, and intermediate products which constitute, and constituted especially in the past, the bulk of these exports. Meanwhile, exports' absorption in this field was particularly strong in the SCEE.

Raw Materials, Agricultural Products, and Foodstuffs

In the case of raw materials, the reason was very simple; industrialization was based, to a very large extent, on those raw materials which the SCEE had at their disposal in their own territories. Thus, growing industrial production meant a growing demand for raw materials. The same could also be said to refer to intermediate products. Pressure of demand was stronger because the use of raw materials and intermediate products per unit of industrial production, by reason of a certain technological gap, has remained relatively high in many branches.

In the case of agricultural products and foodstuffs, another specific factor should be mentioned: a relatively high income elasticity of demand for these products in the SCEE, (10) which results mainly from the still relatively low level of national income per capita and traditional patterns of individual consumption in these countries.

The impact of this demand pressure on the SCEE balance of payments in convertible currencies could be weakened if there were possibilities of ensuring a relatively high rate of growth of agricultural goods, raw materials, and intermediate products in internal production. Unfortunately, this production is usually highly capital intensive, and when there are very strong investment needs everywhere, this is a limiting factor in its development.

Another possibility for weakening SCEE internal demand pressure on balance of payments in convertible currencies might be to increase proportionally mutual supplies of agricultural products, raw materials, and intermediate goods. This possibility has largely been explored; the main source of supply in this field for each SCEE became, and remains, other SCEEs. However, with time, these two factors - exports' absorption, which emerged in every SCEE, and high capital intensity of agricultural and raw material production (11) - started to relatively restrict the rate of growth of mutual SCEE deliveries in this field. Although they were increasing in absolute terms, their share in SCEE global imports tended to decrease (12) which, in turn, strengthened these countries' internal pressure of demand on their balance of payments in hard currencies. Imports of agricultural goods, raw materials, and intermediate products from convertible currency countries tended to increase relatively fast when the growth of exports of these goods - because of exports' absorption and high capital intensity of their production - was relatively restricted. As a result of these trends, and recently because of the additional impact of the Western recession and in some cases of protectionist measures in certain Western countries, a general tendency towards some deterioration of SCEE trade balances in agricultural goods, raw materials, and intermediate products with convertible currency countries could be observed. Some exceptions, however, are Hungary's trade balance in agricultural products and foodstuffs, the Soviet Union's trade balance in energy products, and Poland to some extent.

SCEE Projects

In order to ensure better satisfaction of their demand and simultaneously, to ease their balance of payments pressures in hard currencies, the SCEE have undertaken, especially during recent years, a great number of joint investment projects in their territories, and particularly in the Soviet Union. By the beginning of 1975, joint investments carried out in the latter country only were valued at around $8 billion, and during 1976-80 they may achieve another $12 billion, (13) thus indicating their enormous scale. These projects are concentrated in energy, metals, chemical raw materials, engineering, and electronics. When completed, most with a target date of 1980, they will automatically lessen pressures on SCEE balance of payments with convertible currency countries since they will make possible, in some instances, a certain shift of deliveries from the latter countries towards the SCEE and increase SCEE export possibilities towards these countries.

However, in the shorter run, i.e., until their completion, these joint investment projects, because of the necessity of imports from Western countries, are increasing to some extent SCEE needs for convertible currencies.

Domestic Demand and Technological Gaps

When discussing pressure of domestic demand, it should be mentioned that when on the international market, in general, a buyer's market situation was prevailing in the SCEE, while in many sectors, especially in the past, a seller's market situation prevailed. This discrepancy has tended to decrease the interest of SCEE domestic producers in developing their exports to convertible currency countries since the quality requirements on these latter markets have been higher than those on SCEE domestic markets. SCEE governments by means of various instruments have tried to counteract the influence of the quality factor, but sometimes have not completely succeeded.

Another reason for hard currency, balance of payments constraints on the SCEE is the existence in several fields of a certain technological gap in comparison with Western developed countries. Generally speaking, this factor affects the balances through three channels. First, it limits possibilities of expanding SCEE exports towards convertible currency countries, since it makes it more difficult to respond fully to high quality requirements on those markets or to offer the most sophisticated industrial goods (14) for which international demand, in general, is increasing relatively fast. The result is that the unit prices which the SCEE receive for their industrial products in the convertible currency countries are often relatively low, (15) which additionally contribute to balance of payments constraints on the SCEE. Secondly, the technological gap increases the attractiveness of Western goods and technologies for the SCEE and strengthens pressure on their balance of payments in convertible currencies. Thirdly, in the case of more sophisticated industrial goods, this technological gap relatively limits the possibility of substituting mutual deliveries of the SCEE for imports from Western countries because at the beginning of the 1970s the SCEE undertook on a large scale a policy of a modernization of their economies and the induced demand for foreign equipment was directed mainly towards Western countries. The strength of the impact of machinery and transport equipment on the SCEE balance of payments in convertible currencies during recent years may be seen from the following: the total trade deficit of Eastern countries with Western countries on an f.o.b. basis in 1971-75 amounted to $11.8 billion; total Eastern imports of Western machinery and transport equipment were $26.7 billion; and the trade deficit of the SCEE in latter field was $19.8 billion. (16)

Delays in SCEE Export Potential

Certain inherited delays in developing SCEE export potential should also be mentioned here as one reason for these countries' balance of payments difficulties in their relations with convertible currency countries. It may be recalled in this connection that in the 1950s, because of the cold war, a specific concept of economic growth, and in particular, industrialization being carried out by SCEE at that time, some autarchic tendencies could be observed in these countries' economic policies. The advantages of international specialization did not begin to be discovered until the end of the fifties and the beginning of the sixties. However, under the influence of growing balance of payments pressures, the main emphasis was continuously put in import substitution rather than on building up export potential quickly. It was practically at the end of the sixties and in particular, at the beginning of the seventies that a major change in the approach to foreign trade occurred; the main emphasis, instead of being on import substitution was put on developing export potential. However, this was done too late to counteract previous delays in this field. Consequently, although reasonably fair progress has been achieved since then, there are cases where export production potential is not sufficient to respond to all the possibilities of selling in convertible currency countries.

Last but not least, some difficulties typical of the early stage of industrialization, and/or trade expansion, or resulting sometimes from certain rigidities in the SCEE planning and management system should be mentioned as well, particularly questions of quality of products, delays in developing marketing techniques, insufficient involvement of domestic producers, and end users in export and import transactions, etc.).

External Reasons

Reasons of this kind fall into three main categories: some objective difficulties in entering Western markets on the part of the SCEE, Western commercial policies towards the SCEE, and, more recently, the Western recession.

Objective Difficulties

Concerning the first category of reasons, one has in mind the fact that in many instances and particularly in the case of industrial products, the SCEE were and still are to a certain extent newcomers to Western markets. As such, they encounter the same objective difficulties as any other country, independent of its economic and social system in a similar situation. The SCEE have to enter markets which are already occupied, sometimes for a long time by other suppliers utilizing the developed commercial network and long lasting commercial contacts; the SCEE products are not specially well-known by potential buyers, who sometimes may even have certain prejudices against these products; suppliers from these countries need to obtain knowledge of market requirements and customs, which necessarily takes time, etc.

Under these circumstances, in order to obtain a certain share in the market, the SCEE have to undertake considerable marketing efforts, which give results in a longer run only and are costly, particularly in the early stages when quantities of the products in question sold on the market are small. Sales of Eastern machines may serve here as an example. An analysis of the European Economic Community's imports of 42 items of machinery from the SCEE revealed that well over one half of these imports in value terms consisted of country-to-country flows of less than $1 million per year. (17) One can easily conceive how costly, under these circumstances, is market research and how difficult it is to ensure proper post sales services which are so important in the trade of machinery.

Western Commercial Policies towards the SCEE

As far as Western commercial policies are concerned, difficulties encountered by the SCEE in this area may be divided into two groups.

The first group of difficulties results from measures affecting all countries entering a given Western country's market, independent of their economic and social systems. Because of the specific pattern of SCEE exports, various measures protecting the European Economic Community's agricultural markets have a special importance. SCEE exports have also been affected by various protectionist measures introduced by several Western countries during recent years. The European Economic Community's embargo on beef imports; some of its measures concerning textile imports and quite recently, on steel imports; and import deposit schemes established by some Western countries are examples. New problems also tend to arise for SCEE exports in connection with the creation of a free trade area on industrial products between the European Economic Community and EFTA countries.

The second group of difficulties for SCEE exports results from the fact that in many instances treatment in the trade policy field ensured by the Western countries for the SCEE is and was particularly less favorable than that reserved for other countries.

The second group of difficulties for SCEE exports results from the fact that in many instances treatment in the trade policy field ensured by the Western countries for the SCEE is and was particularly less favorable than that reserved for other countries.

This difference in treatment has found its expression particularly in the application of quantitative restrictions by a majority of Western European countries on many kinds of imports from the SCEE while similar imports from other countries could gain access to the market without any quotas. The importance of this factor has tended to decrease with time since quotas have gradually been removed. Some countries, such as Austria and Switzerland, during recent years have fully liberalized their imports from the SCEE, and others, viz., Norway and Sweden have done this to a great extent. The liberalization was also far-reaching in the main SCEE Western markets, i.e., in those of the European Economic Community (EEC). This liberalization has found its expression, inter alia, in the expansion in the EEC's common list of liberalized products. At the end of January 1970 this list contained 443 entire four-digit tariff headings and at the end of February 1976, 767 entire and 99 partial headings, the number of four-digit headings in the EEC's tariffs is 1,098; i.e., fully liberalized tariff headings by February 1976 constituted 69.9% of their total number. (18) Moreover, several products were liberalized in some EEC member countries, but since they were not liberalized in all its member countries, they could not be incorporated in the previously mentioned common list.

However, one has to take into account that the list of liberalized products, in many instances, contains products which are not a subject of SCEE exports or which play a very limited role for them. On the other hand, among products covered by quotas, there are sometimes products of great importance for SCEE exports to Western countries. Thus, a real degree of liberalization achieved may sometimes be more limited than one could presume on the basis of a number of tariff headings which have been liberalized. In other words, quotas, although they have been removed to a great extent, may even now remain a factor hampering the development of SCEE exports to Western markets and contributing thus to these countries' balance of payments pressures in their relations with convertible currency countries. The same may also be said about the impact of the lack of most favored nation (MFN) treatment for some SCEE in the United States and several protective measures introduced during the last two-three years by some Western countries vis-a-vis imports of certain products from the SCEE.

BALANCE OF PAYMENTS CONSTRAINTS 327

The Western Recession

During recent years, SCEE exports have been heavily affected by the Western recession. As a result of the weakening of demand on Western markets, in 1974 for the first time since the 1950s, the volume of SCEE Western exports dropped by 5% and in 1975 by an additional 2%; at that time, the volume of SCEE imports from the West increased by 11 and 25%. In 1976, the SCEE succeeded in increasing their export volume by 14%, but this increase was too small to compensate for their export losses during the two previous years, the more so in that in the same year the SCEE volume of imports from the West increased by 11%. (19) Under these circumstances, the SCEE, preferring to avoid increasing too fast their indebtedness towards Western countries, have been obliged to considerably strengthen their control over imports from the West. Imports of several products considered not especially essential for achieving the main objectives of SCEE economic policies have been reduced. Moreover, several investment projects considered less urgent have been delayed, which has resulted in a slowing down of imports of capital goods. (20) Although data for the whole of 1977 are not yet available for all the SCEE, data for the first nine months of the year indicate that for the first time since the 1950s the volume of these countries imports from Western countries has dropped somewhat.

It might be added that the Western recession has had another effect; i.e., it has hampered and delayed the implementation of the SCEE concept on which their credit policy was based to a large extent. The concept was to largely draw credits from Western financial sources, to use these credits, <u>inter alia,</u> for development of SCEE export potential, and to repay credits received as soon as possible, maintaining at the same time a relatively high rate of growth of imports from the West. It was generally assumed in the SCEE that the rate of growth of their Western exports had to be considerably accelerated already at the end of the first half of the seventies in order to start to surpass the rate of growth of import during the second half of the seventies, the latter rate remaining relatively high. Because of the Western recession, these projects had to be corrected in a sense that in order to improve their balance of payments situation in relations with convertible currency-countries, the SCEE had to proceed to restrain their import growth from the West.

Mixed Reasons

These reasons for balance-of-payments constraints on the SCEE seem to have their basis in these countries, at the same time in the west, or more generally speaking, in international markets.

Structure of Western Demand

The first factor to be taken into account is a certain inconsistency between the structure of Western demand and the structure of supply of SCEE exports. A positive element in the SCEE export structure is a relatively high share of mineral fuels (SITC group 3) for which Western demand is or at least was dynamic, and prices tend to rise. This share has increased during recent years (in 1970, 16.5%; in 1973, 20.8%; and in 1975, 35.2%), (21) and it was higher than in global Western imports. However, it was a factor favoring the fast development of Western exports only of those SCEE which are exporters of fuels, specifically the Soviet Union and to a lesser extent Poland.

On the other hand, one can see from a comparison of the commodity structure of SCEE Western exports and Western global imports that in the former the share of food, beverages, and tobacco (SITC group 0+1) and of crude materials excluding fuels (SITC group 2+4), for which Western demand is growing rather slowly and which are very sensitive during economic recessions, was much higher than in Western global imports. In Western global imports the share of these two SITC groups taken together, in 1970-1973 was around 23.5-25% and then in 1974 and 1975 it fell to almost 20%; in SCEE Western exports in 1970-73 the same share was about 33%, and then it fell to almost 29% in 1974 and to about 25% in 1975. Moreover, within these two SITC groups, the share of such products as textiles fibers (SITC subgroup 26) and crude fertilizers and minerals (SITC subgroup 27) which are listed as sensitive products on Western markets or at least tend to become products of this nature, was much higher in SCEE Western exports than in global Western imports.

Another characteristic feature of SCEE Western exports is a relatively low share of manufactured products in comparison with the commodity structure of global Western imports, particularly of chemicals (SITC group 5) and machinery and transport equipment (SITC group 7) for which demand on Western markets is usually dynamic. In Western global imports, the share of these two groups was 33-35% in 1970-73, and after a fall in 1974 to 29.5%, it rose to 31% in 1975, and in SCEE Western exports during these years it was around 15-16%. Moreover, in the latter exports, the share of products, such as textile yarn and fabrics (SITC subgroup 65), iron and steel (SITC subgroup 67), and clothing (SITC subgroup 84), which are rather sensitive ones on Western markets, was relatively high. In 1970-75, this share in global SCEE Western exports was to a certain extent higher than in Western global imports, but much higher if only industrial exports were taken into account.

SCEE Terms of Trade with Western Countries

A second factor to be pointed out here was movements in the SCEE terms of trade with Western countries. Their impact on the SCEE balance of payments in convertible currencies depended on a specific country and time. Unfortunately, detailed data are lacking. On the basis of estimations made by the Economic Commission for Europe Secretariat, one may conclude that between 1965 and 1972 changes in these terms were rather moderate, with annual fluctuations ranging from 2.5% in 1971 in favor of the SCEE to 5% in favor of the Western countries in 1972. From 1973 until 1976, these terms were continuously improving, especially in 1974, but mainly under the influence of the Soviet Union's improvement of the terms of trade and to a lesser extent of Poland. (22) In other SCEE, particularly Hungary, these terms have tended to deteriorate, thus contributing to balance of payments pressures in relations with convertible currency countries.

IMPACT OF THE BALANCE OF PAYMENTS CONSTRAINTS ON SCEE'S CHOICE OF PARTNERS IN EAST-WEST TRADE

Existing balance of payments constraints cannot otherwise but be one of the factors influencing the choice of partners by the SCEE. The influence of this specific factor can take different forms. The first possibility to be considered by a central decision maker in the SCEE is such an arrangement or rearrangement of domestic production, investment, and/or consumption which makes a given import from convertible currency countries unnecessary. Such a possibility may exist, however, in the case of products which may be considered as not specifically essential. In a majority of cases, the resignation from imports at all may have limits, particularly in the shorter run, since it may produce distrubances in current production, investments, or in satisfying population consumption needs.

Import Substitution

Under these circumstances, another possibility to be considered is full or partial substitution of some imports from convertible currency countries by domestic supplies and/or imports from other countries not requiring payment in convertible currencies. Here again freedom of action may also be limited, particularly in the shorter run. The production potential in home or in other nonconvertible currency countries may be fully employed, and some additional investments, sometimes requiring imports from convertible currency countries, may be needed notwithstanding the fact that increase of production in that way takes some time. Moreover, the economic calculus may prove that even when such possibilities of import substitution really exist, the whole operation is not profitable. In cases when the possibility of import substitution by supplies from other nonconvertible currency countries is considered, such a possibility may appear to be impracticable since in these countries, convertible currencies may also be scarce and they may prefer to direct products in question to hard currency markets.

If these possibilities are not workable, and given the fact that imports from convertible currency countries are considered necessary, a central decision maker may consider the possibility of exporting to these countries some products initially envisaged for supplying the domestic market or scheduled to be exported to other countries against payments in nonconvertible currencies. But here again, there are limits for such an action. In the case of products envisaged for the domestic market, their export may lead to some disequilibrium in this market. On the other hand, resignation from exports to nonconvertible currency countries may cause some reluctance in those countries to deliver their goods, which could also be exported to convertible currency countries. In both cases, the advantages of imports from the latter countries should be compared with the disadvantages of depriving the domestic market of some goods or resigning from exporting them to nonconvertible currency countries.

When the possibility of import substitution by domestic production and/or deliveries from other countries is not practicable, the central decision maker may encourage enterprises to proceed to full or partial substitution of imports from one convertible currency country by imports from another country offering satisfactory credit facilities and/or favorable conditions of access to its market for products of the country in question. Here, again, freedom in such shifts in import directions may be limited for technological reasons, requirements of the investment cycle, investment and consumption habits, knowledge of relevant markets, and existing commercial contacts, etc.

Import-Export Shifting Patterns

When floating rates of exchanges are prevailing as is now the case, balance of payments constraints also encourage some changes in a geographical pattern of imports and exports depending on changes in rates of exchange of currencies used for settlements. In particular, certain attempts may be observed in the SCEE of some shift of their exports towards countries with strong currencies and their imports towards countries with weaker currencies. However, these shifts have the same limits which were mentioned previously in connection with substitution of trade from one country by trade from another country.

When a given import has to be undertaken, there are some possibilities of maneuvering between firms within a given convertible currency country: a concentration of import transactions in those firms which are able to offer favorable financial conditions, i.e., prices and in the case of some imports, credits on satisfactory terms; and if it is relevant and profitable, to accept sufficient buy-back deliveries from the SCEE in question, or to enter into advantageous cooperation conducive, _inter alia,_ to weakening, directly or indirectly, balance of payments constraints.

Western Counter Deliveries

The interest of the SCEE in counter deliveries to Western markets seems to grow with time, particularly in connection with long-term cooperation deals, the more so when initial deliveries from the West are financed by Western credits. However, this interest does not result only from the SCEE determination to ensure repayment of these credits without causing a burden on the balance of payments. Another reason, and sometimes even the most important one, is the wish to ensure sales during some of the time, and thus, weakening elements of uncertainty, which in a planned economy is a factor of especial importance. When counter deliveries concern elements to be included by a partner in a final product or when co-production and joint marketing occur, the possibility of having certain access to a Western partner's technology, and/or marketing techniques, and commercial network may be another reason for encouraging the SCEE to insist on Western partners' acceptance of these countries' counter deliveries as part of a deal.

Preference for Larger Firms

The interest in such deals necessarily creates for the SCEE a stimulus to choose those partners who are prepared for such cooperation. In the majority of cases, these are larger firms. In comparison with small firms, from the SCEE point of view, they may have several advantages since they may mobilize enormous means (capital, labor, technologies, know-how); have relatively easy access to financial markets; are, in general, sufficiently diversified to find a place among their activities for SCEE counter deliveries; have at their disposal a well-established commercial network, often in several countries; and develop longer-run forecasting and programming, which enable the SCEE to achieve some long-term coordination of cooperation with these firms and to weaken elements of uncertainty in the SCEE economic plans. Moreover, since these firms have an important place in the market, they may more easily receive governmental support for specific cooperation deals, and acting usually in several countries, they may also sometimes avoid certain trade obstacles, etc.

Western Credits

Credits received from the West also constitute one of the factors influencing SCEE choice of partners. This influence depends, first of all, on the type of credits received. In the case of financial "untied" credits, the SCEE maintain complete freedom in deciding how they will disburse money put at their disposal. The choice of kind of import to be financed, as well as the country and firms where money resulting from credits will be utilized, applies entirely to the SCEE. In the case of tied credits, the choice is already determined in a credit agreement. However, it may happen and there have been several cases in practice, particularly in the case of publicly supported credit lines, that credits will not be used since a SCEE may come to the conclusion that terms of a contract, especially prices, offered by firms in the Western country which opens the credit are unacceptable. In such cases, the question of a choice of partner does not appear at all.

FUTURE PROSPECTS

The question arises finally as to what are the prospects for easing balance of payments constraints on the SCEE.

In the nearest future, such an easing does not seem very probable, although the situation may vary depending on a specific country, and the main reasons for this are: lack of perspectives for a considerable improvement in the Western economic conjuncture; possible negative repercussions of recently introduced protective measures in some Western countries against SCEE exports; and the possibility, if the present western recession is prolonged, of new measures of this kind; existing pressure of domestic demand in the SCEE on their imports from and exports to convertible currency countries; and the increasing burden of servicing SCEE indebtedness for these countries' balances of payments. For these reasons, it is probable that in the shorter run the SCEE will continue to constrain to some extent the rate of growth of their imports from convertible currency countries. On the other hand, the SCEE may continue to draw credits from Western financial sources, although probably the scale of these drawings may be smaller.

Favorable Factors

In the longer run, prospects for easing SCEE balance of payments pressures seem to be much more favorable.

On the one hand, there is a factor which will constitute a burden for these balances, i.e., the necessity to ensure servicing of existing indebtedness towards Western countries. However, it seems quite probable that in the longer run the amount of this indebtedness may decrease, or at least may increase more slowly than the increase of SCEE Western exports. Under these circumstances, the burden of indebtedness for SCEE balance of payments would decrease after some time.

On the other hand, there are several factors operating towards improvement of the SCEE balance of payments situation. First of all, completion of several investment projects undertaken during last year may weaken SCEE internal demand pressure on these countries' balance of payments and increase and diversify their export potential, which is already considerably extended and modernized. The same can also be said about the import substitution potential. Again, completion of several SCEE joint investment projects undertaken in their respective territories will allow some substitution of imports from Western countries by imports from the SCEE and will contribute to an increase in these latter countries' export potential. Several cooperation agreements with Western partners envisaging SCEE deliveries for repayment of credits received from the West, as well as other East-West cooperation agreements, will also be a factor favoring the development of SCEE Western exports. A very probably improvement in the economic situation in Western countries will also act in this direction. Yet another favorable factor for expansion of SCEE Western exports is the still relatively low share of these exports in Western markets and in many cases, the existence of reserves for some increase of this share without causing any market disturbances. Growing knowledge of Western markets and of marketing techniques among SCEE producers and exporters will also favor an increase of SCEE exports to the West.

Summary

The extent to which all these possibilities will be employed will largely depend on SCEE ability to better adapt exports to the structure of demand and to the market requirements of Western countries. On the other hand, the employment of the previously described possibilities to a very large extent will depend on Western commercial policies towards the SCEE. If these policies are liberalized, this will make possible not only an easing of SCEE balance of payments pressures, but also achievement on a much higher level of East-West trade and cooperation. It seems that the SCEE policy aimed at fuller participation in the international division of labor is a stable and long-range element of the overall economic policy. These countries' import demand is far from being satisfied, and if they have possibilities for proper expansion of their exports, they will expand their imports relatively fast as well.

TABLE 18.1 - Shares of SCEE in Their Imports According to SITC Groups (Percentage)

SITC Groups	1970	1971	1972	1973	1974	1975
0 + 1[a]	42.8	44.4	36.2	31.0	33.3	27.8
2 + 4[b]	48.0	48.9	49.5	42.9	38.0	45.8
3[c]	90.9	88.6	80.9	75.0	67.4	74.8
5[d]	49.7	52.1	51.6	49.5	35.3	39.2
7[e]	74.3	75.7	75.1	73.5	69.6	64.5
6 + 8[f]	62.3	61.0	60.3	55.4	45.7	48.3
0+1+2+4+3	54.0	55.3	50.7	44.4	42.7	46.5
5+7+6+8	67.1	67.3	67.0	64.4	56.3	55.7

a Food, beverages, and tobacco
b Crude materials, excluding fuels
c Mineral fuels and related products
d Chemicals
e Machines and transport equipment
f Other manufactured goods

Source: United Nations, Monthly Bulletin of Statistics (New York: United Nations, 1970-75).

TABLE 18.2 - SCEE Global Trade (and in Machinery) with the West f.o.b.-f.o.b. Basis ($ millions)

SCEE Global Trade with the West

	Exports	Imports	Balance
1970	7,030	6,940	+ 90
1971	7,761	7,608	+ 153
1972	8,944	10,199	- 1,255
1973	13,392	15,039	- 1,647
1974	19,619	21,028	- 1,419
1975	20,199	27,861	- 7,662
1970-5	76,945	88,685	-11,740
1971-5	69,915	81,745	-11,830

SCEE Trade with the West in Machinery

	Exports	Imports	Balance
1970	630	2,380	- 1,750
1971	827	2,483	- 1,656
1972	947	3,309	- 2,362
1973	1,307	4,699	- 3,392
1974	1,626	6,323	- 4,707
1975	2,191	9,855	- 7,664
1970-5	7,528	29,059	-21,531
1971-5	6,898	26,679	-19,781

Source: United Nations, Monthly Bulletin.

TABLE 18.3 - Commodity Pattern of Western Global Imports (Percentage)

SITC Groups	1970	1971	1972	1973	1974	1975
0 + 1[a]	13.4	13.2	13.5	13.5	10.7	11.8
2 + 4[b]	11.6	10.3	10.2	10.9	9.7	8.5
3[c]	9.8	11.2	11.0	12.0	22.7	22.3
5[d]	6.5	6.5	6.5	6.7	7.3	6.6
7[e]	26.9	28.3	28.3	26.7	22.2	24.5
6 + 8[f]	30.1	29.0	29.2	29.1	26.2	25.0
0 + 1 + 2 + 4 + 3	34.8	34.8	34.7	36.4	43.2	42.6
0 + 1 + 2 + 4	25.0	23.6	23.7	24.3	20.4	20.3
5 + 7 + 6 + 8	63.5	63.9	64.1	62.5	55.7	56.1
5 + 7	33.4	34.8	34.8	33.4	29.5	31.1
26 (textile fibers) + 27 (crude fertilizers)	2.5	2.3	2.5	2.6	2.0	1.8
65 (textile yarn and fabrics) + 67 (iron and steel) + 84 clothing)	11.1	10.9	11.0	10.7	9.9	9.4
$\frac{65 + 67 + 84}{5 + 7 + 6 + 8}$	17.4	17.1	17.2	17.2	17.8	16.8

a Food, beverages, and tobacco
b Crude materials, excluding fuels
c Mineral fuels and related products
d Chemicals
e Machines and transport equipment
f Other manufactured goods

Source: United Nations, **Monthly Bulletin**.

TABLE 18.4 - Commodity Pattern of SCEE Exports Towards the West (Percentage)

SITC groups	1970	1971	1972	1973	1974	1975
0 + 1 [a]	15.9	15.3	16.4	15.7	11.1	9.9
2 + 4 [b]	17.6	17.3	17.0	18.0	17.7	15.5
3 [c]	16.5	19.7	17.8	20.8	29.5	35.2
5 [d]	5.2	5.6	5.5	4.8	6.2	5.7
7 [e]	9.0	10.7	10.6	9.8	8.3	10.8
6 + 8 [f]	28.9	27.0	27.3	27.0	24.6	20.9
0 + 1 + 2 + 4 + 3	50.1	52.4	51.2	54.6	58.3	60.7
0 + 1 + 2 + 4	33.5	32.6	33.4	33.7	28.8	25.4
5 + 7 + 6 + 8	43.0	43.2	43.4	41.5	39.1	37.5
5 + 7	14.4	16.3	16.1	14.6	14.5	16.5
26 (textile fibers) + 27 (crude fertilizers)	3.3	4.0	4.9	4.4	4.8	4.7
65 (textile yarn and fabrics) + 67 (iron and steel) + 84 (clothing)	12.6	12.4	12.6	11.6	10.0	9.0
$\dfrac{65 + 67 + 84}{5 + 7 + 6 + 8}$	29.3	28.7	29.0	27.9	25.6	24.0

a Food, beverages, and tobacco
b Crude materials, excluding fuels
c Mineral fuels and related products
d Chemicals
e Machines and transport equipment
f Other manufactured goods

Source: United Nations, Monthly Bulletin.

NOTES

1. This question in the context of Socialist economies was for the first time analyzed in depth by M. Kalecki, Zarys teorri wzrostu gospodarki socjalistycznej [Outline of the theory of the Socialist economy growth] (Warsaw: 1963), chapter 10.

2. See J. E. Meade, The Balance of Payments, vol. 1, The Theory of International Economic Policy, (London: Oxford University Press, 1951), p. 11.

3. Such statistics have until now been published only by Hungary; they cover the balance of payments with hard currency countries only in 1975 and 1976; see Le Monde, November 15, 1977.

4. See United Nations, Economic Bulletin for Europe, vol. 27, Economic Commission for Europe, 1977, (New York: United Nations) pp. 76-81; vol. 28, pp. 94-101; vol. 29, pp. 117-25 (page numbers from English language version).

5. Another problem is how costly from the economic and social points of view are these adjustments. For example, if because of balance of payments difficulties a State has to limit the rate of increase of imports, the result is a relative decrease in the level of investments and/or consumption, which then can lead to specific economic, social, and sometimes even political consequences.

6. J. Meade, The Balance of Payments, p. 14-15.

7. As these imports have to ensure continuity of current production, they are in the short run very rigid. Thus, in the case of balance of payments difficulties, these imports can hardly be restricted. If it occurs, in comparison with the volume of industrial production, then it means that these difficulties have really appeared. Of course, such an observation is not very relevant for a longer run since changes can take place in production patterns and in the use of raw materials and intermediate goods per unit of production, etc. and some import substitution can occur as well.

8. It is worthwhile noting that the share of consumer goods in SCEE imports from Western countries has usually been much lower than the relevant share in mutual trade between the SCEE them-

selves. One of the reasons is that in relations with convertible currency countries, balance of payments constraints on the SCEE are usually stronger than in relations among the SCEE.

9. United Nations Economic Commission for Europe, <u>Overall Economic Perspective for the ECE region up to 1990,</u> document ECE/EC.AD./17, Geneva, March 1978, p. 44.

10. For example, in Hungary the share of good, beverages, and tobacco in aggregated personal expenditure in 1960 was 53.0% and in 1975 44.8%; in Poland, 65.6 and 52.2%; in Czechoslovakia (expenditure in workers' households only) 52.6 and 42.8%. United Nations, p. 34 [English-language version].

11. Because of the extremely important role played by the Soviet Union as a supplier of raw materials to other SCEE, the tendency towards exhaustion of raw material resources in the European part of the Soviet Union and the necessity to enlarge their exploitation in the Asian part has additionally increased capital intensity.

12. The same occurred, particularly, during last years, in the field of manufactures but the reasons for this phenomenon were more complicated; besides export absorption by growing domestic demand, there was a limited number of assortments of specific industrial products in comparison with the variety of domestic demand, a technological gap in some fields, etc. For figures on the SCEE shares in their imports under various SITC groups, see Table 18.1.

13. See United Nations <u>Economic Bulletin for Europe</u>, Vol. 28, p. 71.

14. In this connection it is interesting to quote from the results of an analysis of factor intensity of Western exports to and imports from Eastern Europe made by the United Nations Economic Commission for Europe. All trade flows were divided into three categories: labor intensive, resource intensive and technology intensive products. It was found that in 1971-74 the shares of the first, second, and third categories in Western exports were: 30, 24, and 46%, while in Western imports they were: 26, 59, and 15%. See United Nations, <u>Economic Bulletin,</u> vol. 28, p. 117.

BALANCE OF PAYMENTS CONSTRAINTS   341

15. Interesting information on this subject is contained in ibid., pp. 119-21, in which it is stated that in all 27 four-digit groups of machinery exported by the SCEE towards Western countries, unit prices were considerably lower than in analogous imports from the latter countries. Besides reasons mentioned in the text above, there were of course some additional reasons for this phenomenon such as difficulties in entering Western markets by the SCEE products, sometimes certain weakness in the SCEE marketing techniques, etc.

16. Source: United Nations, Monthly Bulletin of Statistics. For more detailed figures, see table 18.2.

17. United Nations, "Overall Economic Perspective for the ECE Region up to 1990," p. 101 [English-language version].

18. By the end of 1977, in relations with GATT countries (Hungary, Poland, and Romania excepted), 934 entire and 62 partial headings had been liberalized according to GATT sources. Since February 1976, no major changes in GATT and SCEE countries liberalization lists have occurred, and the mentioned figures reflect quite fairly differences in treatment with the two groups of countries in the field of quantitative restrictions.

19. All figures concerning changes in the trade volumes are from United Nations Economic Survey of Europe in 1977 (New York: United Nations, 1977), part I, chapter 3, table 6.4 (Pre-publication text).

20. Of course, the situation concerning the balance of payments was not the only reason. In some cases, particularly in Poland, changes in investment plans also aimed at improving the situation on domestic markets. In Poland, the share of consumption in national income increased from 62.2% in 1975 and 65.5% in 1976 to 67.2% in 1977, and the share of accumulation decreased at the same time from 37.8 and 34.5% to 32.8%, Maly Rocznik Statystyczny (Warsaw: Central Statistical Office, 1978), p. 44 and Communique on the implementation of the 1977 Plan, Trybuna Ludu.

21. These figures and all others concerning trade commodity structures in the following text derive from United Nations Monthly Bulletin of Statistics. For detailed figures, see Tables 18.3 and 18.4.

22. United Nations, Economic Bulletin for Europe, Vol. 28, p. 114, and Economic Survey of Europe in 1977, Table 6.4, [English-language version].

19 Advanced Technology and the Choice of Trade Partners: The Soviet Policy*

Eugene Zaleski

INTRODUCTION

The term, "technology transfers," has become a fashionable catch-phrase in economic and political discussions of the prospects for technical progress in the modern world. Unfortunately, a wide gap has developed between the definition of these transfers and the statistical evaluation of the flows by which they are supposedly represented.

Technology transfer is generally understood as a process whereby innovations (new products or know-how) developed in one country are conveyed to another country where they are then utilized. (1) Technology, then, is neither a science nor a product, but rather the application of science to the production of goods and services. (2)

Only a portion of these transfers is measurable, i.e., the actual purchase of material goods with the effective application of the imported technology. In practice, there is no way to estimate the transfer of information or the upgrading of qualifications coinciding with the movement of personnel. Indeed, even the measurable part of these transfers has not yet been calculated precisely.

The first estimates made concern research intensive products. A definition of these products was attempted by the OECD in 1970, (3) on which the United Nations seems to have based its 1976 figures. (4) According to these figures: 54% of Soviet imports from ten Western industrialized countries during the period 1965-68 involved research

---

* Translated from the French by Sinclair Robinson, Department of French, Carleton University.

intensive products. This percentage dropped to 43% during the period 1971-74, and these same products made up only 7% of Soviet exports to the same countries in 1965-68 and 8% in 1971-74. (5)

These figures have certain defects. Intensity of research varies for several products included in the same group and for the same products coming from different countries. The OECD is now working on new methods of evaluating expenditures on research and development in relation to gross output, value added, etc.

Research intensive products however, are not necessarily high technology products. The 1970 OECD list includes 50 groups of products, of which 18 are from SITC group 7, while the United States Bureau of East-West Trade lists only 25 groups of products, and they are specified to 5 digits, hence more precisely (see Table 19.1). The two approaches are not mutually exclusive, but, in fact, complementary. All depends on what questions are to be answered.

In practice, given the scarcity of calculations of technology transfers involving either research intensive or high technology products, there is a temptation to simplify the problem and take trade in machinery and equipment (SITC group 7) with a certain number of subdivisions as representative of technology transfers. (6) This approach has the advantage, apart from the relative ease of calculation, of making it easier to link the results to the national investment effort and to the expansion of certain branches of the economy.

Soviet policy on choice of trading partners for technology transfer involves, of course, imports as well as exports. However, Soviet exports of machinery and equipment, especially to Western industrialized nations, are still of minor importance: 2.2% in 1961, 3.6% in 1970, and only 4.3% in 1976. (7) Soviet imports of machinery and transport equipment from these same countries made up 46.2% of total imports in 1961, 39.0% in 1970, and 35.7% in 1976. (8)

We shall thus discuss in particular Soviet _imports_ of Western technology.

SOVIET MACHINERY AND EQUIPMENT IMPORTS: TRENDS AND GEOGRAPHICAL DISTRIBUTION

Machinery and Equipment Imports

Soviet machinery and equipment imports come almost exclusively from two sources: Western industrialized nations, and CMEA members. Table 19.2 gives the distribution.

TABLE 19.1 - High Technology Items

SITC	Description
71141	Jet & gas turbines for aircraft
7117	Nuclear reactors
7142	Calculating machines, including electronic computers
7143	Statistical machines: punch card or tape
71492	Parts of office machinery, including computer parts
7151	Machine tools for metal
71852	Glass working machinery
7192	Pumps and centrifuges
71952	Machine tools for wood, plastic, etc.
71954	Parts and accessories for machine tools
71992	Cocks, valves, etc.
7249	Telecommunications equipment, excluding TV & radio
72911	Primary batteries and cells
7293	Tubes, transistors, photocells, etc.
72952	Electrical measuring and control instruments
7297	Electron and proton accelerators
7299	Electrical machinery, n.e.s. including electromagnets, traffic control equipment, signaling apparatus, etc.
7341	Aircraft, heavier than air
73492	Aircraft parts
7351	Warships
73592	Special purpose vessels, including submersible vessels
8611	Optical elements
8613	Optical instruments
86161	Image projectors (might include holograph projectors)
8619	Measuring and control instruments, n.e.s.

Certain products which might include high technology but which were omitted from the list

7111	Steam generating boilers
71181	Water turbines
71822	Type making & setting machinery
71994	Metal-plastic joints (gaskets)
726	Electromedical and x-ray apparatus
8614	Photographic cameras
8624	Photographic plates, film, etc.
8641	Watches
8642	Clocks

Source: <u>Quantification of Western Exports of High Technology Products to the Communist Countries</u>, Office of East-West Policy and Planning, Bureau of East-West Trade, Washington, D.C., October 17, 1977, pp. 4, 14.

TABLE 19.2 - Soviet Machinery and Equipment Imports at Current prices, SITC Group 7 (in millions of rubles and as a percentage)

	1961	1970	1975	1976
TOTAL	1,565.2	3,753	9,046	10,427
Western Industrialized Nations (a)				
Millions of Rubles	426.9	1,003.2	3,616.9	4,642.0
Percentage	27.3	26.7	40.0	44.5
CMEA Countries (b)				
Millions of Rubles	1,120.8	2,457.3	5,182.2	5,718.2
Percentage	71.6	70.8	57.3	54.8

(a) Belgium, Denmark, France, Federal Republic of Germany (including West Berlin), Italy, Netherlands, Great Britain, Austria, Norway, Switzerland, Sweden, United States, Canada, Japan, Finland. (b) German Democratic Republic, Poland, Czechoslovakia, Hungary, Romania, Bulgaria.

Source: Vneshnyaya Torgovlya USSR (Foreign Trade of the USSR) 1961, 1971, 1976.

It is evident from Table 19.2 that beginning in 1970 machinery imports from the West increased more sharply than those from CMEA countries. The more pronounced increase in Western machinery prices must be largely responsible for this. Prevailing prices in trade inside the CMEA remained relatively stable until 1975, although they have since approached world prices, while prices of CMEA imports from the rest of the world were rising rapidly. (9) However, the volume of CMEA imports from the rest of the world was increasing rapidly as well, by approximately 15% a year during 1970-76, compared to 10% a year in 1965-70. (10) The price differences involved between trade with the West and inside the CMEA seem to have been even more pronounced in the machinery sector than elsewhere. The increase in imports from the West is above all due to the policy of modernization in Eastern Europe. (11)

The breakdown of 1975 Soviet imports of machinery and equipment into various subgroups for all trade and for trade with hard currency countries is given in Table 19.3. It is evident that certain sectors depend heavily on Western imports: machine building and metalworking industries at 66.6% (including the motor industry at 86.5%), oil and gas drilling at 69.6%, mining at 65.3%, the chemical industry at 56.8%, etc., whereas agriculture, electric power, and shipping depend very little on the West. These branches are supplied by Communist partners especially.

Table 19.4 gives the geographical distribution of machinery and equipment imports from the most important Western countries.

It can be seen that Soviet imports come basically from six highly industrialized countries and from Finland. The dominant position is occupied by the Federal Republic of Germany, which supplies 28.5% of all imports from OECD countries. More significant, however, are the changes in the relative importance of the main Western suppliers over the last 15 years. The greatest increase has been in the share of the United States, after a decline between 1961 and 1965, which in 1976 supplied 12.3% of total imports of machinery and transport equipment from OECD countries.

Also shown in Table 19.4 are the frequent variations in the share of various industrialized countries. West Germany, for example, provided a large share in 1961 (31.9%), saw its share reduced to 16.0% in 1970, made a spectacular rise to 33.3% in 1973, and then fell back to 28.5% in 1976. The share supplied by France was greatly reduced from 1961 to 1965, then rose sharply in 1971, and now seems subject to frequent variations.

Later we shall attempt to investigate this variableness in the Soviet choice of machinery suppliers. It should be noted that in 1977 an important change occurred in Soviet imports of machinery and

TABLE 19.3. Soviet Hard Currency Imports of Machinery and Equipment[a] in 1975

ETN number[b]		From Hard Currency Sources ($mn) (c)	Percentage of Same Category of Imports from All Sources	Percentage of All Hard Currency Machinery Imports	Branch Investment Share (%) 1974 (d)
1	all machinery and equipment	4,577	36.5	100.0	...
100-105	machine building and metalworking industries	868	66.6	19.0	9.5
10514	of which, identified as for motor industry	345	86.5	7.5	...
110	electric power industry	5	4.7	0.1	4.2
111	electrical engineering	48	16.5	1.0	...
120,121	mining and ore treatment	88	65.3	1.9	2.1[e]
123	metallurgical industries	219	42.5	4.8	3.5[e]
127	oil refining	60	43.6	1.3	...
128	oil and gas drilling, prospecting, etc.	148	69.6	2.8	6.0

Table 19.3 (continued)

140	food processing	103	32.2	2.2	3.5
144-146	textile, clothing, footwear, etc. industries	210	44.0	4.6	1.8
150	chemical industry	502	56.8	11.0	4.1
151-152	timber, woodworking, pulp and paper industries	98	44.1	2.1	2.0
162-181	agriculture	27	5.8	0.6	25.6
192	shipping	212	14.1	4.6	...

a Identified imports from all hard currency trade partners of goods in the Soviet trade classification "machinery, equipment and means of transport." Non hard currency sources for such imports are the rest of CMEA, Yugoslvaia, and Finland. The total figure in column 1 is based on Soviet data and is not precisely comparable with OECD data.
b Numbers used in the Soviet trade nomenclature, 1971 edition.
c Converted to United States dollars from roubles at 0.7219r = $ the average of monthly Gosbank exchange quotations for 1975.
d Percentage shares of all "productive" investment. This excludes investment in housing and construction work for educational, scientific, and cultural institutions. The figures relate to structure, etc., as well as to machinery.
e Only partial data are available: for coal mining only in the case of mining, for iron and steel in the case of metallurgy.

Source: Philip Hanson, USSR: Foreign Trade Implications of the 1976-80 Plan (London: The Economist Intelligence Unit Ltd., October 1976), p. 64. Columns 1-3 derived from VT SSSR v 1975g. Column 4 from Narkhoz 74.

TABLE 19.4 - The Share of Principal OECD Suppliers of Machinery and Equipment (Group 7) to the Soviet Union

	1961	1965	1970	1971	1972	1973	1974	1975	1976
Total Exports of Machinery and Transport Equipment to the Soviet Union	100	100	100	100	100	100	100	100	100
United States	4.7	1.1	4.4	7.0	5.1	11.8	9.7	12.0	12.3
Japan	-	13.0	10.0	13.0	16.2	9.7	10.0	12.2	13.9
Finland	-	21.0	12.1	7.0	7.0	9.3	9.4	8.4	13.7
France	15.8	5.8	13.8	15.3	9.7	9.7	12.6	12.5	8.4
German Federated Republic	31.9	17.3	16.0	18.7	30.4	33.3	32.9	29.5	28.5
Italy	8.0	6.9	16.9	15.5	10.6	8.9	7.4	8.5	7.3
Great Britain	21.1	10.8	9.8	9.3	8.0	6.0	3.0	4.6	4.2

Source: OECD, Statistiques du Commerce Exterieur (Paris: OECD, 1977).

THE SOVIET POLICY 351

transport equipment. Total Soviet imports from industrialized capitalist countries were reduced by 894 million rubles, or by 8.3%, in 1976, a reduction of 745 million for imports from the United States, 195 million for West Germany, 41 for Switzerland, and 19 for France. (12) There can be no doubt that this overall trend in Soviet imports from Western industrialized nations had a heavy impact on machinery imports. At the present time we have statistics only for the United States. Its machinery exports to the Soviet Union decreased by $231.2 million, or by 38.2%, in 1977 over 1976, more sharply, then, than total exports to the Soviet Union, which dropped only by 29.6%. (13) It is impossible to say at the present time to what extent this reduction in machinery imports from the United States was offset by imports from other Western countries or from the CMEA, but an overall drop in 1977 of Soviet imports of Western machinery does seem probable.

Machinery Exports

We have collected statistics on Soviet machinery exports (see Tables 19.5 & 19.1). Table 19.5 relates only to Soviet exports to OECD countries and is based on Western statistics. Table 19.6 gives data on exports to all "non-Socialist" (the Soviet term) countries and is based on official Soviet statistics.

It can be seen from Table 19.5 that the principal suppliers of machinery to the Soviet Union included in Table 19.4, which in 1976 provided 87.7% of all OECD machinery exports to the Soviets, bought in that same year only 54.9% of all Soviet machinery exports to OECD countries. Thus, the Soviet Union, as is to be expected, is more successful in selling machinery to less industrialized countries.

This is more clearly demonstrated in Table 19.6 which gives figures on Soviet exports to all non-Socialist countries. The total for the three Third World countries, Egypt, Iran, and Syria, is 23.7% in 1976, while the five OECD countries total only 12.6% for the same year.

Generally speaking, the fluctuations in the relative share of importing countries are as pronounced as for exporting countries and seem even more pronounced for certain Third World countries. In the case of Egypt, for instance, political considerations seem to play a preponderant role in the choice of trading partners.

TABLE 19.5 - Share of Principal OECD Importers of Machinery and Transport Equipment from the Soviet Union (SITC Group 7)

	1961	1965	1970	1971	1972	1973	1974	1975	1976
TOTAL......	100	100	100	100	100	100	100	100	100
United States	-	-	1.1	0.7	2.7	0.7	0.8	1.4	0.9
Japan	-	4.6	5.9	6.5	3.4	2.5	3.6	1.5	1.6
Finland	-	36.9	15.3	15.1	14.2	17.3	20.3	24.9	21.3
France	4.0	4.0	8.0	6.2	5.2	6.0	8.9	9.7	8.6
German Federal Republic	9.5	6.0	18.6	9.2	7.4	11.0	2.5	10.0	12.3
Italy	5.0	1.5	5.7	2.2	3.3	4.9	6.6	4.1	3.3
Great Britain	13.5	4.0	5.9	6.6	8.0	9.6	12.3	9.5	6.9

Source: OECD, Statistiques du Commerce exterieur (Paris: OECD, 1977).

TABLE 19.6 - Structure of Soviet Trade in Machinery and Transport Equipment with non-Socialist Countries (in millions of rubles; machinery and transport equipment = 100)

EXPORTS	1970	1975	1976	1977
Total Soviet exports to non-Socialist countries	3,990	9,446	11,575	14,154
Exports of machinery and transport equipment	735	1,198	1,391	
As a percentage	18.4%	12.7%	12.0%	
Share of principal countries (as percentage				
Great Britain	0.1	1.9	1.5	
Italy	0.6	1.2	0.8	
France	0.8	1.6	2.4	
West Germany	3.5	2.1	3.0	
Finland	1.8	7.3	4.9	
Egypt	20.2	7.1	5.8	
Iran	19.5	16.1	12.2	
Syria	4.1	5.4	5.7	
IMPORTS				
Total Soviet imports from non-Socialist countries	3,686	12,702	13,627	12,926
Imports of machinery and transport equipment	1,045	3,852	4,709	
As a percentage	28.4	30.3	34.6	
Share of principal countries				
Italy	16.9	8.0	6.8	
United States	2.1	11.8	13.2	
West Germany	11.7	26.2	23.2	
Finland	11.5	8.1	11.0	
France	14.9	11.0	10.8	

Source: Vneshnyaya Torgovlya SSSR v 1973 godu [USSR Foreign Trade in 1973] (Moscow, 1974), pp. 10, 19, 53-4, 94; in 1975 (Moscow, 1976), pp. 8, 17, 51-52, 91; and in 1976 (Moscow, 1977), pp. 8, 46-7, 83; Commerce Exterieur de l'U.R.S.S., January-December 1977. Appendix to the journal Commerce Exterieur (Moscow, 1977).

HIGH TECHNOLOGY IMPORTS

In Table 19.7, we have attempted a calculation of the share of high technology in the total Soviet imports of machinery from OECD countries.

This share shows a sharp drop in recent years, especially since 1975. It has decreased from 48.3% in 1972, and 44.9% in 1974, to only 33.1% in 1976. This decrease in the importance of high technology products in overall Soviet technology imports from the West is of significance. This reduction could be due to internal technical advances. However, the conclusions of recent Western studies regarding the technological level of the Soviet Union do not seem to support this hypothesis. (14) This trend could also be due to a strengthening of the strategic embargo imposed by the NATO countries under the CoCom plan, but the reverse has occurred. Another factor could be the substitution of imports from CMEA countries. This hypothesis cannot be entirely ruled out, but in view of the decrease in the relative importance of CMEA countries since 1970 (see Table 19.2), this does not seem very probable.

The only explanation which seems plausible involves the overall needs of the Soviet economy. The recent increase in Russian machinery imports likely constitutes a source of capital, on credit as much as possible, and also a security valve for the deficiencies of Soviet engineering industries. In other words, Soviet machinery imports serve above all to accelerate Soviet economic growth, to curb the drop in this growth rate, and provide a kind of spare tire for faults in centralized administrative planning. Catching up in the technological race is most probably of only secondary importance, and as indicated in Table 19.7, the share in high technology products of machine tools for metal, electrical machinery, and electrical measuring and control instruments dropped over the period 1972-76.

Table 19.8 attempts to identify the principal Western suppliers of high technology products to the Soviet Union. The main supplier is West Germany (34-36% of the total during the period 1972-76), followed by Japan and France. The share of the United States was only 6.7% in 1972, but rose to 12.7% in 1976.

Table 19.9 attempts to identify Western nations exporting the largest proportional volume of high technology products to the Soviet Union. It can be seen that the countries which sold more high technology products than machinery both in 1974 and 1976 in general were the Federal Republic of Germany, Belgium, the Netherlands, and Switzerland. This was also true of the United States in 1974, but not in 1976.

TABLE 19.7. High Technology Products and Total Soviet Machinery Imports from OCED Countries (in millions of $ U.S.)

	1972	1974	1975	1976
Machinery and Transport Equipment Imports (SITC Group 7) (from OECD countries) (a)	1,207	2,309	4,576	4,909
Imports and High Technology Products: (b)	582.4	1,036.2	1,583.5	1,627.1
Machine tools for metal (7151)	..	448.8	550.3	576.9
Cocks, valves, etc. (71992)	..	107.8	283.1	252.6
Pumps and centrifuges (7192)	..	107.8	167.4	245.0
Electrical machinery, n.e.s. (7299)	..	119.7	214.3	139.6
Electrical measuring and control instruments (72952)	..	53.4	60.2	69.1
Share of high technology products in total machinery imports from OECD countries (c)	48.3%	44.9%	34.6%	33.1%

NOTE: The term, "Western industrialized," does not include the following OCED countries: Ireland, Finland, Iceland, Portugal, Greece, Spain, Turkey, Australia, New Zealand. These are, however, minor causes for error and are partially evened out in the calculations.

(a) OECD, Statistiques du Commerce (Paris: OECD, 1977).

(b) Quantification of Western Exports, pp. 7, 9.

(c) An approximate calculation since machinery (SITC group 7) and high technology products do not overlap completely. Machinery includes only SITC group 7, while high technology products include optical elements, optical instruments, image projectors, and measuring and control instruments as well (SITC group 8611, 8613, 86161, and 8619). Soviet imports of these four groups totaled only $47.3 million in 1974, $71.1 million in 1975, and $77.8 million in 1976, or 4.6%, 4.5%, and 4.8%, respectively of total Soviet high technology imports from Western industrialized nations.

TABLE 19.8 - Soviet Imports of High Technology Products from Western Industrialized Countries

Country:	1972 ($000)	(%)	1974 ($000)	(%)	1976 ($000)	(%)
United States	39,008	6.7	137,581	13.3	207,109	12.7
Canada	1,330	0.2	729	0.1	8,587	0.6
Japan	83,916	14.4	88,559	8.6	225,506	13.9
Belgium/Luxembourg	2,690	0.5	13,685	1.3	14,390	0.9
France	66,077	11.3	155,501	15.0	177,187	10.9
West Germany	209,484	36.0	352,446	34.0	560,777	34.5
Italy	62,463	10.7	78,713	7.6	136,713	8.4
Holland	2,315	0.4	41,214	4.0	39,148	2.4
Austria	9,036	1.6	20,446	2.0	38,469	2.4
Norway	417	0.1	1,316	0.1	7,231	0.4
Sweden	11,769	2.0	41,197	4.0	49,265	3.0
Switzerland	32,211	5.5	63,511	6.1	100,503	6.2
Great Britain	56,062	9.6	36,391	3.5	53,594	3.3
Denmark	5,662	1.0	4,919	0.5	8,627	0.5
TOTAL	582,440	100.0	1,036,208	100.0	1,627,106	100.0

Source: Quantification of Western Exports, p. 9. Cf. John P. Young, Industry and Trade Administration Office of East-West Policy and Planning (Washington, D.C.: U.S. Department of Commerce), Project No. D-41.

TABLE 19.9 - Relative Share of Western Industrialized Countries in Machinery and Equipment Exports and High Technology Exports to the Soviet Union in 1974 and 1976

	1974		1976	
	Share in Machinery Exports[a]	Share in High Technology Exports[b]	Share in Machinery Exports[a]	Share in High Technology Exports[b]
United States	10.3	<u>13.3</u>	15.1	12.7
Canada	0.1	0.1	0.6	0.6
Japan	10.2	8.6	17.8	13.9
Belgium	0.9	<u>1.3</u>	0.4	<u>0.9</u>
France	14.8	<u>15.0</u>	12.4	10.9
West Germany (including West Berlin)	30.5	<u>34.0</u>	27.0	<u>34.5</u>
Holland	2.5	<u>4.0</u>	1.2	<u>2.4</u>
Italy	8.6	7.6	9.6	8.4
Austria	4.1	2.0	1.9	<u>2.4</u>
Norway	0.7	0.1	0.4	0.4
Sweden	8.2	4.0	4.4	3.0
Switzerland	5.4	<u>6.1</u>	4.2	<u>6.2</u>
Great Britain	3.1	<u>3.5</u>	4.1	3.3
Denmark	1.0	0.5	0.8	0.5
Total	100.5[c]	100.0	100.4[c]	100.0

Note: Underlined figures are shares in high technology exports which are greater than overall share in machinery exports of the same country.

a <u>Vneshnyaya Torgovlya SSSR v 1974 godu</u> (USSR Foreign Trade in 1974), <u>Vneshnyaya Torgovlya SSSR v 1976 godu</u> (USSR Foreign Trade in 1976), Moscow: 1977. Machinery and transport equipment.
b Percentages from Table 19.6.
c Due to rounded figures.

Table 19.10

High Technology Products Exported to the Soviet Union by the main industrialized countries in 1975a
(In thousands of $U.S.)

SITC Group		United States	Canada	Japan	Belgium Luxembourg	France	West Germany	Holland	Italy	Austria	Norway	Sweden	Switzerland	United Kingdom	Denmark	OECD Total	Dept. of Commerce Total
7142	Calculating machines, including electronic computers	39	--	4,773	--	5	355	--	724	18	--	618	448	135	163	7,337	7,281
7143	Statistical machines (punch card or tape)	--	--	12	4	26	36	4	16	--	--	1	1	21	1	341 (b)	14,539
7;492	Parts of office machinery (including computer parts)	969	--	255	--	--	--	--	--	4	--	45	2	1,305	71	2,652	4,064
7151	Machine tolls for metal	1,003	--	14,648	710	4,117	18,775	60	6,860	1.438	--	2,226	3,231	1,206	1	131,622 (b)	448,796
71852	Glass working machinery	170	--	70	4,619	2,954	480	--	22	--	--	1,773	--	813	--	11,102	11,138
7192	Pumps and centrifuges	37,226	256	8,861	199	17,033	16,961	1.502	4,369	407	234	14,503	2,970	2,453	672	114,326	107,823
71592	Machine tools for wood, plastic, etc.	--	279	--	618	241	24,300	12	1,422	137	--	2,758	505	139	--	53,351	30,440
71954	Parts and accessories for machine tools	2,764	--	6,255	575	6,780	8,956	40	2,647	121	102	737	1,515	1,375	7	32,904	31,901
71992	Cocks, valves, etc.	44	--	5,168	11	59,389	19,176	128	20,308	1,961	--	528	549	323	125	108,409	107,340
7249	Telecommunications equipment (excluding T.V. and radio receivers)	1,765	135	5,619	21	2,231	4,920	7	435	166	--	477	40	790	25	20,833	16,808
72911	Primary batteries and cells	1	--	29	--	38	--	--	--	1	--	--	--	38	--	107	107
7293	Tubes, transistors, photocells, etc.	47	4	431	5	1,725	670	--	123	13	--	78	21	97	7	3,222	3,225

358

Code	Description																
72952	Electrical measuring and control instruments	6,929	29	4,570	4	9,120	14,453	1,286	2,648	1,129	129	--	2,896	6,753	3,398	54,178	53,409
7299	Electrical machinery, N.E.S. Including electromagnets, traffic control equipment, signaling apparatus, etc.	13,260	12	6,808	2,169	14,103	59,249	5,601	2,457	688	175	7,145	622	7,241	3	120,436	119,734
7341	Aircraft, heavier than air	439	--	--	--	--	--	--	--	--	--	--	--	--	--	439	439
73492	Aircraft parts	115	6	--	1	--	2	--	2	--	--	--	--	--	116	242	242
73592	Special purpose vessels, including submersible vessels	--	--	--	--	--	--	30,834	--	--	--	--	48	--	--	41,900	30,937
8611	Optical elements	46	--	109	--	45	446	--	--	--	--	--	1	214	8	871	873
8613	Optical instruments	--	--	2,198	11	93	1,237	--	--	179	5	--	--	379	204	4,319	4,322
86161	Image projectors (might including holograph projectors)	14	--	66	1	546	--	17	19	--	--	--	244	17	1	926	927
8619	Measuring and control instruments, N.E.S	2,851	9	3,517	4	4,798	11,418	272	2,921	212	3	2,875	7,060	4,088	341	44,263	41,237
	Specified Total	30,456	474	54,528	8,753	105,616	181,434	39,362	44,973	6,475	648	33,813	20,760	28,946	4,829	753,785	1036,123
	Total calculated by Dept. of Commerce (c)	137,581	729	88,559	13,685	155,501	352,446	41,214	78,713	20,446	1,316	41,197	63,511	36,191	4,919	1036,208 (d)	1036,208

a) OECD Statistiques du commerce, Series C, 1974

b) Unpublished OECD total obtained by the addition of figures published for each country.

c) cf Table 19.6

d) Total for the 14 countries specified in Department of Commerce Statistics, and listed in this table.

Does the Soviet Union have a preference for certain suppliers of high technology products, and what are its motives? Our statistics do not provide an answer. We have, however, attempted a further specification of various high technology products imported by the Soviet Union from each Western industrialized country as given in the figures in Table 19.9. The result is given in Table 19.10. It should be noted immediately that the sample used for Table 19.10, which is based on the trade statistics of the OECD, is more limited than the sample used for the Department of Commerce calculations. The difference is the most substantial for machine tools for metal; the OECD figures give $131.6 million as a total while the Department of Commerce gives $448.8 million, but omit warships. The OECD statistics omit several high technology products such as electron and proton accelerators (7297), nuclear reactors (7117), jet and gas turbines for aircraft (71142), and warships (7351).

A detailed analysis of the reasons why the Soviet Union purchases high technology products from one country in preference to another remains to be done. The statistics given in Table 19.7, showing the share of each Western industrialized nation in high technology exports to the Soviet Union, do not provide an answer. It is not enough to determine that Japan supplied 8.5% of high technology products to the Soviet Union in 1974 (see Table 19.9). We must know which high technology products in particular were bought from Japan.

Table 19.11 provides such calculations. We show which high technology products from each country make up a greater proportion in the Soviet Union than the overall share of that country. For example, in 1974 Russia imported from Japan 65.1% of all calculating machines and electronic computers, and 50.9% of all optical instruments imported from all Western industrialized countries, while Japan's share in overall high technology imports was only 8.6% (see Table 19.11).

There is a clear preference on the part of the Soviet Union for buying a given high technology product from a given country. It is noteworthy that the Soviet Union bought 100% of heavier-than-air aircraft from the United States, 73.6% of special purpose vessels from Holland, 59.0% of image projectors from France, 51.2% of optical elements from West Germany, and 49.2% of office machinery parts from Great Britain.

It is certain that Soviet decisions were influenced by the quality of imported high technology products. Research on this question, using the services of specialists, remains to be done. It is important, however, to show other motives for Soviet choices such as scientific and technical cooperation and the granting of credit by Western countries.

TABLE 19.11 - Principal High Technology Products Exported to the Soviet Union by the Main Industrialized Nations in 1974

Country	Share in total High Technology Exports of the 14 Countries	SITC Group	Share in the Exports of Certain High Technology Products (a)	
United States	13.3	71492	Parts of office machinery	36.5
		7192	Pumps and centrifuges	32.6
		7341	Aircraft, heavier than air	100.0
		73492	Aircraft parts	47.5
Canada	0.1	73492	Aircraft parts	2.5
Japan	8.6	7142	Calculating machines	65.1
Belgium/Luxembourg	1.3	71852	Glass working machinery	41.6
		7299	Electrical machinery	1.8
France	15.0	86161	Image projectors	59.0
		71992	Cocks, valves	54.7
		72911	Primary batteries and cells	35.5
		7293	Tubes, transistors, photocells, etc.	53.5
		71852	Glass working machinery	26.6
		71954	Parts and accessories for machine tools	20.6
Federal Republic of Germany, including West Berlin	34.0	8611	Optical elements	51.2
		7299	Electrical machinery	49.2
		71952	Machine tools for wood, plastic, etc.	45.5
Holland	4.0	7299	Electrical machinery	4.7
		73592	Special purpose vessels	73.6
Italy	7.6	71992	Cocks, valves, etc.	18.7
		7142	Calculating machines	9.9
		71954	Parts and accessories for machine tools	8.0
Austria	2.0	8613	Optical instruments	4.1
		72952	Electrical measuring and control instruments	2.1

TABLE 19.11 (continued)

Country				
Norway	0.1	7192	Pumps and centrifuges	0.2
		72952	Electrical measuring and control instruments	0.2
Sweden	4.0	7142	Calculating machines	8.4
		71852	Glass working machinery	16.0
		7192	Pumps and centrifuges	12.7
		71952	Machine tools for wood, plastic, etc.	5.2
		7299	Electrical machinery	5.9
		8619	Measuring and control instruments	6.5
Switzerland	6.1	7142	Calculating machines	6.1
		8611	Optical elements	24.6
		86161	Image projectors	26.3
		8619	Measuring and control instruments	15.9
Great Britain	3.5	7143	Statistical machines	6.2
		71492	Parts of office machinery	49.2
		71954	Parts and accessories for machine tools	4.8
		7249	Telecommunications equipment	3.8
		72911	Primary batteries and cells	35.5
		72952	Electrical measuring and control instruments	12.5
		7299	Electrical machinery	6.0
		73492	Aircraft parts	47.9
		8613	Optical instruments	4.7
		8619	Measuring and control instruments	11.0
Denmark	0.5	7142	Calculating machines	2.2
		71492	Parts of office machinery	2.7
		7192	Pumps and centrifuges	0.6
		71952	Electrical measuring and control instruments	6.3
		8619	Measuring and control instruments	0.8

Source: Table 19.10

NOTE: (a) Machine tools for metal were not included because of the great discrepancy between OCED and Department of Commerce figures.

ECONOMIC COOPERATION WITH THE WEST AND THE UNMEASURABLE SHARE OF TECHNOLOGY TRANSFERS

The Framework of Economic Cooperation

Until recent years, Soviet economic cooperation with the West was carried on in the classical framework of trade treaties, commercial agreements, credit arrangements, etc. Since the beginning of this decade, new frameworks of cooperation have appeared, which for the first time emphasize cooperation between firms rather than governments and combine technological, commercial, and financial aspects in new institutional arrangements. Some concrete manifestations of these new frameworks are: (a) economic, industrial, and technical cooperation agreements at the governmental level; and (b) industrial cooperation agreements at the level of government and of firms. (15)

In practice, the financial aspect predominates in agreements on industrial cooperation. Such agreements are made less out of a desire for cooperation than because of the acceptance by the Western trading partner of financial arrangements which are favorable to the East. As a general rule, the agreement on the part of the Western partner is to be paid either in the products of the factories sold (compensation agreements) or by means of counter purchases of products not directly related to the product exported by the West.

This element of compensation or counter purchase has become essential to the new type of industrial cooperation. Indeed, the United Nations refuses to include in statistics on industrial cooperation any licensing agreements which are not followed up, at least in part, by counter deliveries of products manufactured under these licenses. (16)

What is of interest to us is less the element of barter or clearing, than the transfer of technology in a broad sense:

1. Sale of machinery as a "measurable" form of transfer.
2. The transfer of information, which is difficult to measure and appears in varying amounts in the different forms of cooperation.

Industrial Cooperation Agreements as a Vehicle for the Transfer of Know-How to the Soviet Union

Industrial cooperation agreements are considered the means par excellence to effect a transfer of know-how. The following categories of agreements are considered to be the most efficient in this regard:

(a) turnkey factories, (b) license with extensive teaching effort, (c) joint ventures, (d) technical exchange with ongoing contact, (e) training in high technology areas, and (f) processing equipment with know-how. (17)

As inactive and inefficient transfers are considered, those cooperation agreements which result in a passive attitude on the part of the supplier include: (a) licenses without know how, (b) sales of products without maintenance and operations data, (c) undocumented proposals, (d) commercial literature, and (e) trade exhibits.

A detailed study of industrial cooperation agreements is needed to determine their active or passive role in the transfer of technology. However, we are confronted with the secrecy which surrounds the vast majority of these representative samples that are available at the present time.

The exact number of industrial cooperation agreements concluded by the Soviet Union with the West is not known. Maureen H. Smith estimates that there are over 160 with Western firms, as well as over 200 intergovernmental agreements on scientific and technical cooperation. (18) Carl H. McMillan estimates that by the end of 1976, the Soviet Union had made 275 general industrial cooperation agreements and 196 specific agreements. (19)

The distribution of these agreements among various Western countries could not be found in our sources. A recent United Nations report on the Eastern bloc as a whole estimates that the breakdown, based on a sample of 658 contracts, is 21.4% for West Germany, 14.4% for France, 9.1% for Italy, 7.4% for Japan, 7% for Austria and the United Kingdom, and 6.2% for Sweden. (20)

As for the relative importance of the various types of cooperation, we have data from the United Nations for a rather complete sample taken on June 1, 1976, which show a certain preference for co-production and specialization contracts, rather than for deliveries of factories (see Table 19.12). According to the criteria given previously, these would not be the most efficient types of transfer, but hasty conclusions should not be drawn.

It should be noted that the study by Carl H. McMillan based on 21 cooperation contracts signed by the Soviet Union in early 1975 attempts to evaluate the components of each contract, i.e., management, equipment delivery, sale of turnkey plants, etc. Of these 21 contracts, 42.9% included the sale of turnkey plants, 57.1% technical assistance, 47.6% licensing, and 23.8% personnel training. (21)
This was, then, an efficient sample from the point of view of technology transfer.

TABLE 19.12 - Different Types of Industrial Cooperation Agreements Made by the Soviet Union

United Nations Sample, 1975, Sample of 275 Contracts for the Eastern Bloc (a)

Licensing	--
Factory deliveries	56.6%
Specialization	34.8%
Subcontracting	4.3%
Joint Ventures	4.4%
Total	100%

United Nations Sample, June 1, 1976, 196 Contracts (b)

Licensing and/or know-how	3.2%
Factory or equipment deliveries	20.4%
Co-production and specialization	61.5%
Subcontracting	4.7%
Joint ventures	7.1%
Common projects or undertakings	1.6%
Tripartite cooperation agreements	1.5%
Total	100%

Sources: (a) *Proceedings of the UN/ECE Seminar on the Management of the Transfer of Technology within Industrial Co-Operation* (Geneva: Economic Commission for Europe, July 1976) ECE/SC TECH./10 Feb. 16, 1976, p. 20. (b) *Apercu de l'evolution recente de la cooperation industrielle* (Geneva: Economic Commission for Europe, 1977).

CONCLUSIONS

The aim of this study has been to show the choices of trading partners made by the Soviet Union for the acquisition and sale of high technology products. We focused on Soviet imports, which are particularly important.

It should be remembered that this is a period of particularly heavy expansion in Soviet imports. From 1961 to 1976, Soviet imports in current prices from OECD countries increased seventeenfold and fourteenfold for machinery and equipment (SITC group 7). There has been a definite opening up to the outside world, especially since 1970. (22)

The expansion since 1970 particularly involves Soviet imports of machinery and equipment from OECD countries. In 1970 these countries accounted for only 26.7% of such imports, and their share rose to 44.5% in 1976, while during the same period the share of CMEA countries dropped from 70.8% to 54.8% (see Table 19.2).

This study has shown that the distribution by country of Soviet machinery imports (SITC group 7) does not permit any valid conclusions regarding Soviet choice of trading partners. The variation observed in the shares of the various OECD countries does not explain the nature of these changes.

We carried on a supplementary investigation comparing overall Soviet machinery imports with imports of high technology products. Despite the imperfection of the statistics, a clear trend can be discerned towards a decrease in the share of high technology products in Soviet machinery imports, particularly since 1972. It is tempting to conclude that the Soviet Union may be more interested in machinery imports as a source of capital, on credit if possible, and as a safety valve for failures in national production than as a means to catch up to the technological level of the West.

Our comparison of statistics on Soviet imports of high technology products with those relating to machinery as a whole raises serious questions concerning the significance of our statistical tool. Those products defined as high technology (see Table 19.1), for example, calculating machines, certainly do not have the same technological level when imported from one country as when imported from another, and even when they are imported from the same country, levels of technical sophistication could differ from delivery to delivery. A study based on national statistics of the West (represented by Series C of the foreign trade statistics of the OECD) should be supplemented by research on specific cases demonstrating these differences, if possible. The real aim of such research would be to <u>isolate the tech-</u>

nological factor in Soviet motivations for choice of trading partners, as opposed to other possible considerations, such as credit, clearing agreements, and political and strategic considerations. In other words, such research should reveal the importance of the technological gap in technology transfers to the Soviet Union.

Another problem raised by this study is that of unmeasurable technology transfers. The nature and quality of industrial cooperation agreements, which serve as the principal vehicles for these transfers, are also discussed. The few studies of such agreements which have been done are in the vanguard of research, but do not provide any definite conclusions. We are, however, tempted to believe that such agreements constitute a powerful means for the transfer of Western know-how to the Soviet Union and the Eastern bloc and are an important factor in the technical development of these countries.

NOTES

1. Technology Transfer and Scientific Cooperation Between the United States and the Soviet Union: A Review. 95th Congress, 1st Session, (Washington, D.C.: Committee on International Relations, 1977), p. 59.

2. J. Fred Bucy, "On Strategic Technology Transfer to the Soviet Union," Current News, Special Edition, August 11, 1977, p. 4.

3. OECD, Ecarts technologiques - Rapport analytique. Comparaisons entre pays membres (Paris: OECD, 1970), pp. 261-62.

4. Bulletin economique pour l' Europe 38, (New York: United Nations, Economic Commission for Europe, 1976), p. 134. It is therefore impossible to make comparisons with the OECD classification.

5. Bulletin Economique pour l'Europe 28, p. 132.

6. Cf. the excellent study of Werner Beitel, "Technological Co-operation with the Soviet Union." In East-West Technological Cooperation, NATO Symposium of March 17-19, 1976, Brussels, pp. 275-313.

7. Calculated from Statistiques du Commerce Exterieur, Series C. OECD, (Paris: OECD).

8. Ibid.

9. Perspective Economique Generale pour la Region de la CEE jusqu'en 1990, Section I, Evolution du Commerce dans la region de la CEE. (Geneva: Economic Commission for Europe, 1977), E.C. AD. (XV)/R.5 Dec. 28, 1977, p. 3.

10. Ibid., p. 3.

11. Ibid., p. 3. The average prices of machinery imported by the Soviet Union from the Western industrialized nations increased by 15% in 1975 and by 2% in 1976. Economic Bulletin for Europe, Vol. 29, Prepublication, p. 83.

12. Commerce exterieur de l'URSS, January-December 1977 (Statistical Data), Appendix to the journal Commerce Exterieur (Moscow, 1977).

13. U.S. Trade Status with Communist Countries, U.S. Department of Commerce, Industry and Trade Administration, Office of East-West Policy and Planning, February 15, 1978, p. 13.

14. Ronald Amann, Julian Cooper and R.W. Davies, eds., The Technological Level of Soviet Industry (New Haven: Yale University Press, 1977).

15. According to Carl H. McMillan, "East-West Industrial Cooperation," in East European Economies Post-Helsinki, 95th Congress, 1st Session, August 25, 1977 (Washington, D.C.: Joint Economic Committee, 1977), p. 1178, an industrial cooperation agreement is concluded when individual producers in the East and West agree to pool funds and coordinate their use in seeking complementary objectives.

16. Rapport analytique sur la cooperation industrielle entre les pays de la CEE, Geneva: 1973, pp. 2, 6.

17. Technology Transfer and Scientific Cooperation Between The United States and Soviet Union: A Review (Washington, D.C.: The Committee on International Relations, 1977), p. 68.

18. Maureen H. Smith, "Industrial Cooperation Agreements: Soviet Experience and Practice," Soviet Economy in a New Perspective, J.P. Hardt, ed. Washington, D.C.: Joint Economic Committee, 1976), p. 771.

19. Carl H. McMillan, "East-West Industrial Cooperation," p. 1186.

20. Apercu statistique de l'evolution recente de la cooperation industrielle, Commission Economique pour l'Europe, Comite pour le Developpement du Commerce, TRADE/R.355/Add. 2, N November 14, 1977, p. 3.

21. McMillan, "East-West Industrial Cooperation," p. 1190.

22. It should be noted that in a nine-year period, from 1961 to 1970, Soviet Imports from OECD countries multiplied by 3.3, and in only 6 years, from 1970 to 1976 by 5.2.
Source: OECD, Statistiques du commerce exterieur, Series C.

20 In Search of a Criterion for the Coalition in International Trade[*]
Henri Dunajewski and Christian Arnal

INTRODUCTION

This study has a three-part objective: (a) to find a praxiological criterion for minimizing the volume and duration of imbalance between export and import plans in world trade, (b) to test the method proposed on a large sample group of countries, and (c) to provide a basis for determining whether present coalitions (CMEA, EEC, Latin America, Asia, etc.) are really the most efficient on the purely economic level.

Based on present knowledge, the problems involved in the objective have not yet been directly examined. However, certain analytical tools have been developed by logicians, mathematicians, and economists which will be exploited in this study. These are in particular:

    1. The praxiological method developed by T. Kotarbinski (1) and J. Zieleniewski, (2) which clarifies the conditions for the juxtaposition of advantages and disadvantages in human activity.

    2. The methods of hierarchical classification. (3) Generally these methods involve the classification of objects in terms of their similarities. In this study, however, classification is in terms of differences between countries, for the simple reason that in international trade two countries are attracted to each other to the extent that their import and export structures are complementary.

---

[*] Translated from the French by Sinclair Robinson, Department of French, Carleton University.

A CRITERION FOR COALITION

3. The theory of triangular trade flows, (4) on which an attempt will be made to extend it to the countries of the world as a whole.

BASIC HYPOTHESES

Let C be a set of countries C_i with $i = 1, 2, \ldots, n-1, n$ and B a set of branches of industrial activity B_j with $j = 1, 2, \ldots, m-1, m$.

Then, let X_i^j be the export intentions (desires, plans) expressed by country i in product category j, and let M_i^j be the import desires of i in this same category.

We are supposing that information on export and import intentions can be attained from worldwide surveys carried on by the United Nations Office of Statistics. Such information, expressed in an international unit of account or simply in United States dollars, can be represented in the form of two figures having n lines and m columns, one for export plans, one for import desires.

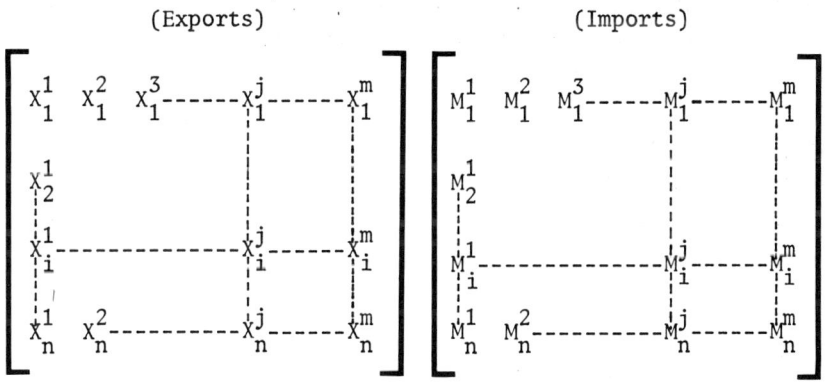

Figure 20.1   Figure 20.2

To a country C_i correspond line i of figure 20.1 and line i of figure 20.2, while to a branch B_j correspond column j of figure 20.1 and column j of figure 20.2.

It is assumed that, inside each B_j, products are perfectly homogeneous or in other words, that for each product there is one and only one corresponding branch j. A product is recognized as identical to another when it meets the same criteria of end use and of composition.

A product which differs from another by one or both of these is classified in a different branch.

As a result of the imperfect information at the disposal of the interested parties, the simultaneous existence of X_i^j and M_i^j cannot be ruled out. Finally, no political constraint is considered in the choice of coalitions. The selection is based exclusively on the economic benefits to be derived by countries from a better organization of the world market.

As for many other theoretical models, the above hypotheses are quite bold. The real world of international trade is much more complex, but any model involves simplifications of reality.

PRINCIPAL CONCEPTS

The total initial imbalance (IM) is the sum of all import and export desires expressed by all countries and in all industrial branches:

(1.0.) $$IM = \sum_{i=1}^{i=n} \sum_{j=1}^{j=m} \left(X_i^j + M_i^j \right).$$

This IM, which does not need to be identified for the purpose of this study, corresponds to the world situation prevailing before any foreign trade contact. Total initial imbalance can also be interpreted as the sum of the initial imbalances of each country, and

(1.1.) $$IM = \sum_{i=1}^{i=n} \left[\sum_{j=1}^{j=m} \left(X_i^j + M_i^j \right) \right] = \sum_{i=1}^{i=n} IM_i$$

IM is also the sum of initial imbalances by branch.

Countries will attempt to eliminate their initial imbalances through trade. Specifically, when two countries enter into commercial relations, a portion of their buying and selling desires is transformed into effective trade flows, leaving unsatisfied only those desires which find no counterpart. It is the sum of these unsatisfied desires which constitutes the residual imbalance (RM).

Let C_k and C_l be two countries which grant trade preference to each other and, thus, together attempt to balance to the maximum extent their respective import and export desires. Only for residual desires will they have to seek other partners.

The residual imbalance ($RM_{k,l}$) which will then characterize the coalition (C_k, C_l) can be written as follows:

(2.0.) $$RM_{k,l} = \sum_{j=1}^{j=m} \left(\left| X_k^j - M_l^j \right| + \left| X_l^j - M_k^j \right| \right)$$

A CRITERION FOR COALITION

The symbol ⌊A⌋ is used to designate the absolute value of the expression A.

It is easily verified that this is the sum of what remains to be imported or exported, either by C_k or by C_1, after maximum bilateral trade balancing. Thus C_k and C_1 remove by means of their trade coalition a portion of their initial imbalances (IM_k and IM_1). However, they are left with the residual imbalance ($RM_{k,1}$).

In the expression of the total initial imbalance (1.1), IM_k and IM_1 are now replaced by $RM_{k,1}$. The decrease in total imbalance ($DM(k,1)$) through maximization of bilateral trade between C_k and C_1 can now be written:

(3.0) $$DM(k,1) = IM_k + IM_1 - RM_{k,1}$$

ALGORITHM OF CHOICE OF COALITION

An iterative method is used. Countries come together for trade in several successive stages t, with t = 0, 1, 2, 3, ..., n-1. Conventionally, stage 0 corresponds to the initial situation in which no trade has yet been carried out.

At each successive stage, two countries are chosen as trading partners. At subsequent stages these countries will appear as a coalition, seeking to satisfy on the world market the residual import and export desires of its two members. Throughout the process, the already constituted coalitions are treated in the same way as countries which are still isolated. The term "country" can thus refer to an actual state as well as to an already existing coalition.

Thus, at each stage, the number of remaining countries is reduced by one unit through the agglomeration of two of them. This type of algorithm is termed "agglomerative." At each stage, also, there is a further decrease in the total initial imbalance (IM), or at the very least, it does not change. The process ends when the import and export desires of all countries have been confronted. Since the number of countries is n, the total number of stages is n-1.

Of course, we cannot simply choose any two countries to form a coalition. We must find a criterion of "proximity." The principle adopted for this choice is based on simple logic: the most substantial trade problems are to be solved first. Thus, we give priority to the most efficient trade coalitions. Each coalition, then, must transform the initial imbalance (IM) into the greatest possible proportion of effective trade flows.

It follows that to a given number of trade coalitions corresponds a maximum decrease in IM, or conversely, a given decrease in IM is obtained with a minimum number of coalitions.

At a given iteration, the coalition (C_k, C_1) is considered the best of all possible coalitions $(C_i, C_{i'})$, if (C_k, C_1) maximizes the reduction of IM.

(4.0) $$\boxed{DM(k,1) \geq DM(i,i') \quad \forall i \neq k \text{ and } \forall i' \neq 1}$$

The above defines the criterion for coalition proposed in this study.

If the need arose, we could establish an additional criterion of proximity which would take geographical distance into account. The criterion of maximization of imbalance reduction would then be supplemented, to an extent to be determined by a criterion of minimization of transportation costs.

DESCRIPTION OF STAGE ONE

This stage begins with the calculation of the imbalance reduction obtained in each possible two-country coalition.

For n countries, there are $\frac{n(n-1)}{2}$ possible coalitions. There are, of course, n possibilities for the first country. There are then n-1 remaining possible partners. This gives n(n-1) possible coalitions. However, in this study, symmetrical coalitions $(C_i, C_{i'})$ and $(C_{i'}, C_i)$ are equivalent, and thus there are only $\frac{n(n-1)}{2}$ pairs to consider. We must now determine which of the $\frac{n(n-1)}{2}$ values of $DM(i, i')$ is the greatest.

Let us suppose that the maximum value of $DM(i, i')$ is attained with the pair (C_k, C_1). This pair is then chosen to form a coalition, and C_k and C_1 achieve a maximum bilateral balancing of their respective import and export desires.

Before proceeding to the next iteration, the residual import and export desires with which the coalition (C_k, C_1) will appear on the world market must be known. To reply to this question, several cases need to be considered.

Let X_k^j be the export desires of C_k in products of branch B_j, and let M_1^j be the import desires of C_1 in products of branch B_j. The following cases can arise:

Case 1: If $X_k^j \geq M_1^j$, it will first be written

$$X_{k,1}^j = X_k^j - M_1^j$$

and $\quad M_{k,1}^j = 0$

A CRITERION FOR COALITION

where $X^j_{k,1}$ represents the residual export desires of the coalition (C_k, C_1) in products of B_j, and $M^j_{k,1}$ represents the residual import desires of the coalition (C_k, C_1) in products of B_j.

Then proceed to compare X^j_1 and M^j_k, X^j_1 representing the export desires of C_1 in products of B_j, and M^j_k the import desires of C_k in products of B_j:

If $X^j_1 \geq M^j_k$, then:

$$X^j_{k,1} = X^j_k - M^j_1 + X^j_1 - M^j_k,$$

and $M^j_{k,1} = 0 + 0 = 0$ (unchanged)

If, on the other hand, $X^j_1 < M^j_k$, then:

$$X^j_{k,1} = X^j_k - M^j_1 \text{ (unchanged)}$$

and $M^j_{k,1} = M^j_k - X^j_1.$

If $X^j_k < M^j_1$, it is assumed provisionally that:

$$X^j_{k,1} = 0$$
$$M^j_{k,1} = M^j_1 - X^j_k$$

The two following situations can arise:

1. If $X^j_1 \geq M^j_k$, then:

$$X^j_{k,1} = X^j_1 - M^j_k + 0$$

and $M^j_{k,1} = M^j_1 - X^j_k + 0$ (unchanged)

2. If $X^j_1 < M^j_k$, then:

$$X^j_{k,1} = 0 + 0 = 0 \text{ (unchanged)}$$

and $M^j_{k,1} = M^j_1 - X^j_k + M^j_k - X^j_1$

These calculations are carried out for the m-1 industrial branches remaining, giving the two vectors (R^m) associated with the coalition (C_k, C_1):

(5.0)

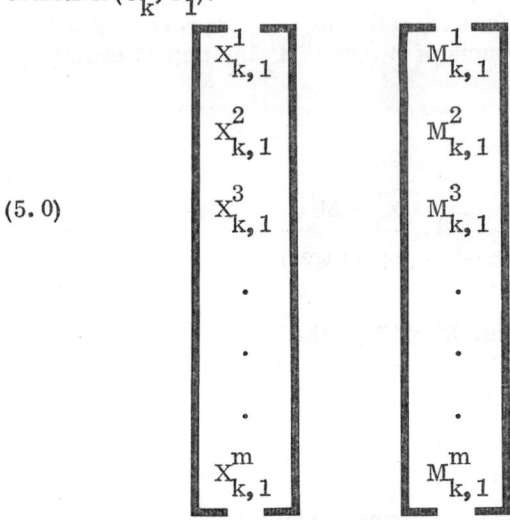

DESCRIPTION OF STAGE TWO AND FOLLOWING STAGES

There are n-1 (number of countries and total number of stages) countries left to consider. The coalition (C_k, C_1) has replaced at the previous stage the two isolated countries C_k and C_1, and now the $\frac{(n-1)(n-2)}{2}$ values of $DM(i, i')$ must be compared. Most of these values are already known from the previous stage. Only the n-2 imbalance reductions $DM[(k, 1), i]$ involving the new coalition (C_k, C_1) must be calculated.

Just as was done at the first stage, a second coalition giving the greatest imbalance decrease has been found. All possible trade is then effected inside this new coalition, which will subsequently appear on the world market only for those export and import desires which were not transformed into actual trade flows between its members. The process stops when all countries have been linked and all possible trade has been effected.

A CRITERION FOR COALITION

MEASURING IMBALANCE REDUCTION

Let DM_T be the imbalance decrease obtained at iteration T of the algorithm. The algorithm has n-1 stages: $t = 1, 2, 3, \ldots, n-1$. If C_k and C_1 are linked at Stage T, then:

(6.0) $$DM_T = DM(k, 1).$$

The algirithm gives us successive partitions of all n countries into n-1, n-2 pairs and coalitions, and finally into one worldwide coalition.

Let Q_T be the quality indicator of the partition of the whole set of countries at Stage T. It is equal in value to the rate of imbalance decrease that was reached at that stage. It is written

(7.0) $$Q_T = \frac{\sum_{t=1}^{t=T} DM_t}{1M}.$$

Q_T increases as the algorithm progresses, rapidly at first since the most efficient coalitions are being formed, then more and more slowly until it stabilizes. Q_T may indeed stabilize before it attains the value of 1, that is before all imbalance has been eliminated.

It is not always possible for the trade among the n , countries being considered to remove all imbalance. This could occur only if the import and export plans of the n countries were globally compatible, <u>ex ante,</u> or if we proceeded to link all the countries in the world <u>ex post facto</u> on the basis of real observed trade flows. In this latter case, there would be a complete elimination of imbalance because imports on one side would be at the same time exports on the other side.

A NUMERICAL EXAMPLE

In order to present a simplified numerical example, it will supposed that the model has only one industrial branch for countries A, B, C, D, E, and F. The export and import desires of these countries are globally compatible. A solution giving total elimination of trade imbalance is possible, using the method presented in this chapter.

Stage 0

At stage T = 0, the volumes of planned exports and imports for countries A, B, C, D, E, F are as follows:

A	
X	M
400	50

B	
X	M
50	300

C	
X	M
250	300

D	
X	M
200	200

E	
X	M
100	100

F	
X	M
50	100

Note: X exports
M imports

The total initial imbalance obtained by adding all exports and imports amounts to 2,100 (IM = 400 + 50 + 50 + 300 + 250 + 300 + 200 + 200 + 100 + 100 + 50 + 100 = 2,100).

Stage One

There are 15 possible combinations for reducing the imbalance:

$$DM_{(C,D)} = \overbrace{250 + 300 + 200 + 200}^{IM_{(C,D)} = 950} - \overbrace{|250-200| - |300-200|}^{RM_{(C,D)} = 150} = 800$$

$DM_{(A,B)} = 700$

$DM_{(A,C)} = 700$

$DM_{(B,C)} = 600$

$DM_{(A,D)} = 500$

$DM_{(B,D)} = 500$

$DM_{(C,E)} = 400$

$DM_{(D,E)} = 400$

$DM_{(A,E)} = 300$

$DM_{(A,F)} = 300$

$DM_{(B,E)} = 300$

$DM_{(C,F)} = 300$

$DM_{(D,F)} = 300$

$DM_{(E,F)} = 300$

$DM_{(B,F)} = 200$

The best possible coalition is that of C, D, for this gives a maximum of DM. We will label this coalition G. It will appear on the world market with the residual imbalances of its members:

G	
X	M
50	100

resulting from the following calculation:

$$250\, X_C - 200\, M_D = 50\, X_G \text{ and}$$

$$300\, M_C - 200\, X_D = 100\, M_G.$$

The quality indicator, that is the rate of imbalance reduction at stage T = 1, is:

$$Q_1 = \frac{800}{2100} = 0.3810$$

Stage Two

We no longer have to consider imbalance reductions for C or D as individual countries, as they now form coalition G. Thus, we have the following situation for countries A, B, G, E, and F at stage T = 2:

A	
X	M
400	50

B	
X	M
50	300

G	
X	M
50	100

E	
X	M
100	100

F	
X	M
50	100

In the remaining set of countries and coalitions the pair for which there is a maximum of trade possibilities must be found. To arrive at the solution, the nine following combinations will be examined

$$IM_{(A,B)} = 800 \qquad RM_{(A,B)} = 100$$
$$DM_{(A,B)} = \overbrace{400 + 50 + 50 + 300}^{} - \overbrace{|400-300| - |50-50|}^{} = 700$$

$$DM_{(A,G)} = 300$$

$$DM_{(A,E)} = 300$$

$$DM_{(A,F)} = 300$$

$$DM_{(B,G)} = 200$$

$$DM_{(B,E)} = 300$$

$$DM_{(B,F)} = 200$$

$$DM_{(G,E)} = 300$$

$$DM_{(G,F)} = 200$$

The A, B pair is the best and will thus form coalition H. This new coalition will appear on the world market with the following residual desires:

H	
X	M
100	0

A CRITERION FOR COALITION

The quality indicator at stage $T = 2$ is thus:

$$Q_2 = \frac{800 + 700}{2100} = 0.7143$$

Stage Three

At the beginning of this stage, there is a set of four countries and coalitions, H, G, E, and F:

H	
X	M
100	0

G	
X	M
50	100

E	
X	M
100	100

F	
X	M
50	100

The imbalance reductions for the six possible combinations are as follows:

$$IM_{(G,E)} = 350 \qquad RM_{(G,E)} = 50$$
$$DM_{(G,E)} = \overbrace{50 + 100 + 100 + 100}^{} - \overbrace{50-100 - 100-100}^{} = 300$$

$$IM_{(E,F)} = 350 \qquad RM_{(E,F)} = 50$$
$$DM_{(E,F)} = \overbrace{100 + 100 + 50 + 100}^{} - \overbrace{100-100 - 100-50}^{} = 300$$

$$DM_{(H,G)} = 200$$

$$DM_{(H,E)} = 200$$

$$DM_{(H,F)} = 200$$

$$DM_{(G,F)} = 200$$

Pairs H, G; H, E; H, F; and G, F, which do not yield maximum imbalance reductions, are eliminated. A choice must be made between G, E and E, F, both of which give DM = 300. Either one can be chosen, but G, E will be selected. It can, moreover, be verified that the choice of E, F at this point would also ultimately lead to a situation where the totality of the imbalance would be removed.

The G, E pair becomes coalition I, for which the set is:

I	
X	M
0	50

The quality indicator at this stage is:

$$Q_3 = \frac{800+700+300}{2100} = 0.8571$$

Stage Four

At the beginning of this stage, there are three countries, H, I and F:

H	
X	M
100	0

I	
X	M
0	50

F	
X	M
50	100

The three possible combinations are:

$DM_{(H, F)} = 100 + 0 + 50 + 100 - 100-100 - 0-50 = 200$

$DM_{(I, F)} = 100$

$DM_{(I, H)} = 100$

The H, F pair is chosen, which becomes coalition J:

J	
X	M
50	0

and $Q_4 = \frac{800+700+300+200}{2100} = 0.9524$

Stage Five

This is the final stage and includes countries I and J:

I	
X	M
0	50

J	
X	M
50	0

A CRITERION FOR COALITION

Pair I, J form coalition K, and all residual imbalance is removed:

K	
X	M
0	0

and $Q_5 = \dfrac{800+700+300+200+100}{2100} = 1.$

Our results can be presented in the form of a "tree" of hierarchical classification (fig. 20.3). The horizontal axis is the scale of the rate of imbalance reduction and indicates the fraction of the initial imbalance which is eliminated.

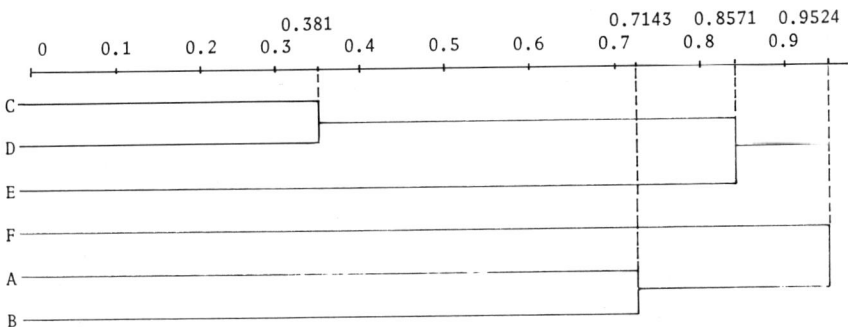

Figure 20.3

C and D remove 38.1% of the initial imbalance (IM) on achieving maximum bilateral trade balancing. When A and B are linked, the imbalance is further decreased by 33.3%. Then E and C, D remove another 14.28%, which gives a reduction rate of 85.71%. The linking of F with A, B removes 9.53% of IM. Finally, the linking of C, D, E with F, A, B decreases IM by another 4.76% and totally eliminates the initial imbalance.

It is easily verified that if another series of coalitions had been chosen, for example, B, F = L; A, E = N; C, L = S; N, S = Y; and D, Y = Z, the quality indicators would have had the following values:

(8.0.)
$$Q_1 = 0.0952$$
$$Q_2 = 0.2381$$
$$Q_3 = 0.4762$$
$$Q_4 = 0.8095$$
$$Q_5 = 0.8095.$$

Q would never attain the value 1.0; the imbalance reduction would not be total. Figure 20.4 shows the difference between the results of the method we propose and the consequences of an arbitrary choice of successive coalitions. The advantages of our method over a choice of coalitions based on other criteria are evident.

PRACTICAL STATISTICAL TEST OF THE PROPOSED METHOD

The model was intended to match the export and import plans of a set of countries. In order to test the model, ex ante, the exact content of the respective plans must be known. Unfortunately such exhaustive information is not available at the present time, even at the level of the specialized services of the United Nations. With the present state of affairs, world trade statistics ex post facto, will have to suffice for the application of the method. (5) This constraint necessarily raises the three following points:

1. The observed flows only imperfectly reflect the initial import and export desires of the countries under consideration. These intentions have had to be adjusted to the concrete possibilities for choice of trading partner and also have often been biased or limited by political preferences.

2. The available statistics have a high level of aggregation making for the heterogeneity of products inside the commodity groups composing a branch. (6) It is not known in fact if the product of

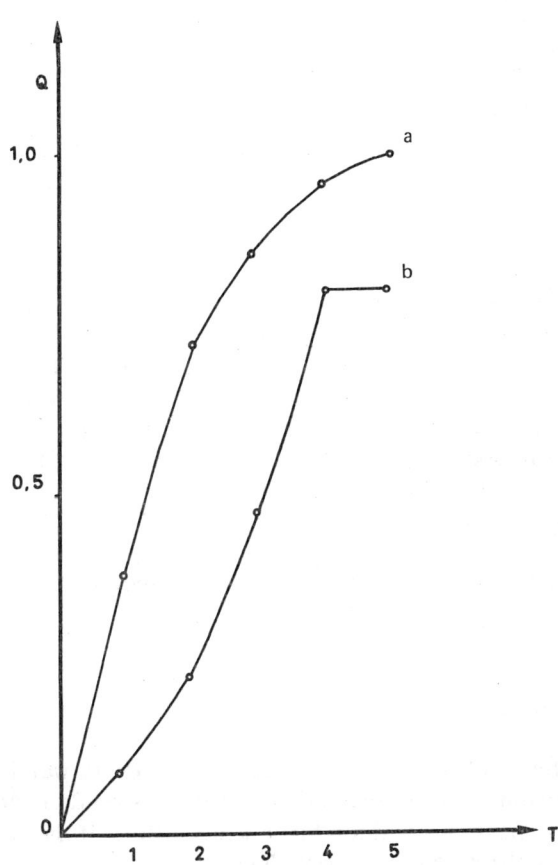

Fig. 20.4. Comparison of proposed and arbitrary method.

(a) Proposed method

(b) Arbitrary method. The curve follows the values of the quality indicators (8.0).

branch B_j sold by country C_1 corresponds to the product of the same branch purchased by country C_2.

3. The observed flows often include re-exports of imports. (7)

The conclusions of this study will thus be valid only within the limits outlined previously.

The test itself is based on statistics for 39 countries listed with their trade figures in Table 20.1. The sample represents 82% of world trade. The criterion for selection was a minimum figure of 4 billion United States $ in either exports or imports for 1974, since 1974 is the latest year for which United Nations international trade statistics were published for the vast majority of these 39 countries. Three exceptions were made, however.

1. Argentina, as the second largest country in Latin America, is included. Its exports in 1974 came very close to the figure of $4 billion.

2. The period of reference for Algeria, Saudi Arabia, Mexico, and Romania is 1973. The 1974 foreign trade of these countries is well above the mark of $4 billion, but the most recent statistics <u>subdivided into commodity groups</u> are from 1973.

3. The German Democratic Republic is not included, although in 1974 both its imports and exports were more than double the cutoff point. The reason is that in its statistical reports the German Democratic Republic does not follow the international classification adopted by the United Nations Statistics Office.

By applying our method we can construct a "tree" of hierarchical classification, as presented in Figure 20.5. (8)

To obtain clearer illustration of branching, we used the scale:

(9.0) $$\hat{Q} = - \frac{1}{\log Q}$$

Note: Q is the linear rate of imbalance reduction.

The "tree" clearly shows countries at present which belong to different economic associations or communities could have found better trading partners outside these associations if the world was not divided into political and military blocs.

Thus, it would be to the advantage of the following paired countries to form coalitions in the first stage:

Federal Republic of Germany - United States	(0.168) (9)
France - United Kingdom	(0.271)
Canada - Holland	(0.353)
Belgium and Luxembourg - Italy	(0.417)

TABLE 20.1 - List of 39 Countries Representing 8.2% of World Trade in 1974

Country	Imports in $1,000	Exports in $1,000
01 Algeria (1973)	4,035,000	4,259,000
02 Argentina	3,674,000	3,930,702
03 Australia	11,086,850	10,787,293
04 Austria	9,022,721	7,161,482
05 Belgium/Luxembourg	29,445,750	28,760,299
06 Brazil	14,162,728	8,669,461
07 Canada	32,296,263	32,783,390
08 Czechoslovakia	7,576,448	7,053,385
09 Denmark	9,364,479	7,683,430
10 Finland	6,850,183	5,521,587
11 France	52,173,808	45,139,346
12 German Federal Republic	68,975,275	89,165,480
13 Holland	32,507,510	32,734,235
14 Hong Kong	6,710,022	6,018,749
15 Hungary	5,574,853	5,128,619
16 India	5,167,132	3,906,068
17 Indonesia	3,858,234	7,426,338
18 Iran	6,543,617	17,792,654
19 Israel	4,237,251	1,824,859
20 Italy	40,681,842	30,251,786
21 Japan	62,094,360	55,537,758
22 Korean Republic	6,844,295	5,081,016
23 Kuwait	1,553,481	10,954,130
24 Libya	2,764,310	8,268,145
25 Mexico (1973)	4,145,600	2,451,995
26 Nigeria	2,756,385	9,169,716
27 Norway	8,413,958	6,274,399
28 Poland	10,488,643	8,320,576
29 Romania (1973)	3,467,899	3,698,499
30 Saudi Arabia (1973)	1,981,039	9,089,355
31 Singapore	8,343,926	5,785,144
32 Sweden	15,820,477	15,909,463
33 Switzerland	14,411,252	11,838,027
34 South Africa	4,720,686	4,906,101
35 Spain	15,820,477	7,675,398
36 United Kingdom	54,149,438	38,661,515
37 United States	100,997,269	98,506,890
38 Soviet Union	24,889,660	27,405,003
39 Yugoslavia	7,519,853	3,804,590

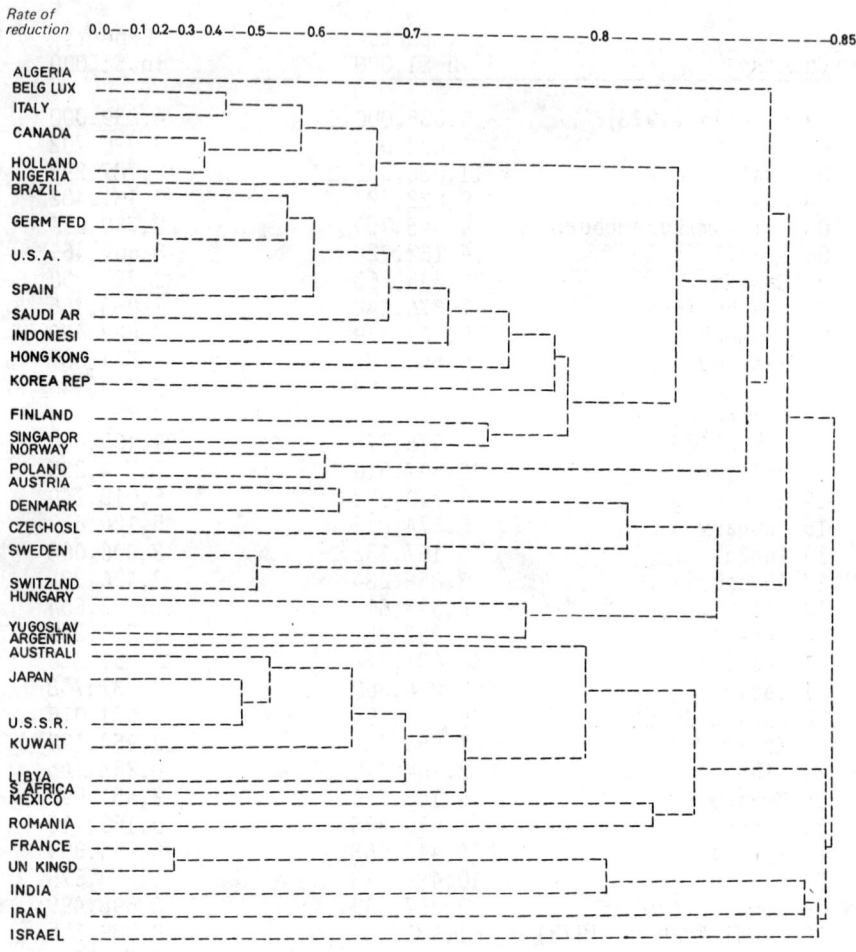

Note: Observations: 39 countries representing 82% of world trade

Variables: ten commodity groups (imports and exports in 1974)

(Inverse of a logarithmic scale)

Fig. 20.5 - "Tree" of hierarchical classification of observations. (The abbreviations used represent the maximum of eight characters for computer processing.)

A CRITERION FOR COALITION 389

Japan - Soviet Union	(0.474)
Sweden - Switzerland	(0.501)
Norway - Poland	(0.615)
Austria - Denmark	(0.633)
Finland - Singapore	(0.750)
Hungary-Yugoslvaia	(0.771)
Mexico - Romania	(0.817)

It would be to the advantage of the above coalitions to link themselves with others, either isolated countries or coalitions. Among the three country coalitions would be the following:

Japan - Soviet Union - Australia	(0.528)
Federal Republic of Germany - United States - Brazil	(0.553)
Sweden - Switzerland - Czechoslovakia	(0.711)
France - United Kingdom - India	(0.804)

Then would come four country coalitions, formed either from two two country coalitions or from a three country coalition plus an isolated country:

Belgium Luxembourg - Italy - Canada - Holland	(0.576)
Federal Republic of Germany - United States - Brazil - Spain	(0.597)
Japan - Soviet Union - Australia - Kuwait	(0.650)
France - United Kingdom - India - Iran	(0.853)

The most efficient coalitions of five countries would be the following:

Belgium and Luxembourg - Italy - Canada - Holland - Nigeria	(0.666)
Federal Republic of Germany - United States - Brazil - Spain - Saudi Arabia	(0.681)
Japan - Soviet Union - Australia - Kuwait - Libya	(0.696)
Sweden - Switzerland - Czechoslovakia - Austria - Denmark	(0.811)
France - United Kingdom - India - Iran - Israel	(0.855)

Below are two coalitions of six countries:

Federal Republic of Germany - United
States - Brazil - Spain - Saudi
Arabia - Indonesia   (0.725)
Japan - Soviet Union - Australia - Kuwait -
Libya - South Africa   (0.737)

The three seven-country coalitions meeting the criterion of maximization of imbalance reduction would be the following:

Federal Republic of Germany - United
States - Brazil - Spain - Saudi
Arabia - Indonesia - Hong Kong   (0.761)
Japan - Soviet Union - Australia - Kuwait -
Libya - South Africa - Argentina   (0.797)
Sweden - Switzerland - Czechoslovakia -
Austria - Denmark - Hungary -
Yugoslvaia   (0.834)

Then, six more coalitions could be formed before we achieved the distribution of all the countries into two large coalitions of 25 and 14.
The first of 25 countries would include:

Federal Republic of Germany - United States - Brazil - Spain - Saudi Arabia - Indonesia - Hong Kong - Korea Republic - Finland - Singapore - Norway - Poland - Belgium/Luxembourg - Italy - Canada - Holland - Nigeria - Austria - Denmark - Czechoslovakia - Sweden - Switzerland - Hungary - Yugoslavia - Algeria (0.849)

The second coalition of 14 countries would include:

Japan - Soviet Union - Australia - Kuwait - Libya - South Africa - Argentina - Mexico - Romania - France - United Kingdom - India - Iran - Israel (0.856).

The balancing of the residual import and export desires of these two large coalitions could result in the formation of a single coalition with an imbalance reduction rate of 0.857 (see Figure 20.5). In other words, only 14.3% of import and export desires would not be satisfied for the 39 countries in our sample, and this without trade with other countries.
Any other choice of partners for coalitions gives us a lower imbalance reduction rate.

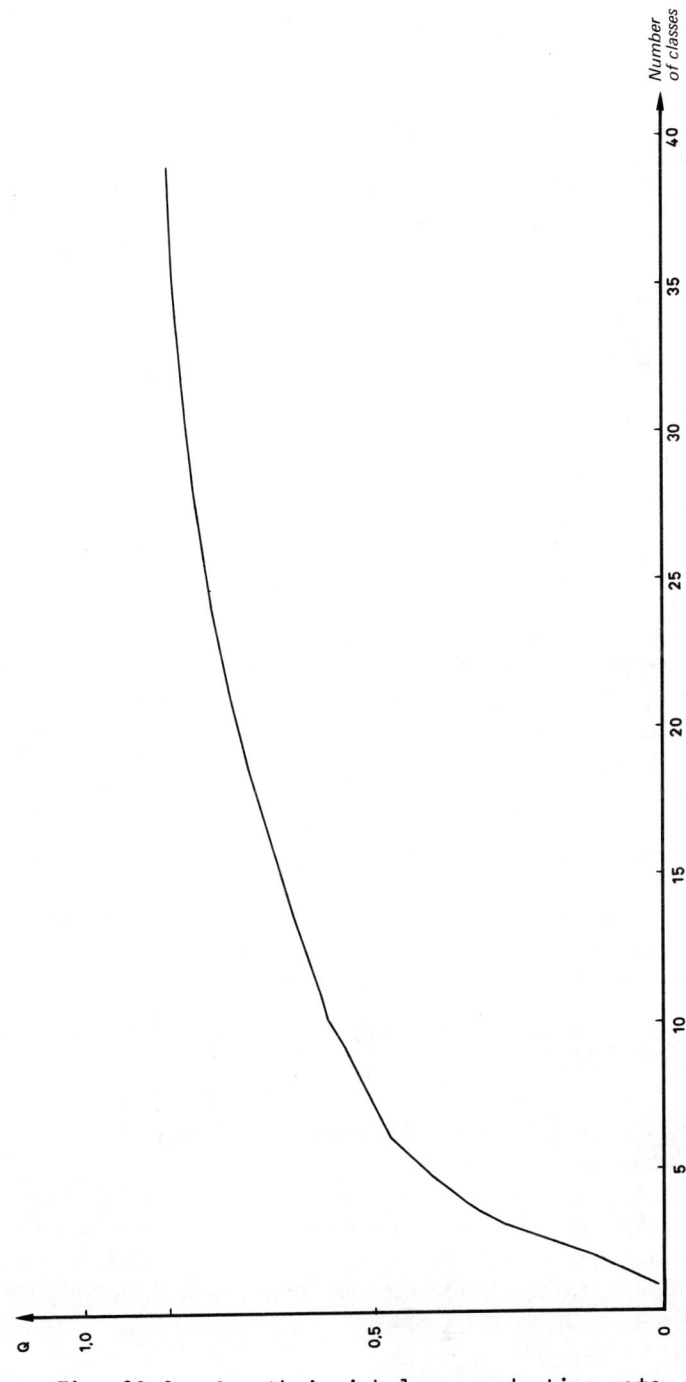

Fig. 20.6. Growth in imbalance reduction rate.

NOTES

1. T. Kotarbinski: Traktat o dobrej robocie, Warsaw: 1955; Mysli o dzialaniu, Warsaw, 1957.

2. J. Zieleniewski: Organizacja respolow ludzkich, Warsaw, 1965.

3. G. Morlat (sous la direction de): Introduction a l'analyse des donnees, Paris: Societe de Mathematiques Appliquees et de Sciences Humaines, 1976.

4. S. J. Huber, Accords bilateraux et transactions triangulaires, Imprimerie St. Paul, Fribourg (Switzerland), 1965; J. Weiller: Accords bilateraux et multilateralisme dans les experiences de pays a systemes economiques differents. Colloque franco-polonais: 27-30 mai, 1974, Paris (mimeographed); "Cooperation industrielle tripartite: Est-Quest-Sud," Politique Etrangere, No. 5, 1976.

5. International trade statistics, frequently four-five years out of date, are classified into 0-9 commodity groups: 0-Food and Animals; 1-Beverages and Tobacco; 2-Crude Metals excluding Fuel; 3-Mineral Fuels; 4-Animal, Vegetable Oil, Fat; 5-Chemicals; 6-Basic Manufactures; 7-Machines, Transport, Equipment; 8-Miscellaneous Manufactured Goods; 9-Goods not classed by kind.

6. In the United Nations classification there is division into subgroups, but few countries publish or provide to the United Nations statistics broken down into subgroups.

7. Yearbook of International Trade Statistics, 1975, Vol. I. (New York: United Nations, 1976).

8. We wish to thank Ms. Michele Brami for preparing the statistical data for computer processing.

9. The figures in parentheses indicate the rates of imbalance reduction appearing on the "tree." It is obvious that these figures are significant only when the algorithm applying to the whole sample is taken into account.

21 Parallels Between Different Systems in International Economic Relations
Detlef Lorenz

INTRODUCTION

This paper has been written from the vantage point of a theorist interested and specialized in international economics. The differentiation of economic systems with regard to trade relevant elements instead of the two classical ones of capitalism and Socialism or market (decentralized) and planned (centralized) economies respectively, started roughly a decade ago; however, it has met with little success so far. Nevertheless, I think Johnson was completely right, when he remarked that the traditional approach "... distorted the conception and analysis of the trade problems and policies ... by diverting attention from other and more relevant characteristics in which the centrally planned economies resemble non-centrally planned or at least non-Communist countries." (1)

Notwithstanding the undisputed significance of the heritage of comparative economic systems analysis it will be necessary to go further in order to (a) take into consideration the realities of the different but interdependent parts of the world economy and (b) draw parallels between different systems instead of underlining well-known differences. It is proposed first to widen the range of analysis with respect to comparative economic systems as well as international economics. Then a few parallels in special fields will be approached directly.

SYSTEMIC COMPONENTS VERSUS COMPARATIVE ECONOMIC SYSTEMS: THE DEVELOPMENT COMPONENT

At first this component seems to be the case with the less developed countries only, i.e., the Third World as an economic system in its own right. From a theoretical point of view, however, this might look different.

First, I think we have to accept the fact that by far the majority of the Third World countries are mixed economies, neither convincingly planned nor typically market led. This very much manifests the development status per se: less developed countries are characterized by underdeveloped systems, too; their systems are not yet determined. Even the new phenomenon of self-reliance seems to have been until now more an expression of defense against the penetration of world market powers (capitalism) than the nucleus of a "self-relying system."

Secondly, development is hardly the privilege of a single system. On the contrary, it has to be a component of every system if not limited to statics or unhistorical dimensions. We find different "stages" of development among market economies of the West, as well as among CMEA countries.

Third, the very special point of the foregoing general statements is the interpretation of the average CMEA country as a kind of underdeveloped country, particularly in respect to international economic relations and in comparison with the First World of the industrialized countries. (2)

THE ECONOMIC POLICY COMPONENT

Within the broad, diversified systems of industrialized market economies there have always existed more or less identifiable subsystems with respect to economic policies, for example, such organized groups of countries as the European Economic Community (EEC) or nonorganized country groups within the Trilateral Commission (OECD).

Besides differences in regard to typical combinations and valuations of the main economic policy targets, even more attention should be paid to differences like those Kindleberger aptly summarized in the term, "capacity to transform." (3) Socioeconomic and historical roots of different, as well as similar, national capacities to transform presumably are of eminent importance as systemic aspects in a world of change and development. If we relate transformation to the openness of countries and add aspects of the actual dilemma of the "trilateral economics of interdependence," we are back to Johnson's "nationalistic economic policies." In his opinion they were the "more relevant characteristics" in which the CMEA countries resemble noncentrally planned countries. (4) Perhaps we can also speak of a propensity to react by neomercantilism, revisiting in some way one of the oldest systems of political economy. This has happened because the national capacity to transform has been weakened and at the same time challenged and strained by international forces, though in different ways and degrees for strong and weak countries. (5)

THE AREA COMPONENT

Economic systems do not seem to be "footloose," but why do they show a propensity to regionalize? Of course, a lot depends on political and historical factors; nobody will deny that. Besides large continental countries like the United States, the Soviet Union, and China, for example, the old and new "Grossraumpolitik" are known. Apparently, in general, political as well as economic influence and elements are narrowly mixed with one another in each regional area. Last but not least, however, the reasons for regional systems of integration have a general and independent economic logic.

Like small countries, economic systems based on too small an area are often more open than it seems tolerable from the point of view of the system's "purity" and efficiency. Dependence as well as interdependence are full of internal and external constraints for nations and systems. No small wonder that there seem to be some parallels between, for instance, trade aversion in CMEA on the whole, self-reliance in less developed countries, "positive" integration policies in the EEC, or even neomercantilist tendencies amongst OECD countries. In complete conformity with the realm of economic policy, theorists have rightly paid attention to so-called optimum currency areas and the optimum size of regions. (6)

THE INTERNATIONAL COMPONENT

Finally, a further component has to be added, i.e., the international component; otherwise there remains a missing link if we want to evaluate economic systems in the context of world economics which can be regarded as the coordination of different conflicting international systems. Subsystems characterized by the systemic components previously discussed naturally have an intra as well as an inter aspect. On the one hand, intrasystemic international economic relations particularly concentrate on integration policy interpreted very broadly, i.e., encompassing market or planned specialization as well as policies of harmonization or development policy often identical with regional policy. On the other hand intersystemic, international economic relations can be roughly divided into three broad categories: (a) relations between adversaries, (b) relations dominated by development gaps, and finally (c) relations caused by different styles and priorities of economic policy systems.

MODERN VERSUS ORTHODOX TRADE THEORY: CATEGORIES OF GOODS AND TRADE FLOWS

Whatever the pros and cons of several new approaches to dynamize and reshape established neoclassical trade theory in its own rights since about 1965, they presumably are better suited to handle problems dealt with in the present paper. In what follows studies that favor a generalizing approach (7) in contrast to quite a lot of more empirically based ad hoc theorizing (8) will be more utilized. In order to hold the analysis manageable within the confines of the paper, there will be a limitation to some strategic issues.

The first issue concerns the "faceless" goods X and Y that were at best characterized by factor intensity. It has become more and more common instead to distinguish different categories of goods, as for instance listed in Table 21.1.

Goods differentiated with regard to quality and functions do not surprise scholars in political economy and CMEA studies. Note, for example, Hirschman, Wiles, Wiczynski, and Goldman, or think of the terms strategic, development, hard core goods, or goods as short-term gap fillers; finally and more specifically, think of grain and R&D goods. (9) The extension of the analysis from these foremost noncompetitive goods (2-4), to ordinary competitive (Heckscher-Ohlin-goods) (1), and differentiated goods (5) dominating intraindustry trade (welfare trade) show the range of trade categories Gray, for instance, recently used in his book (see Table 21.1). Some of these categories will be used later in this chapter.

Besides the essential point that qualitative differences in the kinds of goods count for much in a world where political differences influence the desirability of international trade, a further point is worth emphasizing. That second issue is of a more principal and methodological nature and more than overdue for being expressed explicitly. (10)

TABLE 21.1 - Three Examples Distinguishing Different Categories of Traded Goods

	Hirsch	Gray	Lorenz
1.	a) Heckscher-Ohlin goods or b) Every Man's goods	Ordinary/homogeneous competitive goods	Ubiquitious goods or Heckscher-Ohlin goods
		<u>Noncompetitive respectively availability goods</u>	
2.	a) Ricardo goods or b) Poor Man's goods	Type A: natural resources	Primary goods – mineral and tropical goods (Adam Smith)
3.	a) Product cycle goods or b) Rich Man's goods	Type C: technological expertise	Technological gap goods (Schumpeter/Hufbauer)
4.		Type B: limited availability goods	Supplementary gap fillers: micro and macro (Lorenz)
5.		Differentiated goods	Preference goods (Chamberlin/Linder/Grubel)

Note: Compare also notes 7 and 10.

Orthodox theory mainly wants to know about homogeneous competitive goods produced (available) in every country, ubiquitious or every man's goods. Consequently, merely substitutive exchange has required theoretical interest. But is that the general case? Don't we have far more trade in complementarities in a world of historical development endowed with unequal "partners" and monopolistically/randomly distributed availabilities and product differentiation? For orthodox theorizing the latter trade flows figure too simply to be worth nothing. (11) If there is an appreciation, however, of: (a) the eminent dimensions and quantities of noncompetitive trade flows and (b) the challenging transformation processes when complementary trade flows change into substitutive ones - compare low wage trade or the last stage of the product cycle - the question really arises who or which model is too simple. A preliminary comparison of four theoretical models of trade based on categories of trade flows can be found in Figure 21.1.

DIFFERENT FUNCTIONS OF TRADE

The third issue closely connected with the first and second centers upon the functions foreign trade is expected to fulfill. If allocation of scarce resources according to neoclassical theory in general and the law of comparative costs in particular is the absolute point of reference, then trade performs its first function; it is the instrument of marginal reallocation. More significant than this text book analysis is the general application of foreign trade as a means of competition in domestic markets, including its appearance to check planned economies (Kontrollfunktion) (12) and as a inducement to efficient infant industry protectionism in less developed countries.

Secondly, not necessarily in opposition to comparative advantage but less in accordance with mere reallocation, trade is said to fulfill a growth function. That can be seen manifoldly depending on the export or the import side of international trade and, of course, on different economic and systemic conditions in the respective domestic markets. In many successful dynamic market economies, growth of national income (GNP) has been export led as an outlet for R&D availabilities and intraindustry trade providing static and dynamic economies of scale, raising productivity and gains of trade. (13) Here, however, micro and macro economical growth takes over the primary function, and the division of labor is more or less the byproduct.

The growth function, particularly regarding exports, gets a somewhat different flavor if it is translated into the old vent for surplus version, and this is the third function of trade.

Three cases possibly can be distinguished:
1. The case of export led growth and Keynesian underemployment in industrialized economies, i.e., exports as a necessity of domestic sufficient "dynamics" and employment, possible in stagnant or neomercantilist economies.
2. The case of less developed countries where exports appear "... as a virtually 'costless' means of acquiring imports and expanding domestic economic activity." (14)
3. The case of planned economies where exports are vents for unplanned surplus ("trade proclivity," "exchange of inefficiencies").

The common denominator of all cases seems to be the mobilization of otherwise idle resources. The term, "otherwise," also indicates something of a malfunctioning of the respective systems eventually stimulating international competitive export drives of a problematic nature.

Changing from the export to the import side of the growth function it is necessary to differentiate again. Beginning with the orthodox type of planned economies, there is the well-known function of gap filling. Without suddenly and urgently needed imports, growth or fulfillment of plans could suffer from bottlenecks. Similar things could happen to underdeveloped countries because both types of countries are less "gifted" in regard to transformation capacity (elasticities and diversification). Of more and general importance than these, most often short-term effects and the long-term gap filling by strategic imports of development goods have to be handled. That growth aspect of complementary input imports has equally been stressed for underdeveloped countries and CMEA countries. Recently, the security problem of natural resource imports for industrialized market economies demonstrated the general character of the fourth function of trade, which could be called the supply version of the growth function.

Finally, it might be advisable to consider a separate trade function in close connection with development elements of the world economy and in contrast a shortsighted reallocation analysis. Nurkse once spoke of trade as an engine of growth particularly for areas of recent settlements. (15) Let us go one step further and speak of trade as an engine of development goals, viz., in two different ways: (a) development of economic and social systems, and (b) development of underdeveloped countries. In either case, the hypothesis could be stated that trade performs its fifth function of transition until the respective goals are reached for which the assistance of foreign countries is deemed necessary. Hence, "we have to inquire whether the interdependence is permanent or reversible, or to what degree, for each side taken separately." (16) If trade could be subjected to strat-

I. Microeconomic Models

1. Complementarity of production ex ante (dynamic availability models):

   No availabilities of the same good/input in all or many countries. Supply is monopolistically (randomly) distributed: absolute availability of one country or small groups of countries.

   Trade/exports no means of international division of labor (reallocation). Specialization, however, follows from extensive spill over trade. Expansive allocations accompany world market development. Enlarged/more diversified supply of importing countries (vent for surplus respectively import supply functions).

   Propensity to substitute ex ante complementarities by imitation of supply (parallel prouducation). Complementary trade flows are eliminated by import substitution ex post facto. International time monopolies fade away.

2. Substitutionality of production ex ante (static conventional models):

   Ubiguitous availabilities for all functional homogeneous goods/inputs by all countries (identical physical supplies).

   Trade/exports means of international division of labor (reallocation) which aim at intensifying trade in order to reduce costs by competition. Cheaper instead of enlarged supply of importing countries (function of specialization, i.e.,division of labor).

   Propensity to substitute ex ante substitutionalities by elimination of foreign production. Competitive availabilities of production are substituted by import dependencies ex post facto. Propensity to monopolize internationally by absence of duplicated industries (parallel production).

Model 2 might be supplemented or followed again (dynamic sequence) by model 1, or on the grounds of rising incomes and welfare, both models will be overlapped (partially substituted) by a third model.

3. Dynamic demand and supply model of product differentiation:

Similar conditions of production as in model 2. However, demand and supply (strategic marketing) of functional heterogeneous goods characterized by more or less identifiable gaps of substitution (inputs may be equal or unequal). That means micro economic complementarities of production and trade flows ex post facto as a consequence of demand preferences ex ante. Hence, also, transfer of the extensive elements of model 1. Development of world markets, international specialization as expansive allocation instead of mere reallocation.

How far the model encompasses intensive elements of model 2 depends on the intensity of substitution gaps or on the continuity and individuality of preferences, respectively. Complementarity is guaranteed within a certain band/range only, controlled by competition/substitution in trade and production (latent competition in the meaning of the theory of monopolistic or workable competition).

Product differentiation combines competition with complementarity. The strategy of market/substitution gaps, however, might be due to change into aggresive substitution if as a consequence of filling the supply gaps of a strongly differentiated international demand, the "leeway" of expansion of international trade has become too narrow. "Unfair" competition then intensifies the adjustment problems again that at first were played down by product differentiation and intraindustry trade.

II. Macroeconomic Model (4)

Finally, the micro economic models 3 and 2 could by cynamized by macro economic processes and factors like growth/development, business cycles, inflation, and exchange rates.

In dependence on the respective trade potentials of model 2 and 3 "a state of affairs in which there is a large volume of foreign trade trembling...on the margin of advantageousness...small changes in the wind of circumstances," i.e. macro economic determinates mentioned, create a climate favorable for ambivalent and instable substitutive exchange.

The potential of trade is nonaggressive if macro economic circumstances are of a complementary/supplementary nature, international lags in business cycles, for instance. It is bound to become aggressive in the context of: a) neomercantilistic "liberalizing trade," or of b) tough gaps of development as, for example, between North and South (macro economic low wage trade or vertical competition)

Sources: a) H.G. Grubel, International Economics (Homewood (Ill.): 1977), p. 77, 83-4. b) D. H. Robertson, "The Future of International Trade" (1938). In: Readings in the Theory of International Trade, 2nd ed.., H.S. Ellis and L. A. Metzler, eds., London, 1953), p. 505.

Fig. 21.1 - Comparison of theoretical models of international trade.

egies of political economy to obtain specific objectives and, therefore, be understood as an instrument for that purpose, the degree or intensity of trade relations (interdependence) might indeed depend on the very needs of the limited period of transition. (17) Thus, the much debated questions of dependence and interdependence have to be supplemented by an adequate time element.

SELECTED PARALLELS FOR SOME SELECTED CASES: RISK OF SPECIALIZATION - ADJUSTMENT AND COMPLEX DEVELOPMENT

For a decade or so, no serious quarrel about "Westernization" seems to to have existed in the theory and policy of specialization and integration of CMEA, (18) perhaps because of a dialectic process between reforms and foreign trade. The law of comparative advantage has been accepted in principle, and the easy days of autarchy debates have passed. Integration is no longer a capitalistic matter. At least the "Comprehensive Program" officially recognized and enlarged specialization agreements as a form of Socialist integration. Customs union analysis has been applied, and institutional comparisons between EEC and CMEA have been drawn repeatedly. However, what is really comparable? Do parallels scratch only surface phenomena or should we look for an analysis at more sophisticated levels?
Surely, the application of micro efficiency as the typical market economy criterion might be a fallacy because central planners do not really want that and have not been able to invent reliable allocative indicators either. Presumably, however, not only one but several steps further have been taken by approaches like those of Kojima and Neuberger. Drawing on earlier ideas of Myrdal and Harrod, Kojima elaborated a theory of "agreed specialization." The theory provides systematic arguments for ex ante division of labor on the grounds of intraindustry specialization and economies of scale regarding regions of less developed countries, with explicit application to Eastern and Western Europe. (19) The Kojima theory, therefore, very much overlaps "the third rule of thumb" of Neuberger's "Limited Regret Strategy," where "... decisions can be made on the basis of purely technological coefficients...." (20) Finally the new economics of intraindustry trade strongly based on increasing returns to scale are applicable practically to all systems. (21)
Theoretical as well as empirical research on Gray's "two-way trade" in Western Europe surprisingly showed the dominance of intra over inter industry specialization underlying the phenomenal trade

expansion in the sixties. From research carried out on developed market economies, an answer to an interesting distinction raised by Neuberger seems possible. In 1964 he supposed that "interbranch specialization also requires more sophisticated economic tools" than narrow intrabranch specialization, but also "may involve all the various types of risks." (22) One of the main types of risk, viz., disruption of national plans and costs of adjustment, corresponds closely to the reason put forward to explain successful liberalization in Western Europe: "... Trade liberalization in the European Economic Community... resulted in greater trade expansion and fewer adjustment problems than has been anticipated by analysts who had based their predictions on the more traditional model of interindustry specialization." (23) Hence, liberalization policy might be equally interpreted along the lines of conservative regret strategy instead of laissez faire. Avoidance of strong competition on the grounds of substitutive supplies in mainly HO goods presumably has a parallel in Eastern European countries where "one of the most important factors impeding integration... is the unwillingness of these nations to allow existing enterprises, industries, and sectors to be outcompeted and scrapped." (24)

Last but not least, a further parallel is warranted in the context just mentioned. Socialist theory is very fond of playing down the acceptance of the law of comparative advantage by stressing the necessity of complex development for each CMEA member at the same time. This might be a derivative of the well-known balanced growth strategy in development theory. That requirement is equally to be understood as an _ex ante_ concept, like the Socialist theory of specialization and integration in general. In addition, however, it directly corresponds to _ex post_ protectionism in Western developed countries against fierce substitutive free trade which might lead countries towards more _ex post_ complementarity in production, i.e., being less complex. If we legitimately bring together complex development and indirect social benefits (Nutzeffekte) which is stressed by Socialist trade theory, "these advantages correspond formally to the constraints of free trade in market economies." (25)

PARALLELS IN RESPECT TO EX POST FACTO AND EX ANTE SPECIALIZATION: THE CASE OF COMPLEMENTARITY

The terms _ex ante_ and _ex post facto_ previously mentioned are not limited to planning versus market forces as principles of organization;

historical time and/or development are involved, too. Regarding intergration theory, Balassa distinguised between market and production/development integration. (26) Neoclassical trade theory as well as Vinerian customs union theory take as their premises developed diversified countries which are competing in most industries with one another, their locations of production are known, and the countries have command over the same availabilities. What is left open is the result of foreign trade induced by reallocation processes. Substitutive trade flows determine ex post facto through cost/price competition between identical goods where free trade production and complementarities definitely settle down. Trade is the means of market integration and international competition. Moreover, the higher the volume of trade, the better the success of international or regional integration. (27)

Socialist trade theory, on the contrary, has banned determination of international location via "chaotic" world market competition. Location has not to be the result of time consuming and wasteful resources reallocation; it is fixed ex ante instead in order to avoid Schumpeter's process of "creative destruction." Hence, trade follows as a technical consequence of a planned division of labor, and "unplanned competition" has lost its function as a trial and error process. Thus, in order to get the result of market substitution ex ante, i.e., complementarity or supplementarity in production and trade, Socialist integration has to be seen "as a process of creating complementary and mutually dependent national economic structures which... form one economic complex." (28)

Moreover, a better insight into the appreciation of the importance of the distinction made earlier regarding substitutive and complementary trade flows is gained if it is remembered that particularly intraindustry trade is distinguished by a large content of complementarity, all the more when seen as a limited regret startegy (compare model 3 of fig. 21.1).

SOME MACRO ASPECTS OF COMPLEMENTARITY

The foregoing discussions primarily tried to evaluate the traditional microefficiency aspects of trade and specialization from a broader perspective by bringing to bear on arguments of intraspecialization and microcomplementarity in East and West. Yet, there is something more in favor of the concept of complementarity in international economics.

First, there is a remarkable statement by Neuberger providing systemic parallels in respect to planners' know-how. In order to implement a division of labor, "planners must ask themselves questions that private entrepreneurs need not ask"; therefore they "must take specific, active measures... instead of being able to concentrate on removing artificial barriers, such as tariffs and then permitting individual firms to act upon price and cost differentials." (29) Yet, what about some of the more formidable difficulties EEC integration has been facing for a few years? The nice days of relatively easy "negative" integration and liberalization, i.e. market integration, are over and due to be followed by "positive" integration, i.e. policy integration. (30) In Lipsey's reasoning this parallels the task of regional specialization in Socialist economies. (31) Fallenbuchl in an interesting empirical investigation of "planning" experience in the so-called mixed economies of the EEC countries/industries has also made clear "that the differences in the mechanisms of integration maybe less important than some basically similar national policies...." (32)

Secondly, a short comment on categories of goods which were discussed previously should be in order. Type A and C goods in Gray's classification closely correspond to the first and second "rules of thumb" Neuberger distinguished in respect to advantages of location (raw materials) and technological availabilities. (33) Both categories had been classified as complementary goods by the German economist Heuss nearly a quarter of a century ago. (34) Besides the fact of being more suitable for planning in theory and CMEA practice, macroeconomic dimensions come along when these types of goods are considered as "high priority sectors" (35) more comparable to the so-called "integration industries" in less developed countries than to the narrow lines of intrabranch trade and superficial product differentiation of consumer goods in developed countries.

Thirdly, the macro economic dimension of complementary trade flows has to be interpreted as being of a strategic nature just in the neighborhood of political economy. That is, of course, an old story. Complementary North-South relations between such systems as imperial industrial powers (centers) and colonies or less developed countries (peripheries) have been accused of exploitative nonequivalent exchange by Marxists and dependencia scholars. (36) Recently, comparing types of economic imperialism in West and East, Holesovsky tried to translate the North-South intersystemic special relationship into the intrasystemic East-West context, interpreting the Soviet Union as the imperial center and the satellites of CMEA as the exploited periphery, (37) including a remarkable correspondence in respect to the issue of complementarity. Concerning the CMEA area,

Fallenbuchl equally emphasized the "radical" trade pattern (vertical integration) in a recent empirical investigation: "The CMEA-integration is still very much simply a dependence of individual member countries on trade with the Soviet Union." (38)

Now, for macro complementarities as part of political economy, the most critical issue seems to be the appearance of macro economic terms of trade problems, which are far more a matter of international distribution than a reallocation. Generally, complementary trade flows differ from substitutive ones in that there is no exchange of identical goods, merely differentiated by cost or price relations. This might open the door to conflict and arguments of exploitation, but it is only debatable under certain conditions. (39) Therefore, four separate cases must be distinguished, which at first are symmetrical complementarities without terms of trade disputes.

In case one type A and C goods are exchanged on the basis of roughly equal reciprocal demand or balanced mutual interests. The best known historical example seems to be the classical North-South trade in the nineteenth century. Nevertheless, that pattern is still of great significance, and there are renewed interests which have been enlarged by East-West trade. (40)

Terms of trade conflicts came mainly to the fore when case two reciprocal demand, became unbalanced, for instance, as discussed in Nurkse's famous Wicksell Lectures contrasting the twentieth with the nineteenth century trade pattern. (41) Moreover, if we introduce factor movements, symmetrical complementarities narrow down to questions of equivalance between factor input and factor output, the latter understood as respective payments (by goods) for the factor input. Terms of trade conflicts then partially change into a bargain about investment financing and gains widely known in respect to direct investment policies in the area of natural resources (OPEC) and East European contributions for common CMEA investment projects in the natural resource sector of the Soviet Union.

In addition to symmetrical ones, two cases of asymmetrical complementarities might be distinguished, where the counter trade flow for type A or C goods is of type B or Heckscher-Ohlin goods, respectively.

Type B goods serve as a supplement or gap filler for shortages of domestic supply. This case three is parallel to case one because no essential macro economic terms of trade problems are raised. The important share of Eastern European intra-CMEA exports, particularly to the Soviet Union, in exchange for imports of type A goods might illustrate the case, unless unwanted qualities stand to reason.

Finally, case four is characterized by substitutive imports of Heckscher-Ohlin goods as a counter trade flow for complementary exports, or in other terms, availability gap trade (exports) is paid for by low wage trade (imports). Trade of the low wage type is not only limited to imports from CMEA or less developed countries (new international division of labor), but includes "unorderly" marketing and neomercantilist export drives amongst developed countries as well. Then low wages are often replaced by other means of "unfair" practices in international competition. Although monetary economics heavily influence the trilateral scenarios of the industrial Western countries, many conflicts, however, are closely connected with trade flows and sometimes are the reason for monetary "disequilibrium economics," i.e. structural balance of payments imbalances. (42)

A RETURN TO THE TENDENCY TO REGIONALIZE

Finally, we return to the "international component" of part one, which is apparently closely related to the tendency to regionalize (area component). Contrary to the widely accepted view of the interdependence of the world economy, regionalism gains ground despite several disappointments about integration processes, particularly in developed EEC, but above all in less developed countries. Yet, the phenomenon of regionalism can only be understood properly if we see it in the context of the other two systemic components: development and economic policy. Otherwise, regionalism smacks too much of autarchy barring effective and efficient integration.

The majority, to be sure, still suggests a general worldwide international division of labor, a la Tinbergen, or a global industrial policy, meanwhile "improved" by a few interesting realistic bits of reasoning. (43) Regarding the "question of possible geographical scope of integration," however, the relevant question is not only one of liberal theory (the larger the area the better) versus practice (existing groupings as "jumping off points"). (44) Eventually, since it is far more important, the Linder concept of efficient trade diversion should be remembered. (45) Here, of course, the development component of economic systems arises. Diversion then could be the more justified, either the larger the gap is in respect to the leading region/countries, or the more interdependence threats to the autonomy of national policies. (46)

Particularly if the region's development stages are of a different nature, regions with a "vent for surplus bias" often assist developing regions with a "supply gap bias." But then a conflict might easily come to the fore influencing what in the East-West context is well known as the dispute over centrifugal and centripetal forces of CMEA in respect to intersystemic integration. Balance or imbalance in that case very much depends on the relatively mature region's capacity to absorb, i.e., whether the intersystemic relations are self-liquidating or not. That again could be regarded as a question of the composition of trade flows and categories of goods; or in other words, the potential of micro and macro complementarities in regard to intra and intersystemic trade decides how far substitutional trade is necessary and tolerable, too. Translated into North-South relations, the problem grows into a general phenomenon of the world economy. The problem might even be of actual importance to economic policy groups among industrialized countries of the First World (see fig. 21.1, models 3 and 4 particularly).

NOTES

1. Harry G. Johnson, "Notes on Some Theoretical Problems Posed by the Foreign Trade of Centrally Planned Economies." In International Trade and Central Planning, Alan A. Brown and Egon Neuberger, eds. (Berkeley: University of California Press, 1968), pp. 394 (italics added). See also Peter J. D. Wiles, Communist International Economics (Oxford: Basil Blackwell, 1968). "This book tries to build out the theory and generalized description of international economics... to include Communism; or alternatively to build out Sovietological economics to include all international aspects" (Preface). The relationship between Socialist economies and existing trade models is also briefly touched in the preface by J. C. Brada, ed., Quantitative and Analytical Studies in East-West Economic Relations (Bloomington, Indiana: International Development Research Center, 1976). As the most appropriate studies in the field of comparative economic systems from this point of view, compare for instance Lloyd G. Reynolds, The Three Worlds of Economics (New Haven: Yale University Press, 1971) and Vaclav Holesovsky, Economic Systems. Analysis and Comparison (New York: McGraw-Hill, 1977), chapter 15.

2. See for example Johnson, "Notes on Some Theoretical Problems," p. 394 and recently, Gunnar Adler-Karlsson, The Political Economy of East-West-South Co-operation (Wien: Springer Verlag, 1976). He prefers to speak of "The Semi-Developed East," p. 53. Admittedly, the GDR and CSSR badly correspond to this term. Yet, it also is not just easy to find a "really developed" planned economy.

3. Charles P. Kindleberger, "Foreign Trade and the National Economy," Studies in Comparative Economics, 1 (New Haven: Yale University Press, 1962), chapter 7. See also Knorr's remark in connection with the strains of interdependence and the level of modernization that has been achieved. Klaus Knorr, The Power of Nations. The Political Economy of International Relations (New York: Basic Books, 1975), p. 215.

4. Ibid., particularly pp. 394-7.

5. Cf. for instance Assar Lindbeck, The National State in an Internationalized World Economy. Seminar Paper No. 26, Institute

for International Economic Studies (Stockholm: University of Stockholm, 1973); John Pinder, "The Reform of International Economic Policy: Weak and Strong Countries," International Affairs, 53 (1977), pp. 345-63; Detlef Lorenz, "The Crisis of Liberalization-Policy in the Economics of Interdependence," Intereconomics, 13 (July/August 1978).

6. Beside the vast literature about optimum currency areas, see for example, Richard N. Cooper, "Worldwide versus Regional Integration: Is there an Optimum Size of the Integrated Area?" In Economic Integration, Worldwide, Regional, Sectoral, Fritz Machlup, ed. Proceedings of the Fourth Congress of the International Economic Association, Budapest (London: Macmillan Press, 1976), p. 41-53.

7. H. Peter Gray, A Generalized Theory of International Trade (London: Macmillan Press, 1976). Herbert G. Grubel and P.J. Lloyd, Intra-Industry Trade: The Theory and Measurement of International Trade in Differentiated Products (London: Macmillan Press, 1975). Detlef Lorenz, Dynamische Theorie der internationalen Arbeitsteilung. Ein Beitrag zur Theorie der weltwirtschaftlichen Entwicklung. (Berlin: Duncker und Humblot, 1967). Very similar lines follows the paper by Norbert Kloten and W. Rall, "East-West Economic Interaction: Determinants, Benefits and Limitations." In World Economy and East West Trade, F. Nemschak, ed.; Workshop Papers, Vol. 1, The Vienna Institute for Comparative Economic Studies (Wien: Springer Verlag, 1976), pp. 83-96. See also H. Peter Gray, "Soviet Trade with the West: A Theoretical Note," The ACES Bulletin, 19 (1977).

8. Compare the technological gap (Posner/Hufbauer) and product cycle (Vernon/Hirsch) models. See for example Grubel and Lloyd, ibid., chapter 7.

9. Albert O. Hirschman, National Power and the Structure of Foreign Trade (Berkeley: University of California Press, 1945/1969). Peter J. D. Wiles, "Foreign Trade of Eastern Europe: A Summary Appraisal." International Trade and Central Planning, Brown and Neuberger, eds., pp. 166-73. Josef Wilczynski, The Economics and Politics of East-West Trade (New York: Macmillan, 1969), pp. 259-270. Marshall I. Goldman, Detente and Dollars (New York: Basic Books, 1975).

10. See Lorenz, Dynamische Theorie internationaler Arbeitsteilung, pp. 28-30, 66-84, idem, "Explanatory Hypotheses on Trade Flows between Industrial and Developing Countries." In The International Division of Labour. Problems and Perspectives. International Symposium, H. Giersch, ed. (Tubingen: J.C.B. Mohr, 1974), pp. 83-93.

11. Richard Caves and Ronald W. Jones, World Trade and Payments (Boston: Little, Brown and Company, 1973), p. 11: "Some patterns of trade need almost no explanation... If all trade were of this kind - with each country producing commodities desired by all countries but available only locally - there would be little need for the economist either to expound upon the virtues of trade or to explain the patterns of trade. These would be almost self-evident."

12. Phillip J. Bryson, Scarcity and Control in Socialiam (Lexington, Mass.: D.C. Heath, 1976), pp. 119-20. See also Karl-Heinz Nattland, Der Außenhandel in der Wirtschaftsreform der DDR (Berlin: Duncker und Humblot, 1972), pp. 30-8.

13. The shift from extensive to intensive growth in CMEA countries during the sixties was also accompanied by a revaluation of the contribution of international trade, for example in the GDR. Export led growth and a policy of specialized growth emphasizing the "structural effects" of international trade (Struktureffekte) became rather common. For an interesting discussion including parallel theoretical aspects of trade theory in East and West see Nattland, ibid., chapter 1.

14. Cf. Hyla Myint, "The 'Classical Theory' of International Trade and Underdeveloped Countries," The Economic Journal, 68 (1958), p. 322.

15. R. Nurkse, Problems of Capital Formation in Underdeveloped Countries (New York: Oxford University Press, 1953).

16. Holesowsky, Economic Systems, p. 412.

17. Beside the "foreign transactions between adversaries" dealt with by Holesovsky, ibid., pp. 409-13, supplementing Hirschman's classical study (cf. reference 9) the historical example of the German "Industriestaatdebatte" deserves attention. See Detlef Lorenz, "Die Neue Weltwirtschaftsordnung aus der Sicht

der Indistriestaatendebatte der Jahrhundertwende", <u>Jahrbucher fur Nationalokonomie und Statistik</u> 192 (1977), pp. 49-54. Compare, too, the remark about "stages of interdependence" in Knorr, <u>The Power of Nations</u>, p. 322.

18. Cf. the statement of Holesowsky, <u>Economic Systems,</u> p. 440 and the cautious evalutation by Franklyn D. Holzman, <u>International Trade Under Communism - Politics and Economics</u> (London: Macmillan Press, 1976), pp. 15-20, 46-50.

19. Kiyoshi Kojima "Towards a Theory of Agreed Specialization: The Economics of Integration." In <u>Introduction, Growth and Trade</u>, W.A. Eltis <u>et al.</u>, eds. (Oxford: University Press, 1970), pp. 305-24, particularly pp. 319-22.

20. Egon Neuberger, "International Division of Labor in CMEA: Limited Regret Strategy," <u>American Economic Review</u>, 54 (1964), pp. 513-14.

21. Cf. for market economies and less developed countries Grubel and Lloyd, <u>Intra-Industry Trade</u>, pp. 88-95 and 145-8. In respect to product differentiation these economics at the moment, indeed, lack some realism concerning other systems beside market economies, partly because of different stages of development.

22. Neuberger, "International Division of Labour in CMEA," p. 514.

23. Grubel and Lloyd, <u>Intra-Industry Trade</u>, p. 143, 128. A very strong position is taken by Hufbauer in respect to the severeness of adjustment costs: "Formidable adjustment burdens underlie our pessimism concerning future specialization among the industrial nations or between the industrial countries and the Third World," Gary C. Hufbauer and John G. Chilas, "Specialization by Industrial Countries: Extent and Consequences." In <u>The International Division of Labour,</u> Giersch, ed., p. 9, 19. See also for further aspects H. Peter Gray, "Two-Way International Trade in Manufactures: A Theoretical Underpinning," <u>Weltwirtschaftliches Archiv,</u> 109 (1973), pp. 30-5.

24. Holzman, <u>International Trade under Communism,</u> p. 62. See also Bryson, <u>Scarcity and Control in Socialism,</u> pp. 141-2, and Holesowsky, <u>Economic Systems,</u> p. 389.

25. Alfred Schuller, Osthandel als Problem der Wettbewerbspolitik (Frankfurt/Main: Athenaum, 1973), p. 171. (Translation Detlef Lorenz).

26. Bela Balassa, "Types of Economic Integration," in Economic Integration, Worldwide, Regional, Sectoral, Machlup, ed., p. 18.

27. Lipsey has doubts about the volume of trade as an indicator of success of integration. He rather assumes that "one measure of the success of regional integration is the absense of duplicated industries producing the same product in various member countries...," Richard Lipsey, "Comments," in Economic Integration, Worldwide, Regional, Sectoral, Machlup, ed., p. 39.

28. Zbigniew M. Fallenbuchl, "Industrial Policy and Economic Integration in CMEA and EEC." Discussion Paper Series no. 41 (1976), Department of Economics, University of Windsor, Ontario, Canada. p. 2.

29. Brown and Neuberger, eds., International Trade, p. 508.

30. Cf. reference 5. See also Fritz Franzmeyer, "Widerspruche sektoraler Strukturpolitik in der Europaischen Gemeinschaft und ihre Bedeutung fur den Intergrationsprozess," Vierteljahreshefte 4/1977, (Deutsches Institut fur Wirtschaft Wirtschaftsforschung, Berlin), pp. 207-25.

31. Lipsey, "Comments," p. 37.

32. Fallenbuchl, Industrial Policy, p. 22.

33. Brown and Neuberger, eds., International Trade, p. 513.

34. Ernst Heuss, Wirtschaftssysteme und internationaler Handel (Zurich: Polygraphischer Verlag, 1955), p. 190.

35. Fallenbuchl, Industrial Policy, p. 45.

36. See Knorr, The Power of Nations, pp. 219-36 and chapter IX; see also Detlef Lorenz, "Non-Equivalent Exchange and International Income Distribution," The German Economic Review 8 (1970), pp. 273-94.

37. Holesowsky, Economic Systems, pp. 405-8.

38. Zbigniew M. Fallenbuchl, The Commodity Composition of Intra-CMEA Trade and the Industrial Structure of the Member Countries, in Comecon: Progress and Perspective (Brussel: NATO Directorate of Economic Affairs, 1977), pp. 103-34. In a second study by the same author, however, the pattern of complementarity apparently is also valued as an indicator of the economic and political success of integration. Fallenbuchl, Industrial Policy, pp. 21-3, 40.

39. See note 36.

40. See Adler-Karlsson, The Political Economy of East-West-South Co-operation, pp. 54-5.

41. Ragnar Nurkse, Patterns of Trade and Development, Wicksell Lectures, Stockholm, 1959.

42. Regrettably limited space did not allow parallels to be drawn with regard to monetary fields, for instance the role of fixed and wrong exchange rates and "administered prices" in East and West. Cf. also reference 5.

43. Regarding "the need for an international industrial policy," see Christopher T. Saunders, "New Trends in the World Economy: Their Impact on East-West Relations." In World Economy and East-West Trade, Nemschak, ed., pp. 53-8. Cf. also Fallenbuchl, Industrial Policy, p. 45 with regard to a "global industrial policy."

44. Saunders, ibid., p. 56.

45. Steffan B. Linder, "Customs Unions and Economic Development." In Latin American Economic Integration, M.S. Wionczek, ed. (New York: Praeger, 1966), pp. 32-41.

46. Cf. for example Knorr, The Power of Nations, pp. 218, 322-3.

22 The Influence of the Socioeconomic System on East-West Economic Relations: Poland

Jan Mujzel

INTRODUCTION

This paper will present an analysis of the influence which is being exerted at present and will be exerted in future by the socioeconomic system of the centrally planned economies on the course of the economic cooperation of these countries with highly developed capitalist economies. A general analysis of this problem is, however, an extremely difficult task today. That is due to the fact that there have arisen some important differences between Socialist countries, both in the scope of their economic ties with the West and in solutions applied by their socioeconomic mechanisms. In this situation the analysis will be focused directly on the machanism of the Polish economy and on economic relations of this country with highly developed Western countries. It is believed that some conclusions reached in the process of this analysis will also be, at least to some extent, of a more general nature.

ACHIEVEMENTS

To start with, economic relations of the Polish economy with its developed Western partners will be characterized. Roughly speaking these relations constitute some kind of a mixture of achievements and undoubtedly positive processes on one hand and difficulties and drawbacks on the other one. The list of achievements might be started with the fact that in the last decade the process of opening up the Polish economy to the world economy and intensification of its participation in the international division of labor have become one of the most essential features of the implemented strategy. It reflected a conviction that the share of the Polish economy in the international division of labor did not correspond to the level of development achieved by the country with the gap gradually growing. This disproportion is hampering effectiveness of the economy and may become a force limiting its development prospects. The national income of Poland, estimated according to the SNA method (Systems of National Accounts) and thus the one applied in Western countries, amounted to $2,325 per one inhabitant in 1975. Over the years 1976-77 it rose by another 13% to reach about $2,600 in the 1974 prices. That may be considered to be a decent average level of an industrialized country; on the other hand the share of Poland in the overall value of the world export represented only 1.1% in 1976.

High dynamics of foreign trade was an expression of the previously mentioned policy of opening up the economy to the world system. Export per one inhabitant in current prices grew from $45 in 1960 to $323 in 1976. This dynamics of export growth exceeded the one achieved by many Socialist and capitalist countries. The index of export growth in fixed prices amounted to 443 in 1976 (1960 = 100) as compared with the general world value of 238. The supremacy of export dynamism of the Polish economy over rates scored by majority of other comparable countries became most pronounced over the seven-year period of 1971-77.

The turnover of Poland with highly developed capitalist countries was growing also at a high rate. In the seventies this increase was even distinctly higher than the increase in total trade. The share of developed economies in Polish foreign trade accounted for 29.8% in 1960, 27.1% in 1970, and it rose to 41.4% in 1976. This trend was reversed in 1977 as a result of temporary import restrictions applied by the economic policy in an attempt to improve the balance of trade. In the long-term approach this problem is vividly discussed in Poland today in connection with the economic situation of Western markets in the second half of the seventies and future economic forecasts in this area.

In the last decade there was also a rapid development of higher forms of economic relations, primarily industrial cooperation. Today the majority of leading Polish companies in the electromechanical industry cooperate, sometimes on a large scale, with foreign partners both in Socialist and capitalist countries. This form is especially promoted by the economic policy which is trying to launch various stimulating means and remove barriers on its way of development.

A growing share of electromechanical industry products in total import, especially of investment goods, has been an important feature in the evolution of Polish trade relations with other countries in recent years. That was due to a huge investment effort made in Poland in the seventies. The share of electromechanical products accounted for 29% of the total imports value in 1960, and it increased to 46.2% in 1977.

Wishing to bridge the technological gap faster, the Polish economy in the seventies was a sizeable purchaser of new technologies, not only in the form of machinery and equipment but also licenses and know-how agreements. The number of the so-called active licenses, i.e. possessing valid license agreements, grew from 142 at the beginning of 1971 to 455 at the end of 1976. In the period of 1971-76 the total value of products produced under licenses increased 4.3 times, while the value of direct export of these products increased 2.6 times, reaching the level of $190 million in 1976.

DIFFICULTIES

As mentioned, economic relations of Poland with its developed Western partners represent an area of not only achievements but also difficulties and negative phenomena. High export dynamics cannot overshadow the fact that the present level of export continues to be relatively low and does not correspond with the level of industrialization achieved by Poland. Economies of the German Democratic Republic, Czechoslovakia, Hungary, and Bulgaria were exporting almost or over twice as much per person in 1976. According to the same estimates export volume of highly developed Western countries possessing strong international ties was many times higher than the Polish one.

In the seventies Poland's foreign trade with Western countries was characterized by a relatively high deficit. Foreign trade in the sixties with its general equilibrium has been showing growing surplus of import over export since 1971. In 1976 the total deficit (not only in trade with developed Western countries) amounted to about 3.6 billion dollars decreasing to approximately 2.7 billion dollars in 1977. Trade balance deficit and some indebtedness of the Polish economy were assumed in the development strategy of the 1970s in order to accelerate modernization of the economy and dynamize its all important fields, including also, or perhaps first of all, export. In line with this strategy the Polish economy should show a higher growth rate of export over import in the second half of the seventies, which at the end of the seventies should ensure an absolute surplus of export over import and a gradual reduction of indebtedness. Implementation of this strategy, however, has been encountering serious difficulties. Despite the strenuous efforts of the economic policy, Poland managed to decrease the trade balance deficit only in 1977. The improvement in this field was, however, much below the five-year plan assumptions. To achieve a reduction of trade balance deficit it was necessary to restrict the volume of import, which in turn often produced tensions and difficulties both in industrial production and in the domestic market for consumption goods.

There also appears negative phenomena with respect to changes in the commodity structure of exports. Despite overwhelming growth rates of electromechanical and chemical industries, their share in the overall export in 1976 was almost the same as in 1970. In 1977 Poland only succeeded in achieving a two percentage point increase of the share of electromechanical industry in exports to Socialist and developed Western countries, and after all, it is the electromechanical industry which is charged with the main responsibility for accelerated expansion of exports to meet the needs and possibilities of the national economy. In the six-year period of 1971-76 the share of fuels and energy in Polish exports rose from 12.5 to 18.1%, while in trade with non-Socialist states the corresponding figures were 15.1 and 26.0%, respectively. This phenomenon, combined with the continued unsatisfactory profitability of a number of industrial exports, constituted one of the main causes of the previously mentioned low export growth.

Despite various measures taken by the economic policy, quantitative results scored recently in industrial cooperation with developed Western countries are far from satisfactory. Exports of products turned out on the basis of cooperation agreements were somewhat lower in 1977 than in 1976 and amounted to about $48 million. The share of these exports in the overall value of Polish export stays at the level of approximately 2.5%, while in developed industrial countries it accounts, as a rule, for about 30% of foreign trade turnover.

It could obviously be assumed that the negative balance of Poland in technology trade is a natural phenomenon. The scale of this deficit is, however, rather puzzling. In 1976, 55 licenses were purchased, with the total value of financial obligations during validity of the agreements reaching approximately $160 million. At the same time, only 5 licenses there were sold, with the total value of the agreements amounting to not quite $4 million. Moreover, although the number of home patents obtained by Polish citizens and institutions was growing very rapidly in the seventies, the effects of the patenting of Polish inventions abroad was extremely poor.

Finally, the phenomenon of considerable one-sidedness of Western partners of Polish industry in industrial cooperation and license purchasing should be mentioned again. One multinational Western company accounts for about 40% of Poland's cooperation trade. Over 90% of cooperation trade was concentrated in six countries, and in each of them there takes place deep concentration in some large companies. From among these six countries only relations with the firms of the German Federal Republic are more widely spread. This situation looks similar in the field of license purchases.

CAUSES OF DIFFICULTIES

Difficulties and unfavorable phenomena, which were appearing in the 1970s in the economic relations of Poland with highly developed Western countries, were a result of many complex and most often interrelated factors.

External Factors

The external factors will be discussed first. As a consequence of unfavorable climatic conditions, which were recurring from year to year and were exceptionally long-lasting, crop production in Polish agriculture has not been increasing to any considerable extent since 1974. In 1975 and 1977, it was decreased in comparison with the preceding year by 3.7 and 7.5%, respectively. The rapidly growing demand for meat and other articles of animal origin made it necessary to increase rapidly the import of grain and fodder concentrate. Expenditures for this import grew from $140 million in 1970 to $780 million in 1976.

Export oriented policy was largely hampered by substantial deterioration of economic growth in developed countries of the West in recent years. In the new environment, export expansion of products turned out by the Polish manufacturing industry is encountering intensified restrictions. It should be added here that these restrictions do not reflect solely the strained market situation. Poland's export has been encountering, especially in the second half of the seventies, growing administrative restrictions which reflect the protectionist tendencies in Western countries.

Internal Factors

Nonetheless, external causes cannot be said to account for everything. Performance of the Polish economy in the 1970s was characterized by a number of traditional weaknesses which have not been eliminated. From the point of view of the results of the international exchange, there should be first mentioned here insufficient innovational dynamism and unsatisfactory quality level of production, which primarily concern the manufacturing industries. Despite many efforts of the economic policy, both these processes were far from meeting the requirements posed by foreign trade. One should also add two further problems which were not solved in the seventies, i.e., (a) lack of flexibility and poor initiative showed by industrial and trade organizations and (b) strong supply-demand tensions in some domestic markets creating additional difficulties in maintaining desirable growth rates of export supplies. Under pressure of the market shortages tendencies towards shifting economic resources for the domestic supplies contrary to the provisions of the long-term plans were appearing.

It is worth mentioning here that these unfavorable aspects in the functioning of industrial and trade organizations were appearing parallel to the intensive modernization of their material and labor potential. It was in the seventies that an accelerated process of reinforcement of labor resources took place with new generations better prepared to implement ambitious research and technical tasks. That was also a period of tremendous investment effort. Production capital in all branches of the economy was, to a large extent, renewed and modernized. Thus, significant progress in providing premises for modern innovation-oriented economy was made. Equally big efforts were being made in the 1970s in expanding research and development potential in the industry itself and outside it. The percentage share of the national income earmarked today in Poland for research and development is no smaller than in highly developed Western countries.

We are thus reaching a conclusion that weaknesses in economic relations with Western countries result, to a large extent, from internal systemic solutions. This factor should not be overestimated, but it is believed that it is impossible to perform a correct analysis bypassing this factor.

Traditional Socioeconomic Mechanism

Although the present socioeconomic mechanism was a source of negative phenomena, it also paved the way for many major achievements, a number of which found their way into Poland's history. The point, however, is that the so-called traditional socioeconomic mechanism, which continues to hold a predominant position in the Polish economy, is at present more and more distinctly ill adjusted to requirements imposed by the already achieved level of the economy's development and social aspirations. This refers both to relations with Western economies and to other important economic and social processes. Briefly speaking, it is a factor which acutely hampers satisfaction of the society's needs and improvements of its welfare, the two key targets of Polish economy.

It is not a new problem. Poland has been aware of it for a number of years and for a number of years there have been conducted in Poland and other Socialist countries intensive researches in this sphere. Practical measures aimed at providing at least partial solutions are also being taken. It should, however, be stressed that achievement of a global solution is extremely difficult because it implies control over a big number of complex feedbacks not always well defined by theory, and it is connected with a number of important implications in the sphere of often conflicting interests.

In the period of the past 25 years there were launched at least four times in the Polish economy programs of a far-reaching reconstruction of the mechanism. The latest reform of 1973 provided for creation of the so-called system of large economic organizations. For many reasons development of this system came across serious obstacles, and since the mid-seventies it was being gradually suspended. In 1977 a decision of reactivation of this system in the so-called modified form was made. This decision was made with conditions which are not exactly very favorable at present. Although that is a partial solution it stands to reason that the unquestionable significance of this decision consists in paving once again the way for progressive changes of the mechanism. Moreover, it seems that certain progressive solutions applied by the system of large economic organizations, such as objectivized correlation between wages and effectiveness of the company, introduction of transaction prices into the microeconomic calculus, and economization of industrial associations, found their permanent way into the mechanism of Poland's economy.

DIRECTIONS OF PROBABLE SYSTEMIC CHANGES.

As mentioned, much emphasis is laid on elaboration of future directions of evolution of the Polish economy's mechanism. Teams of experts are employed on the project, and discussions are conducted in various circles. Therefore, some comments on the way in which the probable changes will be affecting our economic relations with highly developed Western states will be made.

It is believed that the broadly accepted confidence in the Socialist company, its entrepreneurship, and rationality is a matter of primary importance. It continues to represent a sizable reserve of effectiveness in our economy. This reserve appears to be even bigger if the fact is considered that in Poland's sociopolitical conditions the company may avoid many negative features which are present in the privately owned company.

Evolution of the Company

The solutions being investigated are aimed at the evolution of the company towards:

1. extension of its time horizon in the field of economic calculus and decisions.

2. promotion of initiatives along with the ability to take reasonable risk, making the company a rational unit not only in the sphere of current processes but also an aggressive one in the development field.

3. promotion of workers' participation in various forms and at different levels (workers' self-management).

Evolution in these directions will produce multilateral effects as regards possibilities of development of economic relations with Western economies. First of all, the importance of ties with foreign partners will be gradually consolidated. These ties should take various forms starting with traditional trade exchange and finally including close cooperation in the production, research, and development areas.

In the Socialist economy central planning constitutes a key element of socioeconomic mechanism. Progressive evolution of the functioning principles of the company and other microeconomic subjects, which is not accompanied by harmonized movements in central planning, cannot produce successful results because it will not generate durable effectiveness. Polish experience, including that of the 1970s, has confirmed that once again beyond any doubt.

Thus the consolidation of the company's position must be accompanied by a profound revaluation of the scope (capacity) of the central plan; the degree to which its structures and especially physical structures are obligatory; and the role of verification of changes of these structures with the help of microeconomic calculus, procedures, and information basis of the central plan. That involves many important and highly complex praxiological and social problems, all of which have not yet been successfully solved by the contemporary theory of planning.

Will that lead, however, to weakening of the central plan position and in a wider sense, of the central management of the economy? That is out of the question. The changes mentioned here should consolidate and rationalize the central management of the national economy, making it a real management corresponding to social needs instead of a purely formal management which is not quite socially effective. One of the important theses of the contemporary theory of the functioning of the Socialist economy continues to be the thesis that there is no conflict between strong central management of the economy and the strong position of the company in the national economy, equipped with wide allocation autonomy, and operating in line with principles of microeconomic rationality. The contradictory character of this relationship formulated in earlier years was practically barring the way for progressive solutions necessitated by the present realities.

Evolution of Organizational Structures

It is expected that the evolution of organizational structures of the national economy will be accompanied by departure from monopolistic schemes in production, the domestic market, and foreign trade. This does not imply a resignation from the policy of establishing a highly concentrated economic organization which groups many plants or companies. In a number of industries or trading networks such organizations constitute a condition for taking advantage of economies of scale and meeting standards of the world economy. But, and this seems to be extremely important, the previously mentioned necessity does not apply to all components of the national economy. In some industries and trade groups the economic policy should aim at counteracting formation of such organizations. Moreover, in some branches in which formation of multiplant organizations is fully justified, such organizations do not have to be launched along principles of horizontal grouping, which in itself is a main source of monopolistic situations. Acceptance of the principle of vertical or some other grouping may appear to be more desirable. Thus, there is a growing conviction that the organizational structures of the Socialist economy require at present much greater flexibility and diversity of forms. Also, the need for wider application of reasonably perceived competition among companies or their groupings in the planned economy is gaining growing popularity. This tendency seems to be of great importance for promotion of international relations because it will contribute not only to improvement of elasticity and effectiveness of Poland's system, but also to enrichment of channels of trade and industrial cooperation.

As to the instruments of the central management of economic organizations, there may be expected a gradual and deep reevaluation of the role of the main direct instrument, i.e., allocation directives. Consequently its scope will be gradually limited and its forms and procedures rationalized.

Regulation of Current Processes

It is believed that there will be a tendency towards complete, or almost complete, resignation from the application of directives in regulation of the current processes. The only exception may be directives concerning export tasks and import restrictions. Most probably it will be necessary to maintain these directives at least for some further time, although in this field some solutions are also discussed which might ultimately lead to larger flexibility in the operational principles of economic organizations.

A matter of the greatest importance continues to be a transition to unconventional forms of directives which do not destroy the initiatives of organizations and verification role of the microeconomic calculus. This is why the proposals to apply directives which would represent the acceptance of propositions submitted by organizations appear to be especially attractive. The field in which these changes may be of special importance are the long-term expansion of organizations and also the general norms of economic effectiveness achieved by them. It seems that along with progress in both these fields there will be changing characteristics of partners in international relations. Partners representing Poland's side should become much more flexible and rational.

Motivation

Passing on to the problem of motivation, which is considered by many to be the most essential component of the central management of economic organizations, two directions of the present search for solutions should be mentioned. The first one is aimed at consolidation and rationalization of the principles on the basis of which the wage fund of the company is coupled with the increase in effectiveness that is achieved as its result. This may consolidate micro economic rationality and open the way for development of self-regulating processes.

The second direction consists in complementing the previously mentioned motivation system with a system of evaluation of managerial staff in economic organizations. In the system for the evaluation of executives there is perceived a big reserve of incentives. Its potential function is sometimes compared to the role played by the organization's drive towards survival in the environment of the private market which constitutes a powerful driving force releasing initiative and efficiency. Since the period of a relatively simplistic enthusiatic treatment of financial measures and micro economic rationality is over, a growing need for wider application of motivation solutions, which enrich and correct the financial measures, is now being recognized. It can be expected that the evolution of the motivation system in both these directions will stimulate the long-term dynamism of economic organizations, which is obviously comected closely with their possibilities in the field of foreign relations.

In the pricing system there are two interrelated tendencies:

1. Bigger than hitherto consistency in the application of transaction prices in import and export, i.e., the prices actually used in foreign transactions, which in the domestic system are not subject to direct interference by central authorities.

2. Smaller and limited interference by central authorities in the pricing policy in the internal markets through exclusion of certain areas of pricing policy from interference, as well as through rationalization of forms and tolls of this interference in those areas where interference is indispensable.

Some changes in the financial system of economic organizations, which are discussed at present, closely correspond to these tendencies. Briefly speaking these changes aim at the simplification of the system and elimination of subject regulations which result in bargaining and excessive freedom of manipulation. This tendency is reflected first of all in the following types of solutions:

1. Putting emphasis on the currency exchange rate at the equilibrium level. In this comection an interesting concept of temporary application of two exchange rates is discussed, one of which would be the so-called commercial exchange rate, which would be supplemented by certain corrective tools in foreign trade designed to prevent import of inflation from Western markets.

2. Consistent application of the import tariff list, compiled in accordance with principles and recommendations of the General Agreement on Tariff and Trade (GATT).

3. A considerable decrease of the role of turnover tax with the tax burden being correspondingly imposed on productive factors. This solution was first applied on a wider scale along with the introduction of the system of large economic organizations in 1973.

4. A growing application of the so-called "fund" rather than "tax" links between economic organizations and the state budget, which may generate desirable elasticity of the system and remove that need for progressive taxation.

5. A consistent elimination of the income effects of directive price changes, along with fixing new product prices, with economic organization taking the risk of effects of price changes negotiated among buyers and suppliers both in domestic and foreign markets.

It seems that these solutions will be able to promote effective rationalization of the economic organizations' activities in the field of international relations and increase the participation of the national economy in the international division of labor.

Horizontal Ties Among Economic Organizations

Finally, some problems of the evolution in the system of the so-called horizontal ties among economic organizations, or more widely in the sphere of the quality of the market should be discussed. The search for solutions leading to the establishment of the permanent buyer's market continues to be the main idea in presently conducted discussions. It would be of great importance for the economic organization's attitude toward export. On the other hand, however, it calls for a more active and open policy with respect to import. Better quality of the market may also be promoted by: securing a higher degree of flexibility with respect to horizontal ties; by eliminating both monopolies, which are operating at present on a wide scale; and eliminating the excessive administrative restrictions.

23 Comments

Richard Portes,
Allen J. Lenz,
Antonio Guccione,
Alan A. Brown,
and Morris Bornstein

As always, Peter Wiles's paper has been found imaginative, stimulating, and worthy of serious disagreement on some points.

Any definition which makes Saudi Arabia small is questionable for an economist. I agree with Wiles's rejection of the criteria of influence over the world money supply or price level. Another unsatisfactory definition, though closer to received theory, is control over the country's own money supply; on this basis, no command economy could be small. On the other hand, it is control over the terms of trade which does seem to be the main point of interest for economists. It is in this respect - not population - that the theory must distinguish between large and small countries, and the one cannot be deduced from the other, nor are they associated empirically with any regularity. Both the natural resource base and the level of industrial development and technological sophistication are too important as determinants of market power, and neither is that closely correlated with population.

Correspondingly, the allegation that economic theory has so far neglected smallness and is essentially "size-insensitive" is false. The existing theories of international trade and monetary relations leave much to be desired, but they surely do not ignore the economically important aspects of smallness. There is a great deal of literature on "small open economies," which has indeed been applied to CPEs (Wolf). This literature focuses on the small country's inability to influence its terms of trade, but also its capability for maintaining employment through exporting.

The point is that any definition must be appropriate to its purpose. We cannot deduce anything a priori from the definition of smallness according to population, yet the supposed consequences are reported to have economic implications. We should, therefore, start from those consequences (influence over terms of trade or domestic money supply, etc.) in empirical applications; we then establish whether they do or do not characterize a given country, whatever its population, and proceed from there. We must recognize that in many respects related to the importance of economics, Saudi Arabia is now considered big and India small.

Professor Wiles's discussion of the effect of per capita income on foreign trade participation confuses cross section and time series. His empirical concern is with cross country comparisons, but his a priori assertions relate to intertemporal changes in economic structure. He does in the end say this is an empirical question, and my impression of the time series data is that they are fairly unambiguous. Over the past three decades, for large countries and small, market economies and CPEs, the elasticities of trade turnover to GNP substantially exceed unity almost everywhere. And some recent trade theory suggests why this should be so as industrialization proceeds and per capita incomes rise (cf. Linder's theory of intra-industry trade in substitutable goods).

I think Professor Wiles may overestimate the difference between the SME and the SCE in liability to the distortions of "self-standingness." It is not at all clear that direct controls are worse in this regard than highly protective and irrational tariff systems, given the "self-standing" policy which motivates both. There is considerable evidence in the literature on effective protection for LDCs of activities with negative value added, i.e., investment decisions just as irrational and costly as Sztalinvaros.

He may also overestimate the impact of distorted relative prices on the effectiveness of specialization through trade. Ex ante comparative advantage doesn't seem to be very important or even meaningful in reference to intraindustry trade. Would even the "best" prices have shown ex ante whether Hungary should specialize in buses and import trucks, or the converse? Here, ex post increasing returns determine "comparative advantage."

Finally, the paper ignores some macroeconomic considerations which are believed to be important. Trade can serve as a "relief valve" at the macro level much more easily for the small country than the large, while conversely, the foreign trade responses of large countries to aggregate excess demand or supply have relatively little effect on domestic macro balance but very strong effects on their small trade partners. I think the trade flows of the small Eastern European countries should be examined much more as a response to domestic macro pressures and the forces which generate them, including, of course, "external" factors like changes in the terms of trade. Here, although it is true that the Preisaugleich shelters the SCE from hot money and the foreign trade multiplier, it is still proportionally more vulnerable, because of its high trade participation ratio to the real income effects of changes in the terms of trade, against which the Preisaugleich gives no protection.

Richard Portes

It is felt that Mr. Kamecki's paper does a very good job of identifying and cataloging the difficulties in measuring balance of payments constraints, the reasons for these constraints, and their impact on the choice of trading partners.

There is basic agreement with his assessment of future prospects, when he concludes that "in the nearest future an easing of the constraints does not seem very probable." His statement that "In the longer run, prospects for easing the SCEE balance of payments pressures seem to be much more favorable" also seems well reasoned.

Further, there is certainly agreement with the conclusion of his paper that, "the Socialist countries import demand is far from being satisfied, and if they have possibilities for proper expansion of their exports, they will expand their imports relatively fast as well."

But, of course, this leaves us with some very interesting questions: (a) How long is the "nearest future" (the period during which the constraints will not ease) going to be; (b) When do we reach the "longer run" when prospects seem more favorable; and (c) How tight are the constraints going to be in the meantime, or in other words, what is the level of the trade going to be in the years just ahead? These questions cannot be answered definitively, but it is necessary to make a few hopefully relevant points. To begin, a very brief review of how today's constraints evolved may be useful. There was a fast growth in East-West trade in the years 1971-76, but much of this growth was financed by accumulating Eastern debt, which now totals 48-49 billion, excluding the Cuban debt. Indeed, according to our estimates, the increase in net debt over the three-year period, 1975-77, was equal to approximately 30% of the value of EE imports during that period.

WHAT ABOUT THE FUTURE?

Starting from current levels of trade and debt, several possibilities seem likely over the next few years. Eastern debt could continue to increase; or to hold down debt growth, Eastern exports could increase while Eastern import growth was restrained or perhaps reversed; or we may see some combination of all three of these trends.

What seems most likely? Will Eastern debt continue to increase? Yes, in all likelihood. Bankers seem willing to lend more. Soviet EE debt is not seen to be high by most standards (debt to GNP, debt/export ratios, etc.). Bankers seem to have faith in the ability of centrally planned economies to service their debt, and given current liquidity of international money markets, additional credit seems available at reasonable rates.

But the Socialist countries seem to be rather fiscally conservative, so it would appear that while their debt will continue to grow in the future, it will probably grow more slowly than in the past, thus putting increased pressure on the export and import variables in controlling their balances of payments.

The centrally planned economies are presumed by bankers to have close control over foreign trade, but it has been observed and Mr. Kamecki's paper confirms this observation that they have much better control of imports than exports. In any event, if one favors an expanding trade between East and West, it will not be achieved by reducing Eastern imports. Rather, as Mr. Kamecki correctly points out in his paper, the crucial factor in future growth of the trade is the East's ability to export to the West, and the key question in determining future levels of East-West trade is, "How fast can Socialist countries' hard currency export capabilities grow?" To get some answers, the Bureau of East-West Trade has been researching Soviet and East European export capabilities.

SOVIET/EASTERN EUROPE (EE) EXPORT CAPABILITIES

From Kamecki's work only a few generalizations can be offered, which will have all the inherent problems of generalizations. With reference to the internal problems cited by Mr. Kamecki:

1. First of all, the most important single constraint seems to be one of supply; East European economies are stretched taut, and they have trouble coming up with items to export. In general, only a relatively slow growth is seen in key export areas that now supply the bulk of Eastern European exports. Further, there is a general inability to take advantage of fast breaking opportunities by reason of the slow response of CPE bureaucracies. There were even reports

last summer of frequent inability to fulfill counter trade contracts.
2. Second, much of recent Soviet/EE dollar value increases in exports has been due to increases in raw material prices, such as the fourfold price increase in oil. Such increases are not likely to be repeated in the near future.
3. It also is important to note the overwhelming importance of Soviet oil/gas supplies in the balance of payments picture of all the EE countries in years immediately ahead. About 45% of hard currency Soviet exports in recent years has come from mineral fuels. There will be obvious effects on Soviet exports if there are no further increases, let alone if exports decrease as per CIA predictions. The importance of Soviet energy supplies to EE countries at subsidized prices is also obvious, as are the effects on their balances of payments if they must turn increasingly to hard currency energy sources.
4. Finally, the existing quality, marketing, style, and servicing shortcomings that the Socialist countries all experience in varying degrees in selling to the West will take a long time to solve.

With reference to the external problems noted by Kamecki, the difficulties in entering new markets due to prejudices are probably declining, but East-West trade is subject to political as well as commercial forces. If political relations sour, e.g., Africa and SALT, both exports into Western markets and credit from Western bankers may be harder to achieve.

TRADE POLICY DISCRIMINATION

Mr. Kamecki mentioned quota restrictions on Eastern exports. He did not mention Western laws, which some see as serious threats to Western imports from nonmarket economies. For example, Western antidumping laws rely for their application on market set prices in the exporting country. Such prices are not available in nonmarket economies. As a substitute, costs may be reconstructed using the costs of a third market economy country, a procedure that effectively rules out the prospect of the nonmarket economy being considered the least cost producer.

THE WESTERN RECESSION

The effects of the Western recession on Socialist country exports to the West are important, but it seems that they can easily be overestimated. Rather, the fundamental constraint seems to be one of Eastern ability to supply saleable items. However, Western recovery would probably affect prices of several raw materials and have important effects in this way, as well as on quantities sold. On the other hand, there are also some positive effects of the Western recession from the Eastern viewpoint; e.g., credit is available in larger quantities and at better rates.

SUMMARY

Then through say 1985, a relatively slow growth in Soviet/EE export capabilities would be expected, even considering the Soviet/EE production expected in the early 1980s. This will probably be accompanied by a continued, but slower growth of debt.

Given these two estimates, then it must be concluded that Western exports to the East will also increase only gradually over the next several years.

Allen J. Lenz

The Dunajewski and Arnal paper, "A Criterion For Coalition in International Trade," is an original and interesting paper if not a completely convincing one. The main problem faced is a highly interesting one, i.e., "...to provide a basis for determining whether present coalitions are ... efficient on the purely economic level." The solution proposed is based on the rule that any two or more countries should enter into a coalition when this choice minimizes imbalance in planned world trade, and actual trade data for 39 countries are analyzed and some coalitions derived.

A difficulty with applied, normative studies is that when their results show the real world to be optimal, the reader is left with the impression that little has been accomplished. On the other hand, if the gap between reality and the implications of the model is too wide, one suspects that some constraints have been missed. The paper under discussion may lean somewhat in the second direction. For example, one reads that Mexico and Romania on the one hand and

Finland and Singapore on the other should join in rather improbable coalitions. To a certain extent these results are due to the exploratory nature of the analysis, and the authors carefully qualify their results, "If the need arose, we could establish an additional criterion of proximity which would take geographical distance into account. The criterion of maximization of imbalance reduction would then be supplemented..." Also some brief reference is made to the possible effects of aggregation over commodities.

However, there are some basic difficulties which would require more careful discussion. A few of these are now pointed out. First, a clear definition of a "coalition" is missing. Second, it is assumed by the authors that in some sense the minimization of imbalance implies the maximization of efficiency. A relation between the two above criteria is impossible to establish, in particular since the analysis is complicated by the assumption that the system is not a competitive one, i.e., "... countries [in a coalition are assumed to] ... grant trade preference to each other...." However if perfect competition is assumed to simplify the analysis, there is no reason why a country which imports a large amount of a certain good should prefer to buy it from a large producer. In reality, I suspect that coalitions, if economically motivated, are based on the possibility for a given region of realizing economies of scale by specializing in certain lines of production, while giving up others in favor of its partners. However, it may well be that in centrally planned economies the minimization of imbalance is, in its own merits, an important criterion.

Finally, it is assumed that the matrices X and M of exports and imports remain unchanged throughout the various rounds of the minimization algorithm. But this would imply a more or less unrealistic assumption that the export and import functions are inelastic with respect to all of their arguments.

In conclusion, the above examples suggest that Dunajewski and Arnal should elaborate with added precision the economics underlying their method. Then their results would turn out to be not only interesting, but extremely useful.

Antonio Guccione

The paper by Professor Lorenz, "Parallels Between Different Systems in International Economic Relations," is an ambitious undertaking. In the first part, he "propose(s) to widen the range of analysis with respect to comparative economic systems as well as to international economics." Then, in the second part, he presents some specific parallels.

The author of this paper is no timid scholar. He firmly dismisses both "the heritage of comparative economic systems analysis" and "orthodox trade theory." Instead of the usual approaches to comparative economic systems, he offers four "systemic components."

First, there is the "development component," which is initially used to identify "the Third World as an economic system in its own right." Does this mean that the study of economic development is simply an aspect of economic systems anslysis? Specialists in neither of these two fields are likely to accept such a view. The author himself appears uneasy about his identification of economic underdevelopment with a specific system, but his further comments about the matter only tend to make his point more obscure. He offers "from a theoretical point of view" three observations. The first two points are fairly clear: (a) "the majority of the Third World countries are mixed economies," and (b) "development is hardly the privilege of a single system." The conclusion of the second point is obvious enough: "We find different 'stages' of development among market economies of the West as well as among CMEA countries." But how does this lead to the third observation: "Thirdly, the very special point of the foregoing general statement is of course the interpretation of the average CMEA-country as a kind of underdeveloped country...."? How can the observation that there are different stages of development among CMEA countries lead to the observation that the average CMEA country is a kind of underdeveloped country? If this is a paradox, and not a contradiction, no hint is given how the paradox might be resolved.

The second systemic component is that of economic policy: "... there have always existed more or less identifiable subsystems in respect to economic policies." Somehow, this economic policy component is associated with Kindleberger's term of the "capacity to transform," which is then related to Harry Johnson's "nationalistic economic policies," and in turn this is connected to a "propensity to react by neomercantilism." It is unfortunately not easy to follow the logical thread connecting the concepts cited in connection with Kindleberger and Johnson which lead to neomercantilism. Students of comparative economic systems might find in this section some suggestions regarding the interactions between the environment and economic policy, although the author does not refer to the literature that attempts to separate conceptual economic policy from the environment and from systemic features of an economy.

Third is the "area component," which leads to the question, "Why do ... [economic systems] show a propensity to regionalize?" The author suggests that the reasons are both political and economic: "Like small countries, economic systems based on too small an area are often more open than it seems tolerable from the point of view of the system's 'purity' and efficiency." Today, however, one is tempted to question the general validity of this proposition. Surely, as we approach the end of the 1970s, we no longer have only one or two isolated islands of economic systems, such as Yugoslavia, Albania, and Cuba. More and more systemic mavericks appear and manage to survive in areas that would seem unreasonably small from an economic standpoint. It is ironic that the current trend toward systemic diversity, regardless of area, should be entirely ignored in a paper that particularly castigates traditional analyses and theories because of their unrealistic abstractions.

The author finally presents the fourth systemic component, what he calls "a missing link" if we want to evaluate economic systems in the context of world economies. This if the "international component." Under this heading he includes both intra systemic economic relations (e.g., integration policies, planned specialization, etc.) and inter-systemic international economic relations. It appears from the discussion that his systemic component is difficult to separate from the other three. For instance, the international component blends into the "development policy often identical with regional policy."

Overall, the analysis of these systemic components tends to be fuzzy. It would have been clearer to refer to some explicit definitions and accepted models of comparative economic systems. The study of this field did make some progress since Harry Johnson's comments a decade ago. Economic systems are not simply differentiated only according to capitalism, Socialism, market (decentralized), or planned (centralized) economies. Refer, for instance, to the decision-theoretical approach of Koopmans-Montias-Neuberger, (1) which enables one to identify systems that may be decentralized in decision making, but centralized in their informational structure (e.g., stock markets). This framework also clarifies the conceptual features of an economic system, as distinguished from policy variables and environmental elements and shifts.

Less will be said about the author's attempt to "widen the range of analysis with respect to ... international economics." It appears that the section "Modern versus Orthodox Trade Theory" tends to oversimplify the contribution of traditional trade theory, and one may wonder to what extent "new approaches ... since about 1965" represent a radical departure from orthodox theory. The paper, for instance, cites Richard Caves to show that "orthodox theory mainly wants to know about homogeneous competitive goods ... [and] merely substitutuve exchange has required theoretical interest." In contrast, Professor Lorenz approves of Harry Johnson's comment which calls for a nontraditional approach. Now one will readily agree that Harry Johnson was frequently outspoken, but not always critical of traditional theory. In fact, he has shared with Richard Caves the distinction of having made single contributions to the modern theory of international trade by building upon orthodox theory. In any case, whether there is a Methodenstreit in trade theory, real or imaginary, to promote the polemics is beyond the scope of these comments.

Professor Lorenz rightly stresses that trade flows differentiating goods by "quality and functions" should be considered. As he points out, complementary trade flows are particularly significant quantitatively as well as strategically. It is not so easy, however, to separate traded goods into the five different categories, as described in the paper. Consider, for example, how one can distinguish goods in the first category, "ordinary competitive Heckscher-Ohlin goods," from those in the fifth category, "differentiated goods." Who is to decide whether goods are homogeneous or differentiated? In his table, Professor Lorenz refers to Chamberlin. According to Chamberlin's definition, however, product differentiation can only be determined by taking into account "all conditions surrounding the sale." Therefore, it is virtually impossible for products produced in different countries to be homogeneous. To sure, the degree of differentiation can vary immensely, and one may set categories of more or less differentiated goods; e.g., as Tobin suggested, one may use the cross elasticity of demand as a criterion. In any case, there is no longer a sharp dichotomy between "homogeneous" and "differentiated" goods. It can be similarly argued that the establishment of the other categories of goods is also more or less arbitrary.

As for the different functions of trade, again it is a useful conceptual approach, but sharp lines of demarcation among various functions are difficult to maintain. Lorenz distinguishes between two main sets of functions with several subdivisions. The first main set of functions is "marginal reallocation [of resource];...means of competition in domestic markets including ... (Kontrollfunktion)." The second set is "a growth-function," which is greatly elaborated. The growth functions on the export side is "translate(d) ... into the old vent for surplus version. This function may appear, for different reasons, in different economic systems; in any case, "the common denominator of all cases seems to be the mobilization of otherwise idle resources...." He adds that "...it indicates something of a malfunctioning of the respective systems...."

On the import side, Lorenz presents "the supply version of the growth function." This includes "gap filling" in orthodox planned economies, but trade may be used also for short-term bottlenecks and in LDCs which are also less able to handle the transformation problem. Trade may be also needed for "long-term gap filling ... of complementary input imports." This function has been relevant for East and South, but more recently also for the West.

This discussion of the different functions of trade is clear and concise. It presents straightforward parallels between different systems.

The second part of the paper is devoted to the discussion of some specific parallels between systems in international relations. Professor Lorenz acknowledges the view of specialists that for a decade or so there has been no serious quarrel in the East with traditional theory of trade and commercial policy; i.e., "The law of comparative advantage has been accepted in principle..." He refers to various examples of rapproachment as, "perhaps of a dialectical process between reforms and foreign trade." Reluctant to accept, however, simple or superficial conclusions, he offers to "look for an analysis at more sophisticated levels." The author briefly refers to various contributions, but particularly stresses what he calls "the new economics of intra industry trade strongly based on increasing returns [which is] ... applicable practically to all systems."

Under the heading of "Risks of Specialization," Professor Lorenz outlines important similarities between the CMEA trade, as discussed by Neuberger, (2) and trade in market economies and LDCs especially, Grubel and Lloyd, Intra-Industry Trade. (3) Unfortunately, the interesting observations are so heavily mixed with cryptic comments that even some of the most useful points become obscure. Parallels are stressed to the point that even observed systemic differences become similarities.

The lines of argument do not become easier to follow as we approach the end of the paper. Thus, under the heading of "Some Macro Aspects of Complementarity," the first point begins with a statement by Neuberger providing systemic parallels. In fact, however, the quotation stresses a systemic difference: "planners must ask themselves questions that private entrepreneurs need not ask." (4) What the paragraph seems to imply is that the systemic difference observed by Neuberger in the early 1960s have given way to similar difficulties in both CMEA and EEC integration. However, as noted by Fallenbuchl, similar difficulties have been encountered by the process of integration under the two systems, not because systemic differences disappear, but because similar national policies have been adopted regardless of them. (5)

Some of the other points which try to stress systemic parallels are more obscure, such as the references to "Type A and C goods in Gray's classification" and "the narrow lines of international trade and superficial product differentiation of consumer goods in developed countries." One may also object to the presentation of systemic parallels and "remarkable correspondence," when one "translates the North-South inter-systemic special relationship into the intrasystemic East-East context. In the traditional North-South relations, the peripheries (colonies) were obliged to provide primary products for imperial centers, while the dependency of the peripheries in CMEA integration was maintained by a flow of primary products from the center, i.e., the Soviet Union.

Determined to find a systemic parallel in trade, Professor Lorenz establishes four Procrustean cases of trade relations. The first two cases he calls "symmetrical" (respectively, complementary and substitutive) and the other two are "assymetrical." Complementary trade flows, whether symmetrical or assymetrical, are "without terms of trade disputes." Thus, for example, "no essential ... terms of trade problems are raised ... in East European intra-CMEA exports, particularly to the Soviet Union." This alleged agreement about terms of trade is attributed to balanced reciprocal demand. Terms of trade disputes appear, according to the argument, when reciprocal demand is unbalanced (including conflicts about investment financing) and with substitutive imports of Hechscher-Ohlin goods (low wage type).

Alan A. Brown

The title of Professor Mujzel's paper, "The Influence of the Socioeconomic System on East-West Relations: Poland," raises an important question, but the paper itself, though presenting interesting information and insights, does not go very far toward answering it. His discussion of Polish foreign trade problems is informative, but his explanation of how reforms in the Polish economic system can be expected to overcome them is less clear.

The first portion of the paper points out Poland's efforts since 1971 to take a greater part in the "international division of labor" by increasing its economic relations with Western industrialized capitalist market economies. In this connection, "industrial cooperation" of various types was emphasized as a vehicle of technological transfer to modernize Polish industrial production, for sale on the domestic market as well as for export to both the CMEA area and the world market.

However, in Mujzel's view, these efforts have not been successful, partly for external and partly for internal reasons. In the external category he includes both bad weather, which reduced Polish agricultural production, and recession and protectionism in the West, which curtailed Polish exports. Among the internal factors hampering Polish exports are shortages on the domestic market, poor quality of Polish manufactured goods, and the lack of aggressive promotion by foreign trade organizations.

As a result, both the level and the structure of Polish exports are unsatisfactory. Export growth lagged behind the expansion of imports, the balance of payments deficit increased, and foreign debt to Western banks rose until annual service absorbed over one-fourth of Poland's hard-currency earnings, according to Western estimates. Furthermore, within total exports, fuels have a larger share and engineering products a smaller share than intended by Polish planners.

The second portion of the paper reports, briefly and in very general terms, on some of the ideas of a small group of specialists who examined possible changes in the Polish economic system intended to improve the performance of the economy, including its export sector. The include the following:

1. Reducing the scope and detail of central planning by replacing, to an unstated extent, direct control through specific binding "directives" and indirect control through more general financial "parameters" like taxes.

2. Modifying managerial performance indicators and incentives to encourage a longer time in decision making and more risk-taking.

3. Relating the level and structure of domestic prices more closely to foreign, i.e., world market, prices through more realistic exchange rates and the use, in the domestic evaluation of exports and imports, of special "transactions prices" equivalent to foreign prices.

However, Mujzel does not explain these and other reform proposals in the detail needed to permit an analysis of their nature or an appraisal of their possible effects on output, cost, quality, investment, innovation, and the level, composition, and geographical distribution of foreign trade.

The design of a sufficiently comprehensive and profound economic reform in an Eastern European, Socialist, centrally planned economy is a formidable task, involving years rather than months of study and negotiation by technical experts and politicians. In turn, the subsequent implementation of a reform requires a determined commitment by a unified political leadership, sufficient "slack" (rather than "tension") in the domestic economy, and a favorable environment in the world economy. (6)

Even in Hungary, where many of these conditions were fulfilled and many of the systemic changes mentioned by Mujzel were adopted, the path of economic reform was far from smooth, and formal and informal central intervention in the economy is much greater than intended when the New Economic Mechanism was inaugurated in 1968. (7)

Moreover, the record of several past attempts at economic reform in Poland is not encouraging. Reform blueprints (models) were incomplete and inconsistent, and they either were not implemented or were soon aborted. (8) Ths most recent reform, based on the creation or large economic organizations, is an excellent example. It was introduced on a limited scale in 1973, but was already substantially curtailed by 1975 as a result of inherent deficiencies, unfavorable developments in the world economy, and internal political problems. (9)

In Poland's present difficult economic and political situation, it is not clear what changes in the economic and political situation, or in place of changes in economic policy, (10) can offer enough promise of improving economic performance to win the necessary political support. The reforms advocated by system remodelers, for example, linking domestic prices more closely to world market prices, making profit the dominant enterprise performance indicator, and establishing new incentive schemes which reward by widening income differentials, appear as attractive technical improvements in the economic mechanism. But they may stand little chance of adoption and wholehearted implementation by a divided political leadership, which considers "muddling through" with the present admittedly unsatisfactory economic system less hazardous than risking the economic, social, and political consequences of a genuine economic reform.

Morris Bornstein

NOTES

1. Tjalling C. Koopmans and John Michael Montias, "On the Description and Comparison of Economic Systems" in Comparison of Economic Systems: Theoretical and Methodological Approaches, Alexander Eckstein, ed. (Berkeley: University of California Press, 1971), pp. 27-78; Egon Neuberger and William J. Duffy, Comparative Economic Systems: A Decision-Making Approach (Boston: Allyn and Bacon, 1976).

2. Egon Neuberger, "International Division of Labor in CMEA: Limited Regret Strategy," American Economic Review, 54 (1964), p. 513-14.

3. Herbert G. Grubel and P. J. Lloyd, Intra-Industry Trade: The Theory and Measurement of International Trade in Differentiated Products (London: Macmillan Press, 1975).

4. Neuberger, "International Division of Labor."

5. Zbigniew M. Fallenbuchl, "Industrial Policy and Economic Integration in CMEA and EEC," Discussion Papers Series, no. 41 (1976), Department of Economics, University of Windsor, to be published in Paul Marer and John Michael Montias, eds., East European Integration and East-West Trade (Bloomington: Indiana University Press, forthcoming).

6. For a comprehensive discussion of the design and implementation of economic reforms in Eastern Europe, see Morris Bornstein, "Economic Reform in Eastern Europe," in East European Economies Post-Helsinki. (A Compendium of Papers Submitted to the Joint Economic Committee, U.S. Congress, 95th Congress, 1st Session) (Washington, D.C.: United States Government Printing Office, 1977), pp. 102-34.

7. Cf. Richard Portes, "Hungary: Economic Performance, Policy and Prospects," ibid., pp. 766-96.

8. The fullest account is Janusz G. Zielinski, Economic Reform in Polish Industry (London: Oxford University Press, 1973).

9. The reform blueprint is explained in detail in Anna Darska, "Le systeme des enterprises pilotes en Pologne," Revue d'Etudes Comparatives Est-Ouest, 6, no. 2 (June 1975), pp. 73-135. Its operation and fate are evaluated in Zbigniew M. Fallenbuchl, "The Polish Economy in the 1970s," in East European Economies Post-Helsinki, pp. 838-46. For a comparison of Polish and Hungarian reforms, see Janusz G. Zielinski, "On System Remodelling in Poland: A Pragmatic Approach," Soviet Studies, 30, no. 1 (January 1978), pp. 3-37.

10. On the differences and the relationships between systemic and policy changes, see Bornstein, "Economic Reform," pp. 108-9, and Antoni Chawluk, "Economic Policy and Economic Reform," Soviet Studies, 26, no. 1 (January 1974), pp. 98-119.

Name Index

Abonyi, A., 48
Adahl, A., 252
Adam, G., 49
Adler-Karlsson, G., 48, 409, 414
Amann, R., 50, 369
Annerstedt, J., 49
Apel, E., 316
Arkwright, F., 86
Askanas, B., Askanas H., 71

Baban, R., 107
Balassa, B., 147, 149, 166, 167, 235, 404, 413
Baumer, M., 74, 107-110
Beck, C., 298
Bergsten, C. I., 109
Berliner, J., 50
Berthoin, G., 109
Bhagwati, J. N., 49
Bell, D., 37, 48
Bettelheim, C., 48
Bogomolov, O. T., 18, 148, 162-163, 166
Bognar, J., 109
Bolz, K., 70, 110
Bornstein, M., 441
Brada, J. C., 291

Brainard, L. J., 72, 165, 168, 169, 217, 283, 291
Brami, M., 392
Brezhnev, L. I., 113
Brougher, J., 72
Brown, A. A., 150, 167, 409, 410
Brown, Archie, 217
Bryson, P. J., 411, 412
Bucy, J. F., 217

Carter, J., President, 33
Caves, R., 411, 435
Ceausescu, N., 30, 33
Chamberlin, E. H., 436
Chawluk, A., 441
Chilas, J. G., 412
Cooper, J., 50
Cooper, R. N., 70, 72, 109, 410

Davies, K. C., 216
Davies, R. W., 50, 369
Delbruch, J., 107
Dhesi, A., 304, 310
Doyle, N., 110
Duffy, J., 169
Dupuy, T. N., 275

Ehlermann, C. -D., 75

Elias, A., 215
Ellis, H. S., 401
Eltis, W. A., 412

Fallenbuchl, Z.M., 405, 406, 414, 437, 441
Fekete, J., 108, 292
Frank, A. G., 34, 47
Franzmeyer, F., 413
Friesen, C., 48, 70
Frobel, F., 49

Galbraith, J. K., 252
Ghosh, D., 217
Goldman, M. I., 73, 396, 410
Gray, H. P., 396, 397, 405, 410, 412
Grubel, H. G., 401, 410, 412, 437
Gutman, P., 86
Gustavsson, R., 49, 50

Haberler, G., 148, 150, 167
Hamm, H., 275
Hanson, P., 47, 48, 50, 73, 349
Hardt, J., 78, 107, 167
Harrod, R., 402
Hasenpflug, 108
Hayden, E. W., 50
Heckscher, E., 396, 397, 406, 436
Heinrichs, J., 49
Heusse, E., 405, 413
Hirsch, F., 110, 397
Hirschman, A. O., 73, 396, 410, 411-412
Hohmann, H. H., 48
Holesowsky, V., 409-412
Holloway, J., 48
Holzman, F. D., 108, 412
Hosoy A, C., 109
Hoxha, E., 259, 274-275
Huber, S. J.,

Hufbauer, G. C., 412

Illig, G., 75

Jacobsen, H. -D., 74, 107-109
Janossy, F., 48
Jelacic, J. E., 215
Johnson, H. G., 393, 409, 434, 435, 436
Jones, R. W., 411

Kaiser, K., 109
Kaldor, N., 49
Kaser, M. C., 48, 217, 256, 259, 274, 275
Kellezi, 259
Kerr, C., 37, 48
Khruschev, N., 313
Kindleberger, C. P., 394, 409, 434
Klotten, N., 410
Knirsch, P., 71, 72
Knorr, K., 409
Ko, S. K., 275, 276, 413, 414
Koh, B. C., 275
Kojima, K., 402, 412
Koopmans, T., 435
Kosaka, N., 109
Kotarbinski, T., 370, 392
Kreye, O., 49
Kupper, S., 75
Kuznets, S., 315

Lambrecht, H., 75
Lange, O., 48
Lara, J., 180
Lawrence, P. R., 143
Lenin, V. I., 313, 316
Levcik, F., 71, 100, 164, 167, 216
Lindbeck, A., 409
Linder, S. B., 407, 414, 428
Lipsey, R., 167, 405, 413
Lloyd, P. J., 410, 412, 437

NAME INDEX

Long, O., 107
Lorenz, D., 397, 410, 411, 413
Lorsch, J. W., 143

Machlup, F., 166, 410
Marer, P., 49, 143, 167, 169, 193, 216, 292
Martos, 74
Maximova, M. M., 147, 162-163, 166, 308, 315
McMillan, C., 72, 74, 149, 151-152, 167, 168, 364
Meade, J. E., 318, 319, 339
Melson, K., 72
Mesa, Lago, C., 292
Metzler, L. A., 401
Michalet, C., 49
Montias, J. M., 49, 168, 435, 440
Morlat, G., 392
Morse, E., 110
Muller, F., 71, 108
Murphy, G. G. S., 275
Murray, R., 49
Mushakoji, K., 109
Myint, H., 411
Myrdal, G., 402

Nemschak, F., 410
Neuberger, E., 156, 163, 167, 402, 405, 409, 410, 412, 413, 435, 437, 440
Nurkse, R., 406, 411, 414
Nye, J. S., 73
Nykryn, J., 252

Ohlin, B., 396, 397, 406, 436
Ortona, E., 109
Owen, H., 109

Palloix, C., 49
Pearson, L. B., 304, 310
Pecsi, K., 168
Picciotto, S., 48

Pinder, J., 410
Polaczek, S., 292
Portes, R., 72, 74, 143, 166, 441
Prebisch, R., 79
Preiswerk, R., 72
Pryor, F. L., 292

Quambusch, L., 108

Raczkowski, S., 292
Radice, H., 49
Raffel, H., 215
Rakosi, M., 311, 312
Rakowski, M., 48
Rall, W., 410
Ravasz, K., 143
Reynolds, L. G., 409
Ricardo, D., 297, 305, 397
Richta, R., 47, 48, 50
Robertson, D. H., 401
Robinson, E. A. G., 298, 301, 315
Ropers, N., 107
Rostow, W. W., 37, 48
Rubin, M., 215

Sanders, A. J. K., 275
Saunders, C. T., 252, 414
Schaetzel, J. R., 109
Schmidt, A., 72
Schuller, A., 413
Schumacher, E. F., 297, 315
Schumpeter, J. A., 404
Searing, M. E., 215
Shehu, Mehmet, 253, 259, 274
Shlaim, A., 107, 315
Schnytzer, A., 274
Shonfield, A., 109
Simai, M., 49
Simons, H. C., 315
Slama, J., 69
Smith, Adam, 397
Smith, Alan, 316
Smith, M. H., 364, 369

Snell, E. M., 73
Stalin, J., 311
Stankovski, J., 72, 100
Stepan, K., 252
Sunkel, O., 49
Sylvain, I. J., 49

Taylor, F., 48
Teal, R., 215
Thalheim, K. C., 48
Thayer, C. A., 276
Theodhosi, 259
Tinbergen, J., 407
Tobin, J., 436
Tucker, R. C., 217

Vajda, I., 49

Ushiba, N., 109

Weiller, J., 392
Wilczynski, J., 143, 252, 396, 410
Wiles, P. J. D., 71, 218, 291, 315, 316, 396, 410
Wionczek, M. S., 414
Wipf, L. J., 291
Wolf, T. A., 72, 215, 291, 427

Yannopoulos, G., 107

Zellentin, G., 107
Zieleniewski, J., 370, 392
Zielinski, J. G., 48, 441
Zoeter, J. P., 72

Subject Index

Administrative restrictions and directives, 309, 311-314, 426, 439
Advanced capitalist countries. See Industrial countries
Africa, 32, 431
Air France, 114
Albania, 253-260, 262, 272-273, 313-314, 435
Algeria, 386
All European Conference on Transportation, 104
Antidumping laws, 431
Antitrust legislation, 129
Arab oil producing export countries, 24
Areas of recent settlements, 399-400
Argentina, 299
Asia, 31, 370
Australia, 226, 269, 305-306
Austria, 55, 114, 195, 201, 224-225, 240, 282, 288, 301, 303, 306, 326, 364
Autarky, 76, 299-300, 311-312
Auto-Dacia (Romania), 115

Balance of payments, 25, 63, 160-161, 317-334, 429-432

Balance of power, 53-54
Bangladesh, 299, 309
Barter trade, 113
Battle Act, 26
Belgium, 303, 306, 354
Belgrade, meeting, 95
Bilateralism, 99, 101, 104, 150, 163, 174-175, 200, 213, 278, 284-285, 303, 313
Bolshevik Revolution, 200
Bowmal, 286
Brazil, 34, 44, 226, 299
Bretton Woods International Monetary System, 41, 94, 101, 106
Britain. See United Kingdom
Bulgaria, 13, 10-11, 32, 55, 70, 114, 158-159, 176, 290, 313-314, 417
Bureau of East-West Trade, 344, 430
Buy-back agreements. See Compensation agreements.
Canada, 70, 84, 201, 226, 230, 282, 299, 302-303, 306
Capital flows, 19, 64-66, 93, 98-99 See also Credits
Central Intelligence Agency (CIA), 187, 431

Central planning, 35, 99, 148, 285, 311, 313-314, 415, 422-424, 425, 439
Chemical industry, 114, 139-141, 177-178
Chemie Linz AG, 114
China, 253-254, 256, 257, 259-260, 262-264, 265, 268, 272-273, 299, 395
Citroen, 115
CMEA (Council for Mutual Economic Assistance), 11, 13, 20-22, 61, 144-147, 150-152, 155-158, 162, 164-165, 170, 172-173, 175, 236, 238, 240, 313, 347, 354, 370, 394, 399, 402-403, 405-408, 434
Comprehensive Program, 20-21, 155-156, 202
countries, agriculture, 5-6
and the Third World. See East-South relations
dependence on trade with the West, 62-63, 67-69, 144-145, 152
economic performance, 6-8, 54
elimination of disparities in the level of development, 10-11, 13, 147
energy, fuel, and raw materials, 7, 79-80, 144-145
international prices, 22, 150, 155-156
joint investment projects, 20-21, 154, 243, 322
joint planning, 148-149
mutual trade, 8-11, 21-22, 24, 150-151, 155-156, 162-163, 164-165, 243-244, 289, 406-407, 437
specialization agreements, 155-157, 164, 243-244
transfer of technology, 8, 11, 20-21

CoCom. See Coordinating Committee.
Cold war, 38, 94, 150, 198, 229, 324
Colombia, 299
Command economy. See Administrative restrictions and directives.
Commercial policy, 103, 232-235, 238, 240, 393
See also tariffs; Quotas; Direct controls; nontariff barriers; and Trade barriers
Commodity and money relations, 163
Commodity inconvertibility, 99-100
Communist parties in the West, 198-199, 213
Comparative advantages, 21, 36, 309-311, 428-429
Compensation agreements, 23-24, 66-67, 114, 123-124, 152, 187-188, 196, 363
Complementarity, 404-407
Complete plants, delivery of. See turn-key plants
Components and parts, 231-232, 246, 248-249
Confederation of British Industry (CBI), 177
Conference on International Economic Cooperation (CIEC), 93-94, 105-106

Conference on Security and Cooperation in Europe (CSCE), 95, 105
Conseil Economique et Social France), 198
Contract negotiation, 121-122
Convergence theory, 37-39
Convertibility, 173
Convertible currencies, 321-323
Cooperation agreements. See Industrial cooperation

SUBJECT INDEX

Cooperation in planning, 250
Cooperation of production. See Industrial cooperation
Coordinating Committee (CoCom), 195, 202, 205, 213, 282-283, 354
Copper, 80
Co-production, 152, 158-159, 177-178, 242, 246, 249, 364
Council for Mutual Economic Assistance. See CMEA
Counter trade, 113-114, 125, 131-132, 135, 140, 142, 363
Credits, 27, 63-64, 327-328
  See also official credit support
CSEPEL Automobile Works, 115
Cuba, 312, 429, 435
Cultural civilizable dependence, 53
Currency exchange rate, 425
Custom union theory, 404
Customs barriers. See tariffs
Czechoslovakia, 6, 38, 55, 60, 61, 70, 101, 114, 136, 161, 224, 236, 238, 241, 243, 245-246, 248-249, 260, 288, 290, 417

Danube River, 32
Davy Power Gas, 115
Decentralization, 313-314, 421-422, 423-424, 426, 439
Denmark, 306
Dependencia theory, 58
Detente, 13, 68, 94, 103, 201-202, 206, 207, 227, 283-284
Developing countries. See less developed countries
Development level, 229-230, 233
Development strategy, 18, 30, 78-79, 319, 415-416, 435
Differentiated goods, 436
Direct controls, 428
Discrimination, 21-23, 231-232, 308, 431

East European chambers of commerce, 177
East Germany. See German Democratic Republic
East-South economic relations, 15, 16-17, 34-35, 79-81, 91, 105-106, 157-158, 436
East-West Development Bank, 101
East-West economic relations, 34, 36, 40-41, 55-58, 60-64, 65-66, 67-68, 92, 96, 101, 105-106, 111, 116-118, 140, 151-155, 161-162, 174-175, 176-177, 198, 228-229, 245, 248, 250-251, 334, 407, 417, 421-423, 431
East-West technology gap, 152, 323
East-West Trade Advisory Committee, 172
Eastern European Business Committee, 139, 171
Economic dependence, 52-54, 62-63, 82-83
Economic integration, 395, 403-405, 407
  See also CMEA integration
Economic rationality, 35-36
Economic reforms, 96, 313-314, 439-440
Economies of scale, 309, 311, 423
Economistic approach, 36-37
Ecuador, 115
EEC. See European Economic Community
Eire, 306
Electric Components for Motor Cars Company, 158
Employment policies in the West, 62
Energy crisis, 1973-74, 15, 18-19, 33
Energy sources, 26, 79-80, 94, 123-124, 431
Eurodollar market, 154

European Economic Community
(EEC), 25, 63, 92, 92-95,
102, 105, 147-149, 155,
224, 234-235, 268-269, 271-
272, 306, 308, 312, 325-
326, 329, 370, 394-395,
402-405, 407
  agricultural marketing regulations, 63, 224
  CMEA agreement, 104-105
Exploitation, 299
Export capabilities of CMEA
  countries, 430-432
Export competitiveness, 76-78
Export oriented development, 44,
  77-78, 332-333

Factor endowment, 299-301
  See also natural resources endowment
Factor movements, 406
FIAT, 78, 158
Financing of East-West trade,
  19, 23, 64, 140, 195-196, 278
  See also Credits; and Official
  credit support
Financial dependence, 53, 63-64
Finland, 55, 158
Floating exchange rates, 42, 331
Fluctuations in the world economy.
  See World economy
Foreign aid, 16, 31, 42
Foreign credits. See Credits
Foreign capital, penetration of,
  14
Foreign direct investment, 13
Foreign Trade Book of Vietnam,
  269, 271
Foreign trade corporation in
  Eastern Europe. See Foreign
  trade organizations
Foreign trade monopoly, 23, 69,
  97
Foreign trade multiplier, 428-429

Foreign trade organizations (FTOs)
  in Eastern Europe, 178, 186,
  420
Foreign trade policy. See Commercial policy
"Foxbat" aircraft, 200
France, 38, 80, 174-175, 176, 198,
  201, 271-272, 282, 298-299, 305,
  360, 364
Free trade, 22-23, 37, 97-98,
  234-235

Gap between the industrialized and
  the developing countries, 5, 29
GATT. See General Agreement on
  Tariffs and Trade.
GDR. See German Democratic
  Republic
General Agreement on Tariffs and
  Trade (GATT), 63, 92-95, 97-
  98, 106, 109, 425
General Motors (GM), 159
Geneva, 176
Geographical factors, 223-225,
  285-286, 305-306
German Democratic Republic
  (GDR), 6, 55, 62, 70, 114, 136,
  161-162, 224, 288, 306, 313-
  314, 386, 417
Germany, Federal Republic of
  (FRG), 55, 59, 62, 69, 158-159,
  201, 207, 209-210, 224, 239,
  262, 282, 283, 284, 288, 298-
  300, 306, 360
Global crisis. See world economic
  crisis.
Global interdependence, 18
Global rationalization of industry,
  44
Gosplan of the Soviet Union, 186
Greece, 306, 308
Group of 77, 31, 93, 102
Group of Ten, 93
Group of Twenty, 93

SUBJECT INDEX

Hard currencies, 46, 179, 287, 322-323
Heckscher-Ohlin goods, 398, 406-407, 435-436, 438
Helsinki Final Act, 23
High technology products, 135-136, 138, 157-159, 344, 354, 360, 364, 366-367, 418-419
Historical factors, 224-225
Holland. See Netherlands
Human rights, 95
Hungary, 6, 8, 36, 55, 63, 66, 77-79, 98, 101, 114-115, 153, 157-159, 164, 175-176, 220, 228, 224-225, 227-235, 286-287, 288, 311, 313-314, 329, 417, 439

IBM (International Business Machines), 172
Iceland, 306
Ideology, 37-38, 68, 69, 96-97, 186, 253, 305-306
Ikarus Czepel Motor Company, 157-158
IMF. See International Monetary Fund
Import substitution, 44, 163, 330-331, 333
Indebtedness of Eastern Europe, 46, 64-65, 92, 333, 429-432
India, 299
Indonesia, 299
Industrial cooperation, 13-14, 45-46, 58, 76-77, 80, 111-113, 120-121, 129, 140-142, 157-158, 174, 176, 177-178, 233-235, 246, 289, 290, 363, 416-417, 438
Industrial countries, 13-14, 16, 34, 41-42, 79-80, 91-92, 96, 105-106, 232, 234-235, 245-246, 278, 344-345, 394, 399, 403, 415-419, 421-422, 438

Industrial policies, 79-80, 103, 231-232
Industrial structure, 81, 230, 231-232, 234, 288-289, 300-301, 428
Industrialization, 10-11, 324, 428
Infant industry, 301
Inflation in the world economy, 18, 36, 42, 63, 425-426
  See also World economy
Integrated raw material progress, 93-94, 113
Integration policies. See Economic integration
Interdependence, 19, 41, 51-55, 65, 67-69, 81-82, 92, 399, 402
International division of labor, 21, 29, 44-45, 47, 76-79, 236, 406-407, 415, 426, 438
International economic cooperation, 18, 20-21, 23, 26-27, 30, 33
International economic order, 14-16, 19, 29-30, 33, 78-79, 92-97, 101-107
International economic organizations, 92-97, 101-103, 175-176
International Energy Agency (IEA), 105
International financial assistance. See Foreign aid
International Investment Bank, 154
International monetary agreements, 103, 425
International Monetary Fund (IMF), 92-95, 101-102, 106, 299, 318
International policies, 26-27, 39-40, 52-53, 69, 240, 431
International specialization of production. See Specialization
International Trade Organization, 94, 102
International trade theory, 37, 424-425, 434-436, 439
Internationalization of production, 80-81, 240

Intra-CMEA trade. See CMEA, mutual trade
Intra-industry trade, 396, 398
Iran, 299
Israel, 309
Italy, 158, 197, 201, 224, 282, 288, 303, 305-306, 364

Japan, 59, 123, 201, 207, 263, 264-266, 268-269, 271-272, 299, 301, 306, 360, 364
Joint marketing, 113, 152, 177-178
See also Marketing
Joint ventures, 112-113, 152, 177-178, 249, 363-364

Keynesian theory, 38, 42, 302, 399
Korean War, 42

Labor Party (Britain), 210
Laissez-faire, 42, 403
Laos, 115
Large countries, 298-299, 427-428
Latin America, 31, 301, 370
Less developed countries, 13-16, 24, 31, 33, 34, 38-39, 43-44, 78-79, 91-95, 97-99, 102, 105, 175-176, 179, 245-247, 351, 394-396, 398-399, 402-403, 405-407, 416-417, 418-419
Licenses, 12-13, 78, 80-81, 124-125, 363-364, 417, 418-419
Lome agreement, 93, 309
London Chamber of Commerce and Industry, 115

Machines and transport equipment, 161-162, 186-189, 209-210, 248-249, 344-347, 351, 354, 360, 363-364, 366, 418

Malcus (Sweden), 115
Malthusianism, 44
Marketing, 233-234, 324-325, 332
See also Joint marketing
Marx's theory, 36
Metalexport (Poland), 115
Mexico, 299, 301, 386
Microeconomic calculations, 165, 421-422, 424
Military considerations, 311
Modernization, 420
Monetary theories, 38, 406-407
Mongolia, 10, 253, 262-263, 272
Monopolies, 423-424, 426
Montedison, 114
Moscow Norodny Bank, 115
Most-favoured-nation (MFN) treatment, 95, 97, 186, 220, 326
Multilateralization, 104, 165, 175
Multinational corporations, 23-24, 44, 45-47, 111, 116-130, 131-142, 145, 154, 170, 301, 305-306, 419

Nairobi UNCTAD conference, 33, 109
Nationalistic economic policies, 394-395
NATO (North Atlantic Treaty Organization), 149
Natural resources endowment, 45, 80-81
Neoclassical theory, 396, 398, 403-404, 435
Netherlands, 201, 302-303, 306
New economic mechanism (Hungary), 285, 287, 439
New world economic order. See International economic order
New Zealand, 306
Nigeria, 299, 306, 309
Nonconvertibility, 162
Nontariff barriers, 96, 98
North Korea, 253, 263, 265-266, 268, 272-273, 312, 314

North-South relations, 34-35, 42-43, 76, 78, 80-81, 93, 105, 236, 238, 247-248, 251, 405-406, 408, 437-438
See also East-South relations
Norway, 273, 306, 326
Nuclear exports, 103

"Oceans" international policy, 103
OECD. See Organization for Economic Cooperation and Development
Official credit support, 195-196, 283-284
Oil and gas supplies, 123-124, 431
See also Energy sources
Oil prices. See Raw materials base; and Energy crisis
OPEC. See Organization of Petroleum Exporting Countries
Orenburg gas pipeline, 20, 154, 242-243
Organization for Economic Cooperation and Development (OECD), 58-60, 93-94, 96, 98-99, 102, 105, 111, 185, 186-187, 193, 196, 205, 306, 343-344, 351, 360, 366-367, 394-395
Organization of Petroleum Exporting Countries (OPEC), 42-43, 92, 102
Organizational problems of corporations, 131-132, 134-137, 138-139, 172
Ostpolitik, 209-210
Overtrading, 311

Pakistan, 299
Peaceful coexistence, 244
Peaceful use of nuclear energy, 103

Philippines, 299
Poland, 10, 55, 59, 63, 65-66, 76, 80, 98, 101, 114-115, 136, 158-159, 286, 288, 290, 299, 314, 328, 415-426, 438-440
Political affinity, 187-188, 196, 198, 206, 213, 278
Political dependence, 52-53
Political relations. See International politics
Pollution of the environment, 103
Portugal, 282, 297, 306, 308
Postindustrial society, 37
Preisausgleich, 300, 429
Pre-Keynesian economics, 38
Price
changes, income effect of, 426
system, 36, 311
international, 14, 18-22, 33, 299-300, 396, 398
Production cooperation. See Industrial cooperation
Production function theory, 47
Prosperity in the world economy, 42, 62
See also World economy
Protectionism, 234, 325, 428
See also Trade barriers and commercial policy

Quality of products for export, 231-233
Quotas, 326

Raba Wagon and Motor Company, 158-159
Raw material base, 236, 285-286
Raytheon, 172
Recession in the world economy, 18-19, 22-23, 37, 62, 332-334, 432
See also World economy
Reforms in Eastern Europe. See Economic reforms

Regional economic integration.
See economic integration
Relocation of parts of industry, 44–45
Research and development (R&D), 61–62, 177–178, 241–242, 246, 249, 301, 396, 398, 420
Romania, 10, 29–33, 55, 63, 66, 70, 76–77, 80, 94, 98, 101, 114–115, 135, 160, 286, 290, 299, 312–314, 386
Russia. See Soviet Union

Sakhalin Island, 123
SALT, 431
Saudi Arabia, 85, 386, 427–428
Scandinavia, 224, 269, 281, 299, 306
See also Denmark, Norway, Sweden
Scientific and technological collaboration, 245, 360
Scientific-technological revolution, 38, 165–166, 306–307
Siberia, 26
Siemens, 286
Sino-Soviet conflict, 253, 312
Size of the corporation: advantages and disadvantages, 126–128, 129, 143, 173–174, 228–229
Small countries, 224–225, 228–229, 236, 238, 297–300, 302–303, 311, 313–314, 427–429
Social science theory, 37, 38, 42
Socialist planning. See Central planning
Sociocultural development, 67
Socioeconomic mechanism, 417, 420–423, 439
Sociopolitical factors, 226–229
South Africa, 299
Soviet energy exports, 22, 59
Soviet oil and gas, 123, 431

Soviet Union, 21, 26, 32, 37, 56, 58–61, 63, 65, 91, 94–95, 103–105, 113–115, 123, 136, 153–155, 158–162, 175–177, 185–188, 193, 195–196, 201, 207–208, 212–214, 223–224, 238, 243, 248, 253, 262–263, 272, 278–280, 282, 283, 284–286, 288, 299, 311–314, 321–322, 328, 351, 354, 360, 363–364, 366–367, 395, 405–406, 438–440
Spain, 282, 299, 306
Special Drawing Rights (SDRs), 96
Specialization, 232–233, 249, 305, 364, 402, 437
Stages of growth, 37
"Stagflation" in the world economy, 20, 41
See also World economy and Inflation in the world economy
State Committee for Science and Technology of the Soviet Union, 115
State monopoly of foreign trade, 287
Strategic embargo, 195, 283
See also Coordinating Committee (CoCom)
Strategy of socioeconomic development. See development strategy
Structural factors, 233–234, 289
See also Industrial structure
Success indicators, 99–100, 424–425, 437
Sweden, 115, 195, 201, 301, 306, 326, 364
Switzerland, 195, 201, 301, 306, 326
Synthetic fibers, 80

Tariffs, 39, 63, 97, 425, 428
Taut planning, 430
Taxes, 425–426
Technical cooperation, 247–248, 306, 308, 364

Technical dependence, 46-47, 52-53, 66-67, 77
Technological gap. See East-West technological gap
Technological leader, 301, 344
Technological progress, 61, 66-68, 78, 99, 116, 165-166, 229-230, 240
Technology trade. See High technology products
Technology transfer, 11, 13, 19-21, 23-24, 26-27, 46, 67-68, 76-78, 94, 113, 116, 124-125, 152, 153-154, 170-171, 247-248, 309, 343-344, 363-364, 366
Third World. See Less developed countries
Tokyo Round, 97
Trade barriers, 20-24, 25-26, 63, 224-225, 246-247, 281, 290
Trade diversion, 331, 333-334
Trade fairs, 140
Trade policy. See Commercial policy
Trade receptivity, 26
Transaction prices, 425, 439
Transferable ruble, 175-176
Triangle Papers, 102
Triangular trade flows, 371
Trilateral Commission, 102-104, 394
Tripartite industrial cooperation, 80, 249
Turkey, 282, 299
Turn-key plants, 66, 78, 245, 248, 363

United Nations, 30, 31, 79, 101-102, 104, 303, 343, 363-364, 371
United Nations Conference on Trade and Development (UNCTAD), 33, 79, 91-94, 110, 236
United Nations Economic Commission for Europe (ECE), 23, 101, 152, 249
United Kingdom, 114-115, 159, 177-178, 185-186, 201, 207, 209-212, 224, 282, 285, 299, 300, 306, 360, 364
United States of America, 25, 37, 40, 55, 80, 85, 92, 95, 147, 153, 186, 196, 201-202, 207, 212-213, 224, 272, 282-283, 299, 300, 306, 327, 354, 395

Venezuela, 301
"Vent for surplus," 398, 407
Vertical integration, 424
Vietnam, 254, 268-269, 271-273, 299, 306, 309, 312
Volga Motor Car factory (Soviet), 158
Volvo, 115, 159

Warsaw Pact, 149
West Germany. See Federal Republic of Germany
West-South relations. See North-South relations
Western corporations, 81, 118-124, 126-130, 137-138, 145-146, 152, 154-155, 171, 186
See also Multinational corporations
Western countries. See Industrial countries
Western markets, 232, 334
Whipsawing, 172
Workers' self management, 422
World economic crisis, 13-14, 28-29, 37, 38-39, 42, 76
World economy, 5, 14, 28, 37, 41, 42-43, 63, 67-68, 78, 92, 97, 108

World economy (Cont'd.)
    fluctuations, 18-19, 22-23, 37, 332-333, 334
    impact of fluctuations on Eastern Europe, 18-19, 22-23, 37, 41-42, 62-63, 431-432
    reintegration of Eastern Europe, 54-55, 78, 96
World political system, world politics. See International politics
World prices. See Prices

Yugoslavia, 32, 101, 299, 301, 306, 312, 435

Zaire, 299
Zhiguli passenger car. See Volga Motor Car factory

About the Contributors

ZBIGNIEW M. FALLENBUCHL   Professor of Economics
University of Windsor
Windsor, Ontario, Canada

CARL H. McMILLAN   Director
Institute of Soviet and East European Studies
Carleton University
Ottawa, Ontario, Canada

ALAN ABOUCHAR   Professor of Economics
University of Toronto
Toronto, Ontario, Canada

CHRISTIAN ARNAL   Faculty of Applied Economics
University of Aix-Marseille
Aix-en-Provence, France

MAX BAUMER   Research Associate
Institute for Economics and Politics
Ebbenhausen, Federal Republic of Germany

OLEG T. BOGOMOLOV   Professor and Director
Institute for the Socialist World Economic System
Moscow, U.S.S.R.

MORRIS BORNSTEIN	Professor of Economics University of Michigan Ann Arbor, Michigan, U.S.A.
ALAN A. BROWN	Professor of Economics University of Windsor Windsor, Ontario, Canada
ANGELA M. CONNING	Chief, East Europe Section Confederation of British Industrial Industries London, United Kingdom
HENRI DUNAJEWSKI	Director Center for the Study of Economic Cooperation with Eastern Countries University of Aix-Marseille Aix-en-Provence, France
AGOTA GUEULLETTE	Research Associate National Scientific Research Center Paris, France
ANTONIO GUCCIONE	Professor of Economics University of Windsor Windsor, Ontario, Canada
PHILIP HANSON	Senior Lecturer Centre of Russian and East European Studies University of Birmingham Birmingham, United Kingdom
JOHN P. HARDT	Associate Director Senior Specialists Division Congressional Research Service Library of Congress Washington, D.C., U.S.A.
HANNS-DIETER JACOBSEN	Research Associate Institute for Economics and Politics Ebbenhausen, Federal Republic of Germany

ABOUT THE CONTRIBUTORS

ZBIGNIEW KAMECKI
Deputy Director
Technology and Trade Division
Economic Commission for Europe
Geneva, Switzerland

PETER KNIRSCH
Professor of Economics
Institute for the Study of Eastern Europe
Berlin, Federal Republic of Germany

G. PETER LAUTER
Professor of Business Administration
School of Government and Business Administration
The George Washington University
Washington, D.C., U.S.A.

JEAN LAUX
Professor of Political Science
University of Ottawa
Ottawa, Ontario, Canada

ALLEN J. LENZ
Director
Office of East-West Policy and Planning
Bureau of East-West Trade
Washington, D.C., U.S.A.

FRIEDRICH LEVCIK
Director
Vienna Institute for Comparative Economic Studies
Vienna, Austria

DETLEF LORENZ
Professor of International Economics
Free University of Berlin
Berlin, Federal Republic of Germany

PAUL MARER
Associate Professor of International Business
Indiana University
Bloomington, Indiana, U.S.A.

JAN MUJZEL
Professor of Economics
University of Lodz
Deputy Director, Institute of Planning
Warsaw, Poland

COSTIN MURGESCU
: Professor and Director
The Institute of World Economy
Bucharest, Romania

EGON NEUBERGER
: Professor of Economics
State University of New York
Stony Brook, New York, U.S.A.

JAROSLAV NYKRYN
: Dean of the Faculty of Management Sciences
Prague School of Economics
Prague, Czechoslovakia

RICHARD PORTES
: Professor of Economics
Birbeck College
University of London
London, United Kingdom

HUGO K. RADICE
: Lecturer
Department of Economics
University of Stirling
Stirling, United Kingdom

ADI SCHNYTZER
: St. Antony's College
University of Oxford
Oxford, United Kingdom

MIHALY SIMAI
: Professor and Deputy Director
Institute for World Economics
Budapest, Hungary

SYLVAIN WICKHAM
: Professor of Economics
University at Paris - IX Dauphine
Paris, France

PETER J. D. WILES
: Professor of Economics
London School of Economics and Political Science
London, United Kingdom

DAVID WINTER
: Partner
Baker and McKenzie, Solicitors
London, United Kingdom

ABOUT THE CONTRIBUTORS

THOMAS A. WOLF	Associate Professor of Economics Ohio State University Columbus, Ohio, U.S.A.
EUGENE ZALESKI	Professor and Director of Research Centre Nationale de la Recherche Scientifique Paris, France

LIBRARY OF DAVIDSON COLLEGE